Remembering Conquest

THE DAVID J. WEBER SERIES IN THE NEW BORDERLANDS HISTORY

Andrew R. Graybill and Benjamin H. Johnson, *editors*

Editorial Board
Juliana Barr
Sarah Carter
Maurice Crandall
Kelly Lytle Hernández
Cynthia Radding
Samuel Truett

The study of borderlands—places where different peoples meet and no one polity reigns supreme—is undergoing a renaissance. The David J. Weber Series in the New Borderlands History publishes works from both established and emerging scholars that examine borderlands from the precontact era to the present. The series explores contested boundaries and the intercultural dynamics surrounding them and includes projects covering a wide range of time and space within North America and beyond, including both Atlantic and Pacific worlds.

Published with support provided by the William P. Clements Center for Southwest Studies at Southern Methodist University in Dallas, Texas.

A complete list of books published in the David J. Weber Series in the New Borderlands History is available at https://uncpress.org/series/david-j-weber-series-in-the-new-borderlands-history.

OMAR VALERIO-JIMÉNEZ

Remembering Conquest

Mexican Americans, Memory, and Citizenship

The University of North Carolina Press *Chapel Hill*

© 2024 The University of North Carolina Press
All rights reserved
Set in Arno Pro by Westchester Publishing Services
Manufactured in the United States of America

Library of Congress Cataloging-in-Publication Data
Names: Valerio-Jiménez, Omar S. (Omar Santiago), 1963– author.
Title: Remembering conquest : Mexican Americans, memory, and citizenship / Omar Valerio-Jiménez.
Other titles: David J. Weber series in the new borderlands history.
Description: Chapel Hill : University of North Carolina Press, [2024] | Series: The David J. Weber series in the new borderlands history | Includes bibliographical references and index.
Identifiers: LCCN 2024005616 | ISBN 9781469675619 (cloth ; alk. paper) | ISBN 9781469675626 (paperback ; alk. paper) | ISBN 9781469675633 (epub) | ISBN 9798890887580 (pdf)
Subjects: LCSH: Treaty of Peace, Friendship, Limits, and Settlement Between the United States of America and the Mexican Republic (1848 February 2) | Mexican Americans—Political activity—Southwestern States—History. | Mexican Americans—Civil rights—Southwestern States—History. | Collective memory—United States. | Collective memory—Mexico. | Mexican War, 1846–1848—Influence. | Mexican War, 1846–1848—Social aspects. | Southwestern States—Race relations—History. | BISAC: HISTORY / Latin America / Mexico | LAW / Emigration & Immigration
Classification: LCC F790.M5 .V35 2024 | DDC 973.6/21—dc23/eng/20240229
LC record available at https://lccn.loc.gov/2024005616

Cover art: *Top*, La Marcha de la Reconquista (copyright © La Raza Staff, from La Raza Photograph Collection [#1000], courtesy of UCLA Chicano Studies Research Center); *bottom*, US Army encampment near Corpus Christi, 1845 (courtesy of Library of Congress).

Part of Chapter 5 was previously published in a different form as "Refuting History Fables," *Southwestern Historical Quarterly* 123, no. 4 (2020): 390–418.

For Sonia, Sam, and Cathy

Contents

List of Illustrations and Maps ix

Acknowledgments xi

Introduction 1

CHAPTER ONE
Contested Borderlands: The US-Mexico War, Treaty, and Immediate Aftermath 16

CHAPTER TWO
Responding to Conquest: Land Loss, Violence, and Repatriation 58

CHAPTER THREE
Asserting Rights, Remembering Loss: Statehood, Property Rights, and Transnational Influences 91

CHAPTER FOUR
Immigrants and Transnational Circulation of Conquest Memories: School Segregation, Lynching, and Shifting Boundaries 132

CHAPTER FIVE
Patriotism and Legacies of Conquest: Segregation, Electoral Politics, and Jury Representation 179

CHAPTER SIX
The Civil Rights and Antiwar Movements: Land Grants, Police Brutality, and the Draft 226

Conclusion 268

Notes 275

Bibliography 321

Index 341

Illustrations and Maps

ILLUSTRATIONS

La Raza magazine with photograph of Manuel Gómez 17

Bird's-eye view of the camp of the army of occupation, commanded by Gen. Zachary Taylor, in 1845 28

Portrait of Francisco P. Ramírez 59

Portrait of Juan N. Seguín 74

Portrait of Juan Nepomuceno Cortina 85

El Tiempo newspaper 106

Portrait of María Amparo Ruiz de Burton, c. 1874–86 124

Portrait of Clemente, Nicasio, and Eduardo Idar 138

Diario del Hogar newspaper 149

The Río Bravo (Rio Grande) and El Chamizal in 1864 167

Portrait of Benjamin Maurice Read 172

Portrait of José T. Canales, c. 1909–10 181

Portrait of Carlos E. Castañeda 186

Portrait of Adina Emilia De Zavala, c. 1908 191

María Elena Zamora in 1906 *Pedagogue* yearbook 199

Photograph of La Marcha de la Reconquista in San Fernando, CA 239

La Causa newspaper 242

Photograph of Brown Beret members on Catalina Island, CA 252

Cover of *La batalla esta aquí* 260

MAPS

U.S.-Mexico boundary before Treaty of Guadalupe Hidalgo 20

Land lost by Mexico from 1836 to 1853 32

The changing boundaries of the Río Bravo (Rio Grande) and El Chamizal in 1899, 1963, and 1980 168

Acknowledgments

This book has taken far longer to finish than I ever imagined it would. I began the research while living in the Midwest, but only completed the writing after moving to San Antonio. As I finish the book, I feel grateful to be near my extended family and immersed in a familiar borderlands culture.

Various colleagues have read portions of this book, commented on conference papers, offered suggestions on fellowship proposals, and given me advice on navigating academia. Since graduate school, I have relied on the advice and support of George J. Sánchez, Sonia Saldívar-Hull, Vicki L. Ruiz, David G. Gutiérrez, and Susan L. Johnson—all exemplary scholars but also generous, nurturing, and encouraging academics. Their example has provided a high standard for which to strive. Among the colleagues who provided suggestions, encouragement, or support are Ernesto Chávez, Vicki L. Ruiz, David Montejano, Leslie Schwalm, Louis G. Mendoza, Susan L. Johnson, Jerry Gónzalez, Ben V. Olguín, Jaime Cardenas, Philis Barragán-Goetz, Billy Kiser, Gabriela Gónzalez, Jason Johnson, Catherine Nolan-Ferrell, Francis X. Galán, Miroslava Chávez-García, Santiago Vaquera-Vásquez, Claire F. Fox, Paul Kramer, Susan Kellogg, José Alamillo, George T. Díaz, Maritza de la Trinidad, John McKiernan-González, Rosina Lozano, Raúl A. Ramos, Amy Porter, Walter Buenger, Ryan Schumacher, Trinidad O. Gonzales, and Ramón Gutiérrez. For the 2018 WHA Conference, David T. Johnson organized a panel with secondary school teachers from California and Texas who developed lesson plans from my research on the Brown Berets. This panel with Frank J. Perez, Jennifer Kendrick, Sam Jezak, Ryan McKinley, and Kurt Kinbacher was very inspiring and motivated me to finish the book. I benefited from Vijay Shah's helpful advice to condense the manuscript. For key assistance in tracking down photographs, I thank Rosaura Sánchez, Mary Ann Irwin, Carlos Cortez, Marie Silva, Xaviera Flores, Kristine Toma, Luis Garza, and Maria Marquez Sanchez.

When I moved to the University of Texas at San Antonio, my History Department colleagues made the transition smoother. I am especially thankful for the friendship and collegiality of Jerry Gónzalez, LaGuana Gray, Wing Chung Ng, and Gabriela Gónzalez. Beyond my department, I am thankful to John Philip Santos, Jill Fleuriet, and Ben V. Olguín for their encouragement.

I would also like to thank various members of La Raza Faculty and Administrators Association and COLFA's Diversity, Equity, Inclusion, and Justice Committee for their hard work to improve the university's climate. At various times, my students have heard some version of the events described in this book and have asked probing questions that have helped me improve its contents. Several former graduate students at the University of Iowa heard my initial thoughts on this project. Katherine Massoth helped sharpen my arguments with incisive questions and key suggestions. I am grateful to the graduate research assistants at UTSA's History Department who helped me with newspaper research, including Delilah Hernandez, Kristel Orta-Puente, Valeria Muñoz, Cindy Chavez, Kathryn Jones, Ahmed Sharma, Kimberly Feathers, Kuba Abdul, José García, Santos Espinoza, Savannah Weeks, and Thomas Holdsworth.

I am thankful for the funding provided by several universities and organizations. My research began with funding from a Career Development Award and an Arts and Humanities Initiative Grant from the University of Iowa. Early in my research, I received travel funding from the Charles Redd Center and UCLA Library Special Collections. At the University of Texas at San Antonio, I received an Internal Research Award, a Faculty Development Leave, and a Stumberg Summer Research Award. To complete my writing, I was fortunate to receive a Summer Stipend and an Award for Faculty from the National Endowment for the Humanities.

I am also grateful for the archivists and librarians who facilitated my research by providing access to manuscripts and processing interlibrary loan requests. In particular, I would like to thank the staff at the University of Iowa Libraries; the Special Collections at the University of Texas at San Antonio Libraries; the Chicano Studies Research Center Library at the University of California, Los Angeles; the Benson Latin American Collection at the University of Texas at Austin, the Houston Metropolitan Research Center, and the Arizona State University Library's Distinctive Collections.

The manuscript benefited greatly from the suggestions of the readers and editors at the University of North Carolina Press. In particular, I would like to thank my editor, Debbie Gershenowitz, and one of the series editors, Benjamin H. Johnson, for their unwavering support for this project.

Finally, I would like to thank my family. My siblings Josúe and Bety and their families have always been supportive of my academic career. My father Raúl was the source of several of the collective memories that inspired parts of this book. However, my greatest source of support and inspiration has come from Cathy, my partner and soul mate since the fateful day we met at

UCLA. As historians are prone to have different views, our stories differ about that day. Regardless, I am forever grateful that we met.

I began this project before my son Sam learned to read. As I finish it, he has become a voracious reader and a bit of a hoarder like his father. In the intervening years, my daughter Sonia was born and has brought much joy to our lives. While learning to parent Sam and Sonia has been one of the greatest challenges in my life, it has also given me much happiness. Watching Sam and Sonia learn Spanish and grow attached to my father during the last years of his life was wonderful. This book grew out of my attempt to understand the life experiences that he and my mother Edelmira shared with their children when they brought us to this country from Mexico.

Remembering Conquest

Introduction

In the summer of 1969, my family moved from Matamoros, Tamaulipas, to Taft, Texas. Opposite its twin city of Brownville, Texas, Matamoros is one of the largest border cities along the Rio Grande, while Taft is a small town north of Corpus Christi. Like many borderland residents, my father's family had been moving back and forth across the Rio Grande for several decades. His parents had fled northern Mexico to escape the turmoil of the Mexican Revolution during the 1910s, then returned to Mexico during the Great Depression. My father, born in Texas, came back to the United States as an adult to work as an agricultural laborer and carpenter in California and Texas. He and my mother eventually moved to Texas so we could live closer to his workplace.

The move introduced culture shock to my brother, sister, and me as we adjusted to our new environment. My adjustment included a memorable encounter with my next-door neighbor, an older Tejano boy, that summer in Taft.[1] I knew very little English, so our conversation was in Spanish. Speaking across a chain-link fence, he asked me where I was from. When my new friend discovered that I had just arrived from Mexico, he brought up the US-Mexico War (1846–48). I remember that we disagreed about the war's causes during that first conversation. His version of the war corresponded to the one being taught in US public schools, while the version I offered reflected the one being taught in Mexico's public schools. I had just finished first grade in Mexico, and my friend had completed second grade in the United States; nevertheless, both of us were already conversant in each country's version of the war.

Our friendly disagreement suggests the influence of collective memories at an early age. Reflecting on this experience years later, I wondered how my neighbor and I had learned about the war at such a young age. I had obtained some rudimentary information from my older brother and sister and from my family's collective memories of the conflict. To my knowledge, my ancestors were not involved in the war, so my siblings learned about this foundational event from oral tradition and through school. My older brother and sister, who were in high school and middle school, respectively, absorbed Mexico's version of the conflict from textbooks and teachers. My sister could recite the names of *los niños heroes* (the boy heroes) who died defending Chapultepec

Castle in Mexico City from US invading troops. In turn, I learned about *los niños heroes* from my siblings. Yet most children educated in the United States (including Mexican Americans) do not learn about these boy heroes in school. My conversation with my neighbor indicates that young children are familiar with their nation's official war memories, but it also reveals the transnational circulation of collective memories. Moreover, it demonstrates that some Mexican immigrants challenged US views of the conflict. Finally, it hints at the multiple influences on collective memories through schools, families, and friends.

My experience illustrates just one of the countless and diverse interactions among individuals, groups, and the public that create collective memories. While our personal experiences shape our immediate recollections of the past, we possess collective memories, or obtain a sense of history, of past events that we did not personally experience but that are shared or influenced by group and public memories. Group memories consist of those held by families, friends, and organizations. We learn about the past from our families and friends, and we also share our memories with others. Public memories circulate more widely within cities, regions, and nations. Individual, group, and public memories influence one another as people learn about the past from their interactions with others. These memories also help establish a sense of self, a personal identity that links individuals to past events. As literary scholar Aleida Assmann notes, "The individual participates in the group's vision of its past by means of cognitive learning and emotional acts of identification and commemoration. This past cannot be 'remembered'; it has to be memorized."[2] Collective memories also provide a sense of group identity, as sociologist Maurice Halbwachs originally posited and historian W. Fitzhugh Brundage and others recently remind us. These scholars explain that social contexts influence collective and personal memories, and their transmission involves the "active labor of selecting, structuring, and imposing meaning on the past."[3] Thus, the collective memories of the US-Mexico War held by Mexican Americans shape their personal and group identity. In addition to their hybrid culture, collective memories of the war often distinguish Mexican Americans from Mexican nationals, Mexican immigrants, and other Latinos.

Remembering Conquest explores the influence of collective memories of the US-Mexico War on struggles for social change among several generations of Mexican Americans across the US Southwest. Its focus is not on the dominant versions of the conflict found in textbooks and transmitted via schools in the United States. Instead, it analyzes Mexican Americans' collective memories, which offered alternative views of the war. The dominant versions of the conflict in the United States emphasize the spread of progress and democracy in the war's aftermath, blame Mexico's refusal to negotiate for the conflict, and consider the war as inevitable. In contrast, the alternative views of the war blame the United States for starting the conflict in order to expand its territory and highlight Mexican Americans' resulting land loss, political disenfranchisement, and social subordination. These alternative views center Mexican Americans' experience by acknowledging the failure of the United States to enforce the citizenship guarantees in the Treaty of Guadalupe Hidalgo, which ended the war. Their collective war memories were transmitted to subsequent generations through oral tradition, newspapers, political speeches, and, in some cases, novels. Mexican immigrants, like my family members, also brought collective memories of the war from Mexico that differed from the dominant US view. As Mexican immigrants shared their collective war memories with Mexican Americans, they participated in a transnational circulation of collective memories through oral tradition, newspapers, and political tracts. These views not only challenged the dominant versions but were invoked by Mexican Americans to remind the nation of the war's continuing legacies. The war instigated immediate intergroup conflict between European Americans and ethnic Mexicans that bore long-term effects by shaping the ways that the latter remembered the aggression and the promises of equality in the treaty that ended the war. The failure of the US government to enforce the Treaty of Guadalupe Hidalgo led to some of these legacies, namely the consequences of Mexican Americans' status as second-class citizens.

In this study, I examine the multiple ways that collective memories of the US-Mexico War motivated Mexican American activists, scholars, and journalists to push for civil rights reforms over several generations from the mid-nineteenth century to the 1970s. Like other historians, I selected certain groups and individuals based on my research findings and the available documentary evidence. For each generation (approximately thirty years), I sought written records that mentioned the war or the treaty as a motivation for civil rights reforms. I looked for documents from various southwestern states and also sought records written by women and men to illustrate geographic and gender diversity. Mexican Americans have never been a monolithic group, so each generation did not have a uniform view of the war. Some who held collective memories of the war did not engage in civil rights reforms. Others who were involved in civil rights movements did not leave records mentioning the war. *Remembering Conquest* focuses only on those Mexican Americans involved in civil rights activism who mentioned the war and treaty. While this group is selective, their collective memories and activism often alluded to the war's effects on the entire Mexican American population. When activists recalled the Treaty of Guadalupe Hidalgo's citizenship guarantees, they referred to the promises made to all Mexican Americans (those incorporated as US citizens in 1848 as well as their descendants and immigrants who qualified for the same citizenship). Similarly, when scholars and journalists traced the war's legacies (i.e., their community's social, economic, and political subordination) to the nation's failure to uphold the treaty since the mid-nineteenth century, they understood that this subordination applied to Mexican Americans as a group. Moreover, while some Mexican Americans might be unaware of these collective memories with alternative views of the war, they nevertheless experienced the war's continuing legacies. For example, Hispanos living in New Mexico or Arizona before 1912 were residents of a US territory, not a state, precisely as a result of the US-Mexico War and the failure of the United States to enforce the treaty.

Remembering Conquest examines the collective memories disseminated among ethnic Mexicans by families, publications, and organizations. My research includes the recollections of landed Californio families who experienced land loss in the war's aftermath, Tejano activists who decried violence and lynchings against Mexican Americans, and Nuevomexicanos who pressed for statehood. I read their war memories in transcribed oral interviews, Spanish-language newspapers, and newsletters of organizations like the League of United Latin American Citizens (LULAC) and the Asociación Nacional México-Americana (ANMA), as well as in the letters and essays of scholars. This book is not a comprehensive study of such memories but instead analyzes the influence of some of these memories on civil rights efforts in communities across the US Southwest. *Remembering Conquest* is also not a social history of such reform actions but rather a cultural and intellectual history of the ways that collective memories spurred these actions. As a cultural history, it explores how land loss and political disenfranchisement shaped the identity (e.g., Hispano in New Mexico and Latin American in Texas), political positions (e.g., statehood in New Mexico), and racial views (e.g., claims to whiteness) held by Mexican Americans. As an intellectual history, *Remembering Conquest* traces how scholars, journalists, and activists deployed collective war memories in varied and often contradictory ways to push their political agendas. It also examines how Mexican Americans disseminated collective war memories, feelings of betrayal, and arguments for statehood to subsequent generations, and the ways that Mexican immigrants and Mexico-based newspapers participated in the transnational circulation of collective memories. To explain such social and political uses of collective memories, *Remembering Conquest* provides selective historical context, yet this narrative is not meant to be an exhaustive social history of the approximately 130-year period (the 1840s through the 1970s). The participants of the Chicano movement are the last generation considered due to the space and time constraints of this book. Additionally, these activists foregrounded the war and treaty more prominently than did previous generations after the first cohort of Mexican Americans in the mid-nineteenth century. Nevertheless, the book's conclusion gestures to the ways that collective war memories persist among subsequent generations. Ultimately, this book explores how various groups in the United States held different war memories and examines the multiple ways in which these memories of the war and its aftermath inspired Mexican Americans' civil rights struggles over several generations.

Throughout various regions during this period, these struggles changed from defending Latino gold miners against violence and decrying land dispossession in California, to struggling for statehood and Spanish-language instruction in New Mexico, to denouncing the disproportionate criminalization and incarceration of Mexicans in Texas. Civil rights actions also included struggling for the right to vote, the right to serve on juries, and an end to public segregation. Mexican Americans' uses of collective memories of the war were not homogeneous, and they changed over time. Various factors (e.g., class status, ideology, and region) influenced the political purposes (sometimes paradoxical) for which Mexican Americans invoked the war and treaty. For example, landed Californios decried their land loss in the postwar period, while working-class miners and journalists denounced the lynchings of miners during the gold rush. Ideological differences explain why some LULAC members deployed memories of the war to claim whiteness, while ANMA activists strategically remembered the treaty's promises to denounce their second-class citizenship. The first group of Mexican Americans, those who had lived through the US-Mexico War, expressed disappointment in European Americans and betrayal by the United States in their remembrances. For subsequent generations, their collective memories focused on the war's negative consequences. The common thread tying these actions together was the belief held by workers, activists, parents, journalists, and scholars that the US government had not enforced the citizenship provisions in the Treaty of Guadalupe Hidalgo. From activists who sought to prevent the lynchings of Mexicans to parents who endeavored to end segregated schools, they shared a strategy of repeatedly citing the treaty's citizenship promises and thus engaging the collective memories of the US-Mexico War. The varied forms of this activism support my argument that collective war memories helped inspire civil rights reforms of various kinds.

In researching collective war memories, I consulted a variety of Spanish- and English-language sources. After the first chapter in the book, which provides an overview of the causes and effects of the US-Mexico War, each chapter focuses on activists within a generation across the US Southwest. For each generation examined in *Remembering Conquest*, I searched for references to the war or treaty in letters, oral histories, newspapers, and organizational documents. For some chapters, the sources created by individuals or organizations were apparent due to the subjects' prominence in Mexican American history; for example, María Amparo Ruiz de Burton wrote about the war's devastating effects in the *Squatter and the Don*, Spanish-language journalists frequently referred to broken citizenship promises in articles on school segregation, and Reies López Tijerina cited the treaty when discussing land grant claims in New Mexico. While Jovita González and Margaret Eimer's (pseudonym Eve Raleigh) *Caballero* focuses on a fictional family's reaction to the US-Mexico War, I chose not to analyze this novel because of the difficulty of placing it within the appropriate generation. Although González and Eimer wrote the novel in the 1930s and 1940s, it was not published until 1996. In cases where the subjects were less well known, I reviewed secondary sources to obtain historical context and leads for primary sources to consult. The wealth of Mexican American historical studies in recent years greatly aided my research. While this scholarship often mentioned the war and treaty only in passing, it nevertheless provided hints that various subjects invoked collective war memories and guided my detailed research. For example, while reading *La Raza* at UCLA's Chicano Studies Research Library, I came across the story of Chicano war resister Manuel Gómez, whom I had coincidentally met when I was a lecturer at the University of California, Irvine, where he was an administrator. This news story led me to consult the various newspapers and magazines where his antiwar poem had been reprinted and to record an oral history with Gómez. Whenever possible, I sought sources authored by women, workers, and immigrants to balance the more well-known sources by men, middle-class professionals, and politicians. I also sought to include activists from various states in each chapter. Although my research was extensive, it was by no means exhaustive, as such a task is impossible for the book's time period.

The lingering influences of the US-Mexico War remain crucial to understanding Mexican Americans' collective memories of the conflict. Despite the existence of monuments, place names, and commemorations of the war throughout the United States, few citizens know the causes or consequences of this "forgotten war," which transformed the nation into a continental power.[4] By contrast, this conflict is prominently remembered in Mexico as having caused the loss of almost half of the nation's territory and as an event that shaped Mexico's relations with the United States for decades. Aware of Mexico's loss and of the unequal power in US-Mexico relations, Mexican immigrants continued to move to the United States because it offered economic, political, and social opportunities often unavailable in Mexico. This apparent contradiction should not surprise us, because Mexicans, like other immigrants, hold a realistic understanding of the opportunities the United States offers while being fully aware of its long and tortured history of racial exclusion and territorial expansion.

In the United States, the war is central to Mexican Americans' collective memories because it created the first generation of Mexican Americans and influenced the identity of their descendants. *Remembering Conquest* compares each nation's histories of the war with Mexican Americans' depictions to illuminate the ways in which alternative histories challenged, modified, or reinforced official portrayals. Historians in Mexico and in the United States often blamed the other nation for the outbreak of the war, while Mexican Americans focused on the war's effects on their community. The war placed Mexican Americans in a liminal space between Mexican nationals and US citizens—neither group fully accepted them as peers or included them in their nation's histories. In contrast, *Remembering Conquest* identifies Mexican Americans' choices of remembered events, explores how memories were transmitted, and analyzes their meaning. By examining the political and social use of memories of war in Mexico and the United States, this book illustrates transnational influences (e.g., the memories and arguments about the war expressed by individuals, journalists, and scholars in Mexico) on the Mexican American community. As historian Peter Novick reminds us with reference to the Holocaust, "a significant collective memory is understood to express some eternal or essential truth about the group—usually tragic."[5] Mexican Americans invoked collective memories of the war to express the tragic failure of the United States to uphold its citizenship promises to them. Finally, this book tracks the multiple ways in which the memories of war have shaped Mexican Americans' struggles for citizenship.

Remembering Conquest is the first to focus on the influence of memories of the war on Mexican Americans' campaigns for civil rights. Historians of Mexico and the United States have explored each nation's war memories and their influence on binational relations but have largely ignored the impact on

Mexican Americans.⁶ Literary scholars have analyzed the narratives authored by ethnic Mexicans who lived through the US conquest and expressed dismay at the unfulfilled promises of US citizenship. These studies have explored the development of internal community divisions, of a nascent Mexican American identity, and of alternative histories.⁷ Yet this scholarship has not considered how subsequent generations modified collective memories to suit their own struggles for citizenship rights. This book focuses on the role of collective memories in processing the trauma of war and fomenting social transformation through political involvement.

Remembering Conquest contributes to the histories of the United States, Mexico, and the US-Mexico War. It explores questions raised by historian Michael Kammen's comment that Americans depoliticize the past in order to avoid contemporary conflicts.⁸ These questions include the following: Which Mexican Americans adopted this strategy to gain acceptance into American society as equal citizens? What were the effects on Mexican Americans who refused to depoliticize the past? How did memories of conquest shape contemporary struggles for civil rights? How does the United States' historical amnesia about conquest influence its relations with descendants of the "conquered" and with Mexico? Popular memories and national histories of war affect international relations and also shape how each nation's population views citizens of other countries.

Not surprisingly, there is a stark difference in the ways the United States and Mexico remember and forget the war. Each country's citizens apply a different label for the conflict. US citizens refer to the "Mexican War" or the "Mexican-American War," while Mexican nationals identify the conflict as the "War of North American Intervention" or the "War with the United States."⁹ Mexican Americans who lived through the war also held different interpretations of the conflict. Such disagreements within and among official, collective, and individual memories are the subject of writer Viet Thanh Nguyen's cogent observation: "All wars are fought twice; the first time on the battlefield, the second time in memory."¹⁰ *Remembering Conquest* posits that the war over the memory of the US-Mexico War has persisted since the conclusion of the conflict as several generations of Mexican Americans have struggled to contest official versions. By exploring the ways that both nations and their citizens deploy memories, this study illuminates the strategic, political, and social uses of memories of war—not just for Mexico and the United States but also for community and national histories globally.

This book engages several issues in memory studies. By analyzing war memories held by several generations, it examines three critical topics in memory studies: the relationship among memories within a community, the transmission and reception of memories, and the connections between social and political issues.[11] In tracing collective memory over time, my study addresses the "politics of memory" by examining how succeeding generations reinforced or modified earlier memories of conquest according to their contemporary social and political contexts.[12] While some studies of collective memory assume that a common identity unites a social group, my project acknowledges that intracommunity divisions determine which events are remembered and shape the reception of these memories. Rather than presuming a monolithic collective memory, my study examines various remembrances among a diverse Mexican American community.

The multiplicity of vernacular and official memories remains central to *Remembering Conquest*. Politics determines which collective memories are expressed as public history at the local, state, and national levels. Influential groups (e.g., politicians, museum benefactors, and local historical societies) deploy their power to shape the institutionalized version of history that is disseminated through monuments, museums, and historic sites. Various scholars argue that public history manifestations of collective memory reflect a shared or consensual vision among the nation's citizens.[13] However, this view ignores the existence of vernacular histories among underrepresented populations (e.g., Mexican Americans and African Americans) that challenge the consensus interpretation. Historian Monica Muñoz Martinez wonderfully illustrates the significance of these vernacular histories and their importance to collective memories in her exploration of the legacies of violence in Texas.[14] Other scholars contend that public history reflects the struggles between competing groups (e.g., political leaders and underrepresented communities) while acknowledging that elites attempt to establish control by suppressing vernacular memories that challenge official histories.[15] This book supports the latter view by focusing on the collective memories of Mexican Americans that challenged official versions of the US-Mexico War and served to foment social activism. As it explores various and competing collective memories among Mexican Americans, the book also acknowledges various official collective memories.[16] Through their interactions, these two types of memories change over time and are influenced by contemporary political and social events. Finally, this study recognizes the importance of understanding contemporary historical contexts to appreciate the reception of both official and vernacular collective memories.[17]

Remembering Conquest examines Mexican Americans' collective war memories as alternative and vernacular histories because they have rarely exercised the power to shape public history. As historian W. Fitzhugh Brundage reminds us, "The resources that any group has available to it dictate the medium of expression used to impart the recalled past."[18] While the dominant European American society leveraged their collective memories of the war to create monuments, hold commemorations, establish historical markers, and curate museum exhibits, these public history avenues remained mostly unavailable to Mexican Americans. Rarely did public history incorporate any of the collective war memories of Mexican Americans, who mostly disseminated their collective memories through oral transmission, newspaper stories, art, and some books.[19] These forms were their available mediums, so it is unsurprising that their oral and written histories shape their collective memories.[20] While Mexican Americans might claim that their collective memories were authentic representations of their community's views, they did not necessarily claim objectivity. Rather, their memories allowed them to create a usable past, to organize meaning from their experiences. The transmission of such memories involves "selecting, structuring, and imposing meaning on the past rather than the mere reproduction of inherent historical truths."[21] Their invocation of collective war memories allowed Mexican American scholars, journalists, and activists to "turn memory . . . into humane action," as historian David Blight reminds us of W. E. B. Du Bois's famous appeal.[22]

Conflicting collective memories of war illustrate how the transmission and reception of memories influence identity. On a long drive across Texas to attend my aunt's funeral in Matamoros, Cristi, my oldest niece, started a conversation about the war with me. She had spent several years living in and attending school in Mexico, where my brother (her father) had worked for several years. By 1993, when our conversation occurred, my brother's family was living in Arlington, Texas, where Cristi was a third grader. Once she understood that I was in graduate school to become a historian, she told me about her experiences attending public schools in Mexico and Texas, and then asked a question that was much harder to answer than any that had preceded it. She explained that when she was in school in Mexico, the other children (Mexican nationals) would associate her with the invading United States when discussing the Texas Revolution and the US-Mexico War. But once in Texas, the other students perceived her as Mexican, so they blamed her for the Alamo and the US-Mexico War.

Cristi wanted to know why this was the case. I recognized her question as one that Mexican Americans often encounter as they try to situate themselves in relation to past events. However, I stumbled to provide a satisfactory answer. My niece's question led me to complicate the European American versus Mexican version of events that she had presented by explaining Tejanos' role in the secessionist struggle in Texas and the subsequent US-Mexico War. I explained that the United States had waged an offensive war against Mexico to obtain the latter's northern territories, and that Mexicans living in these lands had become Mexican Americans after the war. But I sensed that Cristi was not completely satisfied with my explanation. Her question, I realize now, was also about identity. While I offered my interpretation of historical events, my answer did not address identity directly. She was trying to understand the paradox of being a Mexican American and of being caught between two nations.

My conversation with Cristi illustrates how the US-Mexico War continues to influence the identities of Mexican Americans, which is part of its legacy. Neither history of the war that she learned in schools in Mexico or the United States offered a place for Mexican Americans in the conflict but instead implicitly highlighted their in-between status, which persists to this day. Her description of debates with classmates encapsulates the paradox of being a liminal subject when citizens of both nations refuse to fully accept Mexican Americans into their society. My conversation with my niece indicates a more direct influence of public education on children's views of the war, but it also demonstrates how her casual conversation led me to share my collective war memories with the next generation in my family. Her school experiences had forced Cristi to question her place within the histories of the United States and Mexico. These experiences also led her to tell me about conflicting collective memories and gave me an opportunity to offer an alternative version of history and complicate each nation's official version. *Remembering Conquest* does not trace how particular individuals absorbed collective war memories, but it does hint at these transmissions by examining their sources, such as publications, immigration experiences, festivals, and other community events. While these memories do not lead to social activism in everyone, they percolate in communities and can motivate future generations to join civil rights struggles.

Sometimes these memories lead Mexican Americans to challenge official versions of war in minor but consequential ways. While growing up in Texas, I often crossed the international border to visit my maternal extended family, so I was familiar with the interrogation process that my father referenced in a story he often recounted. Throughout his life, my father had crossed this border for economic, political, and social reasons. His family had fled the violence of the Mexican Revolution in the 1910s by crossing into Texas, where he and most of his siblings were born. My father's family made the opposite trip into Mexico to escape the anti-Mexican violence that erupted in Texas during the Great Depression. He attended segregated Texas public schools until the fourth grade, when his family moved to Mexico, where he completed fifth grade before leaving school to work to help his family.

By the 1960s, my father was living in Matamoros with my mother and their three children but commuting to work in the United States. At that time, it was typical for US immigration officers to ask border crossers a few questions about their citizenship and destination before deciding whether to permit them entry into the United States. Most US citizens did not have to show any identification if they answered the officer's questions in English. But my father was a Mexican American worker with limited English proficiency, so he made the habit of carrying his birth certificate (secured in a plastic covering) to show immigration officials. These officers had questioned my father's answers previously. According to my father, one day he experienced a tense interaction with a European American border official who questioned my father's answer about his birthplace. The officer told my father that he had never heard of Hills Prairie (the small Texas town where my father was born) and wondered if it was actually located in Mexico, obviously questioning my father's honesty. So my father answered in a way that recalled the nineteenth-century conflict. My father explained that Hills Prairie was in Texas, but Mexico owned Texas at one time, so perhaps he was born in Texas when Mexico still owned it? The officer did not like my father's bold reply and refused him entry. Undeterred, my father gained entry by traveling to the other international bridge connecting Matamoros and Brownsville. But the story that he retold would bear lasting repercussions.

By recalling this border-crossing story, my father transmitted a memory of one of the legacies of the US-Mexico War to add to my collective memories of the conflict. When my father first relayed this account, it seemed like another cautionary tale of the difficulties of crossing the border. Interacting with US immigration officials at the international border is often fraught with tensions for Mexican Americans despite their US citizenship. While my father recalled a rather uncontroversial fact about the war (i.e., Mexico owned Texas before the United States acquired it), the context of his response politicized this fact. Rather than show meekness and humility in responding, my father asserted his knowledge of history and sarcastically challenged the officer. Deploying a weapon of the weak, he contested state power in an everyday form of resistance along the border.[23]

Recalling my father's story years later, I noticed additional connections to the war. My father's family had fled to Mexico in the early 1930s after learning about the lynching of an ethnic Mexican boy near Bastrop, Texas, where they lived. By using the international border to seek political refuge (as they had done years earlier when they escaped into the United States), my paternal family took part in a process with roots in the mid-nineteenth century, when the US-Mexico War established the present international border. Since then, borderland residents had been crossing the border to obtain political refuge, seek economic opportunity, and maintain social connections for several generations.[24]

According to my family's collective memory of the lynching, my grandmother did not want to raise her family in an environment where European Americans perpetrated such violence with impunity. My grandparents were intimately aware that the Texas legal system did not administer equal justice for all and that Mexican Americans continued to be second-class citizens in the 1930s. My paternal family's return to Mexico was precipitated by one of the war's legacies, namely Mexican Americans' inability to exercise their citizenship rights. Decades later, my father struggled to cross the border because his status as a US citizen continued to be questioned due to the US government's failure to uphold the citizenship promises in the Treaty of Guadalupe Hidalgo. The trauma of war continued to reverberate several generations removed from the original conflict as the "unending US-Mexico War" persisted.[25]

Remembering Conquest explores this trauma of war as expressed in the collective memories of several generations. I have grouped Mexican Americans into five generations that encompass approximately thirty-year periods (1840s–60s, 1870s–90s, 1900s–20s, 1930s–50s, and 1960s–70s) when each group was politically active. The first Mexican Americans, a generation literally created by the war, experienced the war's violence and the subsequent dispossession of their property. They suffered political, economic, and social losses as European Americans displaced them from power and as the war's outcome ruptured their national ties to Mexico. This trauma reverberated among succeeding descendants by influencing their identity and political activism. The war's outcome would shape Mexican Americans' views of their place within the United States as well as their relationship to Mexico. This book analyzes the changes in Mexican Americans' collective memories over time as multiple generations remembered the war and the promises enshrined in the treaty. It concludes by exploring how activists combined collective memories of the war with a vision of the US Southwest as a Chicano homeland, which encouraged entitlement within a Mexican American community often politically and socially marginalized.

Memory and the US-Mexico War

Among the war's legacies are the diverse influences of its collective memories. Reflecting on the US war with Vietnam, Nguyen credits the wounded survivors—the human consequences—for keeping "memories of the war alive when most citizens would rather forget, or, at best, remember in circumscribed fashion."[26] For the United States' war with Mexico, Nguyen's insight about human consequences applies to the first generation of Mexican Americans who kept war memories alive.

After the initial generation, physical consequences no longer appeared in the bodies of Mexican Americans, but they were evident in their lower social, economic, and political statuses resulting from their second-class citizenship. These consequences would bear long-lasting effects over generations, as they influenced how US government officials treated Mexican Americans. Nguyen's premise applies to the US-Mexico War in that the dominant white US population has chosen to forget the war's impact on Mexican Americans and Native Americans, while selectively remembering the vast economic and political benefits accrued by the United States. In Mexico, selective remembering is also evident as the nation recalls the loss of territory and the wounded national pride resulting from the US invasion and conquest. But many Mexican nationals have forgotten the impact on the first generation of Mexican Americans and on their descendants.[27] Thus, it is not surprising that the collective memories of the US-Mexico War and its human consequences have been kept alive by those most affected by the conflict—Mexican Americans. Historian Novick posits, "The most significant collective memories—memories that suffuse group consciousness—derive their power from their claim to express some permanent, enduring truth."[28] For Mexican Americans, that enduring truth is that the consequences of the "unending war" continue to reverberate into the present.

Nations have usually remembered their triumphs in war through commemorations and monuments, but the US-Mexico War memorials in the United States have overlooked the conflict's effects on Mexican Americans. Among some three hundred monuments throughout the United States documented by Monument Lab (an online searchable database), most mention European American soldiers who fought and died in the war, but only one, San Pasqual Battlefield, refers to Mexican American soldiers.[29] Likewise, scholarship on historic sites in the United States does not address the long-term consequences of the war on Mexican Americans. A book in which "leading historians talk about the sites where the past comes alive for them" fails to acknowledge Mexico's previous jurisdiction over the US Southwest, much less mention any historical sites associated with the US-Mexico War.[30] Several recent books on historic sites also overlook the war.[31]

The war began with an armed confrontation between US and Mexican troops on Rancho de Carricitos, located in Mexico's northern territory of Tamaulipas in what is now South Texas. Located on highway 281 between Santa Maria and Los Indios, the historical marker commemorating this event, the so-called Thornton Skirmish, dwells only on the death of US troops by repeating President James Polk's infamous lie, with the label "The spot where 'American blood was shed on American soil,' April 25, 1846."[32] The marker continues its one-sided representation of history by stating, "Here Captain Philip Thornton and 62 dragoons were attacked by Mexican troops."[33] The historical marker sits approximately one mile from the Rio Grande, the current US-Mexico boundary in Texas, but there is no mention of the land being under Mexican jurisdiction in 1846 or of the Mexican national ranch owner's name. The marker also fails to note that General Zachary Taylor's troops, including Thornton, were sent into the disputed area to provoke a fight that would allow the United States to claim that Mexico attacked first.[34]

While many people in the United States have forgotten the US-Mexico War, the conflict remains singularly important for Mexican Americans, as it led to their physical separation from the Mexican nation as well as their loss of social, economic, and political status. The treaty ending the war also provided Mexican Americans with US citizenship, but the treaty's promises were never fully enforced by the United States. Nevertheless, the treaty remains significant for the civil rights objectives of Mexican Americans. As historian Deena González reminds us, "Perhaps New Englanders or other US citizens have forgotten the event [the war], but most Chicanos in the Southwest, and Mexicanos in Mexico, recall it very well; the most informally educated person on both sides of the border has much to say about the war."[35]

Organization of Book

This book begins by examining how a "victorious" nation incorporated a "losing" nation's citizens. The first chapter provides a summary of the events leading to the US-Mexico War, the negotiations over the Treaty of Guadalupe Hidalgo, and the immediate aftermath of the war. The subsequent five chapters are arranged chronologically, with each covering about a thirty-year period, or roughly a generation. Indeed, the US-Mexico War lingers on beyond the twentieth century and is very much alive even today.

CHAPTER ONE

Contested Borderlands
The US-Mexico War, Treaty, and Immediate Aftermath

On a cold day in December, Manuel Gómez stood in front of the Oakland recruiting station and refused induction into the US Army. It was 1969, during the height of the antiwar and Chicano movements. Gómez was a history major at a local university and an activist in both movements. Radicalized by the war in Vietnam, he stood before a crowd of fellow draftees and distributed copies of his letter of protest to the draft board. "It is well known that Mexicans were among the first victims of your empire," Gómez proclaimed. He continued by invoking collective memories of a previous conflict to protest the current war, declaring, "The memory of the Mexican-American War is still an open wound in the souls of my people." His letter described the myriad ways in which Chicanos had suffered discrimination in the United States, including official persecution, land dispossession, language restrictions, environmental destruction, cultural eradication, and incarceration. This discrimination, asserted Gómez, rendered Mexican Americans second-class citizens despite the promises of the Treaty of Guadalupe Hidalgo, which he labeled "a lie." He equated the effects of this treaty to the numerous broken treaties signed by "our Indian brothers." The systematic attacks suffered by both communities led him to declare, "The war did not end. It has continued in the minds and hearts of the people of the Southwest." His letter detailed the ravages of war on the poor, both in the United States and in Vietnam, while the rich in the United States avoided military service. Describing some of the massacres committed by the US Army, Gómez expressed his solidarity with the Vietnamese. "The Vietnamese people are not my enemy," he concluded, "but brothers involved in the same struggle for justice against a common enemy."[1]

Gómez's protest letter illustrates some of the enduring legacies of the US-Mexico War and the power of collective memories. His reference to the war with Mexico was not surprising because Chicano movement activists frequently invoked the treaty, which generated renewed interest among the general public in the war. They highlighted the unfulfilled promises of US citizenship in the Treaty of Guadalupe Hidalgo and the subsequent legacy of discrimination that Mexican Americans experienced. Moreover, the US war

It was from the Chicano that the gringo learned to survive in the hostile deserts of the southwest. From him he learned of water rights and how to cultivate fields and grow crops in a desert climate.

As a reward, the Chicano has received substandard wages, poor education and second-class citizenship. An example of this suppression is evidenced by Cesar Chavez's struggle for the farmworkers. A struggle for wages that would provide at least a semblance of an adequate standard of living.

He has been persecuted by the police as a menace to white society. Chief Parker said that the reason Chicanos are criminals is that they are still too close to their primitive life styles. Thus he virtually declared an open season to hunt down Chicanos.

There are many reasons Chicanos owe no allegiance to this country. One of them is that Americans are not going to Vietnam to liberate the people there from Communism, but rather to enslave them for the American economy. Why should Chicanos fight enslaved people when they find themselves in the same position in the United States.

When the first man was killed, too many had died. For my people, I refuse to respect your induction papers.

Today, December 8, 1969, I must refuse induction into the Armed Services of the United States. Please understand it is difficult for me to communicate my feelings through writing, but nevertheless I will try to let you see through my window.

In my veins runs the blood of all the people of all the world. I am a son of La Raza, the universal Children, and cannot be trained and ordered to kill my brother. When the first man was killed, too many had died. For my people, I refuse to respect your induction papers.

It is well known that Mexicans were among the first victims of your empire. The memory of the Mexican-American War is still an open wound in the souls of my people. The Treaty of Guadalupe Hidalgo is a lie, similar to all the treaties signed with our Indian brothers. The war did not end. It has continued in the minds and hearts of the people of the Southwest. Strife and bloodshed has never stopped between us. This society with its Texas Rangers and Green Berets has never allowed our people to live in peace. The blood is still moist on the land. Too many of my brothers have been killed fighting for a lie called "American freedom," both in our streets and in foreign lands.

My people have known nothing but racist tyranny and brutal oppression from this society. Your educational system has butchered our minds, stung our hearts, and poisoned our souls. You cut our tongue, and castrated our culture, making us strangers in our own land. The sweat of my people watered the fields and their aching bones harvested your food. Today we continue to do your sweat-work for you, with our hands and backs. Though you occupy the land you have not conquered us. I am a free man. I choose my own battles. My fight is here.

In the short time that you have held the land we have felt the pain of seeing beautiful lands turn into parking lots and freeways, of seeing the birds disappear, the fish die and the waters become undrinkable, seeing "Private Property" hung on a fence surrounding lands once held in common, and having our mountains become but vague shadows behind a veil of choking smog.

Your judges armed with the cold sword called law, held in the diseased arm of Justice, have frozen the life of my brothers in your barbaric prisons, scarring them deeply. A man steals to live and you call him a criminal and lock him up worse than an animal. A soldier massacres and pillages a village, and he is made a hero, awarded a medal. I believe that if it is wrong to kill within society then it must also be wrong to kill outside of the society. I am of a peace loving people.

I see rabid leaders of this land live in luxury and comfort while they send my poor brothers to kill in a war no one wants to understand. The helpless and the innocent have lost on both sides as has been the case in all wars. My ears hear the screams of the fatherless children, my heart hurts with the tears of mothers moaning for their sons, my soul shrinks from the knowledge of the unspeakable horrors of Song-My and the rest to come. For the Vietnamese people, I refuse to respect your induction papers.

I cannot betray the blood of my brothers. We are all branches of the same tree, flowers of the same garden, waves of the same sea. The Vietnamese people are not my enemy, but brothers involved in the same struggle for justice against a common enemy. We are all under the same sky. East and West are one.

Photograph of Manuel Gómez, a Chicanx civil rights and antiwar activist, with a copy of his letter of protest to the draft board, 1970. *La Raza* magazine 1, no. 1, La Raza Publication Records, 1001, Chicano Studies Research Center, UCLA.

with Vietnam encouraged comparison with the US-Mexico War. Both conflicts, critics like Gómez maintained, began under false pretenses and led to the oppression of people living on contested land. The use of collective memories of the US-Mexico War by Chicano and antiwar activists was strategic but not unusual, as several generations of Mexican Americans had invoked collective war memories to advance political agendas. More than 120 years after the war's end, Gómez recalled the conflict in a protest against the war in Vietnam. By invoking collective war memories, he demonstrated the enduring power of such recollections and their propagation over multiple generations. The war never ended, he asserted, identifying continued attacks against Mexican Americans as a legacy of this nineteenth-century conflict. Moreover, his characterization of the treaty as a lie pointed to the failure of the United States to enforce the citizenship guarantees for Mexican Americans. He offered a list of discriminatory experiences endured by Mexican Americans as proof of the war's continuation and as evidence that the treaty's citizenship guarantees for Mexican Americans were not enforced. Therefore, the legacies of the war were not only the community's second-class citizenship and land dispossession but also the strategic use of collective memories by several generations of Mexican Americans who pursued various civil rights campaigns.

By invoking collective memories of the US-Mexico War, multiple generations of activists confirmed how much this conflict transformed Chicano history. The importance of this war in generating detrimental legacies of conquest ensured the transmission of collective memories over generations. Each generation remembered the land loss, political disenfranchisement, and social subordination of Mexican Americans in the war's aftermath and reminded the nation of the unfulfilled citizenship promises in the Treaty of Guadalupe Hidalgo. Why is this mid-nineteenth-century conflict so pivotal for Mexican American history? Part of the answer is because the treaty legally incorporated the nation's first Mexican Americans. As the country's first Latinos, Mexican Americans were offered US citizenship by the treaty. Because the Naturalization Act of 1790 declared whites solely eligible for citizenship, the treaty pronounced Mexican Americans to be legally white and also entitled to naturalization. While their incorporation as citizens appeared to be an example of racial justice and a diversification of the electorate, the reality experienced by Mexican Americans demonstrated a retrenchment of racial progress. As citizens of Mexico before 1848, they had exercised various citizenship rights, including owning property and voting. These rights were jeopardized by the US takeover of Mexico's former northern territories. Stymied by the legacies of conquest, Mexican Americans have struggled to exercise their rights as US citizens since the treaty was signed. Activists have repeatedly invoked war memories (and specifically the treaty's citizenship guarantees) in their civil rights campaigns to exercise their rights to vote, retain property, and serve on juries. In addition, civil rights activists have strategically used collective war memories in their campaigns to desegregate public schools, curb lynchings, and expose their disproportionate criminalization. By strategically deploying memories, they have demonstrated the social and political use of collective remembrances.[2] This strategy of remembering the past to address current social injustices also led activists and scholars to challenge dominant historical narratives that excluded or disparaged their community.

Contested Borderlands

Competing national territorial expansions led to the US-Mexico War. By the end of the eighteenth century, Spain had been struggling for decades to populate its northern borderlands in order to defend its territorial claims from French, British, and later US colonists. Poor communications with distant territories and sparse populations of Spanish colonists in those areas hampered the colonial state's efforts to populate its far north. While Spain had attempted to attract colonists to its northern borderlands throughout the seventeenth and eighteenth centuries, Anglo-American colonists quickly moved onto their nation's expanding territory during the nineteenth century. After obtaining independence in 1821, Mexico continued to struggle to control and populate its northern borderlands due to its political instability, lack of finances, and deteriorating relations with Native Americans. By contrast, the US government increased in size and power as the nation's territory expanded and the newly acquired lands experienced a rapid demographic growth. Yet expansion generated internal disunity, especially sectional disagreements over slavery. Territorial expansion had vastly separate aims and bore extremely different results for each colonial and national power. While Spain and Mexico strove to maintain control over their northern borderlands as a defensive measure against other imperial powers, the United States expanded westward as a solution to its domestic political and economic problems. According to the US expansionists, the additional lands would lessen the conflict over slavery and help the nation emerge from its economic depression of the 1830s.[3] Instead, westward expansion only heightened sectional conflicts.

New Spain's northern borderlands were unattractive to potential Spanish Mexican colonists in the eighteenth century because the settlements had

Mexico and the United States in 1824

long remained isolated and distant from its population centers. Spanish colonists struggled to acquire manufactured items, such as clothing and tools, and sufficient military protection from the colonial government. Poorly equipped and rarely paid, soldiers stationed at northern forts often engaged in the Native American slave trade to supplement their meager incomes. Their practice of kidnapping and sexually assaulting Native American women and children worsened relations between Spanish colonists and Indigenous nations. Although Spain claimed vast territories, in reality independent Indigenous nations controlled much of these lands because they greatly outnumbered Spanish colonists and often possessed superior weapons.

Toward the end of the eighteenth century, Spain's new Bourbon leaders adopted a new policy—modeled after the successful French strategy toward Native Americans—of seeking alliances and offering tribute payments to independent Indigenous nations. The new policy decreased raids and led to more peace but came at a financial expense that was difficult to sustain during economic downturns.[4] Such financial constraints would severely hinder Mexico during its independence struggle and its aftermath as the new nation attempted to defend its northern borderlands from the avarice of the United States.

Mexico's independence movement exacerbated the problems in its northern borderlands. The Spanish colonial state's neglect of its far north increased as it became preoccupied with suppressing the independence struggle. Facing increasing military expenditures, the colonial government stopped tribute payments for its Indigenous allies in the northern borderlands. As a result, these former allies renewed their raids on Spanish towns to obtain livestock and weapons. The lack of military support for its northern borderlands failed to improve with Mexico's independence in 1821. The new country fell into disarray after its devastating eleven-year war of independence left it bankrupt and its infrastructure in ruins. The Mexican government failed to reestablish control of its northern borderlands due to its internal political crises and troubled economic situation.[5] The Indigenous raids persisted, while Mexican citizens in the northern borderlands continued to feel neglected by the central government. Moreover, these northern colonists sought trade with European Americans for manufactured items unavailable through Mexican trade channels.[6]

The contrasting laws and racial structures of Mexico and the United States influenced their path toward war. Enshrined in the US Constitution was the belief in white supremacy, demonstrated by the fact that national citizenship was extended only to property-owning white men, while slavery was upheld in the three-fifths clause used to determine representation in the House of Representatives. The United States reinforced these racial preferences in the Naturalization Act of 1790, which permitted immigrants to become naturalized citizens only if they were white. Congress also excluded Native Americans from citizenship when it passed the Trade and Intercourse Act (1790) defining them as "foreign nations." By contrast, Mexico's Constitution of 1824 included some Indigenous people as citizens and eliminated most racial and property restrictions to holding office.[7] Yet Mexico continued to view independent Native Americans as "indios bárbaros" and exclude them from citizenship. Mexico's failure to appease the tribute demands of independent

Indigenous nations would be a major factor in weakening its borderland defenses in advance of the US-Mexico War. By the early nineteenth century, Mexico had become less dependent on African slavery and ultimately outlawed the institution in the 1820s. In contrast, US slavery continued expanding, and European Americans remained committed to white supremacy, as their interactions with Native Americans, African Americans, and ethnic Mexicans would demonstrate. Therefore, most US citizens justified the conquest of Indigenous lands and Mexico's far north (areas inhabited by nonwhites) by their belief in white superiority.[8]

While Mexico faced continuing obstacles to retain control and populate its northern borderlands, the United States flourished as it expanded westward into the newly acquired territories. This westward expansion was driven by several factors, including population pressures. Ninety-five percent of the nation's population was living along the Atlantic Coast in 1790, but that population was shifting westward as it grew. Twenty-five percent of the nation's population lived west of the Appalachian Mountains by 1820, and twenty years later, the majority of the nation's population lived west of the original thirteen states. The rapid population growth in the west manifested in the admission of new states. During the first forty years of the nineteenth century, the United States admitted ten new states, with all but one (Maine) located west of the Appalachian Mountains.[9]

The acquisition of western territory was also partly motivated by European Americans' belief in the nation's "manifest destiny," a term coined by John O'Sullivan in 1845 in the *Democratic Review*. The term referred to the common but not hegemonic belief that the United States possessed a God-given right to expand across the continent and bring the benefits of US democracy, institutions, and culture to seemingly "backward" people. Some scholars describe manifest destiny as part racism and part missionary zeal due to the ethnocentric focus on "superior" whites bringing "progress" to nonwhite people in the western territories. According to recent studies, rather than being a deeply held belief, manifest destiny was actually a strategy by expansionists to distract Anglo-Americans from linking territorial expansion with the goal of expanding slavery. This strategy was partly successful, as many European Americans began to use manifest destiny as justification for the goals of territorial expansion, seeking new western markets, and imposing US institutions and values on conquered peoples.[10]

The rapid westward expansion of Anglo-American colonists had threatened the government of New Spain, which began a colonization program that laid the groundwork for the secession of Texas. The Spanish colonial government sought to increase the number of colonists in its northern borderlands in order to stake a territorial claim in advance of other European powers and to explore potential mineral deposits. To encourage this settlement, the colonial government offered potential colonists land, supplies, and tax breaks. Nevertheless, New Spain's government failed to convince many of its subjects to move to Texas, New Mexico, and California due to these territories' remoteness, isolation, and danger from Indigenous attacks.[11] Because its northern borderlands remained sparsely populated by Spanish colonists, New Spain's government worried about encroachments from other imperial powers. While generally opposed to allowing foreigners to enter its territories as colonists, Spain made an exception when it gained control of Louisiana in the late eighteenth century. New Spain officially prohibited foreign colonization in Texas, but local officials tolerated European American squatters who arrived from Louisiana.[12]

Once the United States acquired Louisiana from France in 1803 (Spain had transferred it back to France in 1800), local officials continued to allow European Americans to settle in Texas as "useful citizens." In the last years before Mexican independence, New Spain's government altered its colonization policy by permitting a group of 300 European American Catholic families, led by Moses Austin, to settle in Texas.[13] After obtaining its independence from Spain, Mexico proposed an official colonization plan to encourage foreigners (European Americans and European immigrants) to settle in Texas. These settlements were also intended to serve as a buffer between independent Indigenous nations and Spanish settlements in New Spain's interior. Mexico's colonization plan also sought to prevent the United States from encroaching on its northern borderlands. To encourage foreign colonists to settle in Texas, Mexico offered several incentives, including land and tax exemptions. In return, the Mexican government required the immigrants to become Mexican citizens, pledge their loyalty to Mexico, practice Christianity (which meant Catholicism because this was the only Christian religion practiced in Mexico), and uphold good habits and morality.[14]

Secession of Texas

Mexico's colonization program became a huge success for European Americans but a disaster for Mexico as colonists flooded into Texas. Participants in the program were required to obtain authorization from the Mexican government to settle in Texas. Some immigrants secured official approval, while others came as part of government contracts between the Mexican government and immigration agents, or empresarios. Under their empresario contracts, immigration agents received land to distribute among recruited colonists. The empresarios were also responsible for enforcing the national laws among their colonists. Some 13,500 families immigrated to Texas under empresario contracts between 1821 and 1835 in order to take advantage of the inexpensive land and tax breaks. Although the colonization plan attracted numerous European Americans, many did not obtain the necessary authorization to migrate. Those who immigrated illegally were often fugitives from the law or from debts in the United States. Historian David Weber ingeniously identified these European Americans as the first "illegal aliens" in Texas, since they entered the territory without permission from the Mexican government. The flood of European Americans led to greater imbalance in the ethnic makeup of non-Indigenous colonists. By the early 1830s, European Americans outnumbered Mexican Texans (Tejanos) by ten to one.[15]

In response to the influx of European Americans, the Mexican government moved to restrict immigration. Mexican officials worried not only about the number of European Americans but also about their lack of acculturation to Mexican society and their rejection of their "naturalized" Mexican nationality. Many immigrants refused to become Mexican citizens, learn Spanish, or abide by Mexico's laws. In order to discourage further immigration from the United States, Mexico outlawed slavery in 1829 (slavery was not significant to regional economies elsewhere in Mexico). However, Tejano elites eager to attract more European American colonists (many of whom were slave owners) successfully obtained an exemption to the outright prohibition of slavery in Texas by persuading the federal government to allow indefinite indenture (a legal euphemism for slavery). The next year, the Mexican centralist national government prohibited further European American immigration into Texas and reimposed taxes on colonists there, favoring a colonization plan that relied on Mexicans from the interior and foreigners from Europe over US citizens. The centralists also sought more power for the federal government at the expense of the states. Since obtaining its independence in 1821, Mexico had witnessed an intense struggle between the centralists and the federalists, who favored more power in state governments under a weak central government. In 1834, Antonio López de Santa Anna, who had previously served as a federalist president, reassumed the presidency as a centralist, abolished the federalist constitution of 1824, and replaced state legislatures with military governments led by appointed leaders. This centralist control of Mexico's government precipitated conflicts with various states, including Texas.[16]

Responding to the increasing centralization of power and to Santa Anna's suspension of the constitution of 1824, Anglo-Texans and Tejanos launched a separatist rebellion. This rebellion placed Tejanos in an awkward position of needing to choose between supporting the separatist rebels or supporting their national government. While a few chose sides (even if it meant fighting against their own family members), most remained neutral. However, both the Mexican government and the Texas rebels perceived Tejanos' decision to stay neutral as a sign of disloyalty. For the Tejanos who actively participated in the conflict, their decision was influenced by political views as well as economic and personal relationships with Anglo-Texans. Other borderland residents, such as settlers living in the Rio Grande towns, indirectly helped the Texas rebels by refusing to aid the Mexican military en route to Texas. Such refusal was based on the Mexican military's continuous pattern of abusing civilians by appropriating their livestock, housing, and food without payment.[17]

Anglo-Texans and Tejanos constituted the Texas rebels who launched Texas's independence. One of the most famous battles occurred at the Alamo, a mission complex in San Antonio de Béxar. In late February of 1836, some 190 Anglo-Texans and Tejanos at the Alamo fought a thirteen-day battle against approximately 1,800 Mexican army troops. The Mexican army won the battle but suffered 600 casualties. All but a few of the Texas rebels were killed in battle or after they surrendered. Among the survivors were families of the Tejano rebels, Anglo-American women, and an African American enslaved man. News of the defeat of the Texas rebels and the execution of survivors at the Alamo and at Goliad, a subsequent battle, fueled anti-Mexican sentiment throughout Texas and the United States. The separatist rebellion concluded on April 21, when some 900 Anglo-Texan and Tejano troops defeated Santa Anna's army of approximately 1,500 in the battle of San Jacinto. The rebels captured Santa Anna and forced him to sign the Treaties of Velasco, in which he recognized the independence of Texas and agreed to remove the Mexican military beyond the Rio Grande. However, the Mexican government never ratified these treaties and refused to recognize the independence of Texas during the republic's nine-year existence.[18]

The actions of the Mexican military during the secessionist struggle and its aftermath instigated anti-Mexican sentiment among Anglo-Texans. In addition to newspaper accounts that condemned the Mexican military, former Texas rebels published personal accounts of the Mexican military's actions during the rebellion, which contributed to the popularization of anti-Mexican views throughout the nation. These sentiments were partly a result of confusing a people (Tejanos) with a government (Mexico), which many Tejanos opposed or from which they were alienated. Violence against Tejanos became widespread as squatters appropriated their ranches, while vigilantes persecuted and murdered innocent Tejanos, believing them responsible for the actions of Mexico's military.

The pervasiveness of anti-Mexican violence is illustrated by Juan Seguín, San Antonio's mayor in the early 1840s. He became a target of vigilante justice due to several disagreements with Anglo-Texan residents. After intervening on behalf of Tejano residents who had been targeted by vigilantes and squatters, Seguín and his family received death threats, leading him to resign and leave for Mexico. Vigilante violence drove other Tejanos away, as many fled to the South Texas border region and, on occasion, into Mexico. The violence against Tejanos was accompanied by their loss of social, economic, and political power. They faced formidable economic and political challenges when Anglo-Texan officials enacted US laws (of which Tejanos were unfamiliar) and when courts and merchants began to conduct business in English. They lost land to Anglo-Texan squatters and retained few political offices as Anglo-Texans became the new elite in most towns outside the South Texas border and El Paso region.[19]

The Texas separatist rebellion and its aftermath led to the beginning of the US-Mexico War. In the Texas republic's first election, Anglo-Texans and Tejanos elected government officials, approved a constitution, and supported the republic's annexation to the United States. However, President Andrew Jackson refused to annex Texas because he feared fierce opposition from Northerners who believed that incorporating Texas would lead to slavery's expansion. In the ensuing years, this opposition continued to block the annexation of Texas. For similar reasons, Jackson delayed official recognition of the republic until the following year, when the United States became the first nation to recognize the independence of Texas. A top priority of Sam Houston, the republic's first president, was to obtain international diplomatic recognition for Texas. Such recognition was necessary to allow the republic to borrow money, obtain credit, sign international treaties, and establish laws respected by other nations.[20]

Although the United States, France, and other European nations formally recognized the independence of Texas, the Mexican government refused to do so. In 1841, Texas sought to expand its territory into New Mexico. The Santa Fe expedition involved Texan troops marching into New Mexico, which remained under Mexican rule, to try to gain control of the lucrative trading houses in Santa Fe. The expedition ended in disaster when the Texans arrived in Santa Fe exhausted from the long trek and quickly surrendered to Mexican soldiers sent to intercept the intruders. Mexican troops subsequently recaptured San Antonio. In response, Texas sent troops to seize several towns along the Rio Grande in the Somervell expedition. Texas officials ordered the militia and volunteers into Mexico to punish it for three raids into Texas. After capturing Laredo and Guerrero, Alexander Somervell, the military general leading the Texas troops, decided to retreat, but some 300 volunteers ignored his orders and decided to press on to Mier (on the south side of the river). The newly formed Mier expedition ended in disaster as Mexican soldiers apprehended the Texans, executed several soldiers, and marched the survivors to a Mexico City prison. These military offensives worsened the already tense relationship between Texas and Mexico. As a result, Texas officials began considering their dormant plan to become part of the United States in order to receive its military protection and economic assistance.[21]

US-Mexico War

Westward expansion and the annexation of Texas became the dominant issues of the 1844 presidential campaign. James Polk, the Democratic candidate for president, attempted to shift the debate away from slavery's advance by running on a platform of westward expansion. His election convinced Congress to reconsider its annexation position after the US Senate rejected the initial annexation treaty early in 1844. The Whig Party candidate, Henry Clay, had initially opposed the addition of Texas but later changed his mind under pressure from Southerners in favor of expansion. Subsequently, John Tyler, the lame-duck president, convinced Congress to approve the annexation treaty that admitted Texas into the Union as the twenty-eighth state in December 1845. The addition of Texas furthered the imbalance between slave and free states, numbering as the fifteenth slave state to the nation's thirteen free states.[22]

The annexation of Texas sparked the outbreak of the US-Mexico War. In response, Mexico broke off diplomatic relations with the United States. Polk pursued two strategies to obtain additional territory from Mexico. His diplomatic strategy involved sending John Slidell to Mexico City with an offer to purchase Mexico's northern territory, including California, New Mexico, and the disputed region between the Nueces River and the Rio Grande (the so-called Nueces Strip). The Republic of Texas had claimed the Rio Grande as its southern boundary but had only exercised jurisdiction over the territory

Bird's-eye view of the camp of the army of occupation, commanded by Gen. Zachary Taylor, near Corpus Christi in October 1845, by D. P. Whiting. Library of Congress.

north of the Nueces River. Polk's military strategy consisted of sending US troops to Texas to prepare for a possible invasion. The troops established camp near Corpus Christi, just north of the Nueces River. After Mexico rejected Slidell's offer to purchase its northern territory, Polk ordered General Zachary Taylor to move US troops into the disputed Nueces Strip. This provocation was intentional, as military leaders and critics would later confirm that Polk's military strategy was to goad Mexico into attacking first within disputed territory. Pedro de Ampudia, the Mexican military commander stationed in Matamoros, ordered Taylor to withdraw his troops. When Taylor refused, hostilities erupted, leaving eleven US soldiers dead. Polk used this incident to ask Congress to declare war after inaccurately claiming "American blood had been shed on American soil."[23]

The declaration of war stirred vigorous domestic opposition. Many Whigs opposed the president's actions, believing that he had led the country into an unnecessary war in a "land grab" from Mexico. They labeled the conflict "Mr. Polk's War," charging that the president had manipulated Congress to declare war and garner public support. Some critics accused Polk of provoking a war against a weaker nation to acquire additional western territory for slavery's expansion. The war would enlarge the power of the slave states according to abolitionists, including Frederick Douglass and William Lloyd Garrison, who believed Polk had been quick to declare war without diplomatic effort. Massachusetts's state legislature passed antiwar resolutions condemning Polk's actions, and several of its residents voiced similar opposition. Among the most famous critics was Henry David Thoreau, who went to jail for refusing to pay a poll tax that he believed would be used to foment a war to expand slavery. In response to his jailing, Thoreau wrote "Civil Disobedience," an essay in which he advocated for a person's right to oppose an immoral government. This influential essay would later encourage antiwar and anticolonial activists in Europe, South Africa, and the United States, as Mahatma Gandhi, Martin Luther King Jr., and others cited Thoreau's essay as inspiration. Abraham Lincoln introduced the so-called Spot Resolutions in the House of Representatives, in which he questioned whether the spot where American blood had been shed was really on US soil. Lincoln and other Whigs believed that the war was an immoral action that threatened republican values. Some Northern Democrats also opposed the conflict because they sought to reserve western territories for free white laborers. Pennsylvania representative David Wilmot attached his Wilmot Proviso to a war appropriation bill in an attempt to bar slavery and indentured servitude from the territories acquired from Mexico. Opposition to the war also emerged from nativists who opposed incorporating some of Mexico's nonwhite Catholic population.[24]

Expansionists overcame sectional and ideological differences by forging a temporary alliance through nationalism. Acquiring Mexico's northern borderlands, they claimed, would supply the nation's growing population with farmlands needed to preserve the Jeffersonian ideal of a republic of independent white yeoman farmers. To obtain support from the North, expansionists manipulated the region's racial fears, convincing slavery's Northern opponents of the advantage of westward expansion—preventing free Blacks and escaped slaves from migrating to Northern cities. Rather, they argued, Blacks would move to western states due to the warmer climate. A partial annexation ultimately proved more agreeable to political leaders who believed the northern borderlands' sparsely settled population would either disappear or eventually identify with US institutions.[25]

In prosecuting the war, the US military launched three major campaigns against Mexico. Stephen Watts Kearny led troops into New Mexico and California, two regions where US troops encountered opposition from Mexican and Indigenous peoples. Taylor directed US soldiers in an invasion of northern Mexico and successfully routed Mexican troops led by Santa Anna in the

Battle of Buena Vista, near Saltillo, Coahuila. The third campaign was an amphibious one commanded by Winfield Scott, who led US troops in an invasion of Veracruz. When the war began, the Mexican government faced several significant obstacles in defending its territories. Following its independence, the country had undergone pronounced political instability due to the struggles between centralists and federalists. The population in Mexico's far north had also experienced devastating financial and human losses due to persistent Comanche and Lipan Apache attacks. Although the Mexican army performed poorly, Mexican civilians engaged in spirited guerilla tactics that slowed the advancing US troops. The US campaign was marred by a series of atrocities, including thefts, murders, and rapes committed against Mexico's civilian population. The principal perpetrators were US volunteers imbued with anti-Mexican views (promoted during the Texas secessionist struggle) and the widespread nativism of US society. Nativism in the United States had assumed an anti-Catholic dimension as a result of the large Irish immigration resulting from the potato famine in the early 1840s. Due to the virulent anti-Catholic bias among US troops and these soldiers' desecration of Catholic churches and abuse of priests in Mexico, several Irish and German Catholic immigrant soldiers deserted the US troops and joined the Mexican side. The Mexicans alternately referred to the deserters as the San Patricios (after the patron saint of Ireland) or the Pelirojos (Redheads). The San Patricios fought valiantly at several major battles, including Buena Vista, Cerro Gordo, and Churubusco, but US troops eventually captured several of the deserters, holding some as prisoners while executing others.[26]

The War's Aftermath and Its Legacy

The war ended after US troops seized control of several urban capitals, including Mexico City. During the war, fervent supporters of annexation, imbued with a belief in the nation's manifest destiny, began advocating for the United States to take the entire territory of Mexico. Most of the opposition to these "all of Mexico" proponents came from Southerners who feared the national consequences of acquiring a large population of so-called mongrel people. Some opponents also objected to the possibility that a large number of Mexicans (whom many considered nonwhites) might be given the same rights as white citizens. When the war ended in February 1848, Mexican casualties numbered some 25,000 people, while the United States had lost 12,500. Under the terms of the Treaty of Guadalupe Hidalgo, which ended the war, the United States acquired over half of Mexico's territory, paid $15 million for land and claims, and secured control over Texas.[27]

Article 5 of the Treaty of Guadalupe Hidalgo established the new international boundary between the two nations. By signing the treaty on February 2, 1848, both Mexico and the United States agreed to transfer some 525,000 square miles of Mexico's northern lands to the United States.[28] US treaty negotiators achieved their goal of establishing the boundary at the Rio Grande and supporting the Republic of Texas's claims to land beyond the Nueces River, even though Texas had never exercised jurisdiction of the so-called Nueces Strip. From one day to the next, the residents of river communities from El Paso to Brownsville, who had been Mexican citizens, became part of the United States. Many of today's US border cities developed after the war as twin towns to older Mexican settlements. For example, El Paso, Rio Grande City, and Brownsville became the twin cities of Ciudad Juárez (known originally as El Paso del Norte), Camargo, and Matamoros.[29] Among the lands transferred from Mexico to the United States by the treaty were the present-day states of California, Arizona, New Mexico, and Texas, as well as parts of Nevada, Colorado, and Wyoming. In response to expansionists who wanted a southern route for the transcontinental railroad, and US officials who sought to reduce the costs for preventing Indigenous raids into Mexico, the two countries signed the Gadsden Treaty (or Tratado de Mesilla) in 1853. In exchange for $10 million from the United States, Mexico agreed to transfer an additional 29,670 square miles of land to the United States, free the United States from complying with Article 11 of the treaty (requiring the latter to prevent Indigenous raids into Mexico), and grant US transit rights across the Isthmus of Tehuantepec in southern Mexico.[30]

The war's end expanded not only US territory but also its population with the incorporation of Mexicans and Native Americans living in the annexed territories. The treaty included provisions for Mexicans in the annexed lands to obtain US citizenship or remain Mexican citizens. According to the treaty, former Mexican nationals who elected to become US citizens were guaranteed full citizenship rights, including freedom of religion and the right to hold on to their property. Unfortunately, the federal government was unwilling to enforce these rights, and many of the nation's first Mexican Americans lost their property to newcomers and often could not exercise their right to vote, sit on juries, or attend nonsegregated schools. The end of the war brought an influx of European Americans onto Mexico's former northern territories, fueled by the promise of land and the discovery of gold in California. As a

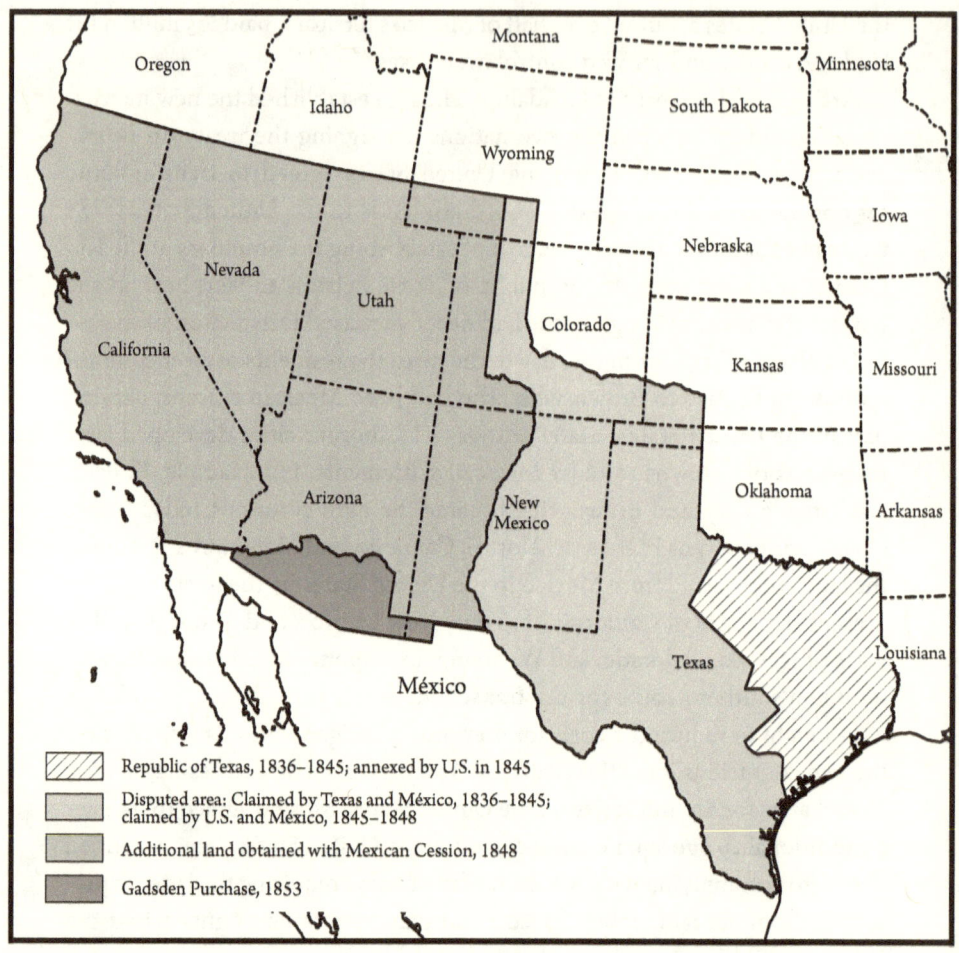

Land lost by Mexico between 1836 and 1853 through war and purchase

result, Mexican Americans became victims of European American vigilantes and squatters who took over their lands, while others lost their property to sheriffs' sales for nonpayment of property taxes and to lawyers' fees for establishing title to their land. Many Native Americans also lost their lands as European Americans encroached on their property and eliminated their livelihood. Additionally, the federal government removed Indigenous nations' sovereignty, waged wars of extermination against them, and forced others onto reservations. Mexican Americans became concentrated in low-paying and low-skilled jobs after the war. Although European American politicians generally replaced them throughout the US Southwest, some Mexican American officials were able to hold on to power in regions where they remained a majority of the population.[31]

The slavery issue became inflamed by the acquisition of additional territories. Determining whether to permit slavery in the recently acquired former territories of Mexico became an explosive political issue. While Texas entered the Union as a slave state in 1845, California joined as a free state under the Compromise of 1850, which also allowed for the populations of the Utah and New Mexico Territories to decide the question of slavery by popular sovereignty at a later time. This compromise also enacted a more stringent national fugitive slave law that angered Northerners by requiring them to help capture runaway slaves. Thereafter, the Kansas-Nebraska Act of 1854 repealed the Missouri Compromise's ban on slavery north of 36°30' latitude and allowed for residents of Kansas and Nebraska to decide on slavery according to popular sovereignty. In the next decade, the United States witnessed several events that led to the Civil War, including the 1856 bloodshed over Kansas's popular sovereignty vote, the 1857 Dred Scott decision, Abraham Lincoln's election, and the subsequent secession of the Southern states. Significantly, this increasing turmoil over slavery was linked to the earlier annexation of Texas as the fifteenth slave state (which further diminished the power of the thirteen free states) and the acquisition of Mexico's former northern territories.[32]

The US-Mexico War continued to reverberate beyond the nineteenth century. Various US military officers obtained valuable experience in the war and subsequently fought in the Civil War, while Mexican officers involved in the war then engaged in their nation's struggle to expel French rulers in the 1860s.[33] Several US and Mexican officers became presidents of their respective nations.[34] The treaty also shaped each nation's interactions with Indigenous nations as both countries sought to diminish cross-border Indigenous raids. The war influenced diplomatic relations into the twentieth century and how each country's citizens viewed their counterparts. The acquisition of Mexico's northern territories increased the nation's diversity as Mexican Americans and various Native American nations became incorporated through conquest. Unlike the Indigenous people, however, Mexican Americans obtained US citizenship with their incorporation into the United States. Therefore, Mexican Americans became the country's first Latinos, the first ethnic group socially considered nonwhite to be given US citizenship, and the first Latinos to be made US citizens at their incorporation into the nation.[35]

Throughout the nineteenth and twentieth centuries, Mexican Americans based many civil rights campaigns and property litigation on Articles 8 and 9 of the Treaty of Guadalupe Hidalgo, which guaranteed property rights and established the terms for US citizenship for the former Mexican citizens incorporated into the United States. Because the treaty enumerated certain rights, several generations of Mexican Americans (especially during the Chicano movement, 1960s–70s) would recall its promises and appeal to the collective memories of the war in various campaigns for full citizenship rights.[36]

Citizenship and Property Rights under the Treaty of Guadalupe Hidalgo

The treaty gave Mexican citizens in the annexed territories three choices concerning citizenship. Some 100,000 Mexicans and several thousand Hispanicized Indians lived in the annexed territories of the US Southwest extending from California through Arizona, Colorado, New Mexico, and into Texas at the end of the war.[37] According to Article 8 of the treaty, Mexican citizens (ethnic Mexicans and Hispanicized Indians whom Mexico viewed as citizens) in these territories could retain their Mexican citizenship, become United States citizens, or delay their choice. For those who did not make a choice, the treaty stipulated that a year (February 2, 1849) after the treaty's passage, these individuals would automatically become US citizens—a type of collective or mass naturalization.[38] Most of the population of former Mexican citizens in the annexed territories remained on their lands and became US citizens. Among the few who chose to retain their Mexican citizenship, some stayed in the United States and others moved to Mexico to either establish new towns or live in existing towns.[39] The Mexican government sought to lure Mexicans who lived in the annexed territories to move to its northern states and create new communities. Mexican officials believed that these communities would function as a buffer zone to protect more established and wealthier interior communities from attacks by independent Native Americans and from incursions by US filibusters.[40] In 1849, one of the first disputes regarding the treaty's enforcement involved the voluntary repatriation of Mexican citizens in the ceded territory. Mexican consular officials submitted diplomatic complaints that New Mexico officials refused to allow Mexican consular representatives to assist Mexican citizens in New Mexico in repatriating to northern Mexico.[41]

The treaty's citizenship guarantees to Mexican Americans became one of the war's legacies. In 1848, only people considered to be white qualified to become naturalized US citizens according to the Naturalization Act of 1790. Thus, by providing citizenship to Mexicans in the annexed territories, the treaty created the first generation of Mexican Americans and made them legally white. State and federal courts now needed to consider Mexican Americans as white "because they were citizens." Mexican Americans became, in the words of legal scholar Ariela Gross, "white by treaty."[42] Moreover, the citizenship provisions in the treaty meant that future Mexican immigrants were entitled to become naturalized citizens because they could claim to be of similar ethnic background as Mexican Americans.[43] With the establishment of birthright citizenship by the Fourteenth Amendment (1868), the children of Mexican immigrants born within the territory of the United States were considered to be US citizens, regardless of the citizenship status of their parents. Thus, the treaty and the constitutional amendment combined to establish the legal path for an increase (beyond biological reproduction) in the size of the Mexican American population from the mid-nineteenth century onward. Mexico's proximity to the United States, its ongoing economic and political problems, US immigration laws, and the United States' continuous need for inexpensive labor ensured that immigration (legal and illegal) from Mexico would endure. However, the federal government failed to enforce the citizenship provisions of the treaty, so Mexican Americans struggled to exercise their rights. The social reality for most Mexican Americans was complicated, as a host of factors, including social position (i.e., their social status, class, gender, and phenotype) and the demographics of the region where they lived, shaped whether they could exercise their citizenship rights.[44]

The treaty's vagueness generated the legal loopholes to prevent the full implementation of citizenship rights for Mexican Americans. The citizenship choices in the treaty resulted from a concerted effort by Mexican government negotiators to protect the rights of former Mexican citizens. The negotiators worried that the racist views of the US public and lawmakers would prevent the newly incorporated Mexican Americans from obtaining justice.[45] The US Senate's modifications of the original treaty draft before its ratification in March 1848 alarmed Mexican lawmakers and threatened Mexico's approval of the treaty. The Senate removed Article 10, which addressed Mexican land grants in the ceded territories and specifically protected Mexican land grants in Texas. The language of Article 10 acknowledged the reality facing many Mexican land grant holders whose property titles were imperfect due to numerous paperwork requirements and the slowness of Mexico's bureaucracy. The deletion of Article 10, as historian Richard Griswold del Castillo concludes, "struck to the heart of a question that would be the basis for hundreds of lawsuits and many instances of injustice against the former Mexican land holders."[46]

Also troubling Mexican lawmakers were the changes to Article 9, which in its original draft "forcefully maintained" the property and civil rights of former Mexican citizens. The US Senate had modified the original draft of Article 9, which included very specific language protecting Mexican Americans' property rights, with a more general and vague statement. The original draft stipulated that former Mexican citizens "shall be incorporated into the Union of the United States as soon as possible" and "with respect to political rights, their condition shall be on an equality with that of inhabitants of the other territories of the United States." The revised statement stipulated that the former Mexican citizens would be "incorporated into the Union of the United States and be admitted, *at the proper time* (to be judged of by the Congress of the United States)" and without any reference to their political rights.[47] The new statement gave Congress the ultimate say about the timing and process of incorporating Mexican Americans into the United States. This power would become the key reason for the long delay in granting statehood to New Mexico and Arizona, as US congressmen feared the incorporation of nonwhite citizens there. Finally, the citizenship guarantees pursued by the Mexican negotiators were not what the Mexican officials believed were in the treaty. US negotiators had probably intentionally misled their Mexican counterparts by writing the guarantees to be legally vague, according to legal scholar Laura Gómez. Mexican legislators did not understand that in the United States, "*federal* citizenship was inferior to *state* citizenship," and the treaty only addressed federal citizenship. According to Supreme Court chief justice John Marshall's opinion in 1828, federal citizens had the protection of the US Constitution but did not have political rights, which were held by state citizens. This distinction between federal and state citizenship would mean that many Mexican Americans (especially those living in the New Mexico territory) would remain second-class citizens throughout the nineteenth century and into the twentieth.[48]

The changes made to Article 9 bore negative long-term consequences for New Mexico's residents. The Mexican Cession included the present-day states of Texas and California, as well as the territories of New Mexico and Utah, which included a vast swath of the ceded lands.[49] While California and Texas joined the Union as states, the rest of the ceded land was designated as parts of the territory of Utah (which included the present-day states of Nevada and Utah and parts of Colorado and Wyoming) and the territory of New Mexico (which included the present-day states of New Mexico and Arizona and parts of Colorado and Nevada).[50] Although portions of other western territories in the Mexican Cession became states in the nineteenth century, New Mexico and Arizona would not gain statehood until 1912. Approximately two-thirds (some 75,000) of all ethnic Mexicans in the Mexican Cession lived in the territory of New Mexico in 1850. The racial makeup of the territory's numerous ethnic Mexicans and Native Americans worried US lawmakers, who opposed the incorporation of "non-white" people, and led them to delay statehood until 1912.[51] Since New Mexico remained a US territory for sixty-four years after its incorporation into the United States, its residents held greatly reduced political rights because they were not state citizens but rather federal citizens. US lawmakers considered New Mexico's residents as dependent people, so they were not permitted to choose national leaders, which meant they could not elect representatives to Congress and could not vote for president. Moreover, they could not even vote for their own territorial governor or other territorial officials, and they had no independent judiciary. While they were permitted to elect representatives to the territorial legislature, all laws passed by that legislature could be nullified by Congress.[52] For these reasons, scholars have characterized New Mexico as a colony and compared it to Puerto Rico, Hawaii, and the Philippines.[53]

The long-term consequences of the removal of Article 10 by Congress were devastating to ethnic Mexican property owners and would shape their memories of the US conquest. During the treaty negotiations, President Polk urged the Senate to delete Article 10 precisely because it addressed the Mexican land grants. Polk did not want to revive the land grant question in Texas, especially since the Republic of Texas had issued new grants to European American colonists after 1836.[54] The distinct approach of US and Mexican negotiators toward the treaty underscored their different perceptions of the ceded territories and their inhabitants. While Polk and other lawmakers took interest in protecting the jurisdiction of Texas over property rights within its boundaries, Mexican legislators worried about protecting the property rights of Mexico's former citizens. For example, during the treaty negotiations, Mexican president Antonio López de Santa Anna rejected an early treaty draft that sought to include New Mexico, arguing that Nuevomexicanos did not want to be part of the United States. Additionally, the United States had annexed Texas illegally and started the war, argued Santa Anna, so the United States should compensate Mexico for seizing Texas.[55] In the view of Mexican treaty negotiators and lawmakers, Texas still belonged to Mexico when the United States decided to annex it. Yet Mexican officials were forced to give up Texas during treaty negotiations after the war's bloodiest battle occurred on the outskirts of Mexico City, Santa Anna resigned as president, and the nation's capital surrendered. The elimination of Article 10 from the treaty meant that Mexican

Americans would struggle to validate their land grant titles for decades. Unsurprisingly, the struggle to obtain their property rights would shape how many of them would remember the US-Mexico War.[56]

Rather than a war that brought progress and democracy, as some European Americans maintained, Mexican Americans would remember it as a war of conquest where the promises of citizenship offered in the Treaty of Guadalupe Hidalgo remained elusive. During an armed rebellion in South Texas eleven years after the treaty's signing, for example, Juan Cortina issued a proclamation asking the government to fulfill its obligations and describing Mexican Americans' disappointment with the promises of citizenship, which he characterized as the "baseless fabric of a dream."[57] Henceforth, the treaty's promises would be cited repeatedly by Mexican Americans as a way to remind the nation to fulfill its obligations. While the collective memories of the war's battles would gradually fade with each subsequent generation, Mexican American activists throughout the nineteenth, twentieth, and twenty-first centuries would often trace contemporary problems to the unfulfilled promises of US citizenship. Rarely would Mexican American activists call for armed revolution, but they repeatedly urged the federal government to simply fulfill its obligations to enforce the treaty.[58]

The promises to protect the property rights of Mexicans in the ceded lands were broken for a variety of reasons. Mexico lacked the power to pressure the United States to abide by the treaty, while the latter lacked the will to enforce the treaty. Articles 8 and 9 contained guarantees to respect the property rights of ethnic Mexicans who chose to retain their Mexican citizenship as well as those residents who became US citizens. After the war, each state and territory established its own process to confirm the Spanish and Mexican land grant titles in US courts. However, confirmation often involved a lengthy process requiring property owners to hire lawyers, incur travel expenses to distant capitals, and pay hefty legal fees. Moreover, many ethnic Mexican landowners held imperfect titles, which meant that they had not satisfied all the legal title requirements to their property while under Mexican jurisdiction. Subsequently, these property owners faced many difficulties obtaining the proper paperwork from the Mexican government to satisfy the legal title requirements in US courts. Even ethnic Mexican landowners who held perfect titles often lost their property while trying to defend themselves from squatters, some of whom had powerful political connections to US lawmakers that influenced lower court decisions.[59] While the process of land title confirmation varied by region, the consequence was similar: many ethnic Mexicans throughout the US Southwest lost their land as a result of the jurisdictional changes introduced by the US-Mexico War. Therefore, one of the long-term legacies of the war was the dispossession of ethnic Mexicans, which would yield bitter memories of conquest for generations. The extent of land loss and its speed varied by region as Mexican Americans living in areas with large numbers of European American arrivals usually lost their land quicker than those who lived in areas with fewer newcomers. Indigenous nations would suffer even greater losses, as few groups were able to hold on to their native lands after the US takeover.[60]

California offers a vivid example of the way that land dispossession varied according to regional demographics. The state's land commission confirmed 604 of 813 (or some 75 percent) submitted land claims, which implied that Mexican Americans were able to retain nine million acres in the confirmed grants. However, the reality was more complicated, as litigation expenses, economic downturns, and legal delays (average appeals took seventeen years) often meant that ethnic Mexican landowners were forced to sell their land to pay their legal expenses. Most Californios were "land rich but money poor," meaning they lacked liquid capital to pay their legal fees.[61] As the gold rush fueled an influx of European Americans, overwhelmed Mexican Americans in Northern California rapidly became a numerical minority.[62] With a few exceptions, such as Mariano Vallejo, Californios in Northern California lost most of their property to newcomers by the late 1850s. In Southern California, land dispossession varied according to the number of European American newcomers. In Santa Barbara, the ethnic Mexican majority maintained political control and their land holdings longer than in areas with a large influx of newcomers (e.g., Los Angeles).[63]

Obtaining confirmation on land titles often depended on legal technicalities that violated the spirit of the treaty. In one infamous case, Dominga Dominguez held a perfect title to Rancho Los Virgenes in Southern California but lost her land because she failed to submit the proper paperwork to the land commission in time. A group of squatters who settled on her land claimed that her failure to comply with the California Land Act of 1851 meant she held no legal title to her property. After the district court and the California Supreme Court initially ruled in Dominguez's favor, the squatters appealed to the US Supreme Court, which issued an extraordinary ruling in 1889 reversing the rulings of the lower courts. The Supreme Court ruled that Dominguez did not hold legal title to her property because she had failed to satisfy the 1851 land act. The court made a surprising admission to justify its decision: if it confirmed her land title as valid under the treaty, the court feared it would establish a precedent that would generate chaos as many other

California landowners with perfect land titles who did not comply with the act might seek to recover their land, which was often already occupied by European Americans.[64] In its decision, the Supreme Court also argued that it possessed no power to enforce the treaty, and that violations of the treaty were the purview of international negotiations. As the country most interested in ensuring that the treaty was enforced, Mexico wielded little negotiating power, so the Supreme Court's ruling left treaty enforcement up to the US government. Therefore, the protection of ethnic Mexicans' private property in the annexed lands "ostensibly guaranteed by the Treaty of Guadalupe Hidalgo," concluded historian del Castillo, "was essentially invalidated."[65]

In Texas, the process of land loss began earlier and was linked to the arrival of European Americans. Tejanos' land loss originated in the nineteenth century and partly resulted from their decision to seek safety during military conflicts. When the separatist rebellion broke out in Texas in the mid-1830s, many Tejanos chose to remain neutral. However, neither the Texas rebels nor the Mexican government considered neutrality an option. Both Texan troops and Mexican soldiers believed that Tejanos who did not support their side were enemies rather than impartial observers. To protect themselves and their families from the military battles, some fled the cities for the countryside or Mexico.[66] After the rebellion was over, the government of the Republic of Texas characterized Tejanos who had fled to Mexico during the conflict as "aliens." According to the republic's constitution, aliens could not own land within its boundaries, so Tejanos who fled were automatically dispossessed of their property.[67] A decade later, the outbreak of the US-Mexico War motivated Tejanos to seek refuge in the countryside or in Mexico once again. After the war's conclusion, they faced various obstacles when they returned to claim their property. Squatters had often settled on their land, so Tejano landowners filed litigation to evict them. Tejanos trying to reclaim their property often sold off part of their land to pay legal fees and back taxes. Still others lost their property to sheriffs' auctions, lawyer fraud, and false lawsuits filed by US speculators.[68]

While US expansionist goals motivated the nation to annex Texas, European American commercial interests significantly influenced the boundaries of Texas. Although the United States had recognized the independence of the Republic of Texas, Mexico had not. During its nine-year existence, the republic had claimed jurisdiction over a vast area, including the so-called Nueces Strip and into parts of present-day New Mexico, Kansas, Colorado, and Wyoming. However, Texas never exercised control over this claimed land.[69] The republic's outlandish territorial claims and the odd shape of the state of

Texas were significantly determined by merchants and land lawyers, according to historian David Montejano. The Rio Grande remained critically important to these two groups, he contends, because they believed the river could link the lucrative Chihuahua–Santa Fe trade to world markets through the Gulf of Mexico. Commercial interests were also attracted to the possibility of controlling the substantial trade through the port of Matamoros, near the mouth of the river.[70] When the United States annexed Texas in 1845, which Mexico considered an illegal action and an act of war, the US government refused to accept the republic's excessive northern claims. However, it did parrot the republic's claims regarding its expansive southern territorial boundaries to the Rio Grande.[71] Thus, the United States claimed the southern boundary of Texas extended to the Rio Grande even though the republic had never exercised jurisdiction over the Nueces Strip.

Jurisdictional issues complicated the property rights of Tejanos and remained a contentious issue between the United States and Mexico throughout the twentieth century. The military conflicts resulting in the independence of Texas and its subsequent US incorporation fundamentally shaped the views of Mexico and the United States regarding the legality of Spanish and Mexican land grants. While Mexico sought to protect the validity of these land grants despite the transfer of jurisdiction to the United States, the latter often relied on arguments that legitimized war and its consequences. In 1855, for example, the US Supreme Court ruled on a land grant case on appeal involving a Mexican citizen who sought to claim two-and-a-half leagues of land owned by her mother, who had fled from Texas to Mexico during the Texas separatist rebellion.[72] A lower court had upheld the property rights of the original grantee citing Article 8 of the Treaty of Guadalupe Hidalgo: "Property of every kind, now belonging to Mexicans not established there, shall be inviolably respected."[73] The Supreme Court reversed the lower court's ruling citing the constitution of the Republic of Texas, which stripped Mexicans of their Texas citizenship if they fled the region during the secessionist revolt, and also prohibited "aliens" from owning property within the republic. So even though the property owner had fled Texas fearing for her life, the Supreme Court justified its decision to strip the former landowner of her property based on the republic's obviously self-interested decision to deny war refugees their citizenship and property rights. The Supreme Court also ruled that the Treaty of Guadalupe Hidalgo did not apply to Texas because the United States had recognized the republic as independent before its annexation to the United States in 1845 and the signing of the treaty in 1848.[74] So in effect, the Supreme Court claimed that two wars of conquest—the secessionist rebellion of Texas and the US-Mexico War—justified European American claims over land that Mexico believed rightfully belonged to ethnic Mexicans.

The issue of whether the treaty applied to Texas remained unsettled, as it was still open to interpretation and to the exigencies of specific legal cases. In the late nineteenth century, the Mexican government continued to argue that US courts were violating the treaty's provisions because Mexico had never recognized the independence of Texas. According to various rulings of the Texas Supreme Court in the twentieth century, the treaty did apply to Texas. So the state supreme court disagreed with the US Supreme Court, but the details of these lawsuits made all the difference. The state supreme court ruled that the treaty applied to Texas in order "to preserve the rights of property owners who had purchased the lands of former Mexican title holders."[75] The purchasers were European Americans. Justice was not blind in these property cases, as the litigants' ethnicity determined if the treaty applied (for European American litigants) or not (for ethnic Mexican litigants). Moreover, the Supreme Court's 1856 ruling on the treaty's applicability to land grant claims in Texas contradicted the Protocol of Querétaro, which was an 1848 agreement between US and Mexican negotiators to clarify treaty modifications (changes to article 9 and deletion of article 10) by the US Senate. The Mexican negotiators included statements to protect the property rights of Mexican title holders in the protocol.[76]

Precisely for this reason, the protocol has remained a source of disagreement between the United States and Mexico. Texas courts have supported the Supreme Court's ruling that the treaty did not apply to Texas but acknowledged that the state's lower courts had confirmed the validity of Mexican land grants based on the treaty and the protocol.[77] Moreover, the issue of Mexican land grants in Texas courts has come up for debate in various binational negotiations during the twentieth century (such as the 1923 Bucareli Conferences on outstanding claims after the Mexican Revolution), with each country sticking to its original argument.[78] Because Texas was admitted as a state rather than a territory, with control over its public lands, then state laws, not federal laws, have determined most land grant claims.[79]

New Mexico's status as a territory meant its residents' property rights depended on the federal government. Unfortunately, this dependence worked against the interests of Nuevomexicanos, as the federal government often delayed rulings on land grant petitions and politicized the process.[80] In 1854, the US Congress established the Office of the Surveyor General to determine the validity of Spanish and Mexican land grants in the territory of New Mexico. The law establishing the surveyor's office stipulated that owners could not sell their property before this federal office confirmed land grant claims.[81] The verification process required landowners to file their claims with the Office of the Surveyor General (few Nuevomexicanos filed such claims in the first years of the office's operation). After the surveyor assessed the validity of the land claims, Congress would decide whether to certify them. However, no judicial review was possible because the confirmation process in New Mexico was completed outside the federal court system.[82]

Surveying the land grants and confirming the claims were very slow and tedious. The entire process often took several decades. By 1880, the federal government had processed only 150 of 1,000 claims filed. The long delays increased the legal fees incurred by Nuevomexicanos, making them vulnerable to land speculators and lawyers, of which the most notorious group was the so-called Santa Fe Ring.[83] This group acquired land grants from Hispanos (as New Mexico's Mexican Americans self-identified) through legal tactics and fraud. Led by lawyer Thomas B. Catron, the Santa Fe Ring included several surveyor generals and territorial governors of New Mexico, who enlarged their properties while in office.[84] Moreover, land grant decisions were affected by national politics. The law establishing the Office of the Surveyor General gave Congress the power to appoint said surveyor, and this politicized the grant confirmation. Some appointed surveyors held virulent anti-Mexican views, which generated additional obstacles. Surveyors also issued decisions that further prolonged the confirmation process. Arguing that his predecessor had been corrupt, one surveyor in the late 1880s revoked the approval of twenty-three previously confirmed land grants. Politics, according to historian Richard Griswold del Castillo, rather than the rule of law and the Treaty of Guadalupe Hidalgo influenced land grant confirmations.[85]

The cumbersome and inefficient land grant confirmation process in New Mexico revealed the goals of the federal government and the desirability of land in the region. Compared to the confirmation process in New Mexico, land grant confirmation in California was rapid. The California Land Act (1851) allowed for a relatively quick confirmation but required claimants to file within two years of the act's passage or risk forfeiting their claims, whereupon the land would become public domain.[86] According to legal scholar Laura Gómez, the differences in the confirmation processes between California and New Mexico illustrated two revealing factors. First, in the view of European Americans in the mid-nineteenth century, California held a higher economic and strategic value than did New Mexico. The discovery of gold had made land in California more desirable to miners and land speculators than in New Mexico. Second, the different racial composition of New Mexico and California influenced the confirmation process. The discovery of gold had led to a rapid influx of European Americans to California, changing its racial composition. While immigrants from China, Mexico, and Chile also arrived, their numbers were dwarfed by the European American population, which became the majority in Northern California within months of the treaty's passage.[87] By contrast, European Americans remained a minority in New Mexico, while Hispanos and Native Americans constituted a majority throughout the nineteenth century. Not only was land less desirable in New Mexico than in California, but it was also harder to control due to its nonwhite majority and the presence of a Hispano elite, which retained some political power.[88]

As the land grant validation process in New Mexico became politicized, Hispano property owners had little recourse and few congressional allies. In the late 1890s, Congress deliberated about revising the land grant confirmation process of the surveyor general. Responding to Hispano pressure, land developers, and railroad companies, Congress began considering a law to settle numerous outstanding claims. So a group of Hispanos asked the Mexican government's plenipotentiary for assistance in speeding up the claims process and also hoped previous detrimental rulings would be reversed.[89] Although the Mexican government was unable to intercede on behalf of Hispano property owners for diplomatic reasons, it did ask the plenipotentiary to intervene in individual court cases if they involved bias against former Mexican citizens. More significantly, the plenipotentiary urged the Mexican government to publicize its concerns for its former citizens to make them aware and ready to oppose violations of the treaty.[90] This episode reveals the vulnerability of Mexican Americans and one of the legacies of the US-Mexico War. Over forty years after the war's conclusion, Hispanos, who had been granted US citizenship by the treaty, were still turning to the Mexican government for assistance with their land claims due to the little faith they had in the US government and the few allies they had in Congress. These Hispanos held negative memories of the US-Mexico War, as it had ushered in a post-conquest era in which they were left on their own to defend their property while enduring the political whims of Congress.

The changes introduced to the land confirmation process in New Mexico led to the establishment of the Court of Private Land Claims in 1891. As more European Americans arrived in the region and established commercial ventures, the land became more desirable than it had been at midcentury. Congress established the Court of Private Land Claims as a federal court designed only to hear land claims, an unprecedented step at the time.[91] The new federal court was unique because it lacked lay juries, which prevented the region's Hispanos from serving as jurors on any of its cases. Appeals were heard by the US Supreme Court, bypassing federal trials and federal appeals courts. Hispanos obtained considerable representation on juries at various levels, but the structure of the Court of Private Land Claims ensured that they would be excluded from its decisions. According to Gómez, this being a federal court and the stipulation that appeals be sent directly to the Supreme Court were two factors intended to transfer as much land as quickly as possible to the public domain.[92] This congressional strategy worked as planned in that millions of acres of land in New Mexico, especially communally owned property, were transferred to the public domain, which favored farmers, ranchers, and the US Forest Service as the main beneficiaries.[93]

While European American elites were divided about whether to promote land ownership as an investment (which favored land speculators) or to promote transferring Spanish Mexican land grants into the public domain, they agreed in their opposition to confirming Spanish Mexican communally owned land grants.[94] The Court of Private Land Claims established strict rules to confirm Spanish and Mexican land grants and stipulated that property owners who did not file a claim within two years would forfeit their property. The confirmation rules on land surveys and corresponding documentation were so rigid that the court construed many land grant claims in New Mexico invalid. Not surprisingly, the court rejected two-thirds of all submitted claims and ultimately confirmed only eighty-two grants, which amounted to 6 percent of the total area claimed by Hispanos.[95] The rejection of the vast majority of Hispano land grant claims by this court reminded the claimants of the bitter legacy of the US-Mexico War and would become part of their collective memory of conquest.

Emergence of New Identities

The end of the war bore long-term implications for Mexican Americans' identities and collective memories. The treaty set a new international boundary that jurisdictionally and legally separated the ceded territories from the Mexican nation. This separation led to the emergence of new identities. It generated divisions within ethnic Mexican communities, especially along the new US-Mexico border. For communities in the El Paso–Ciudad Juárez area or the Lower Rio Grande Valley of Texas that spanned the new international boundary, the war caused the "dismemberment of Mexico in a very immediate way."[96] Before the war, the river attracted ethnic Mexican communities along its banks. Ethnic Mexicans freely crossed the Rio Grande to visit their property, friends, and relatives. The new international boundary physically divided these river communities: their properties were now part of different jurisdictions and subject to distinct legal systems. Regional identities had previously existed among Californios, Nuevomexicanos, and Tejanos dating back to the Spanish colonial period, and national identities remained fragile during the twenty-five-year period that the ceded territories were under Mexican national rule. However, the national identities of Mexican Americans would abruptly change after 1848, when neighbors, friends, and relatives became citizens of different nations. The new international boundary separated Mexican Americans and Mexican nationals, whose distinct citizenship carried significant and immediate implications for the former's social, economic, and political status, all of which declined. Mexican Americans became an ethnic minority in a nation where European Americans dominated social, economic, and political power.

The changes in national identity would also influence each group's collective memories. Mexican nationals would remember the war as a national embarrassment, as a time when the "colossus of the North" invaded their country, took over its capital cities, and forced Mexico to give up over half its territory. However, most Mexican nationals were not personally affected by the Treaty of Guadalupe Hidalgo, meaning that they did not experience a loss of land, a change of citizenship, or the imposition of a new form of government. In contrast, Mexican Americans would view the war as an event that transformed them into a conquered people. Generations would trace many of their contemporary problems (poverty, lack of political representation, inadequate education) to the war's aftermath beginning in the mid-nineteenth century. Unlike Mexican nationals, Mexican Americans would be substantially harmed by the failure of the United States to fulfill the treaty's promises.

The treaty held significant implications on identity issues in New Mexico. The territory's long struggle to obtain statehood influenced Hispanos' identity by encouraging them to emphasize their Spanish ancestry. Despite obtaining legal equality with other US citizens, Nuevomexicanos (like Mexican Americans elsewhere in the ceded lands) did not obtain social equality with European Americans. New Mexico endured a long struggle for statehood precisely because European American lawmakers debated Hispanos' racial background, which many considered to be inferior due to its intermixture. Senator John C. Calhoun argued that Mexicans were a mixed-race people who had inherited the worst characteristics of the Spanish and Indigenous people.[97] In response, a highly racialized language emerged in New Mexico defining, according to historian John Nieto-Phillips, Hispanos as "'Spanish' in race, blood, language, and history, and 'American' in civic identity and national loyalty."[98] Although Mexican Americans elsewhere also claimed a Spanish heritage, Nuevomexicanos emphatically highlighted their ties to Spain in an effort to convince the general US public—and specifically, European American lawmakers—of their "whiteness" and suitability for statehood.[99] Nuevomexicanos identified as Hispanos (not as Mexican Americans) and attempted to distance themselves from Mexican immigrants to avoid the xenophobia directed against new arrivals.[100] This Hispano identity not only generated division with New Mexico's Indigenous people but also enlarged regional divisions with Mexican Americans in California and Texas, where the emphasis on Spanish ancestry was present but not as forcefully pursued.

The treaty's citizenship promises also directly affected civil rights campaigns across the Southwest by defining Mexican Americans as legally white. While legal whiteness technically afforded certain rights, most Mexican Americans actually experienced limited citizenship. For example, the League of United Latin American Citizens (LULAC, begun in 1929) would continually remind lawmakers and the press that Mexican Americans were legally white and therefore deserved full citizenship rights. However, Mexican Americans in LULAC did not claim racial purity or an adherence to white supremacy. Nevertheless, Mexican American civil rights activists' whiteness claims led to various missed opportunities to create alliances with African Americans. This "Faustian pact with whiteness" prevented Mexican American organizations from uniting their civil rights struggles with African Americans for fear of losing the few privileges that the former enjoyed.[101] However, individual Mexican Americans were not indifferent to African American civil rights struggles and in some cases strongly supported those campaigns. But Mexican American civil rights groups did not establish strong, lasting alliances with African Americans until such unions began to develop in the 1940s–70s.[102]

Politics and Voting in the US Southwest

After the passage of the Treaty of Guadalupe Hidalgo, the franchise was theoretically available for Mexican American men throughout the US Southwest, but the reality deviated significantly. The ability to exercise their right to vote varied by state/territory and by individual region according to a number of factors, including the region's demographics as well as the residents' class status and English-language literacy. Mexican Americans tended to exercise the franchise and win elected office in regions where they remained a numerical majority. Variations also resulted from different eligibility requirements for voting in each state/territory. Moreover, Mexican American men in the territories of Arizona and New Mexico could not vote in national elections, while those voters in California, Colorado (after 1876), Nevada (after 1864), and Texas held a right to elect their national representatives and the president.[103] The anti-Mexican violence pervasive across the US Southwest, or the "unending US-Mexico War," yielded additional obstacles as it led to voter intimidation and fewer votes cast.[104] From the beginning of US rule, local officials in California, Texas, and elsewhere challenged the voting eligibility of Mexican Americans by accusing them of being Mexican nationals and thus ineligible to vote. Alternatively, some European American politicians attempted to entice working-class Mexican Americans and Native Americans to vote for them by offering them liquor and money and subsequently marching them to the polls.[105] Finally, Mexican Americans continued to suffer property losses across Mexico's former northern territories and gradually lost political power as a result.

Mexican Americans in Southern California occupied political offices longer than they did in Northern California. Their hold on political power depended on their demographic majorities in various cities. Even within Southern California, where the Mexican American population was larger, their political influence varied. Because European Americans migrated in greater numbers to Los Angeles than to Santa Barbara, Mexican Americans lost political power faster in the former city than in the latter. Nevertheless, from the 1850s through the 1870s, elite Californios obtained a range of local political offices—from superintendent of schools to city councilman to mayor—in Los Angeles, Santa Barbara, and surrounding towns.[106]

The demographic onslaught of European American arrivistes directly harmed Californios' political influence in Los Angeles. In the 1850s, Mexican Americans made up close to 80 percent of the city's population, but their population share dropped to 20 percent by 1880 and then to 10 percent by 1887.[107] As a result, there was a sharp drop in the number of Californios holding political office in the 1860s. Their share held steady until 1880, when the losses increased.[108] The last Los Angeles mayor of Mexican ancestry, José Cristóbal Aguilar, left office in 1872, while Californios' representation in office would cease in the 1880s as they were overwhelmed by the flood of European Americans with the railroad's arrival.[109] Mexican Americans' exclusion from the mayor's office signaled a major transformation in Los Angeles politics. A Mexican American politician would not regain the mayoral post until 2005, demonstrating the long-term consequences of the US-Mexico War.[110] In Santa Barbara, Californios held on to the majority of municipal and county offices through the late 1860s. Despite challenges from European American politicians, Mexican Americans won most elections through the process of bloc voting, uniting behind Californio politicians.[111] However, European American arrivals decreased Mexican Americans' share of Santa Barbara's population from 70 percent in 1860 to 46 percent in 1870.[112] The number of Californio officeholders declined as well through a combination of gerrymandering and disenfranchisement. Moreover, European Americans expelled Mexican Americans from the Democratic Party conventions by the early 1880s, when they ceased holding political office.[113] Although a few Californios served in state offices (as state senators or assemblymen), their political power was increasingly circumscribed by their low numbers in the state's legislature and the growing presence of European American politicians.[114]

The loss of political offices in Texas also varied by region and was complicated by battles during the Texas Revolution and the US-Mexico War. In San Antonio, the site of the infamous Alamo battle, Tejanos quickly became marked as a "suspect class" by Anglo-Texans.[115] Despite several Tejanos' participation on behalf of Texas independence, European Americans suspected them of disloyalty. Most residents—Tejanos and Anglo-Texans alike—refused to take sides in the conflict between the Texas separatist and the Mexican centralist forces, but only Tejanos were suspected of opposing the separatist revolt and therefore of betrayal. European Americans mistook Tejanos' Mexican ancestry as a sign of their allegiance to the Mexican nation, even though they had chosen to remain neutral due to a fear of retaliation from troops on either side, since the battles were often in their hometowns.[116] In this tense environment, San Antonio's first municipal elections after Texas independence resulted in an Anglo-Texan as president of a city council whose remaining members were Tejanos. Throughout the nine years of the republic, Tejanos continued to serve on San Antonio's city council as well as on municipal courts as judges. They also served as county judges, state senators, and state assemblymen.[117]

The precarious position of Tejanos is illustrated by the fate of Juan Seguín. He and his father Erasmo had served as "cultural brokers" between Mexican government officials and various Anglo-American colonists, like Stephen F. Austin and his father Moses Austin when the latter arrived in Mexican-controlled Texas in the 1820s. The Austins and the Seguíns formed a close friendship as Stephen's brother learned Spanish while staying in the Seguíns' home, while Juan Seguín, in turn, learned English while in the Austins' home.[118] Erasmo Seguín held various political offices in San Antonio and strongly supported Moses Austin's successful application for an empresario grant to bring the first Anglo-American families into Texas.[119] During the Texas separatist revolt, Juan Seguín led a company of Tejanos who fought against Mexican troops, including at the decisive battle of San Jacinto, which resulted in the independence of Texas.[120] During the republic period, Seguín served three terms as senator and became mayor of San Antonio in 1841.[121] However, his prominent role in politics changed dramatically in 1842 due to tensions with Anglo-Texans and Mexico's attempt to reconquer Texas.

While carrying out his mayoral duties, Juan Seguín incurred the wrath of the city's Anglo-Texans and was forced to flee to Mexico. Some European Americans disliked Seguín and suspected him of disloyalty despite his military service for Texas independence. Part of the hostility began before Seguín became San Antonio's mayor. While in the military, Seguín engaged in several business transactions (including selling supplies to his own troops) of which local merchants disapproved. Additional tensions resulted from Seguín's land speculation. After Texas independence, speculators had bought land certificates from poor residents who acquired property titles through a headright system open to fraud and abuse. Seguín became a land speculator, allied himself with other Tejano businessmen, and began competing with Anglo-American speculators, who resented him. Finally, European Americans' apprehensions increased when Seguín lent financial support and raised troops for a Mexican federalist ally. His contact with Mexican military and political officials increased Anglo-Texans' suspicions.[122] After becoming mayor, he came to the defense of Tejano residents who complained of attacks by European American vigilantes. Moreover, he evicted several Anglo-Texan squatters from city properties.[123] The breaking point came when Seguín and other Tejanos abandoned San Antonio in response to the city's takeover by the Mexican military in March 1842 in an attempt to reconquer Texas. When Seguín returned to the city, he could not overcome rumors of his allegiance with the Mexican military. In response to threats against his life, Seguín resigned as mayor and fled to Mexico, as did other Tejano residents of San Antonio.[124] The loss of ethnic Mexicans' political leadership signified a new era of political disenfranchisement that would last some 140 years. San Antonio would not elect another Tejano mayor until Henry Cisneros won the mayoral election in 1981.[125]

Tejanos continued winning elected offices in San Antonio throughout the nineteenth century, but their influence and the number of offices they held sharply decreased as they became an ethnic minority. While Anglo-Texans consistently won election as mayors, Tejanos served as aldermen through the

1860s, but their numbers decreased after the US-Mexico War.[126] By 1850, Tejanos had become a minority (46.7 percent) of San Antonio's population, and hence their political influenced waned. Nevertheless, Tejanos obtained municipal, county, and statewide offices. For example, Seguín returned from Mexico and served two terms as justice of the peace, and Angel Navarro served as a state representative during the 1850s.[127] Despite their numerical minority, Tejanos exercised limited political power as Anglo-Texan politicians persisted in courting them as voters.[128] To counter the rise of the Know-Nothing Party in the late 1850s, Tejanos organized within the Democratic Party and established *El Bejareño* newspaper, which published articles defending the community's interests. In response to the so-called Cart War of 1857, *El Bejareño* published articles describing Anglo-Texan attacks on ethnic Mexican cart drivers as well as editorials and letters advocating government intervention to stop the attacks.[129] Tejanos won scattered elected offices until the 1890s, when their political power diminished considerably.[130]

A different political process occurred in the Rio Grande border region of South Texas, where Tejanos remained the majority throughout the nineteenth century. The losses happened later there than in San Antonio because the towns along the Rio Grande did not become part of Texas (despite its claims to the Rio Grande as its border) until the end of the US-Mexico War. Unlike the rapid transformation in San Antonio's demographics, the border towns remained majority Tejano, constituting 80–85 percent of the population in some counties. Nevertheless, Anglo-Texans became dominant along the Rio Grande by dividing political offices between themselves and Tejanos. This arrangement among elites, labeled a "peace structure" by historian David Montejano, permitted Anglo-Texans to "maintain law and order without the constant use of force." Two conditions were necessary for this arrangement to work properly: Tejanos became politically subordinate to European Americans, and a social accommodation was reached by each group's elites. The Tejano elite largely accepted this arrangement in order to maintain control of their property and some political influence in the postwar period. Laredo, seat of Webb County, exemplified the peace structure, as the arrangement led Anglo-Texans and Tejanos to split elected political offices almost evenly. While European Americans captured the majority of county positions, Tejanos obtained the majority of municipal positions.[131]

The loss of political power and social status throughout the US Southwest led to increased criminalization and incarceration of Mexican Americans. With the exception of New Mexico, most areas witnessed a dramatic loss of political power for Mexican Americans as European Americans arrived in larger numbers after the war to become the dominant elected officials. Cultural differences contributed to their criminalization, as European American officials sought to control or eliminate specific ethnic Mexicans' cultural practices considered socially or morally objectionable. In California, the European American dominated legislature passed an anti-vagrancy law (commonly referred to as the Greaser Law) targeting Mexicans, and a Sunday Law, which imposed fines for engaging in "barbarous or noisy amusements" such as bullfights, horse races, and cockfights.[132] Land loss and economic restructuring exacerbated ethnic tensions as the region's Mexican Americans suffered wholesale economic decline after losing their property to European American speculators and lawyers. The loss of their land forced many to become wage workers. This proletarianization assured Mexican Americans' continued subordination as laborers because their opportunities for upward mobility were limited by their race and class.[133]

Ethnic tensions also intensified because European American vigilante groups and law enforcement officials often targeted poor Mexican Americans. Residents of Southern California witnessed these tensions during the "race war" of the 1850s when violence escalated, rumors of Mexican bandits spread, and vigilantes and law enforcement officials targeted Californios (regardless of social class).[134] Mexican Americans' political decline led to their underrepresentation on local law enforcement bodies and juries. They also confronted various obstacles in the newly imposed US legal system. Perhaps the most obvious impediment was many defendants' inability to speak or understand English, in which most courts were conducted. Moreover, because many ethnic Mexican defendants were unfamiliar with US laws and procedures, they could not take advantage of the strategies of delaying trials or moving them to a more favorable jurisdiction. Few Mexican Americans became lawyers until the late 1800s, so defendants rarely had access to sympathetic lawyers or simply lacked the financial means to hire legal representation. This loss of power led to Mexican Americans becoming underrepresented on local juries and as jury foremen. In Los Angeles, only 2 percent of jury members were Mexican Americans, even though they made up 30 percent of the population during the 1860s–70s. In a postwar environment with heightened ethnic tensions, juries dominated by European Americans tended to convict ethnic Mexican criminal defendants and impose harsher sentences than they did for European American defendants. As a result, Mexican Americans became overrepresented in local jails and in state penitentiaries.[135]

The arrival of European American newcomers in the South Texas border region led to restrictions on Mexican cultural practices. As elsewhere, Anglo-

American politicians passed laws to curb "objectionable" social practices. These regulations resembled earlier legislation of the Spanish and Mexican periods in that they were elite attempts at regulating the activities and diversions of the poor. However, this postwar legislation grew out of cultural differences between Anglo-Texans and Tejanos. For example, Anglo-Texan politicians passed ordinances regulating the daily use of the Rio Grande. Since the river was also the source of drinking water, the newcomers objected to Mexicans' habit of washing clothes along the river, ostensibly due to unsanitary conditions. Regulations also emerged from Anglo-Texan characterizations of the Mexicans' laundry practices as primitive and inadequate. More alarming was the latter's tradition of mixed bathing in public, which European Americans identified as proof of Mexicans' promiscuity and moral inferiority. Ordinances restricting cockfights demonstrated moral outrage, as Anglo-Texan officials and journalists cited such diversions as barbaric and evidence of Mexicans' penchant for animal cruelty. Finally, laws regulating fandangos restricted the popular dances, which officials linked to public disorder, crime, and immorality. Ultimately, the new laws led to the racialization of certain cultural practices and the criminalization of Tejanos.[136]

The English-language press played a significant role in criminalizing Tejanos, while the courts and law enforcement officers shared the media's bias. As elsewhere, English-language newspapers in the border region routinely accused Tejanos of various crimes, such as thefts and murders, often without citing any evidence. Typical news stories sensationalized crimes and cited unnamed Mexicans as the perpetrators. Additionally, these news stories often racialized the criminal method or the weapons as ones typically used by Mexicans. The media's pattern reflected a trend of associating Mexicans with delinquency and with a general disregard for human life. Moreover, newspapers criminalized Mexican residences and neighborhoods, thereby concocting the specter of widespread criminal activity and casting suspicion on the entire Mexican community. Influenced by these stories and their own biases, European American vigilantes circumvented the legal process by lynching Tejanos. Similarly, overzealous law enforcement officials often accused Tejanos of crimes before considering other suspects, and officials often shot unarmed suspects attempting to escape. Moreover, the arrival of European Americans in the region led to limited Tejano representation on local juries and legal representation. As a result, Tejanos began filling local jails and the state's penitentiary, where they became overrepresented.[137]

In New Mexico, Mexican Americans' experience in politics diverged from their experience in California and Texas, mainly based on their population.

At the war's conclusion in 1848, some two-thirds of the former Mexican citizens in the annexed lands lived in the territory of New Mexico. The Hispanos remained the majority of the population throughout the territorial period (1848–1912).[138] While residents of New Mexico could not vote in presidential elections or elect their governor (who was appointed by the US president), they did vote for municipal officers and territorial legislators (the president appointed the upper house, but adult white males elected the lower house).[139] As the majority of voters, Hispanos won the bulk of municipal and legislative elected offices. Throughout the territorial period, they made up 66 percent of the upper house (council) and 75 percent of the lower house.[140] A clear sign of their political influence was the established practice of conducting the legislative business in Spanish and then translating it into English, as well as the printing of all laws in Spanish and English. Yet Hispano officeholders remained politically subordinate to European Americans, who made up the vast majority of appointed territorial officials, including the governor. Moreover, the executive branch in the territory held more power than the legislative branch, which differed from states where government branches were coequal.[141]

Hispanos' majority also assured their representation in the legal system. Their substantial participation in the courts and law enforcement distinguished New Mexico from California and Texas, where Mexican Americans held more limited roles. While the overwhelming number of judges and lawyers were European Americans during the territorial period, law enforcement and the courts depended on Mexican Americans, who made up the vast majority of county sheriffs and bailiffs. As in the legislature, court proceedings were translated into Spanish to accommodate Mexican American jurors (who were the majority), and witness testimony was often given in Spanish and translated into English.[142] Elite Hispanos usually served as grand jurors who issued indictments, while their humbler counterparts served as petit jurors who heard trial proceedings and decided on convictions. According to legal scholar Laura Gómez, Mexican Americans' widespread jury participation counterbalanced the legal power of European Americans. Hispano grand jurors checked the power of European American criminal prosecutors, while petit jurors checked the power of European American judges.[143]

Although they remained politically and legally subordinate to European American newcomers, Hispanos nevertheless exercised considerable power in the legislature and the courts. As a result, the pattern of blanket criminalization of Mexican Americans in California and Texas did not occur in New Mexico.[144] The influence of Mexican Americans in the legislative and judicial branches of New Mexico remained significant through statehood in 1912 as the state's constitution made English and Spanish the official languages. Moreover, the constitution required official documents to be printed in both languages and prohibited an English-language proficiency requirement from barring Spanish speakers from holding political office or serving as jurors.[145]

Nevertheless, Hispanos remained second-class citizens in New Mexico throughout the nineteenth century due to their perceived race. Despite their majorities in New Mexico, Mexican Americans remained politically, legally, and economically subordinate to European American newcomers. Part of their disadvantage was New Mexico's continued status as a territory. Although New Mexico applied for statehood ten times between 1850 and 1908, the US Congress rejected the petitions because federal legislators perceived the majority of New Mexico's residents as nonwhite.[146] New Mexico remained a territory for sixty-four years after the US-Mexico War, an extremely long period during which other western territories gained statehood. Unsurprisingly, the population of these other territories held European American majorities. Congress feared that granting New Mexico statehood would permit the Hispano majority to assert their independence and challenge their political subordination.[147] The limited rights of territorial residents meant that the Hispanos and Native Americans of New Mexico remained a "colonized" people despite the citizenship guarantees of the Treaty of Guadalupe Hidalgo.[148] While the political experience of Hispanos in New Mexico differed from the political reality of Mexican Americans elsewhere, they shared a common experience of being perceived as nonwhite by European Americans. According to Gómez, Mexican Americans have continued to be perceived as "off-white" since their forcible incorporation into the United States because they are legally white but socially nonwhite.[149] But unlike other "off-white" groups, such as the Irish, Italians, and Jews, who became "white" several generations after their arrival in the United States, Mexican Americans did not and may be permanently "off-white."[150] Nevertheless, Mexican Americans' tenuous claims to whiteness has generated obstacles to potential alliances with other US racial minorities, such as African Americans, Native Americans, and Asian Americans.[151]

MEXICAN AMERICANS THROUGHOUT the US Southwest lost social, economic, and political power after US annexation in 1848. The first generation would confront obstacles to exercising their citizenship rights that would persist well into the twenty-first century. They struggled to exercise their right to vote, serve on juries, protect their property rights, secure adequate legal representation, and obtain protection from extralegal violence. Their problems (e.g., land loss and limited voting rights) were compounded by the continued arrival of European Americans as the newcomers assumed positions of power and displaced the community's leaders. The obstacles confronting Mexican Americans varied by region, so their civil rights activism also differed. While they lost political power throughout the US Southwest, the loss was more gradual in regions where Mexican Americans remained a large proportion of the population. Regional differences also influenced how collective war memories were invoked. Hispanos in New Mexico were more likely than Mexican Americans elsewhere to assert their Spanish ancestry and claim whiteness in efforts to convince Congress of their suitability for statehood.

Mexican Americans engaged in a range of civil rights campaigns to exercise their citizenship rights. During the nineteenth century, many of these campaigns cited the Treaty of Guadalupe Hidalgo's citizenship guarantees and called for federal and local authorities to enforce the treaty. The first generation also recalled the US-Mexico War as an event that precipitated their economic, political, and social loss. Mexican Americans waged most civil rights campaigns through legal channels, but some pursued extralegal resistance as well. The fence cutting and railroad track removal of Las Gorras Blancas (the White Caps) in New Mexico, as well as the social banditry of Joaquín Murrieta and Tiburcio Vásquez in California, are examples of this extralegal resistance. While armed resistance movements did not explicitly refer to the war and treaty, they often cited the problems caused by the war, and media reports about the resistance cited the treaty's promises of citizenship rights.

Subsequent generations would continue to remember the war and the treaty as they engaged in campaigns to secure rights. This book demonstrates that memories of the war and the treaty have spurred collective actions and civil rights movements across several generations. While war memories often recalled the forcible US conquest, separation of the US Southwest from Mexico, and subsequent property losses, memories of the treaty emphasized unfulfilled promises. The circulation of war memories occurred in various ways. The first generation remembered the war most vividly, as they lived through the US military conquest and witnessed its immediate effects, such as the jurisdictional change, the introduction of a new language and laws, and the arrival and assertion of power by European American newcomers.

Some of these collective memories were passed on from one generation to another through oral traditions and writings. The transmission of collective memories via oral tradition reached local community members and helped explain the struggles of the first Mexican Americans to future generations. The written documents of each generation carried the potential to disperse memories across a broader audience, provide details sometimes lost in oral memories, and compare the experiences of Mexican Americans across various regions. Subsequent generations absorbed war memories as they interacted with other groups, such as Native Americans and European Americans. The collective memories of a community were also influenced by the transnational circulation of memories via recent immigrants and Mexico-based newspapers. Community newspapers, often published in Spanish or as bilingual editions, also played a role in disseminating collective war memories.

For future generations, published memoirs and community histories would serve to disseminate and preserve memories of the mid-nineteenth-century conquest. While subsequent generations invoked the war and the treaty as they pursued collective actions to secure property, suffrage, and legal rights, they also cited the treaty for other causes not necessarily specified in the pact. The clearest invocation was when Mexican Americans cited the treaty to advocate for their language rights, which the treaty did not mention. In cases like language rights, Mexican Americans pursued collective action by invoking the treaty to support claims to what they believed they were entitled to as US citizens.[152]

CHAPTER TWO

Responding to Conquest
Land Loss, Violence, and Repatriation

In 1856, *El Clamor Público*, a Los Angeles–based Spanish-language newspaper, carried several editorials about the long and expensive process undertaken by Californios to confirm their land titles. The editorials' author, Francisco Ramírez, described recent developments to expedite the confirmation process but lamented that the changes were too late for landowners. California's 1851 land act required Californios to prove the legitimacy of their land titles within two years or risk losing the land to the public domain. The expenses from this process forced many to sell parts of their lands. Afterward, these landowners faced additional lawsuits from European American squatters on their land. Ramírez wrote, "Is there no limit to the arbitrariness of the strong over the weak, of the conqueror over the conquered," as he criticized laws to protect squatters, many of whom enjoyed powerful political connections.[1] "Many of the elder Californios . . . now see themselves in the most lamentable poverty and indigence," Ramírez decried, "because of the litigation they have been subjected to in order to prove their land titles." He railed against the fact that "a legislature as hungry as it is unjust has decreed that all lands [with unconfirmed titles] will be considered public property." Ramírez asserted that the legislature's actions violated the treaty and concluded, "Can there be a more bald-faced affront to the solemn treaty of [Guadalupe] Hidalgo?"[2]

Through *El Clamor Público*, Ramírez publicized the myriad ways in which Californios were denied their citizenship rights and waged a vigorous campaign to defend those rights, often invoking the US Constitution and the Treaty of Guadalupe Hidalgo. *El Clamor Público* was the first Spanish-language newspaper in Southern California under the complete control of an ethnic Mexican publisher. Ramírez believed that it was his duty to point out the discrepancy between the rights promised to Mexican Americans and the reality in which they lived. Nevertheless, he wrote about his admiration for the US Constitution and the benefits of freedom of expression, reveling in the freedom of the press to launch his many critiques of state and federal governments. By frequently invoking the treaty in his editorial and columns, Ramírez strategically used remembrances of the war to wage his civil rights

Francisco P. Ramírez, editor and publisher of *El Clamor Público*. Seaver Center for Western History Research, Los Angeles County Museum of Natural History.

campaigns. *El Clamor Público* serves as one of the earliest examples of a Spanish-language newspaper that not only informed its readers about local, national, and international news but also advocated for civil rights on their behalf. But it was only one of many memories of the war.

New Mexico's Statehood Campaign

Spanish-language newspapers were vital in the campaigns to obtain statehood for New Mexico, which often invoked the treaty. The treaty's Article 9 stipulated that residents in the ceded territories who chose not to retain Mexican citizenship would become US citizens and be admitted as a state to enjoy full citizenship rights "at the proper time," to be determined by the US Congress.[3] Until they obtained statehood, residents of territories had limited civil rights and self-government. In the mid-nineteenth century, the US Congress typically approved statehood petitions when a territory's white population was at least 60,000. The 1850 population (excluding Pueblo Indians) of the New Mexico Territory, which included the present-day states of New Mexico and Arizona, exceeded the minimum 60,000 population requirement. However, opposition to granting New Mexico statehood developed in Congress over the territory's antislavery stance and the perceived racial demographics of the territory's residents.

The congressional debates during the US-Mexico War and the negotiations over the treaty bore long-term consequences for New Mexico statehood and for Nuevomexicanos' identity. As Congress deliberated about the amount of Mexico's land to acquire, Senator John Calhoun of South Carolina expressed his opposition to incorporating large parts of Mexico. The United States was a white nation, argued Calhoun, so Mexicans should not be incorporated because they were "Indians" and not Caucasians. He maintained that because the United States was a "government of the white race," incorporating Mexicans would destroy the nation's racial order. Along with other congressmen, he believed that Mexicans, as a mixed race, were less desirable than Native Americans because Mexicans had inherited the worst characteristics of Native Americans and Spaniards.[4] Even congressmen who supported acquiring Mexico's land favored incorporating only its less populated northern territories to avoid aggravating the nation's racial problems.[5] Mexican officials offered a contrasting view during the treaty negotiations. Mexican government negotiators characterized Mexican identity as being based on national citizenship, while American officials viewed it as a racial identity.[6] These divergent views on Mexican identity would continue to shape Nuevomexicanos' identity for decades.

After the war's conclusion, US congressmen made similar arguments to oppose granting New Mexico statehood. Opposition to statehood was present among both Southern and Northern politicians who characterized Mexicans as racial "mongrels" incapable of self-government and not entitled to US citizenship. A typical view, expressed by Michigan senator Lewis Cass, held that Mexicans were "a hybrid race of Spanish and Indian origin, ignorant, degraded, demoralized and priest-ridden."[7] These characterizations of Mexicans defined them as nonwhite and unfit to be US citizens.

Shortly after the signing of the Treaty of Guadalupe Hidalgo, several prominent New Mexican politicians petitioned Congress to convert the territory's military government into a temporary territorial government until statehood was granted. In their petition, the territory's politicians argued that New Mexicans wanted to be protected from the introduction of slaves into the territory. Their antislavery views offended Southern congressmen, who had hoped to admit New Mexico as a slave state. Despite multiple statehood petitions over the next half century, Southern congressmen remained firmly opposed to admitting New Mexico as a free state.[8] From the war's end until 1912, residents held limited rights because New Mexico remained a territory. The federal government considered residents of territories as dependent and therefore not entitled to self-government and not able to fully participate in national politics. They could not elect their own governor, were barred from voting for the country's president, and did not enjoy an independent judiciary; in addition, the decisions of their elected representatives needed approval by the federal government.[9]

To counter such aspersions, statehood supporters emphasized New Mexico's Spanish colonial past. They sought to convince critics that the region's Mexicans and Native Americans were "racially fit" and capable of self-government.[10] Highlighting Nuevomexicanos' "Spanish" ancestry was meant to "whiten" them and persuade federal officials of the territory's eligibility for statehood.[11] Prior to the US Civil War, Hispano territorial legislators developed an argument in favor of statehood based on depicting their ancestors as the region's original settler-colonists. This argument credited Nuevomexicanos' ancestors for bringing "civilization" to New Mexico before the arrival of European Americans. Spanish-language newspapers promoted this new claim by characterizing Hispanos' as "native" to the region. Not only did this argument erase Indigenous peoples' claims to the region, but it also cast Mexicans and European Americans as allies facing a common Indigenous enemy.[12] As historian Anthony Mora explains, claiming "native" status was meant to give Nuevomexicanos "a level of authenticity" and distinguish them from Mexican nationals, who were perceived as foreigners. The region's isolation, Nuevomexicanos claimed, had led their "native New Mexican" ancestors to develop a separate culture from Mexican nationals.[13]

Statehood supporters selectively remembered the Spanish conquest of Mexico's far north by forgetting the extensive process of racial and ethnic intermixing that accompanied this conquest. New Mexico's Spanish-language newspapers, as historian John Nieto-Phillips points out, increasingly began using the term *"hispano-americano"* to refer to Nuevomexicanos' Spanish ancestry and allegiance to the "American" nation.[14] The newspapers employed this term to distinguish the region's Spanish-speaking population from Mexican nationals and from European Americans. They also conveniently forgot the ethnic, cultural, and linguistic links tying them to Mexican nationals.[15]

Mexican Consuls and Advocacy

Memories of the US-Mexico War and the treaty have shaped the advocacy of Mexico's consuls since 1848. The consuls began working on behalf of Mexico's former citizens immediately after the treaty was signed because the treaty's Article 8 provided for Mexicans in the annexed lands to become US citizens or keep their Mexican citizenship by moving to Mexico. Mexico's government sent three commissioners to California, Texas, and New Mexico after the war to assist those who wished to keep their Mexican citizenship and move to Mexico. The territory's governor prevented Ramón Ortiz, the commissioner sent to New Mexico, from meeting with Mexican communities after Ortiz's initial visits were enthusiastically received. The governor justified his decision on the pretense of guarding the public peace. Subsequently, the territory's officials used various administrative obstacles to prevent the territory's Mexican residents from declaring their intention to return and thus receiving assistance from Mexican officials. Moreover, local newspapers refused to publish notices from the commissioner regarding the Mexican government's willingness to help residents return to Mexico.[16]

After the Mexican government sent a diplomatic protest to US officials, the US secretary of state replied that Article 8 did not obligate the United States to receive Mexican commissioners to assist with repatriation purposes. According to Mexican officials, the United States began violating the spirit of the treaty by preventing its commissioners from assisting those Mexicans who wished to repatriate.[17] Some historians posit that preventing Mexican officials from assisting Mexican citizens regarding the treaty's provisions meant that some borderland residents became US citizens against their will.[18] Such historical interpretations demonstrate that the post-annexation period and the treaty's enforcement remained important issues for Mexico. Moreover, these interpretations disseminated Mexico's official war memories among its population and, in turn, among Mexican Americans as they interacted with Mexican immigrants in the United States.

Concern for its former citizens would lead Mexico's consular officials to monitor and protest treaty violations throughout the US Southwest. Mexico would soon learn that the United States would not prioritize enforcement of the treaty's guarantees to its former citizens. During California's gold rush, Mexico's minister of foreign relations, Luis de la Rosa, contacted the US secretary of state to protest violent attacks and persecution of Mexicans. European Americans were responsible for robberies and violent expulsions against Mexicans, stated de la Rosa, condemning these violent actions as treaty violations. The Mexican government asked for reports from its vice-consul in California about expulsions of Mexicans and other rights violations.[19] It also expressed concern about the US government's failure to inform Mexican Americans of their treaty rights and to enforce such rights. However, US officials ignored the Mexican government's protests.

According to Mexican officials, the numerous treaty violations, including widespread theft of property by squatters; injustices of the courts; and extralegal lynchings left Mexican Americans with little recourse.[20] European Americans' violence and threats undoubtedly convinced some ethnic Mexicans to repatriate. Various Mexican consuls in the United States and state governors in Mexico attempted to assist these residents to return to Mexico. Tamaulipas's governor, for example, wrote to the minister of foreign relations in April 1850 to request assistance in relocating some fifty families who had appealed to him for help. Three years later, the Mexican consul in Brownsville, Texas, informed the same minister that a representative had appealed to him for transportation funds and further assistance on behalf of 100 families from Nacogdoches, who wished to repatriate to Coahuila.[21]

Since the mid-nineteenth century, Mexico's government has sought to protect its citizens residing in the United States through its consuls. Among the duties of Mexico's consular officials have been the promotion of trade between Mexico and the United States, the protection of Mexican citizens residing in or traveling through the United States, and the defense of Mexico's interests. The goals of Mexico's consuls have been more difficult to achieve in the United States because its significant ethnic Mexican community has confronted oppression and discrimination since 1848. In countries with smaller ethnic Mexican populations, Mexico's consuls have been more successful in protecting these populations.[22] Since the war's conclusion, Mexico's consular officials have assisted Mexican citizens and Mexican Americans with various legal issues, including immigration, housing, labor, and extralegal attacks. The tensions in the war's aftermath underscored the consuls' importance among ethnic Mexicans confronting the war's consequences, including protecting their property and their civil rights. In the 1850s, for example, the Mexican consul in San Francisco protested the imposition of the Foreign Miners' Tax (which targeted ethnic Mexicans, among others) and the extralegal violence that broke out in California's gold mines.[23]

California's Gold Rush Violence

The discovery of gold in Northern California yielded devastating effects on the state's Mexican and Indigenous people as the European American population surged. Several days before representatives from Mexico and the United States signed the Treaty of Guadalupe Hidalgo, John Marshall, a New Jersey native, discovered gold while constructing a mill for German-born immigrant John Sutter at the fork of the American River in present-day Sacramento.

Marshall and Sutter had immigrated to Alta California while it was still under Mexican control. The discovery of gold set off a massive influx of migrants and immigrants, and would have profound political and economic impacts on California. As its European American population mushroomed, California successfully petitioned to become a state in 1850, while the revenue from gold financed the development of the state and region, including the construction of transcontinental railroads that linked the American West with the rest of the United States. Among the migrants were European Americans and African Americans from elsewhere in the nation, as well as immigrants from China, France, Mexico, and Chile.

As the "world rushed in" to California, the newcomers came into conflict with the region's Native Americans and Californios. European American newcomers launched several genocidal wars against the region's Indigenous people, whose population plummeted from 150,000 in 1846 to 30,000 by 1870.[24] Among the new arrivals were experienced miners from northern Mexico and Chile, whose success in the diggings led to conflict with European American miners. Motivated by a volatile mix of jealousy and nativism, European Americans attacked so-called foreign workers (i.e., Mexicans, Chileans, and Chinese) to expel them from the mines. The vigilantes enlisted the state's lawmakers, who passed the Foreign Miners' Tax in 1850, which charged "foreigners" a twenty-dollar-per-month tax for the "privilege" of mining. This law led many workers to retreat to nearby towns and to Southern California. After the repeal of the 1850 law, a new Foreign Miners' Tax was passed in 1852 targeting newly arrived Chinese miners, some of whom gradually abandoned mining to enter service occupations. The violence and selective enforcement of discriminatory legislation violated the treaty's citizenship guarantees for Californios. In addition to violence, the Californios were forced to confront European American squatters who invaded their lands, killed their livestock, and stole their crops.[25]

The lingering influences of the US-Mexico War and competition over gold diggings increased conflict, leading to European American vigilante violence and a surge in lynchings. The war had exacerbated anti-Mexican sentiments as European Americans confused the politics of Mexico's government with the views of ethnic Mexicans. Mexican Americans experienced hostility from European Americans who blamed Californios, Tejanos, and Nuevomexicanos for policies and military engagements over which borderland residents held little control. In California, the anti-Mexican sentiment expressed itself in nativist newspaper editorials, legislation, and extrajudicial lynchings. Vigilantes often justified the lynching of Mexicans by accusing the victims of murder or theft.[26]

The most common alleged crime of African American and Mexican lynching victims was murder. According to scholars William Carrigan and Clive Webb, the second most common accusation for Mexican lynching victims was theft, while for African Americans, it was "violations of sexual norms."[27] This disparity was due to European American perceptions of African Americans as sexual competitors and of Mexican Americans as "unprincipled, conniving, and untrustworthy." European Americans feminized Mexican American men as belonging to "effeminate" races who were "conquered" in the US West. Despite this disparity, Mexican men were as likely to become victims of mass lynchings (in which groups of Mexicans were lynched at once) before 1890 as were African Americans. In gold rush California, the lynching of Mexicans became spectator events, drawing large crowds who gathered to affirm white supremacy.[28]

While the vast majority of Mexican lynching victims were men, European Americans occasionally lynched Mexican women. An infamous case was the lynching of Josefa Juvera Loaiza on July 5, 1851, in Downieville, California. The conflict began the previous day during the town's Fourth of July celebration. The festivities, coinciding with the first Independence Day celebrations since California statehood, included rowdy intoxicated crowds in this Northern California mining town.[29] On the evening of July 4, a drunk English immigrant, Fredrick Cannon, burst into the house shared by Josefa and her husband José by knocking the front door off its hinges. Josefa, alone at the time, managed to convince Cannon to leave. The next day Cannon returned and was confronted by José, who asked him to pay for the damaged door. Josefa joined the heated exchange and was promptly insulted by Cannon. She dared him to enter her house and repeat the insult. When Cannon entered her home, she stabbed him, and he died. A mob apprehended the couple, set up a hasty "trial," and convicted Josefa of murder despite her claim of self-defense. During her trial, a European American physician testified that Josefa was pregnant in an unsuccessful attempt to defend her.[30] The mob drove José out of town and sentenced Josefa to hang. She refused to be escorted to the gallows on the riverbank, instead walking alone. Unapologetic, she reportedly said, "I would do the same again if I was so provoked." Her lynching was a mass spectacle, as over 2,000 men witnessed the first woman hanged in the state of California.[31]

The hanging of Josefa Juvera Loaiza is inextricably tied to the memories of the US conquest. The circumstances of her hanging have led to various contradictory myths about the events that led to her death. In various European American accounts, she is often identified only by her first name, sometimes as "Juanita," and occasionally simply as "the Spanish woman." The failure to provide her full name, or to refer to her accurately, fits a pattern common throughout the US West whereby European Americans' news accounts and memoirs often omitted the names and surnames of Mexicans. Various scholars point to this practice of "forgetting" or ignoring Mexicans' names as a conscious denial of Mexicans' humanity.[32] These omissions are more apparent and significant when the same narratives that ignore Mexicans' names contain the full names of European Americans. For the assault on Juvera Loaiza, European American accounts usually identify the miner by his full name and occasionally add his middle names (Alexander Augustus). These narratives also cast aspersions on Juvera Loaiza's character by referring to her sexual reputation. They characterize her as a prostitute (in some accounts, Cannon calls Juvera Loaiza a "whore") and question the legitimacy of her marriage (several accounts refer to José as her paramour and a gambler instead of her husband). These accounts further challenge José's masculinity by claiming that he fled and failed to protect Josefa after her arrest.[33]

The tragic experience of Josefa Juvera Loaiza and José Loaiza exemplifies the violence and nativism experienced by non-elite ethnic Mexicans in California and was a legacy of the war. While neither was known to have been a US citizen, their experience in the working-class gold-mining town mirrors the challenges faced by non-elite Californios.[34] European Americans believed that Mexican immigrant and Californio miners were "foreigners" despite the latter's US citizenship, and also expressed anger that Latino miners were more skilled and successful at gold mining. This resentment, along with anti-Mexican views instigated by the US-Mexico War, produced an explosive strain of nativism that manifested itself in mob violence. Throughout the northern mines, from the American River at Sutter's Mill to the Tuolumne, Mokelumne, and Stanislaus Rivers, European American mobs drove Latinos from the most productive mining areas.[35] A combination of violence and the selective enforcement of the Foreign Miners' Tax compelled Mexicans, Chileans, and Peruvians to leave the mines. Mobs initiated killing sprees, resulting in scores of dead Latino miners and abandoned camps.[36] California's southern mines witnessed even worse violence because the vigilantes there were often migrants from Texas, including veterans of the US-Mexico War and Texas Rangers, who felt extreme racial antipathy toward Mexicans.[37] While the wealth and political connections of elite Californios helped them obtain some protection from violence, working-class Latinos could not rely on their status to shield them from mobs, especially given direct economic competition (e.g., jostling over mining claims) between vigilantes and their victims.

José Loaiza mourned Josefa Juvera Loaiza in various ways, but his legal claim against the US government left a written record (and a memory) of the tragic episode that took his wife's life. The vigilante committee that lynched Josefa also ordered José to leave town. He left Downieville and returned to Mexico. From there, following the establishment of the US-Mexican Claims Commission under the Convention of 1868, he filed a claim against the US government "for the lynching of his wife and banishment of himself by a mob."[38] His petition was one of 998 total claims filed, mostly by ethnic Mexicans asserting losses from Indigenous depredations.[39] The commissioners rejected José's claim on June 11, 1875, presumably because he could not prove his legal marriage to Josefa.[40]

In addition to exposing white supremacy in the post-annexation US West, the lynching of a Mexican woman highlights questions about the Loaizas' citizenship and legal issues around the jurisdictional transfer of California. Contemporary newspaper and personal accounts identify the couple as "Mexicans" and identify Josefa as "the Spanish woman" or as a "Mexican woman" without any reference to citizenship.[41] At least one newspaper account refers to Josefa as a foreigner, presuming her lack of US citizenship.[42] The absence of any direct mention of the couple's US citizenship is not surprising, because the majority of European Americans believed that most working-class Mexicans were "foreigners," not US citizens. Thirty years later, *La Voz del Nuevo Mundo*, a Chilean newspaper based in San Francisco, identified Josefa by her maiden name, Juvera, and stated that her birthplace was Atotonilco el Alto, Jalisco, in Mexico, and that José was from Sinaloa. The couple had met and married in San Jose sometime in the winter of 1850 to 1851, but the news account did not indicate when the couple arrived in California or whether either had acquired US citizenship. It is possible that the couple arrived in California before the US-Mexico War and thus acquired US citizenship in 1849 according to the Treaty of Guadalupe Hidalgo.[43] Regardless of the couple's citizenship, they had certain rights (e.g., due process, legal counsel, and jury trial) as residents of California and the United States. The US-Mexico War and the subsequent jurisdictional transfer of California complicated more than the couple's citizenship, as it also called their marriage into question. Just as the validity of property titles granted to Californios by the Spanish and Mexican governments were subsequently questioned in US courts, so too could marriages or common-law marriages be contested when a plaintiff crossed the international boundary. The 1881 news article states that the couple was legally married because Josefa had "sworn eternal fidelity before a competent authority" in San Jose. It also notes that José's claim was denied because he could not prove his legal marriage.⁴⁴ The US-Mexican Claims Commission had placed the burden of proof on claimants like José. Moreover, the jurisdictional transfer of California created several obstacles for José, who had to prove his legal marriage and engage with the US legal system from afar.

The collective memories of Josefa Juvera Loaiza's lynching are significant because they illustrate the effects of the US conquest, the subsequent denial of ethnic Mexicans' rights, and one woman's resistance, demonstrating how a Mexican woman challenged white supremacy by killing her attacker. She paid the ultimate price for challenging the dominant norms, but her example shows that Mexican women were not mere victims but also agents who attempted to defend themselves.⁴⁵ According to one contemporary account, Juvera Loaiza's bravery was evinced in her refusal to be led to the gallows, walking there on her own, climbing the ladder to the scaffold, "and placing the rope around her neck with her own hands."⁴⁶ She also reportedly adjusted the noose around her neck, "releasing her luxuriant hair from beneath it so that it should flow free."⁴⁷ While some European Americans acknowledged her resoluteness, bravery, and dignity in facing her executioners, others claimed that she showed a lack of remorse for killing Cannon and characterized her as "one who thirsted for blood."⁴⁸ Beyond these sensationalist accounts are the larger forces that led to violence. At the most basic level, Juvera Loaiza's lynching poses a dramatic example of violence against women in the post-annexation US West. According to various scholars, this violence included lynching and often targeted women of color.⁴⁹ Previously, this kind of violence had been directed against Indigenous women during the Spanish and Mexican periods of rule.⁵⁰ With the US takeover of Mexico's far north, the targets of this violence expanded to include ethnic Mexican women. Juvera Loaiza's lynching exemplifies the state and federal governments' denial of ethnic Mexicans' rights. These governments were unable and unwilling to enforce their rights to due process, protection from sexual violence, and life.⁵¹

The anti-Latino violence and lynchings in mid-nineteenth-century California spurred civil rights activism by journalists, who wrote stinging critiques in Spanish-language newspapers. Among the most prominent and outspoken was Francisco Ramírez, who established *El Clamor Público* in Los Angeles in 1855, when he was seventeen years old. Born in 1837, when the city remained under Mexican jurisdiction, Ramírez experienced the enormous transition brought about by the US conquest and annexation. Well versed in Spanish, English, and French, he gained writing and publishing experience by working at three different newspapers from the age of fourteen.⁵² A proponent of nineteenth-century Mexican liberalism, Ramírez strongly supported racial equality and abolitionism. In the newspaper's initial issues, he expressed his admiration for the United States, its founding documents, and its laws. He also promoted cooperation among European Americans and Californios and urged readers to become Americanized by learning English and familiarizing themselves with US laws.[53] Despite admiring the United States, he became a frequent critic of the state and federal governments for failing to protect ethnic Mexicans from vigilante violence.[54]

As anti-Latino violence increased, Ramírez's optimism waned and he started denouncing the denial of rights and the lynchings of Latinos. In decrying anti-Latino violence, his newspaper addressed a problem affecting working-class gold miners and laborers. In 1856, Ramírez provided a sobering account of racial tensions and the failure of justice by stressing that Los Angeles had been the "theater of the most atrocious assassinations" for more than six years. He noted that the criminals usually escaped and that justice was almost never served. Ramírez also described daily events following a city deputy's murder of Antonio Ruiz and the deputy's lack of indictment, which provoked outrage among the Mexican community.[55] In one editorial on the subject, Ramírez observed that the occurrences of the previous week had not been seen in California since the US-Mexico War.

Two years after the newspaper's founding, Ramírez was so disillusioned with the nation's democracy that he used the term *"linchocracia"* to refer to a democracy based on lynchings in an 1857 editorial.[56] An astute observer of the contradictions between lynching and democracy, Ramírez delivered this critique to challenge the nation's notions of equality. Mexicans had obtained the same rights and responsibilities as US citizens after the war, he reminded readers, but their hopes in obtaining these rights were dashed by widespread land loss and lynchings. "Only Mexicans have been sacrificed on these shameful gallows raised to launch their poor souls into eternity!" he wrote in August 1856. "Is this the *liberty* and *equality* in the country we have adopted?"[57] As the violence continued, Ramírez urged authorities to protect Mexicans and Chileans from lynchings and massacres.[58] When officials ignored his calls for justice, he resorted to more confrontational tactics, such as publishing the names of the men suspected of lynching several Mexicans in San Luis Obispo in 1858. His frustration with the denial of justice and the complicity of authorities led him to label law enforcement officials as "deaf, dumb, blind, and paralyzed."[59]

In addition to the problems facing working-class Latinos, *El Clamor Público* called attention to the major issue confronting elite Californios: the certification of their property titles within the US legal system. According to

Ramírez, the 1851 land act placed Californio property holders at a disadvantage by requiring them to bear the high costs of confirming their land titles. As the gold rush brought an invasion of European American squatters, Californio property holders faced lengthy and expensive legal costs to confirm their titles. Ramírez highlighted these costs and the steep lawyers' fees incurred by property holders. This complaint explicitly referred to the jurisdictional transfer of Mexico's land to the United States after the US-Mexico War. It also reminded readers of the treaty's promise to respect Mexicans' property rights. Alluding to these court costs and the practice of lawyers asking for payment in land, Ramírez wrote, "When they [Californios] receive patent, if they are not already ruined, they will be very close to it."[60]

While Ramírez advocated for Latinos' civil rights issues, his activism was full of contradictions. He not only was a vocal supporter of the civil rights of Californios but also advocated on behalf of Chileans and embraced the term "*hispano americanos*" in an incipient pan-Latino outlook. By promoting Latino unity, Ramírez hoped to obtain fair electoral representation for Latinos.[61] He made little distinction between Californios (with US citizenship) and Mexican immigrants (without US citizenship).[62] Ramírez was also a strong supporter of abolition and urged lawmakers to prevent slavery from being established in California. He denounced the mistreatment of African Americans, Chinese immigrants, and Native Americans by European Americans. Yet he did not accept the equality of these groups with ethnic Mexicans, and his newspaper was complicit in promoting contemporary racist stereotypes.[63] He characterized Californios as the region's first settlers, while forgetting that Native Americans had previously settled the region. "California has fallen into hands of the ambitious sons of North America," he wrote, "who will not stop until they have satisfied their passions, by driving the first occupants of the land out of the country, vilifying their religion, and disfiguring their customs."[64] Apparently, it was lost on Ramírez that his accusation against North Americans (meaning European Americans) could just as easily apply to Spanish Mexican settlers who pursued similar actions against Native Americans.

Ramírez waged one of the first civil rights campaigns through *El Clamor Público*, motivated by the promises in the Treaty of Guadalupe Hidalgo and the ideals of the US Constitution. The newspaper was unsuccessful in stopping the lynchings of Latinos and the dispossession of Californios, and it closed down in 1859 due to poor circulation.[65] After growing increasingly frustrated over violence and civil rights abuses, Ramírez moved to Mexico only to return years later. He was keenly aware of the war's impact on Californios and of the treaty's promises. Ramírez understood the treaty's bestowal of citizenship rights on Mexicans and continuously called on US and California authorities to enforce such rights. Addressing his fellow Californios, he wrote, "More than any other people, we have certain indisputable rights in the nation where we now live. The Treaty of Guadalupe Hidalgo has conceded to us broad privileges to freely enjoy our rights and property."[66] Yet European American views deeply influenced Ramirez and other Californios' outlook toward African Americans, Chinese immigrants, and Native Americans. By the mid-nineteenth century, the United States had not granted citizenship to these groups, nor did European Americans consider them equals. Subsequent generations of activists would follow Ramírez's example by advocating for the citizenship rights of Mexican Americans while neglecting the rights of other populations of color.

Beyond decrying anti-Latino violence, *El Clamor Público* proposed several strategies for Latinos to claim civil rights and their place within the nation. The newspaper placed the burden of protecting Latinos directly on the federal and state governments. But it also suggested that Californios claim the state as their "native land" as a way of advocating for their belonging. Ramírez's admiration for the laws and government of the United States led him to promote "Americanization" for Californios, who he believed should abandon certain "traditions" that were no longer useful. Similarly, he urged Spanish-language speakers to teach their children English so they could better adapt to the United States.[67] Ramírez pressed Mexican Americans to exercise their voting rights to obtain better political representation. However, Ramírez and other journalists overestimated their ability to exercise these rights and government officials' willingness to enforce several treaty provisions, including citizenship rights. He later grew disappointed in electoral politics and in Californios' support of the Democratic Party due to the party's conservative and racist policies.

By the time *El Clamor Público* shuttered, Ramírez had shifted from an initial focus on the plight of Californios to a broader effort to defend the rights of various Latino immigrants and promote pan-Latino unity. He also developed a strong anti-imperialist stance and came to equate Californios with Tejanos and Nuevomexicanos as colonized people who had endured the US conquest. According to literary scholar Nicholás Kanellos, Ramírez's anti-imperialist, transnational, and pan-Latino views led him to believe that filibustering expeditions threatened other parts of Latin America with a similar destiny as the colonized Latinos within the United States.[68]

Although its five-year existence was relatively short, *El Clamor Público* created a significant documentary record on racially motivated violence against

Latinos and left a groundbreaking legacy of civil rights activism. The newspaper's coverage of violence against Latinos produced an important documentary base for civil rights activists to draw from and for future scholars of violence and lynchings to consult. Several scholars note that historians who rely exclusively on English-language sources to study lynchings assume that racially targeted lynchings were first directed at African Americans and incorrectly date the emergence of this violence to the post-Reconstruction period.[69] *El Clamor Público*'s coverage of lynchings and mob violence targeting Latinos in the mid-nineteenth century corrects this assumption and demonstrates the importance of using Spanish-language sources for understanding US history. At a time when the region's English-language newspapers promoted conservative politics, this short-lived newspaper left an important legacy by disseminating progressive ideas about Californios' national identity, relationship to Latino immigrants, civil rights, and memory of the US-Mexico War. Ramírez engaged in civil rights activism by informing Spanish-speaking newspaper readers of their rights, urging them to exercise their franchise, and reminding them of the promises of the Treaty of Guadalupe Hidalgo.[70]

The civil rights legacy of *El Clamor Público* is important because the newspaper challenged the United States' claims of democratic values with stinging criticism backed up by detailed evidence. Ramírez repeatedly lauded the United States for its system of government, laws, and ideals. Yet he was a strong critic of government officials' failure to enforce its laws and uphold its ideals of equality, justice, and freedom. "We are asking for something that is very just, as they conform to the rights of equality, justice, and liberty that the laws confer to us," he wrote in an 1857 editorial, "like with the privilege of being born here."[71] In addition to publishing sharp editorials, he also republished critical commentaries from other Spanish-language newspapers. "The North Americans pretend to give us lessons in humanity and to bring our people the doctrine of salvation so we can govern ourselves, to respect the laws and conserve order," asserted an editorial reprinted from San Francisco's *La Crónica*. "Are these the ones who treat us worse than slaves?"[72]

According to literary scholar Coya Paz Brownrigg, *El Clamor Público* provides "an early case study of how marginalized groups have used lynching to challenge US claims to democratic values." She credited Ramírez for publicizing the horrors of lynching to change public opinion and press for civil and political rights, the same way that African American activists would pursue a similar strategy several decades later during the post-Reconstruction period. Scholars Carrigan and Webb also compare Ramírez to subsequent African American activists by observing that Ramírez "prefigured the language of

[B]lack civil rights activism" by warning of armed violence if the law was not upheld.[73] For Spanish-language periodicals, *El Clamor Público* served as an important model to advocate on behalf of the downtrodden and disenfranchised. Other Spanish-language newspapers in California (San Francisco's *La Voz del Nuevo Mundo*) and elsewhere in the Southwest (Tucson's *El Fronterizo*) would subsequently engage in similar activism to promote the interests of their Spanish-speaking readers.

The Last Nineteenth-Century Mexican Mayor of San Antonio

Anti-Mexican violence, land loss, and dashed hopes were also topics of a memoir published in 1858 by Juan Nepomuceno Seguín. In the memoir, he describes his experience as a supporter of the Texas secessionist struggle, during the ethnic turmoil of the Republic of Texas period, and in the aftermath of the US-Mexico War. Although set thousands of miles away in Mexico's northeastern borderlands, Seguín's memories touch on themes consistent with the experience of Californios. His efforts to establish political alliances and welcome European Americans to Texas in the 1830s only to be accused of disloyalty and threatened with death mirror the experiences of the Californios in the 1850s.

Like some Californios, the Tejano elite played a significant role as cultural brokers between European American arrivistes and the Mexican government. The Spanish colonial government and the independent nation of Mexico instituted colonization programs to attract European American immigrants to Texas after failing to entice sufficient Spanish Mexican colonists from central Mexico to its northern borderlands. The Spanish government began an empresario system that established a contract between the government and an individual immigrant by which the empresario would obtain land in exchange for settling between 150 and 800 families on the property. The colonial government sought these immigrants to establish Spain's claim to the land ahead of other European and US powers, and to use the colonists in borderland settlements as a shield against Indigenous attacks. Seeking to expand their commercial ties to European Americans and to increase their region's population, the Mexican Texan elite in San Antonio established personal relationships with various immigrants and often vouched for their character and honor in communications with Mexican federal officials. Since the colonization laws required that European American participants be of good character, the Mexican Texan elite's positive portrayal of these colonists was key to their acceptance as empresarios by Mexican government officials.[74]

Juan N. Seguín by Thomas Jefferson Wright, 1838. Seguín supported the Texas separatist rebellion, served as a senator during the Republic of Texas, and held several elected positions in San Antonio, including mayor. The State Preservation Board, Austin, Texas.

Despite his alliances with prominent European Americans and his active support for the secessionist struggle, Seguín faced charges of disloyalty and death threats, which forced him to flee his native land. After Texas's independence, Seguín was the only Mexican Texan senator in the republic. During his three terms as senator, Seguín served on various committees on military affairs and also advocated for the Spanish-language translation of the republic's laws. After resigning his senate seat in 1840, he joined Mexican federalist troops led by Antonio Canales in an unsuccessful campaign against the centralists. Upon returning to San Antonio, he won election as mayor but became engulfed in several conflicts with Anglo-Texans, yet he won reelection as mayor in 1841. Tensions with the arrivistes escalated when Seguín attempted to protect some Tejanos from attacks by squatters and was subsequently the target of rumors of assisting Mexican troops during the disastrous Santa Fe expedition of 1841 and the Mexican army's invasion of San Antonio in 1842. Facing death threats from European American squatters and political enemies, Seguín resigned as mayor to escape to safety in Mexico in 1842. The social and political situation had changed drastically within six years of Texas's independence. Seguín's experience illustrates how one of the rebellion's heroes and a sitting mayor felt so alienated and without government protection that he left his native land for refuge among his previous enemies.

Seguín's time in Mexico complicated his relationship with Anglo-Texans because he was forced to serve in that nation's military. According to his memoirs, the Mexican government imprisoned him but offered military service as a way out. Far from his relatives in San Antonio and with no way to provide for his family, he chose to serve in Mexico's army. Yet his role in the military was not as a regular soldier or officer. General Adrián Woll placed Seguín in charge of the Defensores de Béjar (Béxar Defenders), consisting of Mexican Texan refugees. An auxiliary unit to the Mexican army, the Defensores de Béjar were charged with scouting and transporting supplies. The roles given to Seguín and other Tejanos indicate that the Mexican military did not completely trust them with more serious missions. Not surprisingly, the Mexican Texans in the Defensores de Béjar had been responsible for similar tasks when they fought for Texas's secession. This similar role is another indication that neither the Mexican nor the Texas military officials were assured of Tejanos' loyalty, placing them in the in-between status that Mexican Americans would occupy in succeeding generations.

The Defensores de Béjar accompanied General Woll's troops in their 1842 attempt to retake San Antonio. Seguín and the other Defensores were blamed for killing three Anglo-Texans, which added to the enmity toward Seguín. During the US-Mexico War, Seguín led the Escuadrón auxiliar de Béjar (Béxar Auxiliary Squadron), composed of some members of the Defensores de Béjar. According to historian Raúl Ramos, Seguín's participation was probably required of his military impressment, but he was likely also motivated to defend Mexico because of his support for Mexican federalists and his conflicts with European Americans.[75] They patrolled the Rio Grande from Laredo to Presidio Rio Grande in order to guard against river crossings and Indigenous attacks. Seguín and his troops (many formerly from San Antonio) were involved in the Battle of Buena Vista, among others.[76] Despite his Mexican military service, Seguín chose to return to San Antonio after six years away. His return was facilitated by political connections with several Anglo-Texan political leaders, including Sam Houston and President Anson Jones. Settling near his father's ranch, he resumed his political career by becoming justice of the peace in Bexar County and precinct president. Seguín played a key role in establishing the Democratic Party of Bexar County in opposition to the Know-Nothing Party, which propagated xenophobic, anti-Catholic, and anti-Masonic views. In 1869, Seguín won election as Wilson County judge but served only one year before accompanying his son Santiago to Mexico.[77]

Seguín began his memoirs by acknowledging his native-born status, and his military service and political office holding in the Republic of Texas. By identifying himself as a native of "San Antonio de Béxar" and using the Spanish-language name for the city, he was asserting his sense of belonging and reminding readers of the city's Spanish colonial origins. This information was significant in 1858, when the city was undergoing a demographic shift as more European Americans became residents and officeholders. Similarly, he reminded readers that he fought for the republic from the independence struggle's inception to its conclusion at San Jacinto. This information established Seguín's devotion to the Texas cause at a time when European Americans were questioning his loyalty. Finally, Seguín reinforced his service as an elected senator in the republic. His election to statewide office demonstrated his political connections and knowledge of the republic's early laws in contrast to his critics, who "falsify historical fact with which they are imperfectly acquainted."[78]

Seguín's illustrious political and military career as well as elite standing did not shield him from spurious charges of disloyalty. European Americans would level similar charges of disloyalty at Mexican Americans elsewhere in the US Southwest after the war. Seguín acknowledged that "scribblers and personal enemies" had been attacking him, which motivated him to write his memoirs. Unfortunately, these men had obtained a degree of credibility due to "their origin and recent domination over the country." He identified his enemies as a few European Americans but was careful not to accuse all newcomers.[79]

Seguín's memoirs describe the republic's unfulfilled promises, as Tejanos were unable to exercise their rights as Texas citizens due to an increase in ethnic tensions with the influx of European Americans after 1836. Among the arrivistes were European American military officers who, he contended, were jealous of the esteem and trust that Anglo-Texan military leaders bestowed on him. The newcomers' racial bias increased this jealousy, according to Seguín, who wrote that "some envied my military position, as held by a Mexican." He characterized San Antonio as "the receptacle of the scum of society," as it was overrun by "American adventurers" and "many bad men, fugitives from their country." These newcomers attacked Mexican Texans, who appealed to Seguín. "At every hour of the day and night," wrote Seguín, "my countrymen ran to me for protection against the assaults or exactions of those adventurers."[80]

As mayor, Seguín maintained an obligation to protect his constituents from attacks, but he also felt an affinity for the victims because they were his "countrymen." Explaining his plight, he wrote, "Could I leave them defenseless, exposed to the assaults of foreigners who, on the pretext that they were Mexicans, treated them worse than brutes?"[81] He usually convinced assailants to stop, but occasionally he resorted to force. Unsurprisingly, European American adventurers, who were accustomed to exerting their will on people of color, resented the intervention of a Tejano mayor on behalf of his constituents. By calling the assailants "foreigners," Seguín employed a term used by Mexican Texans to disparage interlopers. Unlike European Americans who arrived before 1836 and nurtured friendships with Mexicans, the newly arrived adventurers did not assimilate into Mexican Texan society. The newcomers' attitude and indifference to the existing culture would be repeated elsewhere in the US Southwest after the US-Mexico War.[82]

Seguín described competition over land as the root of the ethnic conflict that exploded with the arrival of European American officers and adventurers after Texas's independence. The jealousy directed by the recently arrived US military officers at Seguín spread to "straggling American adventurers, who were already beginning to work their dark intrigues against the native families, whose only crime was that they owned large tracts of land and desirable property."[83] These adventurers terrorized Tejano families into abandoning their property, while squatters filed lawsuits against the owners. Seguín believed that squatters and land speculators attacked him because, as mayor, he became "an obstacle to the accomplishment of their villainous plans." He also pointed to the "land suits which still encumbers the docket of Bexar County" as proof of the adventurers' nefarious plans to "deprive rightful owners of their property."[84] Land conflicts and European Americans' attempts to deny property rights to Mexican Americans remained a constant during the Republic of Texas years and continued after the US-Mexico War.

Seguín's memoirs illustrate Mexican Americans' common experience of being caught between two competing nations. European Americans suspected Tejanos of remaining loyal to Mexico after Texas's independence due to the latter's ethnic background. Significantly, the newcomers did not question the loyalty of other Anglo-Texans (e.g., empresarios and their colonists) who had previously pledged their allegiance to Mexico—primarily due to their status as white Americans. European Americans' habit of confusing ethnic identity for national allegiance helped topple Seguín, a sitting mayor and revolutionary hero with an extensive social network among the Anglo-Texan and Mexican Texan elite. The rumors that Seguín helped the Mexican military, which exacerbated these suspicions, would not have carried the same weight had they been leveled at an Anglo-Texan mayor. Seguín believed that

Mexico's General Rafael Vázquez, who led the 1842 attempt to retake San Antonio, had initiated the rumor of Seguín's assistance to his troops. Some scholars believe that Vázquez initiated this rumor to force other Tejanos to side with Mexico.[85] While some Mexican Texans helped the Mexican army in its attempt to regain control of Texas, many Tejanos remained neutral in the conflict but nevertheless became victims of violence and forced dispossession due to spurious charges of disloyalty.[86]

These suspicions also bore tragic consequences for Seguín, who suffered social, economic, and political losses despite his illustrious military and political service to the Republic of Texas. Seguín considered himself to be a "foreigner in my native land" as a result of the hostility accompanying San Antonio's demographic changes. "Exiled and deprived of my privileges as a Texan citizen," he wrote, "I was outside the pale of society in Texas." He identified alienation and a lack of civil rights as a common experience for many Mexican Texans as European Americans flooded into Texas. Lacking protection from the Texas government and unable to exercise their rights, Seguín contended that he and other Tejanos were free to "seek protection elsewhere" by fleeing to Mexico. He justified his decision: "I had been tried by a rabble, condemned without a hearing, and consequently was at liberty to provide for my own safety."[87] Tellingly, he characterized the efforts to drive him away as unlawful and defended his own choice to seek protection elsewhere. He demonstrated that the denial of citizenship rights and the lack of state protection were widespread among Mexican Texans. This pattern would recur and be remembered by subsequent generations of Mexican Americans.

The publication of Seguín's memoirs held short-term consequences for the author. Seguín wrote his memoirs in Spanish and had them translated and published in English in 1858.[88] The translation coincided with his efforts to rehabilitate his political career, so by the time of their publication, Seguín had once again won local elected office after returning from Mexico. Perhaps more importantly, he published his memoirs during a period when he was attempting to take advantage of various military pension programs for his service during the Texas insurrection and in various campaigns against Native Americans.[89] According to Seguín, he wrote his memoirs to defend himself against false charges, demonstrate his patriotism, and explain his difficult decision to fight on Mexico's behalf. His return from Mexico had been facilitated by Anglo-Texan politicians and military leaders, so his memoirs were partly meant to appeal to a larger Anglo-Texan and English-speaking audience. However, Seguín also sought to convey his individual memories to fellow Tejanos.[90] The memoirs brought immediate benefits as Seguín became the county judge of Wilson County in 1869 and managed to collect part of his pension. Shortly after serving as a judge, he moved to Nuevo Laredo with his son, who served as that border town's mayor. Returning to visit relatives and apply for a pension in Texas during the 1870s and 1880s, he agreed to the Texas Veterans Association's request to write about his experiences and also gave interviews to journalists about his role in Texas's secessionist struggle.[91]

His memoirs also caused long-term effects for Mexican Texans and Mexican Americans. By publishing his memoirs, Seguín contributed his individual memories of betrayal and unfulfilled promises to Tejanos' collective memories of loss. The memoirs provide an early example of the difficulties confronted by generations of Mexican Americans whose loyalty to Texas and to the United States would be questioned despite exemplary political and military service. They offer a personal reflection on the effects of conquest and the bitterness and disappointment among Mexican Texans. Seguín's ethnicity marked him as suspect despite all his accomplishments, social networks among the Anglo-Texan elite, and wealth. The dominant Texas society valued European American newcomers with fewer political and military accomplishments more than they valued Seguín, because Tejanos, regardless of achievements and status, were not afforded the same rights as European Americans.

Seguín's memoirs confirm that suspicions about the loyalty of Mexican Americans began before the US-Mexico War. In addition to his contemporary audience, Seguín wrote his memoirs for future generations seeking to understand the plight of Mexican Texans in the aftermath of the secessionist rebellion.[92] These future generations would realize that the suspicions would continue to fester in the postwar period, with lasting consequences. According to literary scholar Genaro Padilla, Seguín's memoirs are "the prefigurative narrative of the forms of personal and cultural schizophrenia witnessed in succeeding Mexican American autobiographies."[93] He expressed pride in his heritage but also sought to fit into an Anglo-Texan society that disparaged his culture. Similarly, he was disappointed with his treatment by Anglo-Texans whom he defended and fought alongside to establish a republic but who failed to advocate for Mexican Texans' civil rights. The false accusations against him and the need to prove his loyalty to Texas, he confessed, "wounded me deeply."[94] Ultimately, the memoirs provide evidence of the collective trauma suffered by the larger Tejano community in the periods after the secession of Texas and the US-Mexico War.[95] In this manner, the memoirs help disseminate a collective memory of a community's wounds—not solely from these wars but also from the postwar impact on people forced to feel collectively like foreigners in their own land.

Elite Californios' Land Loss

Seguín's attempts at accommodation with European Americans, the accusations of disloyalty against him, and his memories of betrayal match the experience of elite Californios. Among the Californios who sought accommodation with European Americans was Antonio María Pico. Socially and politically connected, he was a cousin of ex-governor Pío Pico and related by blood and marriage to the prominent Vallejo and Castro families. During the Mexican period, Pico served several terms as alcalde (mayor) of San José, a member of the territorial legislature, and a militia captain. After US annexation, Pico continued his political service by becoming a member of the constitutional convention in 1849, a presidential elector in 1860, and a receiver of the Los Angeles Land Office in 1861. When the US Civil War broke out, Pico leveraged his influence and his own money to organize a company of Californios in support of the Union.[96] Yet despite Pico's willingness to support European Americans, he suffered devastating property losses as a result of squatters, lawyers' fees, and costly delays in confirming his land title.

In 1859, Pico and forty-nine others sent a petition to Congress describing their dashed hopes in the promises of US citizenship stipulated in the Treaty of Guadalupe Hidalgo. The petitioners documented the difficulties in securing title to their Spanish and Mexican land grants in California. Describing themselves as California residents and some as US citizens, they identified as former citizens of Mexico. This acknowledgment cited the jurisdictional transfer from Mexico to the United States as the original cause of their problems. While most petitioners were men, at least eight women (including one widow) also signed, indicating that these women were heads of households or major property owners. The majority of the petitioners were Spanish-speaking Californios, who stressed their disappointment at the broken citizenship promises.[97] They asserted that few Californios opposed the US invasion due to the assurances by officers of the US Army and Navy for their protection and security. These officers also outlined the potential advantages of becoming US citizens. Californios welcomed European Americans, according to the petition, because they felt alienated from Mexico's government and admired US prosperity and government. Moreover, the petitioners believed in the treaty's promises. Few remained "in California as Mexican citizens," as was allowed by the treaty, but instead became US citizens and "conducted themselves with zeal and faithfulness and with no less loyalty" than other US citizens.[98]

The petitioners described problems in confirming their land titles under a new legal system and facing a flood of land-hungry European American newcomers. The jurisdictional change generated several legal issues for property holders who had grown accustomed to "the rural and pastoral life." Acknowledging that some were ignorant of Mexican laws, they described mounting problems with the US legal system being conducted in English and based on different property and tax laws. California lacked lawyers properly trained in US law, and its elected judges were "incompetent and ill-fitted to occupy the delicate position of forensic judicature." The passage of the Land Act of 1851 compounded the problems by compelling landowners to submit their Spanish and Mexican land titles to the Land Commission for confirmation. In doing so, they incurred "enormous fees" from lawyers, which forced the landowners to sell their property to cover these expenses.[99]

Pico and others confronted new challenges with the arrival of gold rush migrants, who began squatting on the petitioners' lands, killing their cattle, and destroying their crops. Aggravating these problems were onerous new state property taxes, which, if left unpaid, would result in the state selling off the land. This led landowners to mortgage their property in order to pay such levies. However, the mortgages proved insufficient because the land had depreciated due to its uncertain status as squatters staked claims to the property. Thus, the owners were forced to either borrow money at exorbitant interest rates or sell their property incrementally. Had the state respected their land titles, they concluded, such a process would have increased the fame of the "conquerors" and won the faith and respect of the "conquered."[100]

Describing their dashed hopes in the treaty, the landowners deployed collective memories of the war and US annexation to push for their civil rights, primarily protection of their property. The petitioners acknowledged their US citizenship and their faith in Congress to resolve their problems. Significantly, they did not appeal to Mexico's government for assistance even though some petitioners were not US citizens.[101] While the petition compiles a long list of travails from the jurisdictional transfer to the United States, the document is not overly bitter or accusatory. The native Californians remained hopeful that their representatives would provide some assistance to resolve their legal problems. Their war memories seemed benign and free of the trauma of armed conflict. Perhaps because these native Californians cooperated with the "conquerors," they did not experience (or they strategically forgot) unpleasant war memories. Nevertheless, they remembered the war as an "invasion" of Mexico that led to the appropriation of its northern territories in the subsequent "conquest." The woes of land loss, litigation expenses, confusion over a new legal system, and the violence of squatters who arrived with the gold rush seeped into their words. Their memories of conquest demonstrated cultural trauma as they were "thrown among those who were strangers to their language, customs, laws, and habits."[102] The petition supplies detailed testimony of the broken promises of military officers and the treaty. This documentation highlights the Californio elite's contemporary civil rights concerns and would prove useful for future generations as evidence of the unenforced property rights resulting from the US conquest.

Expulsions of Ethnic Mexicans in Texas

As the Californios were struggling to retain their property, a different type of civil rights struggle in Texas became a concern for Mexican consuls. In fall 1853, a newspaper from the Gulf Coast of Texas near present-day Port Lavaca published a short article describing the expulsion of ethnic Mexicans from nearby Matagorda County. According to the *Indianola Bulletin*, the "people of Matagorda county have held a meeting and ordered every Mexican to leave the county." The newspaper acknowledged that "strangers" might consider this action wrong, but they believed it was "perfectly right and highly necessary" for several reasons. Those residents expelled were lower class or "Peon Mexicans," who had no fixed housing, claimed the *Indianola Bulletin*, but rather wandered around the plantations to woo African American women. The newspaper also accused ethnic Mexicans of stealing horses and helping African American women escape to Mexico. The news story closed with a comment about the mildness of this expulsion compared to a possible appeal to "Lynch law."[103]

In response to this expulsion, the Mexican consul stationed in Brownsville, Texas, wrote to a state senator and to Mexico's foreign minister in Washington, D.C., to seek additional information and protest this violation of civil rights. The consul called the expulsion "cruel" and "illegal," and the attackers people who ignored the need for justice. The consul's letter to state senator Robert Kingsbury asked for additional details on this attack and to find out if the victims were naturalized US citizens or Mexican citizens. He also alerted Kingsbury that if some victims were Mexican citizens, the consul would be notifying the Mexican diplomatic delegation in Washington.[104]

The consul's intervention derived from the ethnic tensions resulting from the US-Mexico War and the treaty's promises. The expulsion of Mexicans from Matagorda County was not an isolated incident, as similar events had occurred elsewhere in the Southwest. For example, European Americans drove Mexicans from various parts of Texas in the aftermath of the Texas Revolution, as well as from California's northern gold mines in the 1850s.[105]

The reasons given for driving Mexicans from Matagorda County were not unique because Tejanos' alliances with African Americans had previously caused resentment and anxiety among European Americans in Texas.[106]

Mexican officials would repeatedly intercede on behalf of ethnic Mexicans after the war. This example highlights the consular officials' difficulties in determining the citizenship of ethnic Mexicans because Mexican Americans and Mexican nationals often lived in the same communities, intermarried, worked alongside one another, and held similar political views. By contacting the state senator and Mexico's foreign minister in Washington, D.C., the consul made Mexican Texans aware that Mexico's officials were actively pressuring the United States to honor the treaty and respect the rights of their current and former citizens. Additionally, the news article made Tejanos elsewhere aware of a civil rights violation and the consul's advocacy. Spanish-language newspapers throughout the Southwest took notice of similar incidents. The press would report on civil rights abuses and urge consular officials to defend ethnic Mexicans' rights. In 1853, the consul could not prevent ethnic Mexicans from being expelled from Matagorda County or from other locations, but they put politicians and European Americans on notice that Mexico's government was monitoring and protesting civil rights violations. For Mexican Texans, the consul's actions reminded them of the legacies of the US-Mexico War, including the promises of US citizenship enshrined in the treaty.

Articulating Land Loss and Armed Rebellion in South Texas

Among the Mexican Americans who lived through the US conquest and remembered the treaty, Juan Nepomuceno Cortina is one of the most famous because he was a land grant heir who led a six-month rebellion in southern Texas. During the rebellion, Cortina and his followers issued a series of proclamations that outlined the denial of civil rights as the basis for their armed revolt. Born in 1824 in Camargo, Tamaulipas, where his father was an alcalde, Cortina had deep ties to the *villas del norte*, a group of towns which the first Spanish Mexican colonists of the region established along the Río Bravo (Rio Grande) in the mid-eighteenth century. As a reward for participating in colonizing the region, Cortina's great-grandfather, José Saldívar de la Garza, received the Espíritu Santo land grant. This Spanish land grant (some 261,276 acres) was located north of the Rio Grande and was the site of Rancho del Carmen (owned by Cortina's mother) and Rancho San José (owned by Cortina). Shortly after his birth, Cortina's parents moved to Matamoros, a river city near Rancho del Carmen where Cortina would grow up and become an experienced vaquero. His skills and general demeanor endeared him to rancheros and workers alike. While he did not obtain a formal education, he became a charismatic leader through his ties to social and political elites. In addition to his great-grandfather, Cortina's ancestors included military and political leaders of Nuevo Santander and Nuevo León. His great-great-grandfather, Blas María de la Garza Falcón, had been the presidio captain in Cerralvo, Nuevo León, and his maternal grandfather, José Manuel Goseascochea, had been a military officer in Spain and served in the colonial army in New Spain's northern borderlands.[107]

Prior to the US invasion, Juan Cortina obtained military training by participating in several military expeditions against local Indigenous nations, such as the Tampacuas, Karankawas, and Apaches. Cortina gained more formal military experience after joining the Defensores de la Patria (Defenders of the Motherland), which were tasked with defending the river towns from Indigenous attacks. When the US-Mexico War broke out in April 1846 at El Rancho de Carricitos, not far from Rancho del Carmen, Cortina was serving in the Defensores de la Patria. With vast knowledge of the landscape, he served as a scout for Mexico's military as US troops moved illegally into the Nueces Strip to instigate a provocation. Likely part of Mexico's cavalry forces at the war's first two battles—Palo Alto and Resaca de la Palma, both of which occurred just north of the river—he remained active in the National Guard during the war, receiving a promotion to sergeant while serving in Monterrey. As part of Mexico's military, Cortina joined other local men who resisted the US invasion.[108]

After the war, he returned to Rancho San José and began the process of adapting to the new government. His older half brother Sabas Cavazos became a respected merchant and held several county and municipal offices, while his younger brother José María Cortina became a tax assessor in Brownsville. Cortina helped his brother and other European Americans win elected office by encouraging Tejanos to vote for them.[109] Besides tending to his ranch, Cortina drove cattle and transported equipment for the US Quartermaster's Department and for various merchants. European Americans accused him of engaging in cattle rustling on both sides of the Rio Grande, and he was implicated in various murders but never convicted.[110]

A Brownsville marshal's pistol-whipping of a Mexican Texan worker in July 1859 sparked a rebellion after Cortina attempted to stop the abuse but was rebuffed and insulted by the law enforcement officer. In response, Cortina shot the marshal, rescued the worker, and rode out of town on his horse. Cortina viewed this incident as part of a postwar pattern in which European

Juan Nepomuceno Cortina, a land grant descendant who led an 1859 rebellion to protest the denial of Mexican Americans' civil rights. General Photograph Collection, University of Texas at San Antonio Special Collections.

American lawmen and civilians routinely abused Tejanos. European American dominated municipal governments passed restrictions on various Mexican working-class cultural practices, such as fandangos, gambling, and cockfighting. Officials fined violators, and the local press exploited such incidents to disparage the poor. Newspapers routinely accused unnamed Mexican Texans of murders and cattle theft without corroboration. Such accusations cast blanket suspicion on working-class Tejanos. Moreover, European American dominated local courts imposed higher sentences on Mexican Texans than on European American criminals for the same crime. The rising incarceration rates in the border region were mirrored across the state as the number of Tejanos in local prisons and state penitentiaries rose. Aggressive law enforcement tactics, shootings, and extrajudicial lynchings of Mexican Texans resulted in a community under siege. Tejano elites suffered land loss as squatters and speculators took over their land, while lawyers demanded payment in land for securing title to their property. Although these conflicts had simmered for years, the pistol-whipping provoked a full-scale rebellion that engulfed the region several months later.[111]

In September 1859, Cortina led a group of Mexican Texans and Mexican nationals in taking over Brownsville after a Mexican independence celebration in Matamoros. Composed of seventy-five men, the Cortinistas (as the rebels came to be known) combed the town for European Americans who had murdered Mexicans with impunity. The rebels shot several enemies, fought off local law enforcement officials, and freed prisoners from the county jail. Feeling overpowered, Brownsville authorities secured assistance from Mexican National Guard troops. Matamoros's political and military leaders were critical in persuading the Cortinistas to relinquish control of Brownsville by that evening. During their six-month rebellion, the rebels issued several proclamations to explain their goals and their complaints. These proclamations, along with the rebels' victories, caused the Cortinistas' numbers to swell to some 350 to 600 men. Many more residents on both sides of the river supported the rebels with supplies and logistical information. By the end of the rebellion, some 150 rebels had perished while approximately 15 European Americans had been killed. A combined force of Texas Rangers and US Army troops eventually defeated the Cortinistas, but the insurrection had depopulated many of the region's towns and ranches. US military authorities accused the rebels of targeting European American owned ranches and charged the Texas Rangers with attacking and plundering Tejanos' ranches. The rebellion exposed simmering ethnic tensions, provoking widespread fear of a race riot among the region's European American minority. Most importantly, the insurrection demonstrated that the border's ethnic Mexicans protested their racially motivated persecution and the injustices of the post-annexation period.

The rebels' proclamations stressed the detrimental consequences of the US failure to enforce the Treaty of Guadalupe Hidalgo. The first proclamation began by flatly stating that Mexican Texans had encountered persecution and theft "for no other crime... than that of being of Mexican origin."[112] Here, then, was one of the first complaints about the war's results: European Americans' increased legal and extralegal discrimination toward Mexican Americans. Californios and Nuevomexicanos would voice similar complaints about direct and tangible long-term consequences: their loss of economic, political, and social power. The proclamations identify the persecutors as a specific group of men ("a perfidious inquisitorial lodge") who sought to "persecute and rob us."[113] They assert that "with a multitude of lawyers, a secret conclave" formed "for the sole purpose of despoiling the Mexicans of their lands and usurp them afterwards."[114] The Cortinistas' assertion addressed racial discrimination in Texas society, specifically in the justice system. They cited the lack of justice for Tejanos to justify their rebellion ("supremacy of the law has failed") and claimed a "sacred right of self-preservation" to defend themselves from attacks.[115] The proclamations ultimately conclude that the United States failed to guarantee their citizenship rights as outlined in the treaty.

One consequence of the nation's refusal to enforce the treaty was the widespread loss of land. Fashioning a unique argument based on views of Mexican nationals toward Mexican Texans ("their old fellow citizens"), the Cortinistas asserted that Mexican nationals regretted not only the loss of the nation's land but also the unjust treatment toward Tejanos. They alluded to their hopes of living in "tranquility" while "enjoying the longed-for boon of liberty within the classic country of its origin" where "our hopes hav[e] been defrauded in the most cruel manner in which disappointment can strike."[116] In one of the most poetic passages, the second proclamation declares that the United States' annexation of Texas led to the arrival of "flocks of vampires in the guise of men [who] came and scattered themselves in the settlements, without any capital except the corrupt heart and the most perverse intentions" to rob and burn the houses of their relatives in Mexico and trick Tejanos out of their land titles.[117]

The proclamations demonstrate that Mexican Texans sought to contest law enforcement's targeted prosecution and criminalization as well as the legal system's devastating impact on a conquered people. The documents pinpoint the rebels' enemies by identifying specific individuals by name and by occupation (deputy sheriff, marshal, jailer). Justice officials failed to enforce the law to protect Tejanos and unfairly targeted them for prosecution. In response, the rebels shot two European American men accused of killing Mexicans with impunity. Addressing Mexican Texans, the rebels contended, "Inviolable laws, yet useless, serve, it is true, certain judges and hypocritical authorities, cemented in evil and injustice, to do whatever suits them, and to satisfy their vile avarice at the cost of your patience and suffering."[118]

The rebels' actions to free prisoners after storming the jail demonstrated their belief that Tejano prisoners were being unjustly punished. They addressed these unjust punishments and increasing incarceration throughout the state: "through witnesses and false charges, although the grounds may be insufficient, you may be interred in the penitentiaries if you are not previously deprived of life by some keeper who covers himself from responsibility by the pretence

[sic] of your flight." District courts tended to issue longer prison sentences (often in the penitentiary) to Mexican Texans than to European Americans accused of the same crime.[119] Summarizing their community's lack of protection from local and state officials, the second proclamation stated, "Many of you have been robbed of your property, incarcerated, chased, murdered, and hunted like wild beasts, because your labor was fruitful, and because your industry excited the vile avarice which led them."[120]

The rebels' statements also indicate the emergence of a Tejano identity within eleven years of US annexation. The proclamations describe the continuous immigration of Mexicans into the United States as a result of Mexico's internal political turmoil. Economic need and politics, according to the Cortinistas, motivated this migration, as Mexico's unrest had led to widespread poverty. The Mexican Texan community included "some because they were born therein, others because since the [T]reaty [of] Guadalupe Hidalgo, they have been attracted to its soil by the soft influence of wise laws and the advantages of a free government." Some of these migrants were "induced to naturalize," according to the Cortinistas, because they were "desirous of enjoying the longed-for boon of liberty within the classic country of its origin" and "flattered by the bright and peaceful prospect of living therein." The rebels viewed themselves as representatives of a Tejano community that shared "our identity of origin, our relationship, and the community of our sufferings." Ultimately, the proclamations acknowledge the development of a distinct identity for Mexican Texans apart from Mexican nationals based on different citizenship. The edicts infer that Mexican nationals might have felt reassured about their former fellow citizens (now Mexican Americans) living in "tranquility" in the conquered territory.[121]

Yet these hopes have been but the "baseless fabric of a dream" due to persecution and discrimination in the United States. In turn, this ordeal had led some to migrate to Mexico seeking refuge, but these migrants have "returned as strangers to their old country to beg for an asylum." In these explanations of migration and return migration, the rebels implicitly recognized that ethnic Mexicans (whether US citizens or not) had experienced acculturation in the United States to a degree that they considered themselves "strangers" upon returning to Mexico. Ultimately, the declarations function as conduits of collective memories that identify "a group, giving it a sense of its past and defining its aspirations for the future."[122]

The Cortinistas' proclamations demonstrate a strategic use of collective memories to advance Tejanos' civil rights. By invoking the US-Mexico War, they highlighted the consequences of conquest on Mexican Texans' status as

US citizens. The rebels' insurgency and their declarations provided concrete evidence of their demands a mere eleven years after the war's end. The proclamations invoked the war's human repercussions and the treaty's unfulfilled promises to justify the Cortinistas' rebellion and other civil rights struggles.

Surely some rebels understood that without the justification for the rebellion, the explanation offered by European American officials and the press would go unchallenged. By publishing these proclamations, the rebels were constructing a collective memory and organizing the past to emphasize their rebellion's importance.[123] While the declarations explain the injustices perpetrated against Tejanos in considerable detail, they remain silent about the myriad ways in which the region's Native Americans had suffered at the hands of Spanish Mexicans and European Americans.

This discerning emphasis on the specific effects of conquest revealed not only the civil rights priorities of Mexican Texans but also their selective memory. Like Mexican Americans elsewhere in the US Southwest, the Cortinistas ignored their ancestors' violent conquest, enslavement, and decimation of Native Americans but highlighted the detrimental impact of the US westward expansion on Mexican Americans.[124] This selective memory of conquest would be repeated by multiple generations of Mexican Americans, who conveniently "forgot" their ancestors' role in conquering Indigenous people. The proclamations also construct a homogeneous Tejano community by overlooking internal class and gender divisions that fractured Mexicans' unity before and after the war. While the proclamations listed various grievances affecting both the elite (e.g., property losses) and the working class (e.g., criminalization and imprisonment), they stressed the loss of land that mainly affected wealthy Mexican Texans.

The rebels' statements helped propagate war memories among their contemporaries and for future generations. In 1859, the proclamations circulated on both sides of the border, in both Spanish and English. On the US-side of the border, English-language newspapers published the translated edicts with very critical commentary about the rebels' identity and citizenship. In addition to reading leaflets, Mexican nationals probably learned about the proclamations through word of mouth in Mexico. Years later, US congressional reports on the troubles along the US-Mexico border published the rebels' edicts. Undoubtedly, illiterate residents listened to others reading the proclamations and to comments from the crowd about the rebels' specific complaints. This oral transmission surely influenced the reception of the rebels' war memories, as did further discussion among other community members and the reaction of the English-speaking press on the Texas side.

In summary, the rebels' complaints were read or heard by English- and Spanish-speaking working-class and elite members of the border region shortly after the rebels published them. Because the proclamations were published in multiple sources, the rebels' complaints and their view of war rememberances bore long-term effects on various collective memories: those recollections held by Mexican nationals, Mexican Americans, and European Americans. While each of these groups read or listened to the proclamations, their interpretations of the rebels' complaints varied considerably by class, ethnicity, and citizenship. For Tejanos and other Mexican Americans, the Cortinistas' proclamations demonstrate an early history of civil rights struggles, demand for justice, and selective use of war memories.

VIOLENCE AND LAND LOSS were common experiences for the first generation of Mexican Americans after the US-Mexico War. Spanish-language newspapers and journalists played instrumental roles in publicizing the plight of this first generation and in advocating for their civil rights. While elite Mexican Americans invoked the treaty to protest the federal government's unwillingness to enforce their property rights as citizens, journalists and Mexican consuls cited the treaty to advocate for the rights of working-class gold rush miners and ranch workers who fell victim to vigilantes. Ethnic Mexicans appealed to Mexico's consuls for assistance to fight their expulsions and persecution, but they quickly realized the consuls' limited power to confront the US government's unwillingness to enforce the treaty provisions. Spanish-language newspapers, consulate reports, and a few memoirs documented the denial of US citizenship rights for the working poor. In New Mexico, newspapers advocated for statehood and also helped shape Hispano identity by adopting ethnic terms that foregrounded Spanish ancestry while forgetting the multiethnic origins of its population. Likewise, journalists in California and Texas noted the US conquest's effects on ethnic Mexicans while forgetting the devastating effects of the Spanish conquest on Indigenous peoples. While most civil rights activism was peaceful, the Cortina rebellion in Texas involved an armed insurrection that advocated for the rights of property owners and against the criminalization of workers. Although the advocates of civil rights reforms in the first generation came from different socioeconomic classes, they shared an understanding that the US government was failing to honor its promises in the treaty. As organic intellectuals, they established precedents for future generations of parents, activists, and university scholars to emulate in civil rights campaigns.

CHAPTER THREE

Asserting Rights, Remembering Loss
Statehood, Property Rights, and Transnational Influences

In March 1881, *La Gaceta*, a Santa Barbara, California, newspaper, published an article about the events leading up to the outbreak of the US-Mexico War and a description of some of the battles. After describing the war's first two battles in Texas—Palo Alto and Resaca de Guerrero—the article summarized clashes between *mexicanos* and *norteamericanos* in New Mexico and Nuevo León before turning to California. Under the subtitle "Alta California," the newspaper carried a one-paragraph description of a battle between Californios and US troops. "Having this state been invaded without any [Mexican] troops intended for its defense, a victory in the city of Los Angeles was obtained due to the patriotism of captain José María Flores," the article stated, "who defeated the enemy on September 26th and 27th with a handful of valiant men in such a manner that led them [the enemy] to capitulate."[1]

This summary reminded its readers not only of the war's battles but also of Mexico's earlier jurisdiction over California. The paragraph began by noting that US troops had invaded Alta California. The term "invaded" unequivocally characterized the conflict as a war perpetrated by the United States on lands owned by Mexico. This point was reinforced by referring to US troops as the "enemy." Using "Alta California," the Mexican government's term, explicitly reminded readers of Mexico's claim to both Californias (Alta and Baja). The accounts of battles in New Mexico and Texas also reminded readers about Mexico's control over those lands, demonstrating the resistance of Mexico's troops and civilians to the US invasion. The article exalted Flores's patriotism and the devotion of the so-called Californio lancers who joined Flores in resisting the invaders. However, these Californios had exhibited their loyalty to Mexico, not to the United States. By recalling Californios' previous allegiance, the article underscored how the war had severed their previous national ties to Mexico. A reprint of a series that originally appeared in Mexico-based newspapers in the war's immediate aftermath, the article was likely republished in a contemporary Mexican newspaper where the editors of *La Gaceta* read it. Over thirty years after the conflict's conclusion, the publication of this US-based newspaper article exemplified the transnational circulation of war memories.[2]

Across the Southwest borderlands, Spanish-language newspapers continued advocating on behalf of ethnic Mexicans throughout the nineteenth century. This chapter explores how these newspapers cited the treaty's promises to remind readers of their citizenship rights, encourage them to vote, and inform them of various civil rights struggles, including land grant confirmations, Spanish-language use, statehood for New Mexico, and anti-Mexican violence. It also analyzes the role of Hispano politicians in reminding constituents of the treaty in pushing for New Mexico statehood and land title confirmation. The struggle to validate property titles in Arizona drew in the Mexican consuls, who attempted to stop anti-Mexican violence and helped Mexicans wishing to repatriate. The chapter also explores the written and oral memories of elite Californios in which they recall their experiences with land loss and dashed hopes of exercising full citizenship rights. It concludes with an examination of María Amparo Ruiz de Burton's *The Squatter and the Don*, which describes the extensive loss of land based on the author's own experience and her conversations with Californios. These varied sources demonstrate the persistence of collective war memories, their transmission, and their strategic use in distinct civil rights struggles.

Transnational Circulation of War Memories

War memories circulated across the international border through visits, migration, and newspapers. When individuals crossed the border to visit family and friends, they shared remembrances of the war and of its effects on the ethnic Mexican population in the annexed lands. This process occurred more frequently in regions where populations lived closer to the international border, such as the lower Rio Grande region of Texas, the El Paso area, and other twin cities. While visitors could share such memories during short trips, the transnational circulation of war memories tended to occur when Mexican nationals immigrated to the United States or Mexican Americans immigrated to Mexico because these immigrants stayed for longer periods (in some cases permanently).[3] A third avenue for the transmission of memories was newspapers. It was common for Spanish-language (and occasionally English-language) newspapers to carry articles that originally appeared in Mexico's weeklies or to publish original articles with news on Mexico. Such articles might inform US readers of the Mexican government's views of the war in retrospective pieces or of lingering issues about the treaty's enforcement, such as cross-border Indigenous raids. Newspapers in Mexico also covered developments in the United States. Some of these articles focused on issues surrounding the treaty's enforcement, such as the land confirmation process or the inability of Mexican Americans to exercise full citizenship rights. The transnational circulation of war memories informed Mexican Americans of Mexican nationals' views of the war and of lingering treaty issues, while Mexican nationals learned of the war's consequences on the contemporary lives of Mexican Americans.[4]

Some US Spanish-language newspapers published direct references to the war via historical summaries. Over a five-week period in 1881, *La Gaceta* published a detailed retrospective series titled "Historical Notes—Notable Occurrences about the War between Mexico and the United States." This weekly series reproduced extracts from the *Calendario de Ontiveros*, a calendar with brief historical summaries that originally appeared in Mexico. The series began with a description of the annexation of Texas, the declaration of war, and the initial battles. Subsequent issues contained summaries of additional battles throughout eastern and central Mexico (e.g., Cerro Gordo and Churubusco). The series ended with Mexico's surrender after US troops captured Mexico City and Mexico's decision to sign the Treaty of Guadalupe Hidalgo. This segment explained the territorial limits established by the treaty and the US monetary payment for the ceded territory. It also outlined the choice of Mexican or US citizenship for the Mexicans living in the annexed territories and the guarantees of US citizenship rights (i.e., liberty, property, and religious freedom). For those residents who chose to remain Mexican citizens, the article described the funds set aside by the Mexican government to pay for their transportation and resettlement in Mexico. The article closed with the departure of the US Army from Mexico City and other capital cities.[5]

This retrospective series offered Mexico's view of the conflict to Spanish-speaking readers in Southern California and reminded them of the war's consequences. Originally published in Mexico City in 1849, the series' reappearance thirty-two years later suggests that José Arzaga, the editor and publisher of *La Gaceta*, sought to remind readers of the conflict and its consequences. Advertised as "the only paper published in the Spanish language in Southern California outside of Los Angeles," the newspaper claimed a large circulation in the section of the state "where Spanish is extensively spoken" in order to lure advertisers.[6] It is unclear why Arzaga chose to reprint Ontiveros's summaries from among several *calendarios* published as war retrospectives. His choice to republish a Mexican author's view of the war demonstrates the transnational circulation of ideas, history, and literature. The Ontiveros *calendario* was part of the popular literature of Mexico (including almanacs and forecasts) that circulated among all social classes and underwent various style changes over the years.[7] So its republication in *La Gaceta* led to a cultural transmission across the border, which allowed readers in Southern California to enjoy Mexican popular literature and reinforce Mexico's cultural traditions.

This series clearly intended to remind Spanish-language readers of the damages caused by the US invasion as well as the treaty's promises. Offering a Mexican perspective, it described the annexation of Texas as an "atrocity" and the movement of US troops into Mexico as an "invasion." In the last installment, Ontiveros summarized the significance of the series: "This is in excerpt the most interesting part of the treaty, and what needs to be kept in mind continuously in order to reflect on the sad state to which the internal disorders led us, and to calculate the immense sacrifice that the previous government had to make in order to end a war of innumerable consequences."[8] The Mexican government had not been "indifferent to the future of Mexican families that lived in the annexed territories," Ontiveros informed readers, and had allocated funds for their transportation to Mexico if they chose to keep their Mexican citizenship. In this way, Mexican Americans learned that Mexico's government had expressed concern for their welfare and sought to assist them. While obviously sympathetic to Mexico's government, the republication of this series helped remind the first generation that lived through the US conquest of their rights and disseminate war memories among the next generation of Mexican Americans living in Southern California.

Readers' reactions to the war retrospective series were not published in *La Gaceta*, but the contemporary historical context of Santa Barbara provides some clues for the editor's decision to publish the series. After the war, the denial of citizenship rights for working-class Mexican Americans became evident, although wealthy Mexican Americans escaped some of the immediate problems, and elite Californios in Santa Barbara held on to their property longer than did Los Angeles residents.[9] Nevertheless, the widespread loss of property among Californios was well-known by the time the series appeared. Mexican Americans in Santa Barbara had experienced profound changes due to US annexation by the early 1880s. They rarely served on local juries, and their political power had diminished considerably with the influx of European Americans. Although Mexican Americans made up about 21 percent of the city's electorate, they were no longer influential in municipal elections. Dismissive of Mexican Americans' electoral power, European American politicians had expelled them from the county's Democratic Party convention. This rejection infuriated Arzaga, a fervent Democratic Party supporter, who wrote a scathing editorial decrying the Democrats who "excluded them [native Californios] completely, as if they did not need them for anything and did not consider them among citizens they represented or worthy of occupying any public post."[10]

By the early 1880s, the city's working classes had become increasingly impoverished, while elite Californios had suffered considerable property losses.[11] Moreover, Mexican Americans had become concentrated in Pueblo Viejo, the old downtown barrio, and were residentially segregated from the European American arrivistes. The predominance of European American newcomers manifested as their cultural celebrations replaced Mexican public activities. While Mexican cultural events did not disappear, bullfights and Sunday dances had been outlawed, and Santa Barbara witnessed an increase in "gringoized Mexicans" and the emergence of "Spanish clubs" that emphasized Spanish ancestry over mestizo roots.[12] These losses led to an outmigration of Mexican Americans to other cities in California or the Southwest, while others participated in colonization ventures to northern Mexico, which remained popular in the 1880s.[13] These social, economic, and political losses undoubtedly motivated Arzaga to publish the five-part retrospective in order to remind Mexican Americans of the war's long-term consequences and to underscore the US government's promises of full citizenship. Arzaga probably hoped that informing his readers about their rights under the treaty would motivate them to demand their citizenship rights.

Statehood, Language, and Land in New Mexico

Reminders of the treaty's citizenship guarantees appeared often for Nuevomexicanos who advocated for statehood, used the Spanish language in local governments, and confirmed their land titles in the late nineteenth century. The war and the treaty continued to affect their daily lives several decades removed from the war. Statehood advocates based their campaigns on the treaty's promises of eventual incorporation of the annexed lands. Nuevomexicanos witnessed the former Mexican lands of Texas, California, Nevada, and Colorado become states from the mid-1840s through the mid-1870s. When Congress rejected their statehood petitions, Hispanos undoubtedly recalled its power to determine their fate. The treaty specifically addressed this power in Article 9 with the phrase, "incorporated into the Union of the United States and be admitted, *at the proper time* (to be judged of by the Congress of the United States)." Similarly, landowners who struggled with long delays and paperwork to confirm their land titles were reminded of the treaty and must have wondered if its promises to protect their property would ever be fulfilled. As more European Americans arrived in the region, they questioned the use of Spanish in conducting local government affairs. To confront these challenges, various Nuevomexicano politicians and newspapers cited the treaty's guarantees.[14]

The statehood campaign involved various politicians, their political parties, and numerous civilian supporters. Between 1889 and 1895, New Mexico's politicians introduced four different bills for statehood. While these bills were widely supported by New Mexicans, the US Congress rejected them for various reasons. Congressmen maintained that most New Mexicans did not support statehood, which had sharply divided the electorate. Legislators continued to believe the majority of the state's population (Nuevomexicanos and Native Americans) was not prepared for self-government due to their racial background.[15] In challenging this latter charge, Nuevomexicanos cited their long history of self-government under Spanish and Mexican jurisdiction.

Statehood supporters presented their arguments through newspapers, which carried their letters, description of party conventions, and statehood petitions to Congress. The railroad's arrival in 1879 dramatically increased the number of Spanish-language newspapers.[16] By the 1890s, several Spanish-language and bilingual newspapers advocated for statehood as an answer to the territory's lack of political power and changed Nuevomexicanos' views in support of statehood.[17] Newspapers reported on the statehood bills introduced by their (nonvoting) congressional representative, as well as congressional debates on the bills. Several of these news articles noted the war and treaty, reinforcing conquest memories among readers. In 1889, *El Tiempo* described a statehood bill introduced by Antonio Joseph, the nonvoting congressional representative for New Mexico. Describing Joseph as a "champion of New Mexico, who always guards the interests of his people," the article explained that he had introduced the bill as soon as Congress had approved the act to admit the territories of the Dakotas, Montana, and Washington.[18]

The admission of these territories would figure again in Representative Joseph's remarks in 1892, when he reminded Congress of the treaty's promises. He repudiated criticism about the supposed lack of affinity for US institutions among New Mexico's "foreign-born" population. Statehood critics had characterized the territory's population as "foreign-born" due to Nuevomexicanos' use of Spanish and racial ancestry.[19] Alluding to the war and its long-term consequences, Joseph made a forceful pro-statehood argument. Over forty years had elapsed since the conclusion of the US-Mexico War when he submitted this report in 1892. Joseph creatively employed the recent admission of former territories as states as proof of the bias exhibited by Congress and the US press against New Mexico. Citing the 1880 census population figures, Joseph noted that the percentage of the foreign-born population of the Dakotas, Montana, and Washington far exceeded the percentage of New Mexico's foreign-born population.[20]

Joseph asked rhetorically if a New Mexican who had given up allegiance to Mexico over forty years prior held less allegiance to the United States than a recent immigrant held to European monarchs. By addressing allegiance, he identified one of the lasting legacies of the war: the accusation of disloyalty. To emphasize his point about Nuevomexicanos' allegiance, Joseph noted that some 8,000 New Mexican soldiers had fought for the Union. This number surpassed the combined total of troops from the territories and states of Nebraska, Nevada, Colorado, Washington, North Dakota, South Dakota, Montana, Idaho, and Wyoming. Wealthy New Mexicans, he noted, also lent money to the US government at the request of the military. After forty years of US citizenship, Joseph concluded, it was too late to dispute the devotion of New Mexicans to the United States. The charges of disloyalty and lack of affinity for US institutions were obviously hollow, based more on racist views about Nuevomexicanos than on facts about the population's actions.[21]

Nuevomexicanos' loyalty and ability to self-govern also figured in statements in favor of statehood by other politicians, who also cited the war and treaty. In 1890, various newspapers published a statement written by José D. Sena in which he listed twenty reasons to vote for New Mexico's constitution advocating for statehood. Representing Santa Fe, Sena was a delegate to the constitutional convention. He began by stating that it was time to demand that the United States fulfill its promises to incorporate New Mexico as a state as stipulated by the Treaty of Guadalupe Hidalgo. The treaty, he asserted, had served as the greatest inducement for Nuevomexicanos to embrace the rights of US citizens while renouncing their rights as Mexican citizens. This group of new citizens, Sena posited, deserved respect and the fulfillment of these promises. When the United States annexed New Mexico and established a territorial government, Sena insisted, the federal government understood that the territory's residents held the necessary qualifications to obtain the status of "complete" US citizens. His argument acknowledged that both Nuevomexicanos and the federal government made their respective decisions with the understanding that the territory could eventually obtain statehood and fulfill one of the treaty's promises. Sena also addressed critics who disparaged New Mexicans' ability to self-govern by describing their centuries of self-government under Spain and Mexico and their three decades of territorial government. Moreover, he addressed charges of disloyalty by highlighting those residents who served in the Civil War and provided food for Union soldiers.

Statehood, according to Sena, would make specific rights and objectives easier to obtain. He urged readers to support statehood because he believed it would allow New Mexicans to more easily obtain payment from the federal government for damages caused by raids by Indigenous peoples. This argument referred to the treaty's stipulation that the US and Mexican governments reimburse each other for raids launched from their respective lands. According to Sena, statehood would also facilitate the federal government's payment to New Mexico's militias, which served during the Civil War, and for provisions given to the Union army. Sena believed that statehood would also help Nuevomexicanos obtain confirmation of Spanish and Mexican land grant titles. He alluded to several outrages suffered by landowners due to the government's delay in title confirmation. By bringing up raid damages, Civil War reimbursements, and title confirmation, Sena explicitly linked several civil rights issues to statehood and, more importantly, reminded readers of the treaty's promises. His statement's publication in multiple newspapers suggested that editors sought to disseminate Sena's significant arguments among a broad audience and propagate collective war memories.

New Mexico's statehood struggle received support among Hispanos beyond the territory's boundaries. In 1889, Colorado state senator Casimiro Barela authored a memorial on New Mexico statehood. The state senate and house approved the memorial without amendment and forwarded it to Congress with the governor of Colorado's signature. Born in New Mexico, Barela maintained friends and family there. According to the memorial, the territory's residents had renounced their Mexican citizenship due to the treaty's guarantee that they would be incorporated into the United States and admitted as a state. The memorial explained that New Mexico had sought statehood several times, including in 1874 when Colorado also applied for statehood. It acknowledged that Congress approved the bill granting statehood to Colorado but rejected the bill in support of New Mexico's statehood. Colorado's residents supported New Mexico's bid for statehood because they co-mingled with people in the territory and because their commerce and interests were allied. In support of New Mexico's bid, the memorial emphasized the loyalty of the territory's residents, their service as soldiers and creditors during the Civil War, and their dedication to US principles and institutions. The memorial's approval by Colorado's state legislature demonstrated the popularity of New Mexico's statehood petition, the joint interests of Colorado and New Mexico, and an awareness of the treaty's promises among Coloradans. In turn, newspaper coverage of the passage of the memorial reinforced war memories and the treaty's promises among the state's residents.²²

Advocating for the memorial's passage, Barela delivered a senate speech recalling the war and treaty. He explained that the US-Mexico War forced Mexico to cede its northern territories via the Treaty of Guadalupe Hidalgo. By agreeing to the treaty, Barela maintained, the United States pledged to incorporate the territories' former Mexican citizens and grant them full rights of US citizenship. He voiced his "profound sympathy towards the citizens of that territory" by acknowledging his birth in New Mexico and identifying his parents as among the territory's residents who gave up their Mexican citizenship. His parents were part of a group of former Mexican citizens, Barela explained, who had "waited in vain ... for the redemption of this promise [of full US citizenship] which was so solemnly extended and which guided them to such an action." He offered his parents as exemplary of the first generation of Mexican Americans in New Mexico who grew disillusioned with the US government's failure to fulfill the treaty's promises. Barela's memorial was part of a larger effort to pressure the federal government to honor its promises to his parents' generation.²³

Barela's speech also disputed criticisms of Nuevomexicanos by reminding his audience of the treaty's statehood promises. According to opponents of statehood, Hispanos were not qualified to assume the duties and responsibilities of citizenship because they were ignorant and easily manipulated by "American adventurers," who used them as pawns to obtain power. "I resent this accusation with the deepest scorn," wrote Barela, adding that the territory's Mexican population had increased in education, autonomy, and intellect since 1848. The US government, he averred, had not stipulated that the territory's residents had to increase their wisdom and virtue to obtain statehood. According to Barela, the federal government only required New Mexico to contain a population "that would entitle any other territory to be admitted as a state." He also brought up General Kearny's and President Zachary Taylor's declarations in support of statehood for New Mexico during and immediately after the war. To address loyalty, Barela reminded legislators that New Mexico's first state constitution in 1850 had prohibited slavery and that the territory had supplied more soldiers for the Union than other territories, including Nebraska, Nevada, and Colorado. Then he posed a rhetorical question: "Who can say upon reviewing the record, that the Mexican population of that territory is not capable of exercising all the rights of sovereignty and American citizenship?"

In subsequent comments to his biographer, Barela discussed Articles 8, 9, and 10 of the treaty in detail to explain the lack of civil rights for Nuevomexicanos. "Neither has the United States made a good faith effort to respect this [the civil rights of New Mexico's inhabitants]," contended Barela, and additionally the United States has "sought to forget it for their own convenience." This comment reveals his purpose in reminding his audience about the war and treaty. While the federal government sought to forget its commitment to enforce the treaty, Barela emphasized Mexican Americans' need to preserve their collective war memories and to advocate for their civil rights as promised by the treaty. The denial of rights guaranteed under the treaty, he stipulated, was evident in the failure of the federal government to confirm Spanish and Mexican land grant titles, which had led many owners to lose their lands through "chicanery and in some cases by force." He also indicated his belief that statehood opponents were motivated by politics and racial hatred.[24]

When Barela wrote his 1889 memorial bill, he was a civil rights veteran who often remembered the war and the treaty in his activism. He had served in political office for twenty years in various positions, including as a member of the territorial legislature and as a state senator. Barela had championed the civil rights of Hispanos, the need to confirm Spanish and Mexican land grant titles, the teaching of Spanish in schools, and the publication of the state's laws in Spanish.[25] During a debate on a bill that would have penalized raisers of small livestock, Barela defended the state's assembly for publishing documents in Spanish after a newspaper criticized the practice and attacked the Mexican community. The state's constitution allowed for the publication of its laws in Spanish for twenty-five years after obtaining statehood, Barela explained. He also elaborated on Mexicans' long history in the Americas since the Spanish colonial period. He cited the "disastrous" US-Mexico War and the treaty, and characterized Mexican Americans as the "adopted" children of the United States who would faithfully defend its constitution.[26] When a Colorado county judge issued a ruling stipulating that all jurors speak English, Barela helped organize a meeting and a petition opposing it. The petition cited the treaty to justify Hispanos' right to continue to serve on juries without English-language proficiency.[27] His frequent references to the war and treaty in the legislation that he authored and the speeches that he delivered demonstrate that Barela was concerned with keeping war memories alive to document the war's adverse repercussions.

By the turn of the century, Barela had become the president pro tempore of Colorado's state senate, and he continued to address the war's long-term consequences. In a Fourth of July speech at the Las Animas County Courthouse in 1898, he countered accusations by politicians and newspapers that Hispanos sympathized with Spain in the Cuban War of Independence (or the so-called Spanish-American War).[28] Barela recalled that Hispanos had been subjects of Spain, then citizens of Mexico, before becoming US citizens as a result of the US-Mexico War. He explained that the United States had obtained a vast amount of Mexico's northern territories through the Treaty of Guadalupe Hidalgo and cited the choice contained in Article 8 of the treaty: that people in the annexed lands could remain Mexican citizens or become US citizens. The vast majority of residents of New Mexico Territory chose to become US citizens. He expressed disbelief at the accusation that Hispanos would sympathize with Spain after living as loyal US citizens for fifty years. As he had often done, Barela reminded the audience of the 8,000 Nuevomexicano soldiers (including some from present-day Colorado, which was part of New Mexico Territory at the time) who had fought on the Union side during the Civil War, noting also that companies of Hispanos were serving in the US military during the present war. While Barela's speech intended to forcefully demonstrate Mexican Americans' patriotism and allegiance to the United States, it also effectively brought up one of the long-term consequences of the war and treaty.

Unfortunately, the US public's continued suspicion of Hispanos' disloyalty, based on their ethnic ancestry, would persist into the next century. After the Cuban War of Independence, Barela sponsored a memorial bill to send to Congress advocating for the return of war trophies captured by US troops during the US-Mexico War. The war trophies had first been obtained from Spanish troops by Mexican soldiers during Mexico's independence war. In a speech supporting this bill, he sought to address some of the long-term consequences of the US-Mexico War on international relations. Returning these captured war trophies, he contended, would help endear the United States to Mexico's citizens and improve diplomatic relations. Barela was ultimately successful in convincing US officials to return the war trophies. Moreover, his speech and newspaper coverage of the memorial bill ensured that war memories continued to circulate across the nation fifty years after the war's conclusion. Through his legislative efforts and civil rights activism, Barela sought to remind the nation of Hispanos' collective memories of the war and its legacies.[29]

The treaty was also cited by various Hispano politicians and Spanish-language newspapers in their efforts to defend Nuevomexicanos' Spanish-language use. By remembering the treaty's promises, they not only reinforced Hispano collective war memories but also challenged the nation's attempt to forget its commitment to enforce the Treaty of Guadalupe Hidalgo. While the treaty did not mention Mexican Americans' language rights, various activists have interpreted it as granting such rights.[30] In 1884, for example, a large contingent of Colorado's Hispanos rallied to oppose county judge Caldwell Yeaman's ruling excluding monolingual Spanish speakers from serving on juries in his court. Some 1,500 county residents gathered in a *junta de indignación* (mass meeting of indignation) to hear speeches by several community leaders, including Barela, who denounced the ruling.

As a committee member, Barela helped issue a petition criticizing the ruling. The petition appeared in several newspapers throughout Colorado. The committee's resolutions demanded respect for Hispanos' rights as US citizens and urged residents to remember the treaty and the rights guaranteed therein.[31] The *junta de indignación*, the drafting of the resolutions, and the petition's publication demonstrated how Hispanos in Colorado were motivated by memories of war and the treaty to campaign for civil rights. According to historian Rosina Lozano, about 1,500 people (or 15 percent of the county's population) attended the *junta de indignación*, which demonstrated widespread support for language rights. Therefore, the petition's references to the war and treaty reached a large audience. The resolutions demonstrated the attendants' political sophistication, Lozano suggested, as they combined a mass demonstration with a published account that recorded their criticisms for posterity. Barela took his activism to the state senate, where he authored and led the successful passage of a bill to nullify the judge's ruling.[32]

In 1892, New Mexico congressional representative Joseph also cited the treaty in defending his constituents' Spanish-language use. Congressional opponents of statehood used Nuevomexicanos' culture, including their Spanish language and Catholicism, to deny statehood during the late 1880s, and European Americans accused most Hispanos of not knowing English. Many Nuevomexicanos spoke Spanish, Joseph admitted, and elderly people might not speak English; however, the vast majority of people under thirty years old, he insisted, spoke English and were rapidly overtaking Spanish-language speakers. As part of this acculturation, Joseph contended, Nuevomexicanos understood the importance of learning English, which was taught to schoolchildren. He also added a bit of foresight: the Spanish language will always "be dear to those who descended from the first settlers of New Mexico ... and its familiar use may never be wholly eradicated."[33] Citing Article 9 of the treaty, he brought up its promises of eventual statehood to residents of territories. The treaty, he pointed out, did not include a requirement that all territorial residents speak English before statehood could be granted. A congressional decision to reject statehood for New Mexico until every inhabitant was literate in English, Joseph concluded, would be a violation of the treaty.[34]

When a bill attacked Nuevomexicanos' Spanish use, various Spanish-language newspapers cited the Treaty of Guadalupe Hidalgo to oppose the proposal. In October 1890, Republican senator William Stewart of Nevada introduced legislation that sought to prohibit monolingual Spanish speakers from serving in any territorial government office or as jurors (both petit and grand) in any court of the territory. In response, *La Estrella Mejicana*, a Democratic Party newspaper, strongly criticized the bill as unconstitutional. Establishing such prohibitions for monolingual Spanish speakers, according to the newspaper, would violate the spirit of the treaty. The newspaper excoriated Senator Stewart for his proposal and labeled the Republican Party as an enemy of Hispanos. It also published the state's Democratic Party platform, which favored statehood and accused the federal government of ignoring New Mexicans' rights for the speedy confirmation of their land titles as guaranteed by the treaty. In its endorsement of Joseph's reelection, *La Estrella Mejicana* published his support for statehood and the expeditious resolution of New Mexico's land titles.[35]

El Nuevo Mexicano, a Republican Party newspaper, also condemned Stewart's bill as unconstitutional, as an "insult to our most sacred rights, and as an unjust and illegal blow to the treaty between Mexico and the United States." However, the newspaper also accused Joseph, a Democrat, of secretly urging Senator Stewart to introduce said bill and of previously working furtively with other senators to oppose a bill to confirm the territory's land grants.[36] These charges painted Joseph as opposed to two important civil rights issues (Spanish-language rights and land grant confirmations) for the territory's Hispanos. The county's Republican Party platform, which the newspaper published, also favored statehood but supported Mariano Otero for congressional representative. Despite the political invectives against the opposing party, both newspapers agreed on the unconstitutionality of Stewart's proposed bill, which would violate Mexican Americans' rights granted by the treaty. This agreement signals Nuevomexicanos' consensus on the treaty's significance to defend their civil rights. Moreover, the newspaper coverage of the proposed bill and the discussion of the treaty helped disseminate Hispanos' collective war memories to a wider audience across New Mexico.

The race for New Mexico congressional representative indicated that discussions about land grant confirmations, statehood, and Spanish-language rights were often linked to the treaty. Various politicians and newspapers reinforced these links in their speeches and editorials. Colorado state representative Barela brought up the treaty and the urgency of confirming land grants in a speech for a memorial bill sent to the US Congress advocating for the establishment of a separate court to adjudicate Spanish and Mexican land grants. He emphasized that "the United States owes a debt to Mexico to confirm to its citizens those valid land grants that are protected by the Treaty."[37] Congress passed the bill and established the Court of Private Land Claims in 1891.[38]

Subsequently, the territory's newspapers reported on this new court and the procedures for submitting claims. The *Santa Fe Daily New Mexican* printed the congressional act establishing the court in its entirety. It stipulated that newspapers in Colorado, Arizona, and New Mexico publish the act in English and Spanish. While the act avoided a direct reference to the war, it implied its consequences by referring to "lands within the limits of the territory derived by the United States from the Republic of Mexico," encompassing the territories of New Mexico, Arizona, and Utah, as well as the states of Nevada, Colorado, and Wyoming. Officials established the court to adjudicate Spanish and Mexican land grant claims according to various laws, including the Treaty of Guadalupe Hidalgo.[39] The bilingual *Independent Democrat* also printed portions of the act and explained that it pertained to all people who had become US citizens as a result of the treaty.[40] A common argument employed by several pro-statehood politicians and newspapers was that obtaining statehood would help New Mexico resolve the confirmation of land grant titles. By linking these issues and by citing the treaty, statehood proponents repeatedly propagated Hispanos' collective memories of the war and its consequences.

The confirmation of Spanish and Mexican land grants remained a significant issue throughout the nineteenth century. In New Mexico, property owners struggled to acquire title confirmation for reasons beyond their control. The federal government contributed to delays as it failed to appoint a surveyor general, who would be responsible for investigating each grant title's legitimacy, until 1854. Moreover, Congress gave itself ultimate authority to issue final decisions on all land claims. This condition caused more delays by requiring Congress to issue a final judgment after the surveyor-general approved land titles. Not surprisingly, these bureaucratic delays were devastating for New Mexican grantees. Although they had submitted more than 1,000 claims by 1880, the surveyor general had sent only 150 of these claims to Congress, which in turn had made decisions on only 71. Numerous delays and lawyers' fees increased the grantees' financial burden, as did property taxes. According to historian David Weber, more than 80 percent of New Mexican grant holders lost their land due to delays, litigation costs, and the challenges of adapting to a new legal system in a different language.[41] Landowners forfeited their property in New Mexico, as elsewhere in the US Southwest, through a combination of legal and illegal means, including working with lawyers who often demanded land as payment for their fees. Not surprisingly, "the land grant business became the territory's major industry," attracting numerous lawyers and making several into major land barons.[42]

Throughout the nineteenth century, Spanish-language newspapers in New Mexico continued referring to the treaty in articles on land title litigation and property losses due to Indigenous depredations. The importance and lucrative aspect of land grant title litigation was clearly shown in the front-page advertisements that appeared in Las Cruces's *El Tiempo* during the 1880s. Over several months, E. N. Ronquillo advertised his services (e.g., legal counsel and notary public) and listed various issues with which he had experience, including claims for attacks by Native Americans and Spanish and Mexican land grants, which the advertisement indicated were "provided by the Treaty of Guadalupe Hidalgo."[43] *El Tiempo* also carried occasional news stories about land grants that mentioned the treaty. In April 1885, it summarized several treaty articles regarding the international boundary at the Rio Grande and explained diplomatic exchanges about the river's changing course.[44] While the news stories on land grants probably interested only elite Nuevomexicanos, pieces on Indigenous attacks held widespread appeal. These articles reminded readers of the changing jurisdiction over New Mexico due to the war and of the continuing significance of the treaty.

A more direct, potent reminder of the war's consequences appeared in Santa Fe's *Boletin Popular* in 1886. That May, the newspaper carried an account of Mexico's total acreage loss from the war and compiled a list of the number of square miles in each territory (New Mexico and Arizona) and state (California, Nevada, Utah, Colorado, and Wyoming), portions of which had once been part of Mexico. It indicated that the treaty transferred over 522,500 square miles from Mexico to the United States, to which was added an additional 45,400 square miles acquired through the subsequent Gadsden Treaty. The newspaper also printed a short essay on pending laws regarding confirmation of Spanish and Mexican land titles.[45] The next year, another news story summarized the latest developments in the litigation regarding a contested Mexican grant of 60 million acres that eventually became part of the Maxwell Land Grant.[46] Such articles reminded readers of the ongoing consequences of the war, the significance of the treaty, and the declining power of Hispanos in New Mexico.

By the end of the century, some journalists had become frustrated with the US failure to enforce the treaty. In an editorial calling on the federal

EL TIEMPO.

Publicado todos los Jueves en la tarde, en LAS CRUCES Condado de Doña Ana N.M.

TERMINOS DE SUBSCRICION
Por un año ....
Por Seis Meses ....
Por Tres Meses ....

M. VALDEZ, Editor y *Propietario.*

PRECIOS DE AVISOS
Por Una Pulgada $1.25
Por Cada Subsecuente Insercion ... $1.00
Noticias Locales por Linea .... .10

Los anuncios, remitidos y comunicados de interes general se publicaran gratis; los particulares á precios convencion. Estos últimos no se admitiran sino con la responsiva de la oficina.

Las suscriciones se recibiran al contado en esta oficina.

EL TIEMPO, Las Cruces, N. M.

VOL. III.   LAS CRUCES N. M., JUEVES, ABRIL 30, DE 1883.   NO. 23.

Dr. Jas. P. Booth.
MEDICO
y Cirujano, en Partos.
Oficina en la calle 1ª casa D. G. Ascarate
Las Cruces N. M.

Dr. G. Butschofsky
Avisa á todo habitante de este lugar como á los de afuera, haber abierto una gran
Exelente Votica.
La que pone á la órden de la persona que guste visitarlo.
Plaza principal.
Las Cruces, N. M

DR. FRASER
MEDICO
Cirujano, en Partos.
Calle principal, cerca de la Botica del Dr Gutschofsky.

John D. Bryan.
ABOGADO Y CONSEJERO en Leyes.
LAS CRUCES, N. M.
Practicará en todas las Cortes del tercer Distrito Judicial. Dará atencion especial á l'ágencion de Minas, á negocios de oficinas de Planes y Colecciones de Clientes.

Vengan al Salon
HISPANO-AMRICANO por cerveza fina, mejores licores, vinos y cigarros y afable servicio.
Calle principal Hillsboro N. M
BLAS CHAVEZ CO.

W. H. H. LLEWELLIN
U. S. COMMISSIONER
South Fork P. O., Lincoln Co. N. M.

Antonio Luera.
OFRECE AL PUBLIO
Cumplimentar
EN
CARROCERIA Y CARPINTERIA
Toda clase de obra en esta proffecion, si que se despachara pronto y espelita á los que nos patrocinen; teniendo la satisfaccion de dar igu to en mi Oficina, á toda persona que mandara algun encargo a precios modicos baratos, mas que ninguno otro.
LAS CRUCES N. M.

Mancion del Ejecutivo.
Washington, Diciembre 3 de 1884

Convencion entre los Estados Unidos Mexicanos y los Estados Unidos de América, respecto de la linea divisoria entre los dos paises, en la parte que sigue el lecho del Rio Grande y del Rio Gila.

Por cuanto en virtud del tratado de Guadalupe Hidalgo concluido el 2 de Febrero de 1848, entre los Estados Unidos Mexicanos y los Estados Unidos de América, algunas porciones de la linea divisoria entre los dos paises siguen el centro del canal del Rio Grande y del Rio Gila, con el fin de evitar las dificultades que puedan ocurrir por los cambios del canal á que dichos rios están sujetos por causa de fuerzas naturales, el Gobierno de los Estados Unidos Mexicanos y el gobierno de los Estados Unidos de América, han resuelto concluir una convencion que fije reglas para resolver esas cuestiones, y han nombrado sus plenipotenciarios.

El Presidente de los Estados Unidos Mexicanos, á Matias Romero, Enviado Extraordinario y Ministro Plenipotenciario de los Estados Unidos Mexicanos, y el Presidente de los Estados Unidos de América á Frederick T. Frelinghuysen, Secretario de Estado de los Estados Unidos.

Quienes despues de haberse mostrado sus respectivos plenos poderes, y encontrándolos en buena y debida forma, han convenido en los siguientes articulos:

Art. I.—La línea divisoria será siempre la fijada en dicho tratado, y seguirá el centro del canal normal de los citados rios, apesar de las alteraciones en las riberas ó en el curso de esos rios, con tal que esas alteraciones se efectuen por causas naturales, como la corrosion lenta y gradual y el depósito del aluvion, y no por el abandono del canal existente del rio y la apertura de uno nuevo.

Art. II.—Cualquiera otro cambio ocacionado por la fuerza de la corriente, ya sea abriendo un nuevo canal ó en donde haya mas de uno, haciendo mas profundo otro canal que no sea el que se marcó como parte de la linea divisoria al tiempo del reconocimiento hecho conforme á dicho tratado, no producirá alteracion alguna en la linea divisoria, tal como fué fijada por los reconocimientos de la comision internacional de limites en 1852; pero la linea fijada entónces, seguirá siendo el centro del canal original, aun cuando éste llegue á secarse del todo, ó á obstruirse por el aluvion.

Art. III.—Ningun cambio artificial, en el curso navegable del rio, ya sea por la construccion de jetties, muelles u obstrucciones que tiendan á desviar la corriente ó producan depósitos de aluvion, ó por el ese dragas para hacer más profundo un canal distinto del primitivo del tratado, cuando haya más de uno, ó para abrir nuevos canales con el objeto de acortar la distancia por agua, se permitirá que afecte ó altere la linea divisoria que determinó la comision de 1852, y á la que fija el articulo I de esta Convencion bajo la limitacion que en él se menciona. No se considerará como cambio artificial la proteccion de las riberas de uno ú otro lado, contra la corrosion, cuando se pongan losas de piedra ó de otro material, que no proyecten sobre la corriente del rio.

Art. IV. Si se hubiese construido ó se construyere un puente internacional sobre cualquiera de los rencionados, se marcará el punto de dicho puente que quede exactamente sobre el centro del canal principal, segun se ha determinado en este tratado, con un monumento á proposito, el cual denotará la linea divisoria por lo que haga á los objetos de dicho puente, no obstante los cambios en el canal que puedan ocurrir despues. Pero todos los derechos que no sean los que se tengan sobre el puente mismo, ó sobre el terreno en que este edificado, se determinarán en el caso de algun cambio subsequente, de acuerdo con las disposiciones generales de esta convencion.

Art. V.—El derecho de propiedad sobre las tierras que pudieran quedar separadas por causa de la formacion de canales nuevos, de la manera que se define en el articulo II de esta convencion, no se afectará por esta causa, sino que las expresadas tierras continuarán perteneciendo á la jurisdiccion del pais á que ántes pertenecian.

En ningun caso, sin embargo, afectará ó restringirá este derecho de jurisdiccion, que ambas partes se reservan, el derecho de navegacion comun á los dos paises, conforme á las estipulaciones del articulo VII del referido tratado de Guadalupe Hidalgo; y el expresado derecho comun de navegacion continuará sin ningun menoscabo. por todo el canal principal que sea navegable de hecho en los expresados rios, desde la boca del Rio Grande hasta el punto en que el Rio Gila cesa de ser limite internacional, aun cuando una parte del canal de dicho rio pueda con motivo de los cambios previstos en esta Convencion, llegar á comprender en el territorio de una de las dos naciones.

Art. VI.—La presente Convencion será ratificada por ambas partes, de acuerdo con respectivos procedimientos constitucionales, y las ratificaciones se canjearán en la ciudad de Washington tan pronto como fuere posible.

En testimonio de lo cual los Plenipotenciarios infrascritos lo han firmado y sellado.

Hecho por duplicado en la ciudad de Washington, en las lenguas española é inglesa, el dia doce de Noviembre de mil ochocientos ochenta y cuatro.
—*M. Romero.—Frederick T. Frelinghuysen.—La Nueva Era.*

Francia y China.

Al fin se ha asegurado la paz entre Francia y China. El resultado ha demostrado la tonteria del alarde hecho contra el Ministerio de Ferry cuando se recibieron las noticias de una derrota Francesa en China. El Ministerio Brisson ha hecho la paz sobre la base propuesta por el Ministerio Ferry antes de la derrota de los Franceses. Es un hecho que el nuevo Ministerio aun no se habia formado cuando vino la noticia que el Ministerio de Ferry habia concluido un tratado de pas. La Francia es muy impaciente bajo reversos para su propio bien. Naciones en guerra deben esperar de cuando en cuando golpes no muy agradables.

El Tiempo newspaper, published in Las Cruces, New Mexico, with an 1885 article on the Treaty of Guadalupe Hidalgo. Hispanic American Newspaper Database.

government to appoint a Nuevomexicano as the next territorial governor instead of a European American transplant, Albuquerque's *El Nuevo Mundo* listed various ways that the US government ignored the rights of Nuevomexicanos. "Never has Washington thought to fulfill the obligations under the Treaty of Guadalupe Hidalgo," began the blistering editorial. The efforts of the Spanish-language press have been in vain, it continued, because their eloquence and justice have crashed into the indifference of Congress and the presidency. "The telegraphs, railroads, telephones, electric lighting, and in a word, 'the American progress,' has not brought to New Mexico," continued the editorial, "more than ruin and misery." It then shifted to portray Hispanos as the "legitimate owners" and "civilized colonists" who needed to defend themselves against nomadic Native Americans who "infested" the land. "The vandalism of the fierce savage," the editorial inveighed, "was substituted by the 'scientific' pillage of the enlightened 'gentleman.'"[47] The editorial perpetuated a common Hispano viewpoint by portraying their ancestors as the original settlers while disparaging Native Americans and discounting their previous settlement of New Mexico. While focusing on the deleterious effects of the US conquest, it ignored the devastating consequences of the Spanish conquest on Indigenous peoples. The editorial engaged in selective forgetting—a convenient amnesia emulated by future generations. This forgetting of Native Americans' long presence in the region fit the dominant narrative advanced by Spanish colonial administrators and contemporary US officials. Yet by publishing such a searing indictment of the US conquest, the newspaper also selectively remembered the "endless US-Mexico War" and its long-term "ruin and misery" while advocating for Hispanos' rights (promoting the selection of a Nuevomexicano territorial governor).

Mexican Consuls and Treaty Rights in Arizona

The war and treaty remained on the minds of Mexican Americans throughout the US Southwest as they appealed to Mexican consuls for assistance in exercising their rights. In the 1850s, Mexican consuls helped families in the annexed lands wishing to repatriate to Mexico, and they defended ethnic Mexicans under attack from European Americans during California's gold rush. The Mexican consuls' advocacy reflected the national government's views about the war and the treaty. In turn, this advocacy helped disseminate knowledge about the Treaty of Guadalupe Hidalgo among several generations of Mexican Americans, who further spread memories of the war and the treaty via newspapers, word of mouth, and activism.

Interethnic relations between European Americans and Mexican Americans in Arizona were partly shaped by demographics and became progressively worse as the European American population increased. Like others in the northern borderlands, Arizona's Mexican citizens had experienced decades of neglect by Mexico's central government, including a lack of military protection from Indigenous raids. After 1848, an increase in Apache attacks, which had begun before the war, motivated some Mexican Americans to turn to the United States for military protection. Arizona was tied administratively to New Mexico until 1863, when it became an independent territory. The lack of commercial enterprises in the territory's desert climate and the constant threat of Native American attacks impeded the growth of the European American population, which attempted to accommodate to Mexican American society. A few intermarriages tied ethnic Mexican and European American elites, and US mining companies needed ethnic Mexican mining laborers, so interethnic relations were relatively positive, although not conflict-free. The two ethnic groups were also united in their common defense against Apache attacks. Nevertheless, mistrust existed among ethnic Mexicans and European American officials, as vigilante committees administered extralegal punishments and indiscriminately targeted ethnic Mexicans in the absence of legal courts.[48] In the 1870s, a copper-mining boom began attracting more newcomers who exhibited less tolerance for ethnic Mexicans, especially as the European American population surpassed that of Mexican Americans. Ethnic relations deteriorated further with the arrival of more European Americans, and these relations plunged after 1880, when the completion of the transcontinental railroad and the "pacification" of the Apaches led to a flood of newcomers.[49]

As Arizona's European American population became the majority in some cities (like Tucson) by the 1870s, their migration created problems for some Mexican American landowners. These property owners, who had been Mexican citizens until 1848 (or 1854), received some assistance from Mexican government officials stationed in Arizona. In the mid-1870s, the Mexican government established a consular office in Tucson to facilitate the growing mining trade between Sonora and Arizona and to protect the increasing number of Sonorans who immigrated to work in Arizona's mines.[50] In addition to the "pull" of mining and ranching employment, political instability and the Apache wars in Mexico had served as "push" factors for Sonorans immigrating to Arizona. Robberies, lynchings, and random violence inflamed racial tensions between European Americans and ethnic Mexicans (i.e., Sonoran immigrants and Arizona's Mexican Americans). Unsurprisingly, reactions to

Mexican "bandits" who attacked European Americans was more extreme than when European American "cowboys" assaulted Mexicans. In 1878, for example, after Mexican "bandits" staged a series of attacks, European Americans organized a vigilante committee (calling themselves "minute men"), while Tucson's English-language newspaper, the *Arizona Star*, urged the vigilantes to lynch the guilty parties. In response, Tucson's Mexican consul, Manuel Escalante, attempted to halt vigilantes from targeting Sonoran immigrants and perpetrating indiscriminate lynchings. Escalante asked the acting territorial governor for protection by US troops because the local police had failed to stop previous attacks on Mexicans.[51]

The Mexican consul also intervened in property disputes harming elite Mexican Americans. In 1878, Escalante wrote to the Mexican secretary of the Foreign Ministry to describe Mexican Americans' legal and extralegal challenges in southern Arizona. Escalante began his letter by identifying the "execution of the treaties" that occurred when "part of the Mexican territory passed into United States control" as one of the most important matters affecting Mexicans in Arizona. He reminded his superior that the United States had agreed to "respect and protect the property of Mexicans" in the ceded territory in the Treaty of Guadalupe Hidalgo and the Gadsden Purchase. Escalante explained that the US Congress had passed a law "for the examination and assessment of title deeds" in New Mexico in 1854, and that this law applied to Arizona once the latter was established as an independent territory.[52]

Calling this law "completely useless in achieving the objective the treaties had proposed," the consul described the frustrating experience of Mexican landowners over the last twenty-four years. He averred that the process of confirming Spanish and Mexican land titles in California and New Mexico, while different and imperfect, had allowed several title confirmations to be resolved. The crux of the problem in Arizona, according to Escalante, was the law's lack of enforcement due to Congress's failure to allocate funds to pay for a surveyor. He urged the Mexican government to lobby the US government to revise this 1854 law because it was extremely detrimental to Mexican American property owners. Characterizing them as helpless to stop squatters from invading their land, the consul cast landowners as powerless because their titles were "not honored nor confirmed" and held no legal value. Despite the property owners' precarious land rights, Arizona officials forced Mexican Americans to pay taxes on property to which they did not have "official" title. Escalante characterized this situation as "horrendous and unfair" because Mexican Americans were not considered owners except for the purpose of collecting taxes. This process was repeated until the landowners, frustrated with the uncertainty of their land titles, either sold their property or lost it at auction.⁵³

The consul's intervention demonstrated the Mexican government's efforts to pressure the United States to enforce the treaty's promises and its willingness to assist Mexican American civil rights efforts. Escalante urged Mexico's government to demand that the United States honor the treaty or risk a continuous loss of land for Mexico's former citizens. The US government had assumed that all Mexican land titles were invalid, contended the consul, and required their owners to prove otherwise. According to Escalante, the government's assumption exposed its intent not to honor the treaty.⁵⁴

Mexican consuls exerted some influence over their nation's policies but ultimately had little power to sway US officials. Nevertheless, a sovereign nation (Mexico) sought to help its former citizens obtain the civil rights promised by the treaty. Significantly, the Mexican consuls' intervention reinforced Mexican Americans' collective war memories. The consuls presented Mexico's interpretation of the war and treaty, which in turn influenced how Mexican Americans remembered these events. Despite the consuls' unsuccessful efforts, Mexican Americans understood that the Mexican government believed their civil rights were being chronically violated and that the United States was ultimately responsible for treaty enforcement.

This awareness was strengthened by the Mexican government's further efforts in the 1870s on behalf of its former citizens. Mexico's Foreign Ministry conducted an 1878 investigation into the violation of Mexicans' property rights in the United States by asking each consulate to submit a detailed report on the enforcement of the treaty's land title guarantees.⁵⁵ This investigation raised the consuls' profile among Mexican Americans and alerted them of Mexico's efforts in defending their civil rights. Through this investigation, Mexican consuls publicized their efforts to gather additional title information and interview the aggrieved landowners. In 1884, the Mexican Foreign Ministry conducted an additional investigation into abuses of Mexican agricultural workers in Texas counties along the Rio Grande. Unfortunately, the US government ignored these reports, and Mexican officials subsequently did not pursue them through diplomatic means.⁵⁶ A survey of the Foreign Ministry's records demonstrates that consular officials continued to defend the rights of Mexican nationals living in the United States with respect to the immigrants' experience with racial discrimination, abuse by local authorities, and poor working conditions.⁵⁷

However, the consul's advocacy began to change in the late nineteenth century. Additional investigations by Mexico's Foreign Ministry in 1888 and

1901 focused on the abuses of Mexican immigrants' judicial rights, but the United States ignored these complaints, and Mexico failed to further pursue them.[58] As president Porfirio Díaz cultivated US foreign investment, his consular officials were less likely to criticize US domestic policies. Additionally, the role of Mexico's consulates became more complicated with respect to ethnic Mexican labor organizing. While Mexico's consuls have sometimes helped Mexican workers, they have also refused to advocate on workers' behalf on various occasions when the Mexican government's promotion of trade clashed with laborers' rights.[59] At the turn of the century, the Díaz administration was consumed with domestic problems as it faced increasing internal opposition to its reactionary land consolidation and mechanization policies, which generated rising levels of landlessness and unemployment. The priorities of the Díaz administration were to attract foreign capital and promote trade, rather than to defend ethnic Mexicans in the United States.

As political turmoil and the Mexican Revolution occupied the attention and resources of Mexico's government, its consuls repeatedly failed to protect the interests of ethnic Mexicans in the United States.[60] Nevertheless, the consuls' early advocacy of Mexican Americans' civil rights helped disseminate the Mexican government's views on the Treaty of Guadalupe Hidalgo and reinforced memories of the war and its devastating aftermath among Mexican Americans. Newspaper coverage in Mexico of the consuls' efforts also led to the transnational circulation of memories of conquest as Mexican nationals learned of the persistent obstacles confronting Mexican Americans, while Spanish-language newspapers in the United States informed Mexican Americans of Mexico's continuing efforts on treaty enforcement on their behalf.

Transborder Civil Rights Advocacy for Tejanos

The press in Mexico not only reported on the developments in the United States but also advocated on behalf of Mexican Americans' civil rights. By reporting on civil rights abuses, Mexico's newspapers engaged in transborder civil rights advocacy, ensuring that Mexican nationals became aware of Mexican Americans' welfare. This advocacy often cited the long-term consequences of the US conquest, thereby reinforcing the dissemination of collective war memories. Spanish- and English-language newspapers circulated along both sides of the US-Mexico border, influencing the views of the border's residents, politicians, and activists. From the end of the US-Mexico War to the post–Civil War period, a variety of Spanish-, English-, and French-language newspapers appeared in the southern Texas and northeastern Mexico region.[61] By the late 1870s, newspapers in the Matamoros/Brownsville region included news stories about civil rights issues in Texas.

In an 1876 *El Progreso* editorial on US civil rights abuses, the editors mentioned the Treaty of Guadalupe Hidalgo and challenged Texas's official narrative. Like other regional newspapers in Mexico, the Matamoros-based *El Progreso* focused mainly on political and economic developments. However, the January 1876 editorial waded into Tejanos' civil rights by describing a speech by Colonel John S. Ford published in Corpus Christi's *Weekly Times*. According to *El Progreso*, Ford had delivered a speech on the roots of the ethnic tensions in the so-called Nueces Strip. Ford had moved to Texas in 1836 and joined the state's military, later becoming a newspaper editor, a Texas Ranger, and an elected official.[62] According to Ford, the "peace" guaranteed by the treaty existed only on paper because the hostilities had never been suspended after the war. These hostilities, he claimed, were caused by Mexicans who took cattle and land in the Nueces Strip. These Mexicans, Ford continued, blamed European Americans for stealing and possessing their property illegally. Ford identified Juan Cortina as the principal leader responsible for advocating this view, promoting hatred between the two "races" and killing several US citizens (meaning European Americans). Cortina, according to Ford, maintained his high position in Mexico's military precisely due to the hatred that he professed against the American "race." Ford had harped on Cortina's exploits since being sent to the border in 1859 to quell Cortina's rebellion but failing to capture him. In addition to cattle "bandits," Ford continued, Mexican military troops had invaded the Nueces Strip to steal livestock. Ford charged that these incursions had been occurring uninterrupted and led to assassinations and rapes of *americanos*. In his account, he dismissed or ignored all the attacks and injustices suffered by Tejanos.[63]

El Progreso refuted Ford's assertions and accused him of engaging in dishonor and slander. Spurning Ford's words, the editorial disputed his view that Mexico harbored cattle thieves and enemies of the *americanos*. A fraction of Mexicans expressed enmity toward some European Americans, the editorial maintained, due to Mexicans' conviction that they have been victims of unjustified expropriation. No distinction was made between Mexican nationals and Mexican Texans (with US citizenship), so *El Progreso* was probably referring to Tejanos who owned land in the Nueces Strip. It asserted that Mexican Texans well knew that the Treaty of Guadalupe Hidalgo had established the boundary between the two nations and that the Nueces Strip was now part of the "great American republic." Tejanos' animosity, emphasized *El Progreso*, was not due to Cortina's actions but was caused by their land loss and their inability to obtain justice through the courts. While the editorial agreed that some Mexicans participated in cattle theft and that Texas residents needed protection, it disagreed vehemently with Ford's accusations against the Mexican military. *El Progreso* accused Ford of false and malicious aspersions against the Mexican military. Although Mexico's military was not an exemplar of morality, the editorial advanced, neither could it be compared to the Texas Rangers, which brought horrible memories to Mexico. The reference to the Rangers recalled their participation in the US-Mexico War, in which they committed numerous atrocities against Mexican civilians.[64]

The editorial demonstrates the transnational flow of ideas, political views, and interpretations of history by challenging Ford's specific arguments and his generalizations about Mexicans. *El Progreso* contested his arguments about the origins of hostile ethnic relations and his generalization that all Mexicans hated European Americans with a detailed account of the land dispossessions and injustices suffered by Tejanos. Importantly, it refuted Ford's dominant narrative that Cortina was responsible for fomenting hatred. Because *El Progreso* was read on both sides of the border, its editorial reminded Mexican Texans and Mexican nationals of the treaty and alluded to Mexico's memory of the war. By rebuking Ford's account, which coincided with the official interpretation promoted by the state of Texas, *El Progreso* engaged in a transnational challenge of the dominant historical narrative in Texas.

The editorial's remark about the sad history (from Mexico's perspective) of the Texas Rangers illustrates the convergence of Mexico's views on the Rangers' atrocities during the US-Mexico War with the experiences of Tejanos who had suffered from the Rangers since the republic's early years. This editorial demonstrates that the newspapers' civil rights advocacy crossed international borders. It disseminated a strong rebuke of Ford's interpretation among citizens, politicians, and civil rights activists on both sides of the international boundary. Such advocacy was not lost on Mexican Texans, who read the editorial and understood that Mexican nationals were aware of the civil rights abuses in Texas. The newspaper's rebuke of Ford is also significant for Tejanos because Ford would spend the final years of his life writing and publishing historical articles that promoted Texas's dominant narrative.[65] Therefore, Mexican Texans' collective memories of the war and treaty were shaped not only by individual and community memories but also by the transnational flow of memories of war promoted by Spanish-language newspapers. While most Tejanos undoubtedly opposed Ford's take on the source of the border region's ethnic conflict, they likely agreed with his claim that hostilities had never been suspended because the "unending US-Mexico War" continued to cause devastating effects on their communities.

Californios Speak Back

The war and its effects were also embedded in the individual and community memories contained in the Californio *testimonios* collected in the 1870s. While researching the history of California, Hubert Howe Bancroft sent his agents to obtain the recollections of Californios. His agents interviewed sixty-two elders and recorded their words in a series of dictated memoirs. These dictations cannot be considered solely authored, as Bancroft's agents not only guided the interviews with specific questions but were also responsible for writing and transcribing the answers.[66] As historical documents, the *testimonios* provide documentary evidence of the Californios' mediated views of the US conquest and the post-annexation period.[67] They were not widely read until the late twentieth century because the interviews, with a few exceptions, were not published but rather kept in Bancroft's private collection. The views expressed in these interviews are examples of conversations (both oral and written) about the collective memories that Californios shared with their contemporaries. Several elders also wrote letters to Spanish-language newspapers about their experiences under US rule.[68] These views influenced contemporaries to press for civil rights, and the subsequent publication of the *testimonios* would lead to civil rights activism among future generations.

Like other Californio elites, Felipa Osuna de Marrón hailed from a military family that was among the first Spanish colonists to Alta California. Her paternal grandfather was a member of the Portolá expedition from Baja to Alta California in 1769, which left a Spanish military presence in San Diego and Monterey.[69] Born in 1809 in San Diego, where her father had served as a presidial solider and mayor, Felipa Osuna married Juan María Marrón, a sea captain and ranch owner. Marrón became justice of the peace and later served as an administrator of mission San Luís Rey when the US-Mexico War began. After Marrón died in 1853, Osuna de Marrón managed their land holdings on their ranch and continued to live in the San Diego area. When she was interviewed by one of Bancroft's agents in 1878, she defended her husband from accusations that he profited from his mismanagement of mission property and recalled the couple's experience during the US invasion.[70]

Osuna de Marrón's memories of the US-Mexico War demonstrate that she and her husband attempted to remain neutral during the conflict, but they also reveal Californios' divided sympathies. Like other ethnic Mexican women, Osuna de Marrón helped hide prominent Californios whom the US military pursued. She hid José Matías Moreno, Governor Pío Pico's secretary, when US troops arrived at her home. Pico, who was her cousin, and Moreno used their social connections among elite Californios to escape to Mexico.[71] After helping hide Moreno, Osuna de Marrón and her husband attempted to continue their ranching operations but were repeatedly drawn into the military conflict by both sides. Californios who opposed the US invaders captured her husband and unsuccessfully pressured him to join their resistance. Despite attempts to remain neutral, Osuna de Marrón acknowledged that she feared the undisciplined US troops.[72]

The Marróns eventually secured a travel pass from US officials that allowed them to move freely without being arrested by US troops. To secure this pass, the Marróns needed to pledge not to take up arms against the United States. At the same time, Osuna de Marrón and her husband complained about the rebels who stole their cattle to support their resistance. The rebels suspected that the Marróns had been communicating with and helping US troops and targeted their cattle in response. The Californios' divided sympathies were evident within her family, as her brother, Leandro Osuna, had fought US troops at the Battle at San Pasqual, during which he killed a US captain.[73] This battle, near San Diego, was a significant blow to US efforts to quash the resistance. After growing tired of losing their livestock, the Marróns sold most of their remaining cattle to Commodore Stockton for his trip from San Diego to Los Angeles. The Marróns subsequently cooperated with US officials for the rest of the war.[74]

Although Osuna de Marrón shared the prevailing Californio view about Native Americans' subordinate status, her conquest memories expressed sympathy for their plight. In her memoirs, she mostly followed the Californio practice of referring to Natives without acknowledging their individual names and the nations to which they belonged. However, in describing a plot that she had uncovered, she referred to a Native American laborer who worked as her gardener by his first name and identified his Indigenous nation. She had discovered the plot—to steal from and murder a neighboring merchant and kidnap the merchant's wife—because she understood the Indigenous language of the local Natives who visited the gardener. Unaware that Osuna de Marrón understood their language, the workers discussed the specific time and date of their plan. Osuna de Marrón shared these details with her husband and the neighboring merchant, who in turn arrested the laborers and informed local authorities. Local officer Macedonio González and his troops arrived to search for additional plotters. Their violent search and massacre of several Native Americans deeply disturbed Osuna de Marrón. She felt remorse about disclosing the plot due to the harsh punishment endured by the local Native communities, but she justified her actions by claiming that had the Natives carried out their attack, several people would have been kidnapped or killed. The harsh repression, she acknowledged, stopped further raids.[75]

Osuna de Marrón's conquest memories demonstrate Californios' divided sympathies while also confirming her position as part of the Spanish Mexican conquest of California's Native Americans. Like the Tejanos who attempted to remain neutral during the secessionist Texas revolt in 1836, the Marróns faced difficulty remaining uncommitted during the US invasion. Their attempted neutral stance indicated a desire to continue pursuing their economic activities without interference from larger political developments. Thirty years after the war's end, Osuna de Marrón possibly remembered this "neutrality" for political purposes. Namely, she might have chosen to emphasize her and her husband's neutrality to remain in the good graces of European Americans after her husband's death. Nevertheless, her recollections confirm that the reactions to the US invasion varied even within families, as her brother and cousin actively opposed the US invasion. Osuna de Marrón's memoirs also reflect more complicated interactions with local Natives than those of other Californios. She expressed remorse about informing authorities regarding the Indigenous plot due to the repression that her decision unleashed. Yet she acknowledged her position as part of the dominant (conquering) group by admitting that she benefited from the Natives' punishment due to the subsequent decrease in raids. Her memoirs illustrate the profound changes experienced by many Californios as a result of the US-Mexico War, which transformed them from conquerors of Native Americans into a conquered people.

Ethnic tensions among Californios, Native Americans, and European Americans were also the subject of the memoirs of Antonio Franco Coronel. Born in Mexico City, Coronel arrived in northern Alta California with the Hijar-Padrés expedition in 1834 as part of some 300 colonists who established a colony in Sonoma, just north of San Francisco.[76] Educated in Mexico, Coronel obtained several political posts in California, including superintendent of schools and mayor of Los Angeles in the 1850s. During the US-Mexico War, he was among the Californios who resisted the invasion.[77] He would subsequently participate in the gold rush and describe the ethnic tensions that ensued. He provided detailed accounts of his travels to different locations along Northern California rivers in search of placers, interactions with diverse groups of miners, and various strategies for finding gold. His recollections confirmed observations from contemporaries about the ease with which some miners obtained gold, gambled away their earnings, and transferred their gold to women who provided food and other domestic services.[78] In addition to noting the dramatic changes caused by the massive influx of newcomers, Coronel recounted various tense interactions among miners from diverse backgrounds.[79]

Coronel's memories report indiscriminate violence during the gold rush. Through his travels in Northern California, Coronel visited several prominent Californios, including Mariano Guadalupe Vallejo and Andrés Pico, and learned about the lingering tensions caused by the Bear Flag Revolt (1846), an attempt to establish a separatist republic during the US-Mexico War.[80] European Americans in Sonoma, for example, continued to resent Juan Padilla for his alleged role in imprisoning several Bear Flag Revolt participants. This animosity led them to attack Padilla, which left him badly beaten and requiring medical attention.[81] European American threats against Padilla continued even while he recovered under Coronel's supervision. Such lingering hostility from the secessionist revolt still plagued postconquest California and become inflamed with the competition over gold diggings. The influx of diverse immigrants, competition over gold, and an undercurrent of xenophobia among European Americans incited ethnic tensions. European Americans grew increasingly angry with Sonoran immigrants whose previous experience as miners helped them obtain more gold in shorter periods of time than neophyte miners.

Driven by this animosity, European Americans violently expelled "foreign" miners such as Californios, Native Americans, Chinese, and Sonorans from the diggings. Coronel attempted to avoid this hostility but witnessed several violent attacks and lynchings that ultimately led him to consider abandoning the mines. Several European American merchant friends convinced Coronel's group not to leave by promising to vouch for them and issuing credentials confirming their citizenship.[82] The group remained in the mines a bit longer but eventually fled due to violence. Coronel returned to Los Angeles, where he won elected local and state offices. His elite status allowed him to exercise some of his citizenship rights for a limited period before European Americans assumed almost complete control of local government in Los Angeles and around the state.

In addition to describing European American violence against Californios and Sonorans, Coronel explained that Native Americans were subject to forced labor, brutal attacks, and massacres. Sonoran miners traveled with Native captives whom they tied at the ankles to prevent their escape at night.[83]

These captives, likely from northwestern Mexico, had accompanied the Sonoran miners to California. While Coronel acknowledged the captives' lack of freedom, he was more troubled by the massacres of Natives perpetrated by Sonorans and European Americans. He outlined the prevailing view that murdering a Native American in cold blood was considered equal to killing a rabbit.[84] Appalled by the indiscriminate killing of Indigenous people, Coronel occasionally sought to intervene. He refused to hold Indigenous captives and also deterred violent attacks against Natives. While not responsible for this violence, Coronel shared Californios' views that Natives should be subordinate laborers. He acknowledged employing at least two Indigenous servants.[85] Tellingly, Coronel noted the ethnic background of various immigrants but did not acknowledge Indigenous nations or identify any of them by name. By contrast, he identified most European immigrants by country of origin and many of them by name. Such elision of Natives' background and personhood remained common among Spanish Mexican colonists throughout the borderlands.

Although Coronel's memories of the US conquest acknowledged the mistreatment and second-class status of Californios, he conveniently forgot his own role in the conquest of Native Americans. Describing a trade between his party and Indigenous people, he noted that the transaction was heavily in the Californios' favor, as their blankets were valued well below the gold supplied by the Natives. Afterward, one of Coronel's servants followed the Natives to determine the location of their gold diggings. Coronel and his servants took over the diggings without any doubt or guilt about the Native Americans' prior claim to the placer.[86] While he did not mention any violence against the Indigenous miners, the latter probably understood the threat had they resisted or attempted to expel the Californios. Coronel acknowledged several additional trades in which he or other Californios obtained gold from Natives in exchange for manufactured items worth considerably less than the nuggets.[87] The refusal to acknowledge Native claims to land and gold diggings resulted from Californios' views of Indigenous peoples as subordinate and inferior people who did not use the land properly. These views also shaped the Californios' selective memory of the Spanish conquest when they conveniently forgot their roles in committing atrocities against Indigenous people.

Another descendant of Spanish colonists who wrote about the Californios' complex reactions to the US conquest was Juana de Dios Machado. Machado, born at the presidio at San Diego, hailed from several generations of military families who took part in the Spanish conquest of Alta California.

Her maternal and paternal grandparents had arrived in 1781 to help found Los Angeles. Her first husband was a presidial soldier at San Diego who was killed in Sonora in the mid-1830s. Several years later, Machado married Thomas Wrigthington, a European American sailor from Massachusetts who had arrived in San Diego in 1833.[88] Wrigthington acclimated to Californio society, becoming a Mexican citizen and serving as a *juez de paz* in the 1840s. During the US-Mexico War, some San Diego residents (both Californios and European Americans) sided with the invading troops, including, not surprisingly, the Wrigthingtons. After US soldiers commanded by General Kearny suffered a stunning setback and various casualties at the Battle of San Pasqual in December 1846, they sought shelter at the Wrigthingtons' house. Machado de Wrigthington's brother would subsequently help guide the invading troops to San Diego.[89]

Machado de Ridington's memoirs confirm the divided reactions to the US invasion. Like Osuna de Marrón, Machado de Ridington described the resistance offered by various Californios to Commodore Stockton's arrival in San Diego. She confirmed that the Californio troops were able to defeat US soldiers at various battles and to inflict several casualties at San Pasqual. The details on the battles, casualties, and names of military officials demonstrate that the war and its outcome generated considerable attention. Machado de Ridington's family obtained passes from US officials, allowing them to travel freely during the war. In an apparent act of gratitude, her brother served as a guide for US troops heading to San Diego.[90] Although Machado de Ridington asserted that her brother did not take part in military combat, he provided critical assistance to US troops. Her husband Thomas also joined the "Battalion of California Volunteers" led by John C. Frémont.[91]

Machado de Ridington's memories of the US conquest reveal Californios engaging in the earlier conquest of the region's Native Americans. She expressed the Californio belief in their superiority over Indigenous groups and described various armed conflicts with them. She recalled her father's role as a presidial soldier in an assault on an Indigenous group near San Diego. The assault was meant to punish Natives accused of stealing horses from another Indigenous group allied with San Diego's presidio. Two of the Natives accused of horse theft, she claimed, were probably "runaway Christianized Indians," alluding to the captivity of some mission Natives. Machado de Ridington participated in the dominant society's pattern of criminalizing the conquered population by choosing the terms "thieves" and "habitual delinquents" to refer to the accused. Moreover, she described horrific acts against Natives without expressing any qualms about the violence. After killing a Native American in battle, her father took the victim's scalp and ears to present to the presidio's commander. Scalping was "customary at that time," according to Machado de Ridington, so she failed to condemn the practice.[92] By omitting the names and nations of Indigenous people while carefully noting the names and background of Californios and European Americans, Machado de Ridington joined other Californios in treating Native Americans as inferior people whose individuality was not necessary to acknowledge. She also confirmed Osuna de Marrón's memory of discovering a plot and the subsequent retribution massacre of Natives by Macedonio González. However, unlike Osuna de Marron, Machado de Ridington expressed no sympathy for the Natives killed.[93] The tensions between Natives and Californios continued during the US-Mexico War and led Native Americans to kill eleven Californios, who had fled from US troops and were short on supplies.[94]

Like other Californio *testimonios*, Machado de Ridington's remembrances allude to the transition of Californios from conquerors to conquered as a result of the US-Mexico War. She evinced little sympathy toward the Indigenous people while describing their conquest, punishments, and subjugation. Most revealing is Machado de Ridington's characterization of Indigenous raids as criminal atrocities rather than as Native resistance to the Californio conquest. As literary critic Rosaura Sánchez observes, the *testimonios* often pair descriptions of Indigenous raids with acts of retribution by Californios.[95] Machado de Ridington characterized Indigenous raids as "barbarous" and the vigilante response by Californios as "justified." She related attacks and massacres of Native Americans in deliberate and detached terms. Her casual attitude toward violence against Natives as well as her inattention to identifying their full names and nations reflected her sense of superiority as part of the conquering group. While venting outrage about various Indigenous attacks against Californio communities, Machado de Ridington did not express any animosity or outrage at the US invasion. At the time of her interview with Bancroft's research assistant, Machado de Ridington boasted four daughters, two granddaughters, and a cousin who had married European American men.[96] Her family's political and social alliances with European Americans help explain the absence of any criticism about the US conquest. While she chose to "forget" the Spanish-Mexican conquest of Native Americans, she did not denounce the American conquest, as did other Californios. Her reactions demonstrate not only the range of reactions to the US conquest among Californios but also the multiple and varied influences shaping these reactions. Like other Californios, Machado de Ridington died in poverty after losing her property due to the new U.S. property laws.[97]

Mariano Guadalupe Vallejo also established political alliances with European Americans, but the newcomers' betrayal and attacks left him bitterly disappointed. Like other Californios, Vallejo hailed from a storied military family. His paternal ancestors had served as soldiers for the Spanish Crown during the initial colonization of Hispaniola and Hernán Cortés's expedition to Mexico.[98] His father arrived as a soldier in 1773 with the initial expedition to settle Alta California and was rewarded with a large land grant north of Monterey. Born in 1808, Vallejo followed in his father's footsteps by joining the military, obtaining high-ranking posts, and acquiring land grants. By the 1830s, he had become the commandant general, or military governor, of Alta California under Mexican jurisdiction. His vast landholdings (some 225,000 acres) made him the largest landowner in the region. He warmly welcomed European Americans, admired the US government, and had sought to make Alta California a US protectorate before the US-Mexico War. Nevertheless, Vallejo became one of the first targets of European American separatist rebels, who arrested him during the Bear Flag Rebellion. After US annexation, he served as a delegate to California's constitutional convention and became a state senator in the first legislature. However, his allegiance to the US government did not protect him from the avarice of lawyers, speculators, and squatters. Following the pattern of fellow Californios, Vallejo lost most of his land and died impoverished in 1890.[99]

Vallejo remembered the US conquest as a betrayal for the Californios and described their marginalization in the post-annexation period. He vented his sense of betrayal and disappointment about the US-Mexico War and the false promises in the nation's ideals.[100] Denouncing the US military invasion of California and the subsequent war with Mexico as a "conquest," he identified the numerous newcomers to his home region as the "conquerors." Vallejo used terms such as "our country" and "owners of this land" to claim that he and other Californios were native-born landowners overrun with new immigrants, whom he characterized as immoral intruders.[101] Like other elite landowners, he denied Native Americans' claims to land and also omitted any criticisms of the Spanish conquest and usurpation of Indigenous lands. Vallejo conveyed the community's disappointments in vivid terms. He decried the English language, US laws, and European Americans as obstacles to "us owners of this land," and antagonistic to "our" interests and rights. These rights were not important to the conquerors, Vallejo insisted, who sought their own advantage and not Californios' interests. He scoffed at the European Americans' promises to close jails and abolish unjust Mexican laws in favor of promoting primary schools so that Californios would reach the heights of

European Americans. Vallejo starkly exposed European Americans' hypocrisy and expressed his dismay at the contrast between the nation's ideals and the lived experiences of Californios, who came into daily contact with European Americans who claimed superiority.[102]

Vallejo leveled anger and disgust at the widespread loss of land endured by the Californios. He cited the Treaty of Guadalupe Hidalgo and blamed European Americans for not honoring the property rights guaranteed therein. Characterizing the arrivistes as shrewd and "full of guile," he blamed them for scheming to defraud Californios of their land and hindering his fellow landowners with lawsuits that the US Supreme Court often resolved in the squatters' favor.[103] He felt incensed that some Californios lost land because they could not afford additional lawyers' fees after the newcomers appealed state court decisions to the Supreme Court.[104] Like others of his generation, Vallejo traced many of Californios' problems with land titles to the arrival of arrivistes during California's gold rush.

He reserved the strongest ire for European Americans, whom he condemned as squatters and petty lawyers who arrived with hardly any clothes but were full of petulance, daring, and disrespect. According to Vallejo, European American newcomers claimed that land grants distributed by presidial commanders were invalid. The targeted rancheros confronted a severe disadvantage in court due to the different customs, laws, and language of the "Yankees," often emerging from court "almost naked."[105] Vallejo identified the arrivistes' scheming and characterized the US legal system as a major obstacle. He also explained the rise of social bandits, like Joaquín Murrieta, by averring that several of Murrieta's followers were disaffected youth (who ignored wise counsel) from more than 200 Californio families victimized by squatters and lawyers. The injustice suffered by Californios had led to violent resistance, Vallejo maintained, but this option was limited, as many youth had been sentenced to death by local tribunals, become victims of the widespread lynch law, been confined to the San Quentin penitentiary, or been placed in mental asylums.[106] Vallejo's conclusion about the negative outcomes of resistance demonstrated his awareness of settler colonialism's "elimination" process, which deployed incarceration as a way of limiting dissent to make way for land acquisition. Yet Vallejo chose to forget Californios' role as settler colonists who eliminated Indigenous resistance to make way for Spanish acquisition of Native American lands.[107]

Vallejo acknowledged the economic benefits from the change of government but contended that the damages had been greater due to the US government's broken promises to uphold the Treaty of Guadalupe Hidalgo.

While agriculture and commerce had expanded with US rule, these benefits had been accompanied by a decline in residents' morals resulting from the arrival of immoral newcomers who had obtained government support. Vallejo believed that the state and federal governments played a crucial role in the moral decay by supporting the newcomers' activities. He also faulted the federal government for not assisting the Californios after its promises "seduced" them into granting initial support to US troops. This argument indicated that Vallejo and other Californios regretted their initial support for US annexation after realizing that the new government had no intention of upholding the treaty. Vallejo introduced what seems to be a tangent by questioning why the French and German languages were taught in San Francisco's schools but not the Spanish language. He attributed this disparity to voting strength by positing that the state's "Tudor" population accounted for 30,000 votes, while the Spanish-speaking population accounted for only 4,000 votes. Vallejo's incisive analysis linked the effective exercise of the franchise to political power.

To conclude his memoirs, he stated that future generations would agree with him about the broken treaty promises. Here, then, is Vallejo's ultimate memory of conquest: European Americans did not treat the Californios as fellow US citizens but rather as a "conquered population."[108] While he questioned the usefulness of complaining about the broken promises and expressed resignation about the Californios' dispossession, he stayed resolute about providing a meticulous account of post-annexation life for future generations of Californios. His exhaustive description of broken promises and contradictions between the nation's ideals and the Californios' reality helped disseminate his memories of conquest to subsequent generations and inspired some contemporaries to pursue civil rights reform.

Writing and Remembering Land Loss

The collective memories of conquest that Californios shared with contemporaries were influential in shaping the views of María Amparo Ruiz de Burton, whose ancestors had taken part in the conquest of Baja California before her family moved to Alta California. In addition to conversations with Mariano Guadalupe Vallejo, Ruiz de Burton also exchanged letters with him, his family, and other elites. Moreover, she was related by blood or marriage to several prominent families.[109] From these prominent leaders and residents, Ruiz de Burton learned about their sense of betrayal after initially cooperating with European Americans, their anger at their dispossession by squatters

María Amparo Ruiz de Burton, c. 1874–86, author of *Who Would Have Thought It?* and *The Squatter and the Don*. California Judicial Center Library.

and US courts, and their resentment at the failed promises of US citizenship. These collective memories as well as Ruiz de Burton's own experience with land loss would shape her private letters and publications.

Ruiz de Burton's literary contributions exemplify strategic uses of memories of conquest and transnational influences. Her grandfather, a lieutenant in the Spanish colonial army, became governor of Baja California in 1822, and her great uncle led the presidio at San Diego. Both men received land grants for their service in the army. Born in Baja California in 1833, she received her education from a private tutor from Spain. In 1848, María Amparo Ruiz and her family moved to Monterey. The next year, she married Henry Burton, a lieutenant in the US Army, a Connecticut native, and a West Point graduate. While living in Monterey, she developed a long-standing friendship with Vallejo. Her letters to him and his family included details of quotidian life, friendships, political discussions, and social observations. In an 1859 letter to Vallejo's son (Platón), Ruíz de Burton expressed her view of the unfulfilled promises of US citizenship: "It cannot be denied that the [C]alifornios have reason to complain. The Americans must feel it; their boasted liberty and equality of rights seems to stop when it meets a Californian.... They can crush us with impunity, they know it and broke their faith so solemnly pledged at Guadalupe Hidalgo.... How shameful this, in the conquering, the prosperous, the mighty nation!"[110]

Lieutenant Burton was subsequently transferred to San Diego, where the Burtons purchased the 8,926-acre Rancho Jamul after US courts rejected its original owners' property title. The original owners were none other than Pío Pico, the former governor of California, and his family.[111] After another military transfer in 1859, the Burtons moved to the East Coast, where Ruiz de Burton socialized with several military and political elites, including President Abraham Lincoln. Upon her husband's death in 1869, Ruiz de Burton returned to San Diego and developed extensive ranching industries. She eventually received title to Rancho Jamul but lost all the land during the 1880s when 160 squatters and creditors filed lawsuits against her estate. For several years, Ruiz de Burton filed lawsuits in local, state, and even federal courts (including the US Supreme Court) and traveled to Washington, D.C., to lobby Congress on behalf of Californio landowners.[112]

This background helps explain her literary output. She published her first novel, *Who Would Have Thought It?*, in 1872. This novel examines race and class relations during the US Civil War and enjoys the distinction of being the first English-language novel by a Mexican American author. In her second novel, *The Squatter and the Don* (published in the 1890s), a Californio family with a large ranch near San Diego confronts European American squatters. In her novels, Ruiz de Burton employed "disguised autobiographical fiction," because this genre of writing offers a "safer space than memoir" for ethnic minority writers to offer a counternarrative about the past. As historian Hannah Ewence observed, memory fiction can serve to represent "not only the author's memories, but a spectrum of memories for a whole community."[113] *The Squatter and the Don* represents a "spectrum of memories" of the Californio elite, thus serving to disseminate one community's collective memories of conquest, which countered the traditional triumphalist narrative of US westward expansion. Ruiz de Burton blamed the squatters' racial prejudice against Mexicans as an important part of her critique of the US conquest. She also sharply criticized corruption caused by the alliance between railroad companies and state officials.[114] Notably, the novel takes the view of the Californio elite, largely ignoring the experiences of poor and working-class Californios and Native Americans.

Ruiz de Burton's friendship with Vallejo and her own landowning experience shaped *The Squatter and the Don*. The novel's protagonist, Mariano Alamar, not only shares a first name with Vallejo but also endures very similar experiences.[115] Like Vallejo, Alamar owned a vast amount of land in California but lost it gradually as a result of US laws and squatters' claims. The novel depicts the Alamar family's dispossession, financial ruin from lawsuits against squatters, and corresponding loss of racial and class status.[116] The social and economic decline of the fictional Alamar mirrored the fall suffered by Vallejo and many other Californios. Both Vallejo's memoirs and Ruiz de Burton's novel can be considered declension narratives that depict a traditional Californio society beset by adversity as a result of the US conquest. In both narratives, Vallejo and Ruiz de Burton depict pre-annexation Californio society as idyllic and attribute their postconquest loss to European Americans' arrival.

Ruiz de Burton considered herself part of the elite, so her own landowning experience also influenced the novel. Her financial straits were exacerbated by her husband's death, which left Ruiz de Burton with two young children and few financial resources besides her husband's military pension.[117] After spending ten years on the East Coast, she returned to San Diego with her children only to discover that Rancho Jamul was heavily in debt and invaded with squatters.[118] By 1882, Ruiz de Burton had endured ten years of litigation against various squatters claiming land on Rancho Jamul. She also faced significant debts from two groups of creditors, failed business ventures, and impending financial ruin from her legal costs.[119]

Her novel offers a sharp critique of the economic and political changes introduced by the US conquest of California. By focusing on the intertwined lives of the landowning Alamars and several families of squatters (the Darrells and the Mechlins), Ruiz de Burton described the devastating impact of the arrival of numerous land-hungry European Americans in California, the Treaty of Guadalupe Hidalgo, and California's 1851 Land Act.[120] Through descriptions of the legal and illegal ways in which Californios lost land after the US conquest, the novel criticizes the US legal system, the nation's political culture, and its failure to enforce the promises of US citizenship in the treaty. It depicts Mariano Alamar attempting to protect his land while understanding, as a pragmatist, that Congress and California's legislature had passed laws favoring squatters because European Americans could deliver more votes than Californios.[121] This realization mirrored the views of Vallejo and other Californios who knew that their postwar political decline stemmed from their lost economic fortunes and their low population numbers in contrast to the surge of European American migrants. Ruiz de Burton also took aim at the railroad monopolies by describing their unfair practices and the political corruption from which they profited. Her critique highlighted how the railroad monopoly's unfair business practices and corruption hurt Californios and non-Californios alike, with devastating consequences for the entire country. Despite her harsh denunciation of corporate monopolies, she did not reject the entire capitalist system, instead advocating for its reform.[122]

Nevertheless, Ruiz de Burton called for Californios' integration into the social and cultural fabric of the United States through the experiences of the fictional Alamar family. In one scene, Mariano Alamar expresses his disappointment at not being recognized as an equal US citizen. He feels discouraged not only by the US failure to uphold its treaty obligations but also by Mexico's abandonment of its former citizens and by its lack of enforcement power. Like Vallejo, Alamar ultimately identifies the Californios as a "conquered" people.[123] For Alamar and other Californios, the US-Mexico War did not introduce democracy and progress to California but was rather a war of conquest that failed to uphold democratic principles for the "conquered" population. The novel depicts the Californios' decline in class status and their loss of the privileges of whiteness.[124] This loss mattered to the Californios because whiteness conferred US citizenship rights after 1848. Other scholars note the apparent contradiction in Ruiz de Burton's novel, which harshly criticizes the US legal and political system while also expressing the Californios' goal of integration into US society.[125] This apparent contradiction dissipates if we acknowledge that the Californios' most significant criticisms were about the US legal and political systems' inability to enforce the rights guaranteed by the Treaty of Guadalupe Hidalgo. Had Californios been able to exercise full citizenship rights, they would have believed themselves to be more fully incorporated into the nation.[126]

Alongside their struggle for citizenship rights was a desire to gain social and cultural acceptance by European Americans. Ruiz de Burton addressed this goal by portraying several intermarriages between Californio and European Americans in a positive light. According to scholar Elisa Warford, marriage is a common rhetorical device in literature, used to elide assumed differences between people of different cultures. Unlike other nineteenth-century novelists,

Ruiz de Burton characterized cross-cultural marriages between European American men and Californio women as successful. Moreover, unlike her contemporary writers, she also provided examples of European American women marrying Californio men, which overturned the patriarchal view of only Californio women being suitable partners for the European American conquerors. In a private letter to Mariano Guadalupe Vallejo, she deemed such unions as leading to mixed-race offspring who possessed better qualities than their parents, an idea that was common among her contemporaries.[127]

The Squatter and the Don expresses Californios' collective memories and a call to correct injustices. By describing the devastating effects of the US conquest from the Californios' view, the novel differs sharply from other nineteenth-century romance novels, which offered the perspective of the US conquerors.[128] Ruiz de Burton inhabited a unique position as part of this "conquered" population while at the same time claiming access to military and political elite circles (through her husband) on the East Coast. According to literary scholars Rosaura Sánchez and Beatrice Pita, *The Squatter and the Don* poses a counterhistory for the Californio population, which "by 1870 was a marginalized national minority, precluded from agency, and whose voice and history were effectively muzzled if not erased."[129] The Alamars' experiences with land loss and their negative views of the immorality instigated by European Americans exemplified the views shared by Ruiz de Burton's Californio contemporaries, such as the Vallejos, Picos, and Alvarados, to whom she was related by family or marriage.[130] Unlike other nineteenth-century US novels and travel narratives that depict Californios as inferior and culturally backward, Ruiz de Burton extolled this population as cultured, capable, and moral. She also contradicted contemporary portrayals of the Californios as stuck in the past and destined to vanish in the face of the US conquest by characterizing the Alamars as adaptable to the US capitalist economy.[131] Moreover, she avoided depicting all European American newcomers as the enemies of Californios, instead singling out squatters, lawyers, and corporate monopolies. In the novel, Mariano Alamar acknowledges that his best friends are European Americans, whose sentiments and views he admires.[132]

Ruiz de Burton sought to cast some European Americans in a positive light to attract non-Californio readers. These characterizations help explain her goal of informing European Americans of the adverse effects of US conquest on Californios. She makes this goal explicit in a scene in which a European American settler (a member of a family who buys land from the Alamars) acknowledges that he did not know that the Californios' rights were being trampled and that the United States was not enforcing the treaty.[133] Ruiz de Burton's goal is made clear by her decision to publish her novel in English in order to obtain a wide readership and generate a source of income. She wrote her novel as an informative vehicle to unite non-Californios and Californios against the injustices plaguing the state. While the book did not lead to a mass reform movement, it did document Californios' collective memories of the US conquest through a fictionalized account of their experiences. Several contemporary European American newspaper critics praised Ruiz de Burton's prose and storyline as engaging. Moreover, California readers made the novel moderately successful in the nineteenth century.[134] It also served as a model of fiction with "a political purpose," as described by contemporary book reviews, or as "social reform fiction" for future Mexican American writers, novelists, and activists.[135]

IN THE LATE NINETEENTH CENTURY, Spanish-language newspapers continued to promote collective war memories and advocate for the civil rights of the second generation of Mexican Americans. By republishing articles on the war from Mexico's newspapers, the US-based newspapers demonstrated their role in the transnational circulation of war memories. Mexican immigrants also helped disseminate war memories across the international border. The arrival of immigrant miners and ranch workers in Arizona and Texas led to conflicts with European American vigilantes. In citing the treaty to advocate for immigrants' judicial and Mexican Americans' property rights, Mexican consuls helped disseminate war memories in diplomatic correspondence and news articles outlining their efforts. The consuls defended the property rights of Mexico's former citizens by reminding the United States of its citizenship promises in the treaty.

Hispanos' advocacy for New Mexico statehood demonstrated the regional variations in remembering the war and treaty. They joined Mexican Americans in California and Texas in citing the treaty to advocate for confirmation of their land grants, but Hispanos' strategic use of collective war memories differed because they remembered the treaty's promises of statehood and protection from Indigenous raids. Moreover, politicians, journalists, and residents in New Mexico began interpreting the treaty as guaranteeing their continued use of the Spanish language. The *testimonios* of elite Californios contained their memories of the failed promises of citizenship as they recounted their inability to exercise property rights. These recorded memories illustrate how written and oral conversations among the first and second generation of Californios transmitted collective war memories. Such remembrances highlight

Californios' divided reactions to the US conquest, as some resisted, others cooperated with US forces, and still others attempted to remain neutral. These *testimonios* also reveal the Californios' bitter memories of the US conquest and their strategic amnesia of their role in the conquest of Indigenous nations.

Ruiz de Burton's experience and her novel are exemplary of the collective memories of war among the second generation of Mexican Americans under US rule. She experienced the US-Mexico War as a teenager and absorbed memories of pre-annexation California from an older generation who lived through the war as adults. The elder Californios were part of the first generation of Mexican Americans to live under US rule and ask the United States to live up to its ideals and promises. Ruiz de Burton shared grievances with another first-generation Mexican American who lived thousands of miles away in southern Texas. Juan Cortina was ten years older than Ruiz de Burton and experienced the war as an adult. His rebellion in 1859 was one of the first violent reactions to the US conquest, and his proclamations encapsulate some of the disappointments of the first generation. The Cortina rebellion and Ruíz de Burton's literary contributions demonstrate the ways that some Mexican Americans deployed memories of conquest to press for civil rights. This generation elected municipal and state representatives, filed lawsuits in pursuit of justice, and issued civil rights appeals to state and federal officials.

Yet the lives of Cortina and Ruíz de Burton were full of contradictions. Both portrayed Mexicans as victims of US conquest but neglected to discuss Mexicans' roles as conquerors of Indigenous nations. Cortina was very critical of US annexation, particularly the second-class citizenship of Tejanos, yet he remained silent on the violence that his ancestors had inflicted on Indigenous people and on his role in exterminating a band of Karankawa Indians. Likewise, Ruíz de Burton's writings exemplify Mexican Americans' collective memories of land loss and their inability to obtain justice within the US legal system. Her choice to "forget" her grandfather and grand-uncle's role in the conquest of Indigenous nations would also be repeated by subsequent generations who held the US accountable for the violent conquest of Mexicans while absolving (or simply ignoring) their Spanish and Mexican ancestors for their violent conquest of Native groups. Similarly, Ruíz de Burton was critical of US westward expansion, yet she married a military officer who participated in this expansion. In their denunciations of the US failure to enforce the Treaty of Guadalupe Hidalgo's promises of citizenship for Mexican Americans, Cortina and Ruiz de Burton ignored internal class divisions by conflating the views of the elite and poor. Finally, both Cortina and Ruíz de

Burton pose early examples of Mexican Americans with transnational family connections who employed collective war memories to advance civil rights. Their proclamations, letters, and novels would complement newspapers, congressional reports, diplomatic correspondence, and immigrants' oral interactions with Mexican Americans to reinforce the collective memories of future generations.

CHAPTER FOUR

Immigrants and Transnational Circulation of Conquest Memories
School Segregation, Lynching, and Shifting Boundaries

On December 24, 1910, Clemente Idar published an article in *La Crónica* about the segregation of ethnic Mexican schoolchildren in Texas. *La Crónica*, a Laredo-based Spanish-language newspaper, planned to present the Mexican consul with proof of school segregation. "Do not believe that we are seeking a scandal," Idar wrote, "we are merely claiming a right." Various immigrant children of other races, asserted Idar, do not confront obstacles in attending public schools across the nation. He then posed a series of questions: "So why are they imposed on Mexican and Mexican American children? By virtue of which right, or which constitutional principle? Are they [ethnic Mexican children] not recognized as a white race? Has the Treaty of Guadalupe Hidalgo been forgotten?"[1]

In the early twentieth century, newspapers in Mexico and Texas published articles about the exclusion of ethnic Mexican children from Texas public schools. These articles highlighted the welfare of the children of Mexican nationals living and working in Texas, as well as the rights of Tejano children. Laredo's *La Crónica* characterized this exclusion as indisputable and widespread across the state, and more common outside the border counties. Moreover, the newspaper published various articles connecting the denial of public schooling to the lack of enforcement of various citizenship rights, comparing the experience of Mexicans to that of other immigrants, and urging various Mexican American organizations and the Mexican government to stop blatant discrimination.[2]

Like previous generations, journalists and activists strategically recalled collective memories of conquest to motivate ethnic Mexicans to engage in civil rights campaigns. Newspapers, especially Spanish-language circulars, also became conduits for the propagation of memories of conquest. While discussing school exclusion, vigilante violence, and other forms of discrimination, Mexican American activists, as well as the press in Mexico and Texas, referred to collective memories of the US-Mexico War and to the citizenship rights enshrined in the Treaty of Guadalupe Hidalgo and the US Constitution.

Reinforcing Collective Memories of Conquest

As immigration from Mexico increased in the late nineteenth and early twentieth centuries, the collective memories of conquest held by Mexican immigrants and Mexican Americans would intermingle and reinforce each other. Developments in Mexico and Europe led to a change in the composition of the US immigrant labor force. Emigrants had begun leaving Mexico in the middle of the nineteenth century to escape their debts, obtain higher wages in the United States, and flee the nation's political instability. This emigration stream increased during the last third of the nineteenth century as the economic policies of Mexico's dictator, Porfirio Díaz, increased landlessness and unemployment.[3] The flow of Mexican immigrants rapidly accelerated with the outbreak of the Mexican Revolution in 1910. Emigrants fled the military conflict and the forced enlistment by various armed factions. Approximately one-tenth of Mexico's population (some 1–1.5 million people) emigrated to the United States, attracted by social stability, political refuge, and economic opportunities.[4] While the majority of immigrants arrived to work in the US Southwest's burgeoning railroads and expanding agricultural fields, some ventured into the Midwest to labor in agricultural and industrial occupations.[5]

The arrival of numerous immigrants did not meet with a uniform reaction from Mexican Americans. Historians Albert Camarillo and David Gutiérrez identify three sets of factors that provoked tensions between Mexican Americans and Mexican immigrants. The first consisted of economic competition. As more immigrants arrived, they often competed for jobs and housing with Mexican Americans.[6] Blaming recent arrivals for their inability to obtain better wages and working conditions, Mexican Americans increasingly came to view immigrants as economic threats. This competition led various Mexican American organizations and most labor unions to oppose further Mexican immigration. The second set of factors involved the internal heterogeneity of the ethnic Mexican population. Despite sharing some traditions, language, and ethnic backgrounds, Mexican immigrants differed socially and culturally from Mexican Americans in significant ways. Each group often acted on their differences when they perceived the other group as a threat. The large immigration stream further increased ethnic Mexicans' internal heterogeneity. The "external prejudices" of European Americans were the third set of factors. Because most European Americans could not readily distinguish between Mexican Americans and Mexican immigrants, European Americans' disdain for one group affected the other. Therefore, some Mexican Americans sought to distance themselves from Mexican immigrants in an effort to avoid this racism.[7]

The massive migration from Mexico at the beginning of the twentieth century bore significant cultural impacts. Drawn by social networks and familiar cultural practices, most Mexican immigrants settled in long-standing Mexican American communities such as San Antonio, Tucson, and Los Angeles, or in smaller communities along the border. Their arrival increased the number of Spanish speakers in each community, the number of customers frequenting the stores catering to Mexicans, and the readership of Spanish-language newspapers. Mexican music and other forms of popular culture were reinvigorated by the immigrants' arrival, as were ethnic restaurants and cultural celebrations.[8] As Mexican immigrants made friends, intermarried, and socialized with Mexican Americans, the former introduced the latter to a distinctly Mexican nationalist version of history. The influences ran in both directions, but the effect of Mexican immigrants on the society and culture of Mexican Americans was prevalent. In addition to personal interactions, the influence of Mexican immigrants was transmitted via mass media. During the last third of the nineteenth century, the creation of *mutualistas* (mutual aid societies), which assisted recent immigrants in adjusting to life in the United States, emerged as an important development—an emergence that became evident in Spanish-language newspaper articles by Mexican exiles and immigrants.

Mutual Aid Societies and Memories of Conquest

Among the first organizations to promote civil rights reforms were the *mutualistas*. These working-class self-improvement societies began appearing throughout the US Southwest in the post-annexation period but increased sharply during the 1870s.[9] Members consisted of both Mexican nationals and Mexican Americans. Among the founders were Mexican immigrants who modeled the organizations after mutual aid societies in Mexico.[10] The organizations promoted unity and cooperation among ethnic Mexicans, regardless of nationality. While immigrants joined *mutualistas* to help them adjust to their new country, Mexican Americans often sought membership to shield them from "economic and racial discrimination."[11] As their name implied, the organizations provided their members with mutual aid to surmount social and economic obstacles. One of the principal member benefits of *mutualistas* was death insurance, which gave the surviving family financial and logistical assistance to conduct a proper burial. In addition, *mutualistas* offered illness insurance, legal aid, loans, and job-seeking assistance.[12] Some societies also established newspapers, schools, and libraries, and held night-school classes. Seeking to promote cooperation in their communities, the *mutualistas* rented their meeting halls or auditoriums to barrio organizations at little or no cost. They also helped organize celebrations on Mexican national holidays and often named their organization in honor of Mexican patriotic figures to increase cultural retention.[13]

The mutual aid societies also promoted various civil rights reforms among ethnic Mexicans. They assisted members (and community residents) with court cases involving civil or criminal charges. Because few Mexican Americans served on juries, *mutualistas* viewed the Texas legal system as unjust. The societies often helped with legal fees and bail for indigent ethnic Mexicans facing criminal proceedings or jail.[14] La Liga Protectora Mexicana of San Antonio dispensed legal advice directly to members and through a weekly article in *El Imparcial de Texas*. Among the topics were legal advice about tenants' rights, workers' compensation, sharecroppers' rights, laws about personal loans, and voting rights. La Liga also helped members prepare for citizenship tests, understand adoption procedures, and remember children's compulsory attendance at free public schools.[15] Similarly, the Alianza Hispano Americana, one of the largest mutual aid societies with branches in various states, vigorously defended its members' legal rights, encouraged immigrants to become US citizens, and enthusiastically informed members of their civil rights.[16] While the *mutualistas* avoided confrontational politics that might have garnered unwanted attention from the English-language press, they protested various discriminatory measures, such as segregated swimming pools and theaters, as well as derogatory stereotypes in movies.[17] Therefore, the *mutualistas* helped inform Mexican immigrants of the legacies of conquest that continued to affect the ethnic Mexican community.

The legacies of conquest figured prominently in the aims of these mutual aid societies. Their goal of mutual protection from European American society was best elaborated by members of the Colorado-based Sociedad Protección Mutua de Trabajadores Unidos, which emphasized "the need to organize to protect themselves from the considerable discrimination that had already developed in the county of Conejos and in this part of south-central Colorado ... since the treaty of G-H [Guadalupe Hidalgo] in 1848."[18] This statement indicated that some *mutualistas* deemed the US-Mexico War as a war of conquest with tragic consequences for ethnic Mexicans living in the annexed territories. While some *mutualistas* chose descriptive names alluding to their goal of mutual protection, such as El Paso's Unión Fraternal

Mutualista La Protectora or Phoenix's La Liga Protectora, other mutual aid societies made deliberate choices to name their organizations after Mexican national heroes, such as Miguel Hidalgo, Benito Juárez, and Ignacio Zaragoza. *Mutualistas* chose Hidalgo (the father of Mexico's independence movement) and Juárez (Mexico's first Indigenous president) as organization names with the purpose of reminding members of their national and ethnic ties to Mexico.[19] Additionally, several Texas-based *mutualistas* were named after Zaragoza, who was originally from Goliad (La Bahía), Texas, and was a hero of the battle of Cinco de Mayo against the French. By choosing the name Ignacio Zaragoza, these groups invoked a time when Texas was part of Mexico and also proudly remembered a Tejano who fought for Mexico's sovereignty. By contrast, the state's historical accounts in the late 1800s offered little recognition of Mexican Texans' contributions to the state's early history.

By naming their organizations after Mexican national heroes, *mutualista* members fostered collective memories of conquest and preconquest collective identities. In honoring Zaragoza, the *mutualistas* offered, according to historian Julie Leininger Pycior, "an implicit challenge to the account of Texas history put forth by the victors."[20] Because mutual aid societies often celebrated Mexican national holidays, they helped reinforce Mexican culture. In New Mexico, the Hermandad Penitente, a mutual aid society established during the 1700s with civil and ecclesiastic functions, went underground after the US conquest. The need for the Penitente to go underground symbolized the impact of conquest on New Mexico's Hispano community.[21] Members continued their religious and self-help practices after 1848, but they did so in hidden ways because the US Catholic Church had outlawed the group. New Mexico's Hispanos undoubtedly saw the Penitente as a reminder of a preconquest era when the landowners were Mexican and Indigenous.

The Idar family, based in Laredo, was instrumental in promoting mutualism and in organizing and publicizing various civil rights reforms. Nicasio Idar, the family patriarch, was born in Texas, lived part of his life on both sides of the US-Mexico border, and maintained transnational friendships. Idar had worked as a yardmaster on Mexico's northeastern railroads for twenty years, helping to establish a railroad union in 1890.[22] After rejoining his wife and children, who had remained in Laredo, Idar began working as a journalist for *La Crónica* and later would become its publisher. Clemente, Jovita, and Eduardo Idar would join their father as writers, helping transform *La Crónica* into a leading voice for respectability politics as a means to achieve Mexican American civil rights.[23] Respectability politics were based on the modern concept of progress, which involved using self-improvement and community uplift to better the Tejano community. According to historian Gabriela González, this approach "presupposed that there was something inherently wrong with the aggrieved party [Tejanos] and that in order to attain rights, they had to meet a certain cultural standard."[24] The Idars believed that self-improvement and community uplift would allow Mexican Texans to achieve the same moral and cultural ground as European Americans and thereby obtain civil rights. Their struggle to desegregate schools for Mexican children was part of a strategy of uplift by promoting proper education.

The Idars supported various self-improvement organizations, including *mutualistas* and fraternal lodges. According to historian Emilio Zamora, the Idars espoused a "Mexicanist sense of unity and purpose" in their efforts to organize ethnic Mexicans to fight against various forms of discrimination.[25] Through *La Crónica*, they sought to shame the Mexican government into action by highlighting news stories of school exclusion, civil rights abuses, and vigilante killings that targeted ethnic Mexicans. Yet *La Crónica*'s editors and writers repeatedly vented their disappointment in the Mexican government's inaction in the face of repeated civil rights violations. In a November 1910 article on the segregation of Mexican schoolchildren, the editors charged Mexico's government of not caring for the numerous immigrants in the United States. It was up to Mexican Americans and Mexican immigrants, they contended, to unite and improve their situation, because neither group could count on the Mexican government's assistance.[26]

Mexican Consulate and School Segregation

The frequent press reports on school exclusion eventually came to the attention of Mexico's ambassador, Francisco de la Barra, in Washington, D.C., who asked the Mexican consul in Laredo, Miguel Diébold, to research the issue. Diébold completed his research on Webb, Zapata, and Duval Counties by November 1910 and reported to de la Barra that no evidence of school segregation existed. However, his report had one caveat—some monolingual Spanish-speaking Mexican children were segregated in public schools until they learned English.[27] In response to this conclusion and its optimistic (but erroneous) report, the Idars launched a vigorous campaign to refute the consul's investigation in *La Crónica*. Clemente Idar criticized the perfunctory report by averring that state law did not require segregating monolingual Spanish-speaking children. He also characterized the report's assertion that

Clemente, Nicasio, and Eduardo Idar. Nicasio Idar was the editor and publisher of *La Crónica*, a Spanish-language newspaper based in Laredo, Texas. Three of his children, Clemente, Eduardo, and Jovita, worked as journalists for *La Crónica*. General Photograph Collection, University of Texas at San Antonio Special Collections.

most school directors and teachers in the region were ethnic Mexicans as absurd.[28] The Idars subsequently asked readers across Texas to send complaints about school segregation to submit to the Mexican consul.[29]

According to *La Crónica*, school segregation was one of the legacies of conquest. Idar strongly denounced Diébold's report because it focused only on three border counties (with majority Mexican populations) and did not examine school segregation in the state's interior counties, where school exclusion was prevalent.[30] "Exclusion is not only by decree, but also by isolating students to separate neighborhoods, as in Pearsall, Devine, Kingsville, Del Rio, Asherton, Kyle, etc. and where small school buildings are constructed (dimensions: 20 × 20 feet)." Idar elaborated that "when they attend official schools, and the American children insult them, when they quarrel with them, slap them, . . . they forget (forever) to nourish their minds with the sacred bread of knowledge."[31] He outlined a pattern of residential segregation as well as harassment preventing ethnic Mexican children from obtaining an education. "We know that the exclusion of the Mexican children in Texas is a fact," Idar concluded, "in some parts by express and direct prohibition, and in others indirectly, through bad treatment, through humiliation and antagonism."[32] With these arguments, Idar linked school segregation and discrimination against ethnic Mexicans to their second-class citizenship and the country's failure to enforce the treaty.[33]

Newspaper coverage of Mexican schoolchildren's exclusion noted geographic differences. Along the border, residents praised Mexican teachers for providing education to the region's children. However, the ethnic Mexicans residing in the interior counties felt isolated and abandoned according to news articles. Their exclusion was more conspicuous and indisputable in the interior counties. In December 1910, *La Crónica* published letters from readers in Guadalupe and Frio Counties on school segregation. The newspaper had previously requested letters to determine the condition of the state's public schooling.[34] In response, parents wrote to the newspaper asking for recommendations for Mexican teachers. According to *La Crónica*, these concerned parents sought to hire their own teachers "to impart the bread of knowledge to their children who are not admitted into the public schools, or if they are, the American teachers do not make any effort to teach them, it being very common to find children who have attended the schools for four or five years without knowing any English."[35] Rather than displaying ignorance or lack of interest about public education, ethnic Mexicans took active steps to hire teachers to supplement the inadequate education received by their children.

Education for All?

As the Idars waged their journalistic campaign to end segregated schools, the Texas Superintendent of Public Instruction gave a speech that selectively remembered the Texas rebellion by placing public education as a defining cause of the revolt against Mexico. In a speech at the Texas State Teachers Association meeting in Abilene on December 28, 1910, F. M. Bralley, the state's superintendent, opined, "Texas has a unique history in that her people, while yet belonging to the Mexican government, rebelled and gave as a principal reason the failure of their government 'to establish any public system of education.... Our fathers, the only people in the history of the world who rebelled and went to war over the proposition that *education is for all.*"[36] Clemente Idar and other activists found Bralley's speech appalling. Bralley distorted the reasons for the state's secessionist rebellion by claiming that the rebels sought public education for all the state's residents when most African American and ethnic Mexican schoolchildren remained segregated. Idar published the speech and exposed Bralley's hypocrisy: "public school officials boasting that Texas seceded from Mexico on the principle of equal educational opportunities for all, when they themselves were responsible for segregating ethnic Mexicans into separate schools."[37] The state's educational system "does not have the slightest tinge of democracy," explained Idar, since democracy would not deprive Mexicans the pleasure of enjoying these 'equal educational opportunities.'"[38]

The state superintendent's selective memory of the Texas rebellion gave Idar an opportunity not only to challenge the superintendent's interpretation but also to advance an alternative collective memory. Bralley's audience consisted of 700–800 mostly white teachers and school officials, a receptive group for his selective memory of the Texas rebellion.[39] Notably, he failed to mention several reasons for the rebellion: the tensions between Mexico's federalists and centralists in the mid-1830s, the territorial expansion of the United States, and the growth of slavery. Mexico had outlawed slavery in the 1820s and had rescinded the exemption for the importation of slaves in Texas when the separatist rebellion began. Claiming that Mexico's failure to establish a system of public education as the main reason for the rebellion was a convenient fiction to appeal to public school teachers.

Tejanos contested Bralley's attempt to become an architect of memory. After his speech appeared in newspapers, readers vigorously challenged his arguments. Idar forcefully refuted Bralley's assertion of the causes of the Texas rebellion and also emphasized that the Anglo-Texan rebels obtained the support of US citizens living in Texas and, most importantly, the US government. Therefore, Idar provided the historical context to understand the rebellion while Bralley made ahistorical arguments without proper context. Texas's government did not provide public education for all its citizens, Idar noted wryly, and Mexican Texans could not expect support from the United States if they rebelled against the Texas government. By publishing parts of Bralley's speech and then rebutting his most outrageous arguments, Idar was reminding *La Crónica* readers that collective memories of the Texas rebellion held by Anglo-Texans and Tejanos diverged. His readers were Spanish-speaking Mexican Texans who held alternative collective memories of the rebellion and its tragic consequences. Significantly, Idar's disagreement with Bralley brought up Mexico's prior jurisdiction over Texas and the contested history of the republic's birth.

San Angelo's School Boycott

The small West Texas town of San Angelo became a site of the struggle over segregated public schools and memories of conquest. The town's local campaign became an international issue when the Mexican consul became involved and press coverage cited the Treaty of Guadalupe Hidalgo's guarantees of citizenship rights. In 1910, the city's European Americans, African Americans, and Mexicans attended separate schools. San Angelo's dominant white population held very condescending views of working-class Mexicans to rationalize the city's segregation. According to San Angelo's white residents, Mexicans were a "race of mongrels" who resigned themselves to gambling, drinking, and immoral sexuality. They characterized Mexicans as "incapable of education," unable to understand politics, susceptible to political bosses, and unconcerned about their livelihood, preferring to live on handouts.[40] Not surprisingly, Mexican children received poor instruction from unprepared teachers working at physically inferior schools. After constructing a new school building for white students in 1910, the city decided to move ethnic Mexican children to the abandoned white school. Mexican parents showed their displeasure quietly by refusing to give the names of their school-age children to a census enumerator that April. These parents believed that Mexican children were not receiving the benefits of an equal education, which was funded by the state on the basis of each city's population of school-age children.[41] By withholding their children's names, the parents were decreasing the number of children enumerated in the census and thus lowering the city's portion of the state's education funds. A committee of four parents and an attorney met with the school board in early June to advocate for integration.

If full school integration was not approved, the parents insisted that the separate schools for white and Mexican children be on the same grounds so the children could at least socialize.[42]

The parents took more drastic steps later that month. In June 1910, 300 ethnic Mexicans met to demand the city's white schools admit their children. The attendees included a cross-section of San Angelo's ethnic Mexican community, who heard parents deliver speeches in English and Spanish calling for integration.[43] According to *La Crónica*, the parents planned a lawsuit to press their "demand that Mexican children be admitted in the Schools of the City with the *white* children."[44] Parents undoubtedly found inspiration in various news articles that outlined their rights under the US Constitution and the Treaty of Guadalupe Hidalgo. *La Crónica* reminded readers of ethnic Mexicans' claims to whiteness and alluded to the US government's strategic attempts to neglect the treaty: "Has the Treaty of Guadalupe Hidalgo been forgotten?"[45] The school board was surprised at the Mexican parents' census protest and their determination.[46] To appease the parents, the board acknowledged past problems with inferior school facilities and poorly trained personnel, promising to improve the facilities and hire competent teachers. However, it rejected the parents' main demand. The board's president stated, "If Mexicans were given access to the schools, this would demoralize the system of public schools."[47] He made the board's sentiment explicit: "The proposition of intermingling the whites and Mexicans would be a terrific blow to our school system and create a world of discord."[48] By refusing to integrate the city's schools, the board confirmed its decision to prioritize the interests of white parents. Ultimately, it proposed to establish two "Mexican schools" in older buildings, which would be "just as good school facilities as [those for] the white children."[49] However, the board underestimated the resolve of the Mexican community. Through their attorneys, the Mexican parents forcefully rejected the board's "separate but equal" proposal because they believed separate schools would not provide the advantages of integration.[50]

Motivated by knowledge of their citizenship rights, San Angelo's ethnic Mexican parents asked the Mexican consul for assistance and also organized a school boycott. The parents sent a representative to meet with Enrique Ornelas, the Mexican consul in San Antonio, to report their experience with school segregation in San Angelo.[51] The Mexican consul spoke with the state's governor, the Mexican government, and US president William Howard Taft. The parents, the consul stipulated, were law-abiding citizens who were justified in their demands because their children were enumerated in the school census, which was used to allocate school funds, but did not receive the full benefits of education. The consul encouraged the parents by reinforcing their argument linking the payment of taxes to the rights to an equal education: "The Mexicans pay taxes to the state, county, and municipalities, and their children are entitled to the same educational advantages as the children of [white] American parents."[52] According to the *El Paso Herald*, the San Angelo dispute became an international issue and was likely to become as significant as the exclusion of Japanese children from schools in San Francisco, California, in 1906.[53]

The majority of parents kept their children from attending the segregated schools to pressure the school district to integrate the "white" schools. Parent Florentino Muñoz explained their decision: "We will not send our children to the separate school. It doesn't benefit them any."[54] Moreover, seven ethnic Mexican children attempted to enroll at one of the white schools, but school officials refused to admit them.[55] But the ethnic Mexican families stood firm in their school boycott. Because no ethnic Mexican schoolchildren attended the segregated schools in 1910, the city reassigned the teachers to the "white" schools. In an effort to educate their children during the public school boycott, ethnic Mexican parents enrolled their children in Immaculate Conception Academy, a local Catholic school, where their tuition was waived. Unfortunately, the children were still segregated in "Mexican rooms," where they were taught by a separate teacher.

While some parents possibly viewed this arrangement as an improvement because their children might interact with white children attending the same school, this separation demonstrated that the Catholic Church (like the San Angelo school board) was more responsive to requests from white parents than those from ethnic Mexican parents.[56] The boycott began to waver as a few parents chose to send their children to the segregated Mexican schools. In 1911 and 1912, enrollment in the Mexican schools rose gradually but then declined after 1913, when the Mexican Presbyterian Mission School opened and enrolled many students. This school was part of the Presbyterian Church's outreach effort to ethnic Mexicans.[57] No students attended the public Mexican schools in 1914. After 1915, however, enrollment in the Mexican schools gradually increased again, while some children continued attending the Catholic or Presbyterian schools.[58] Unfortunately, the boycott ended without convincing San Angelo's school board to allow ethnic Mexican children to enroll in the "white" schools, as it steadfastly refused integration.

The parents' activism against school segregation reinforced their commitment to exercise their citizenship rights while introducing some to collective memories of conquest. By appealing to the Mexican consul, the parents converted a local issue of segregated schools into an international concern over the rights of Mexican nationals in San Angelo and the denial of Mexican Americans' citizenship rights. The Mexican consul advocated on behalf of Mexican nationals, but his efforts also assisted Mexican American children. Conversations with the Mexican consul and newspaper coverage of the segregation controversy reinforced the parents' argument that their children were being counted in the census, which determined San Angelo's school funding, but were not benefiting from that funding. Additionally, the consul and various newspapers, such as *La Crónica* and *El Regidor*, characterized the parents as taxpaying and law-abiding residents whose children were not receiving a proper education. Many parents repeated the link between their obligation to pay taxes and the city's responsibility to provide all residents with the same benefits.

Conversations with the Mexican consul and newspaper stories on their desegregation struggle exposed parents to discussions about the Treaty of Guadalupe Hidalgo. Moreover, various Texas and Mexican newspapers cited the treaty and its citizenship guarantees when discussing the San Angelo school desegregation case. Although some parents were aware of the treaty, the newspaper coverage and conversations with the Mexican consul undoubtedly made more parents aware of these rights. The ethnic Mexican parents read newspaper coverage of school desegregation cases in which journalists, like the Idars, contended that the treaty in conjunction with the Naturalization Act of 1790 made Mexicans legally white. "Why are they [ethnic Mexican children] not admitted with the American children," Nicasio Idar demanded, "despite that the Treaty of Guadalupe Hidalgo specified that we would be recognized as a white race."[59] In 1897, a federal judge had made this precise argument when he granted naturalized US citizenship to Ricardo Rodríguez, a Mexican national living in San Antonio, based on the treaty.[60] According to the US Supreme Court, the question of ethnic Mexicans' legal classification as white continued to be unsettled into the 1930s.[61]

Lynching of Mexicans and Unjust Legal Trials

During the month in which *La Crónica* published an editorial against the Mexican consulate's inaction on school segregation, news of a vigilante murder demonstrated journalists' deployment of collective conquest memories to defend the welfare of ethnic Mexicans in Texas. From Los Angeles to Tampa, the Spanish-language press carried articles that called the killing "savagery" and "barbarism."[62] Newspapers reported on the tragic death of twenty-year-old Antonio Rodríguez in Rock Springs, a town west of San Antonio. Authorities had captured Rodríguez after he was accused of killing Effie Greer Henderson on a local ranch. While Rodríguez was in custody, a vigilante mob broke into the jail, abducted Rodríguez, and burned him alive.[63] In an editorial titled "Barbarisms," *La Crónica* denounced the lynching by an "enraged horde of savages who did not respect the law or [human] rights."[64] In their trenchant critique, the editors stressed that the case revealed much about the proclaimed "civilization" in "this land of democracy." According to a summary of the killing, the assailants had not been arrested and authorities had not ordered an investigation into the murder of Rodríguez because the coroner had concluded that "*unknown* persons had burned alive an *unknown* Mexican."[65] The editors doubted the assailants would be brought to justice, and indeed neither the county nor the state ever convicted anyone for the lynching of Rodríguez.[66]

While condemning the murder in Texas, some Mexican dailies urged federal officials to use diplomacy to ask for justice, while other newspapers criticized the Mexican government's tepid response.[67] Within days of Rodríguez's murder, impromptu anti-American protests rocked Mexico City, involving attacks against American-owned businesses, destruction of US flags, and attacks against European Americans living in the Mexican capital.[68] Protests soon spread to other cities in Mexico with demands that Mexico's president, Porfirio Díaz, pressure the United States to investigate the crime, arrest the murderers, and ensure Mexican immigrants' safety.[69] These spontaneous actions conveyed Mexican nationals' widespread outrage and their sympathy toward the experiences of Mexican immigrants. The lynching and subsequent protests gained international attention as newspapers in the United States, Mexico, and other parts of Latin America covered the protests and subsequent diplomatic efforts to diffuse tensions.[70]

The reactions to the Rodríguez murder demonstrated the limits of transnational links among ethnic Mexicans as well as the continuing legacies of conquest. Journalists and residents in Mexico City and other major Mexican cities denounced the killing, confirming their concern for Mexican immigrants. "Antonio Rodríguez has perished within the flames," a Mexican newspaper declared, "fueled by barbarism and hatred."[71] According to another Mexico City daily, *El País*, this act of "savagery by the americanos" proved that "in the United States, Mexicans have no guarantees and immigration is highly dangerous."[72] However, for the editors of Laredo's *La Crónica*, the protests in Mexico City were a double-edged sword. While the demonstrations proved Mexico City residents' concern for immigrants, the editors also acknowledged the limits of such sympathy by noting that the anti-US demonstrations made it more difficult for ethnic Mexicans to survive in Texas because the suspicion and discrimination against them would continue until tempers calmed down. The increased

US-Mexico tensions, *La Crónica* elaborated, resulted in the lack of hospitality and denial of work for ethnic Mexicans throughout the state because employers often hired African Americans in their place.[73]

This negative view of demonstrations was partly shaped by the Idars' "politics of respectability," which led them to believe that anti-US demonstrations did not contribute to positive portrayals of Mexicans in Texas.[74] In an editorial, *La Crónica* acknowledged the stark reality that commentators in Mexico ignored: the very different political context of ethnic Mexicans as subjugated minorities in Texas compared to residents of Mexico City. Moreover, *La Crónica* faulted Mexico City's residents for forgetting the "numerous calamities in Mexico" that initially caused their fellow citizens to emigrate. Mexican nationals' lack of understanding of immigrants' plight, the editors concluded, underlined the lack of unity among ethnic Mexicans. The allure of higher wages and secure jobs in the United States combined with the political and economic turmoil in Mexico had fueled this migration since the mid-nineteenth century. Mexican nationals, *La Crónica* continued, also failed to consider Tejanos as part of their ethnic group. These conclusions spoke to the schism caused by the US-Mexico War, a rupture that led to different social, cultural, and economic realities in the United States than in Mexico. Unlike Mexican nationals who held various positions of power in Mexico, Mexican Americans and Mexican immigrants lived and worked as subjugated ethnic minorities in the United States.[75] This situation revealed how Mexican nationals in Mexico could not completely grasp the subordinate status and precarious position of ethnic Mexicans in the United States.

As protests spread from Mexico City to other areas, the US press grew alarmed by reports of riots, anti-American rhetoric in major Mexican newspapers, and attacks on American-owned businesses. Some European Americans feared a connection between the anti-US protests and border insurrectionists with ties to Francisco Madero, who sought to overthrow Mexican dictator Porfirio Díaz.[76] According to US newspapers, the protesters chanted, "Death to Americans!" and "Down with the gringos!" as Mexico's police forces arrested hundreds and shot others in attempts to disperse the unruly crowds.[77] The real danger of the student-led protests, feared the *New York Times* in a revealing editorial, was the possibility that middle-class student demonstrators would incite the lower classes, whom the US press portrayed as extremely unruly and very capable of indiscriminately attacking European Americans and destroying property.[78] Moreover, the anti-American protests fueled suspicions about ethnic Mexicans' supposed hatred of European Americans and their inability to control their anger.[79] These fears had been common since the Texas revolt and the US-Mexico War, which led European Americans to doubt the loyalty of Tejanos and other Mexican Americans, leading to their criminalization.[80] In 1910, collective memories of conquest continued to influence interpretations. However, European Americans and ethnic Mexicans drew on their collective memories to interpret the past and present in divergent ways.[81]

Rodríguez's murder and its aftermath offered vivid examples of how interpretations of current events are shaped by each group's collective memories. The US press chose to focus on the anti-Americanism and violence that the lynching had unleashed. But Mexican American journalists interpreted the lynching and the US inaction to pursue the vigilantes as part of a pattern of injustice dating back to their incorporation into Texas and the nation. The lynching, according to Mexican and Latin American newspapers, confirmed the United States' condescending views toward Latin America, which justified its expansionists policies.[82]

Accusations of disloyalty and criminality against Mexicans increased in the 1910s as European Americans worried about the disturbances of the Mexican Revolution.[83] Tensions surged as rumors circulated of attacks on European Americans in Mexico and as Mexican refugees streamed into Texas. "Anglo Texans justified their violence against Mexicans living in the United States," according to historian Nicholas Villanueva Jr., "by highlighting the anti-American threat that the revolutionaries represented."[84] In addition to instigating vigilante actions, various European Americans wrote to their representatives complaining about threats that Mexicans posed to the state and the nation. In a letter to Texas congressman John Nance Garner, an Anglo-Texan expressed common fears about the turmoil in Mexico and cast doubt on Mexican Americans' allegiance. However, the writer made little distinction between Mexican nationals, Mexican Americans, and Mexican immigrants. Moreover, he harped on the perceived threat of ethnic Mexicans' supposed race prejudice based on inaccurate memories of conquest:

> The fact remains, and will ever remain, that the Mexican, whether he be naturalized, [or a] native-born Mexican American, still retains and stubbornly maintains race prejudice against the American People. It is innate in them and Hell can't eradicate it. This feeling has existed with that *nationality* [emphasis added] ever since ... the Treaty of Guadalupe Hidalgo of 1848 when the territory ... was ceded to the United States. ... Mexican children have been taught that this territory was STOLEN from them by Americans—Mexican histories repeat it, their statesmen herald it, and their priests communicate it.[85]

This passage is an incredible example of projection onto all ethnic Mexicans a racial animus toward European Americans that was partly applicable in reverse.[86] This writer confused ethnicity with nationality by suggesting that all ethnic Mexicans shared the same nationality and all learned Mexico's version of the US-Mexico War in school. This was untrue, since Mexican Americans learned the US version of the war in US public schools. Perhaps he was referring to ethnic Mexicans' collective memories of conquest transmitted across generations? While families taught such collective memories to their children, their intention was not to promote race animosity but rather to transmit a forgotten history, inspire pride, and highlight their ancestors' roles. By claiming that racial hatred explained anti-Americanism, this writer and other US journalists discounted more immediate causes, such as the consistent failure of US authorities to punish vigilantes for the lynching of ethnic Mexicans.

In falsely linking anti-US protests to racial hatred of European Americans, the writer ignored ethnic Mexicans' anger toward an unjust US legal system that repeatedly failed to punish killings of Mexicans. Appearing above a 1910 news article titled "The Lynching of Antonio Rodríguez," a cartoon in Mexico City's *Diario del Hogar* illustrated the direct cause of the anti-American protests. The foreground showed a dapper man (labeled "pueblo" or "people") using a rolled-up newspaper marked "popular protests" to hit Uncle Sam (who held a club labeled "savagery"), while the background showed a mob burning Rodríguez in Texas within a crude map of the United States and Mexico.[87] According to the cartoonist, the anti-US protests were a direct response to the murder of Antonio Rodríguez. Especially infuriating to Mexican nationals was the initial refusal of Texas officials to investigate Rodríguez's lynching.[88] Memories of conquest did not fuel anti-Americanism but rather reminded Mexican nationals and Tejanos of Mexico's mid-nineteenth-century loss in a war of conquest, the power of US racial hierarchy, and the United States' failure to uphold the Treaty of Guadalupe Hidalgo's citizenship guarantees.

In the devastating editorial "Yankilandia," *Diario del Hogar* accused the United States of satisfying its "barbarous appetite" with the lynching of Rodríguez. Sarcastically referring to Yankee "civilization," the editorial remembered the US-Mexico War: "The traces left by your putrid plants that in 1847 as starving vultures you unleashed on Alta California, Texas, New Mexico, etc. are not yet erased."[89] For this newspaper, as well as others critical of the US response, the lynching was part of a long pattern of hostility and imperialist expansion by the United States.[90] In struggling to exercise their civil rights, Mexican Americans did not express anti-Americanism but rather

Diario del Hogar, a Mexico City newspaper, with a 1910 article on the lynching of Antonio Rodríguez. Readex, World Newspaper Archive.

demanded that the United States live up to its ideals and enforce its promises of citizenship—a standard reformist goal rather than a revolutionary one. For Mexican American activists and journalists, this struggle involved holding the nation accountable to the laudable ideals enshrined in the US Constitution and the Treaty of Guadalupe Hidalgo. One month after the lynching of Rodríguez, *La Crónica* cited the failure of the United States to enforce the treaty's citizenship guarantees.[91] Yet in its initial reporting on the lynching of Rodríguez, the editors of *La Crónica* criticized the anti-American protests in Mexico as counterproductive for ethnic Mexicans in the United States and urged Mexican nationals to pressure their government to use diplomacy with the United States to obtain justice for Rodríguez's murder.[92] The Idars preferred diplomacy to demonstrations.

Seven months after Rodríguez's murder, another vigilante lynching led to widespread outcry from Mexicans in Texas and Mexico. Newspapers published details of the murder, and several reported on ethnic Mexicans' demands for authorities to punish the perpetrators.[93] The press reported the savage lynching of Antonio Gómez, a fourteen-year-old ethnic Mexican boy on June 19, 1911, in Thorndale, Texas. Incensed to find Gómez cutting a shingle with a knife outside his garage, Charles Zieschang, a German American resident, snatched the tile away and assaulted the boy, who shielded himself from the blows while holding his knife. In the altercation, Gómez's knife accidentally cut Zieschang, who subsequently died from the heart wound. A Thorndale constable arrested the boy, but some 100 vigilantes abducted Gómez, dragged him by a chain around his neck, and lynched him.[94] In *La Crónica*, Nicasio Idar described this tragedy in painstaking detail, asserted the boy's innocence based on the state's penal code, and stressed the state's history of racial hatred and lynching of Mexicans. While careful not to accuse all Anglo-Texans of racism, Idar inveighed: "We do not know to what to attribute such deep-rooted hatred that a great part of the Texan-American population feels for the Mexican element."[95] Lamenting the lack of influence of the Spanish-language press in stopping these tragedies, Idar pessimistically predicted that the Mexican consulate would do nothing because the Díaz government wanted to maintain friendly relations with the United States while facing the insurrection of the Mexican Revolution.[96] "The child was lynched," Idar concluded, "not to punish a crime he had [allegedly] committed, but rather plainly and simply because he was Mexican."[97]

In a subsequent issue, Nicasio Idar explained how the vigilantes would likely escape punishment because no local jury would find them guilty. The failure to punish several vigilantes during the previous year undoubtedly influenced the outlook of civil rights activists. None of the accused who burned and lynched Antonio Rodríguez in 1910 were punished, which soured Idar's hope for a just resolution in the lynching of Antonio Gómez.[98] English-language newspapers appeared to confirm Idar's suspicions by outlining several obstacles to bringing the perpetrators to justice. According to the *New York Times*, Mexican officials had identified twenty-five vigilantes from the testimony of several witnesses, whom they were protecting from death threats. Moreover, the Mexican government condemned local and state officials' inability to punish the guilty. "The Texas state officials," concluded the article, "[have] failed to produce evidence pointing to the leaders of the mob, [so] the matter is to be referred to Washington."[99] The governments of Texas, the United States, and Mexico, asserted Idar, could not convict the vigilantes but could provide lawyers to argue the case and stress the enormity of the tragedy.[100]

According to Idar, local juries ultimately held the power to convict, but given local European American residents' anti-Mexican bias, the vigilantes would surely escape punishment. "They [jurors] will discard the case completely," anticipated Idar, "as until now we do not recall any American who has been punished for the lynching of a Mexican."[101] After identifying the vigilantes as German Americans, Idar suggested boycotts of German-owned businesses in Mexico and urged Tejanos not to seek revenge but rather to join fraternal organizations (such as Masonic lodges and Order of the Knights of Honor) in a show of unity.[102] For Idar, the only possible response was for ethnic Mexicans to educate themselves and to organize.

Hanging of León Cárdenas Martínez

A subsequent death sentence against a Mexican boy focused more scrutiny on legacies of conquest, namely the legal system's bias and the criminalization of ethnic Mexicans. In July 1911, authorities arrested León Cárdenas Martínez Jr., a fifteen-year-old, and forced him, at gunpoint, to confess to murdering a white woman near Pecos, Texas. US and Mexican newspapers publicized the developments in this case, which included various irregularities, due to the youth's age and the death sentence imposed by the court. Among the most vocal was *Regeneración*, the official organ of the Partido Liberal Mexicano. Published in Los Angeles by Ricardo Flores Magón, the newspaper decried a litany of injustices suffered by ethnic Mexicans in the United States, including segregated facilities, biased juries, segregated schools, and racial hatred.[103] After intense lobbying by various ethnic Mexican organizations (including San

Antonio's Mexican Protective Association and the Partido Liberal Mexicano) and several Mexican consulate officials, the Texas governor delayed Cárdenas Martínez's death sentence so his attorneys could appeal. However, the state's court of criminal appeals rejected the case, so the attorneys appealed to the US Supreme Court, which dismissed the case citing technical errors. Subsequently, Texas's governor ignored various appeals and clemency petitions citing Cárdenas Martínez's age (state law prohibited the death penalty for minors) and allowed state officials to execute him by hanging on May 11, 1914.[104]

Many observers believed that the youth did not receive a fair trial. "The Mexican peons in this state," wrote the *Houston Post*, "have felt the vengefulness of violated law to a harsher and more exacting degree than even the negroes."[105] According to the newspaper, Mexicans on trial faced hostile white juries who were motivated by the animosity expressed in the phrase "Remember the Alamo" and referred to ethnic Mexicans as "greasers."[106] In *La Crónica*, Clemente Idar underscored the legacies of the US conquest, the widespread loss of land, and the deteriorating economic position of ethnic Mexicans in the war's aftermath: "Texas-Mexicans have produced with the sweat of their brow the bountiful agricultural wealth known throughout the country, and in recompense for this they have been put to work as *peones* (peons) on the land of their forefathers."[107] With these comments, *La Crónica* was reminding readers of the legacies of conquest and also inspiring action. The inability to prevent the death sentence of Cárdenas Martínez, the earlier lynching of Antonio Gómez, and the ongoing school desegregation efforts motivated various activists to organize a conference in the fall of 1911 to unify various civil right campaigns.[108]

El Primer Congreso Mexicanista

The goal to coordinate various ethnic Mexican associations created the impetus for El Primer Congreso Mexicanista (the First Mexicanist Congress), held in Laredo in September 1911. Spearheaded by the Idars, this political conference sought to highlight their community's many social problems, including continued economic setbacks, school segregation, ongoing loss of Mexican culture and Spanish-language use, lynching, and general social discrimination.[109] For months before the conference, the Idars published a series of articles in *La Crónica* calling for unity among Mexican immigrants and Mexican Americans to confront their various obstacles. The articles described recent lynchings, school segregation struggles, and the biased legal system. As members of fraternal lodges and mutual aid societies, the Idars had extensive social networks through which to publicize the upcoming Laredo conference.[110] Through these networks and *La Crónica*, they encouraged masonic lodges, mutual aid societies, and civil rights organizations to send representatives to the conference.[111]

The delegates attending El Primer Congreso Mexicanista emphasized unity, affirmed a Mexicanist identity, and recalled collective memories of conquest. In reinforcing the need for unity, several speakers called on Mexican Americans to use their citizenship rights to defend Mexican immigrants, since US politicians were generally unhelpful. Tejanos were justified in distrusting elected officials, contended attendee J. M. Mora, because politicians made numerous pledges to obtain votes but never fulfilled their promises.[112] Another common point of agreement was support and affirmation of a Mexicanist identity, which served to unite ethnic Mexicans regardless of citizenship status. The conference, held during the week of celebrations for Mexican Independence in September, inspired various speakers to praise Mexico and laud its heroes.[113] According to historian Gabriela González, attendees promoted a transnational Mexicanist identity through their speeches and discussions. One speaker made this point explicitly while also referring to the legacies of conquest: "And don't think that because we cross the river, because we live in this land that once belonged to us, or because we enroll . . . in registries that *la raza* will be lost. . . . We are Mexicans here and in any other part of the world."[114]

Such comments linked memories of conquest with immigration, ethnic identity, and acculturation. Speakers recalled the recent lynchings as one of several forms of discrimination against ethnic Mexicans. Hortencia Moncayo mentioned the lack of punishment for the lynching of Rodríguez and the ongoing struggle to save Cárdenas Martínez from a death sentence.[115] The Congreso led to the founding of two organizations: La Gran Liga Mexicanista de Beneficencia y Protección (Great Mexican League for Beneficence and Protection), a statewide group formed to fight against discrimination, end school segregation, and promote morality and uplift among its members, and La Liga Femenil Mexicanista (League of Mexican Women), a woman's group dedicated to education, various charitable projects, and cultural redemption.[116] While these organizations, like the Primer Congreso Mexicanista, were in existence for only a few years, they helped inspire civil rights activism among a broad cross-section of ethnic Mexicans.

The Primer Congreso Mexicanista demonstrated that collective memories of conquest continued to motivate civil rights reform efforts among transborder activists. Since the mid-nineteenth century, ethnic Mexicans had faced increasing obstacles in their attempts to exercise full citizenship rights. The activism exhibited by ethnic Mexican attendees identified various forms of discrimination (from nonrepresentative jury service and school segregation to land loss and violence) as legacies of US conquest. Mexican immigrants and Mexican Americans, the activists asserted, faced similar issues of discrimination in the United States, as neither the US Constitution nor the Treaty of Guadalupe Hidalgo were enforced for ethnic Mexicans. Finally, the Mexican identity promoted at the Primer Congreso Mexicanista emphasized cultural retention, bilingual language skills, and unity among immigrants and Mexican Americans—issues embraced by future civil rights activists.

The *mutualistas*, fraternal organizations, and journalists in attendance also encouraged the transnational circulation of collective memories that reminded attendees of Mexico's previous ownership and jurisdiction over Texas. By citing their previous landownership in Texas, the activists, like contemporary Nuevomexicanos, simultaneously erased Native Americans' claims and recognized their Spanish Mexican ancestors' role as settler-colonists. Such counternarratives challenged the architects of Texas's memories, which characterized all Mexicans as recent immigrants.

Civil Rights and Memories of Conquest

School segregation was part of a larger pattern of civil rights violations, some which began with the US conquest. Various newspapers had documented discriminatory actions against Mexicans, including restrictions on entering public places, enforcement of the poll tax, criminalization, and lynching. In June 1911, Nicasio Idar, writing in *La Crónica*, linked the lynching of the fourteen-year-old boy in Thorndale, Texas, to the broader denial of civil rights for Mexican Americans, including vigilante killings, thefts, public school exclusions, and public segregation. After describing the misunderstanding that led a mob to lynch Antonio Gómez, Idar surmised, "The barbarous acts of cruelty and savagery committed against Mexicans, burning them alive or lynching them without bringing a charge, excluding them from public schools, robbing them infamously of their work, insulting them in a million ways, awakens compassion for the Mexican people, and hatred and aversion for the American people."[117] By no means was Idar advocating racial hatred; he was merely trying to explain its emergence. Idar used this violent tragedy to expose various civil rights issues resulting from the lack of enforcement of Mexican Americans' citizenship rights. In the state's interior, signs reading "Only white people" were widespread in hotels, restaurants, and barbershops that excluded Mexicans. Idar cited vigilante killings, housing evictions, and school exclusions among the most important civil rights abuses against Mexicans.[118]

Seizing on the inaction of the US and Mexican governments to respond to civil rights abuses, the Idars encouraged ethnic Mexicans to understand their rights. After accusing Mexican consuls of inaction regarding explicit discrimination and violent attacks, Idar encouraged readers to organize, gather funds for lawsuits, and urge the US government to punish the offenses.[119] In an earlier article about the lack of access to public education, Clemente Idar made a broader argument about the denial of civil rights. Despite their US citizenship, Mexican Americans did not enjoy the privileges and guarantees of the federal Constitution, he contended.[120] In addition, Idar believed that US officials also denied Mexican nationals the rights and prerogatives conferred to them by the Treaty of Guadalupe Hidalgo. Mexican Americans and Mexican nationals found themselves in a similar situation in the United States, Idar concluded, meaning without the rights to which they were entitled.[121] By invoking the treaty, Idar was recalling nineteenth-century collective memories of the US-Mexico War as well as asserting the civil rights of Mexican Americans. His reference to the treaty reminded Mexican American readers of their rights or introduced others to the treaty as one of the foundations (besides the US Constitution) of their rights. Moreover, references to the treaty served to bring up Mexico's prior claim to the US Southwest, which the war of conquest severed from Mexico. These references not only propagated collective memories of conquest among new generations of *La Crónica* readers but also informed them of their rights and responsibilities, which the US government was failing to respect. Ultimately, *La Crónica*'s articles on civil rights struggles buoyed Mexican Americans' sense of purpose to fight for their rights.

La Crónica linked the similar circumstances of Mexican Americans and Mexican nationals to race and citizenship. While these groups were citizens of different nations, they shared similar experiences in the United States because European Americans treated them as racial inferiors. The racial problem in the United States, according to the newspaper, was a question of color. Because Mexicans "belonged to a multicolor Latinized race," observed the editors, Mexican immigrants entered a decidedly hostile US environment, which directly led to the denial of their civil rights.[122] According to *La Crónica*, most European Americans did not believe Mexican Americans could be upright, responsible, and faithful citizens. Therefore, these discriminatory practices resulted in a situation in which ethnic Mexicans were "beggars of nationality."[123] In this view, Mexican Americans could not exercise their citizenship rights due to the racial hostility of European Americans, while residents in the United States stripped Mexican immigrants of their nationality because the Mexican consulates failed to protect their interests in the United States. By linking the oppression of Mexican Americans and Mexican immigrants, *La Crónica* made a strong case for unity. If European Americans treated Mexican Americans and Mexican nationals the same (partly because most whites could not distinguish them), then the two groups should unite to fight their discrimination.

The denial of civil rights included prohibiting Mexican children from attending the same public schools as white children. Seizing on this prohibition, *La Crónica* added school segregation to a long list of grievances and invoked memories of conquest. The exclusion from public schools, explained the editors, contradicted the implicit acknowledgment of Mexicans as "white" in the Treaty of Guadalupe Hidalgo, which had bestowed US citizenship to Mexicans during a time when only white people could exercise citizenship.[124] By highlighting the government's long-standing disinterest in enforcing the treaty, the journalists also encouraged Mexican Americans to become involved in civil rights struggles.[125] Clemente Idar wrote, "As US citizens of Mexican origin, it is our duty to interest ourselves in every public issue affecting the interests of our co-nationals of equal origin [Mexican immigrants]" due to "links of blood that unites us, our duty as journalists, and above all, because the rights of man do not recognize jurisdiction nor racial distinctions."[126] By citing the treaty, the journalists invoked the legacies of conquest as factors in preventing equal public education for ethnic Mexicans and called for transnational solidarity.

In opposing the exclusion of Mexican children from public schools in Texas, the Idars demonstrated a clear understanding of the rights of Mexican Americans and public school funding. Although Tejanos were US citizens and taxpayers, the state ignored their rights and segregated their schoolchildren. Mexican nationals were also paying state taxes, but their children were excluded from white public schools. Thus, Mexican Americans and Mexican immigrants confronted the same problem with school segregation. The articles on school exclusion characterized these discriminatory actions as unjust for ethnic Mexicans as a group. The editors cited both the federal Constitution and the Treaty of Guadalupe Hidalgo as legal documents conferring US citizenship rights. Because the treaty implicitly defined Mexican Americans as legally white, according to the Idars, then all ethnic Mexicans were legally white, even those without citizenship. Ruling on the naturalization case of Ricardo Rodríguez in 1897, Texas district judge Thomas Maxey agreed that Mexican immigrants were legally classified as white and thus eligible for naturalization. "Federal courts interpreted the treaty to require all future Mexican immigrants to be eligible for naturalization," noted legal scholar Ariela Gross, who concluded that Mexican Americans had become "white by treaty."[127] Thus, Mexican immigrants, like Mexican Americans, held a legal right to send their children to white schools. The Idars faulted federal and state governments' unwillingness to enforce these rights. Like other journalists, the Idars strove to make their audience aware of their citizenship rights in order to motivate them to join civil rights struggles.[128]

La Crónica cited the payment of the state's poll tax by Mexican Americans and African Americans as an additional reason to claim their right to admission to the same public schools as white children. By paying poll taxes, reasoned the editors, Mexican Americans and African Americans were directly funding public schools, as the state funneled a portion of the poll taxes to the state's public education fund. School exclusion, *La Crónica* advanced, was particularly unjust, since taxes paid by these citizens were used to hire teachers and construct school buildings, which Mexican Americans and African Americans could not attend.[129] The state of Texas, the Idars sarcastically observed, "rewarded" Mexican Americans and African Americans for paying poll taxes by isolating them in dirty neighborhoods and keeping them ignorant (i.e., denying them education). Ethnic Mexicans' payment of property or commerce taxes also contributed to the state's public school fund, according to the newspaper, and further entitled them to access public schools.[130] Through these contentions, the editors not only informed readers of their rights but also sought to motivate ethnic Mexicans to fight for their children's access to public schools.

The Idars highlighted other immigrants' struggles and the treaty to advocate for ethnic Mexicans' access to public schools. In several articles meant to pressure the Mexican government into action in support of Mexican immigrants, Clemente Idar cited a 1906 case in which the San Francisco Board of Education adopted a policy of segregating Japanese students in public schools. The involvement of the Japanese government, Idar implied, introduced changes designed to generate respect for Japanese schoolchildren. Calling for a complete investigation by Mexico's secretary of exterior relations, he predicted that a meticulous examination of various Texas counties where ethnic Mexican children had been directly excluded would confirm his newspaper's research.[131] He also compared Mexican children to other immigrant children. In Idar's view, the children of Japanese, Irish, Scottish, English, and Italian immigrants did not confront the obstacles ethnic Mexican children faced when attempting to enter the nation's public schools.[132] While Japanese American parents would probably disagree with Idar's view, his overall point was that ethnic Mexicans were not accepted into public schools as were other immigrant children. Posing a rhetorical question, he asked by virtue of what constitutional principle were Mexicans and Mexican Americans barred from public schools. His reasoning then shifted dramatically to an appeal to whiteness: "Are we [ethnic Mexicans] not recognized as a white race? Has the Treaty of Guadalupe Hidalgo been forgotten?"[133] By linking Mexican Americans' citizenship rights to claims to whiteness, Idar ensured that his newspapers' readers understood that the treaty effectively defined Mexicans as legally white.[134]

In invoking the treaty in these rhetorical questions, Idar not only asserted Mexican Americans' rights to US citizenship but also pointed to the US government's selective memory of the US-Mexico War. While the United States obviously "remembered" the treaty's setting of new international boundaries, it selectively "forgot" the parts of the treaty covering the rights of Mexican Americans. The US government failed to enforce the treaty's guarantees and did not promote awareness of these rights among the public.

In contrast, Mexican Americans and Mexican nationals had not forgotten the treaty's promises, as was evident in news articles published in Mexico and the United States. Among Mexico's newspapers that addressed the exclusion of ethnic Mexicans from public schools in Texas was *El Eco de la Sierra*, published in Puebla, Mexico. *El Eco* complimented Idar and *La Crónica* for their campaign to publicize ethnic Mexicans' exclusion from public schools. Beginning in the mid-nineteenth century, *El Eco* contended, the United States had failed to abide by the treaty's provisions—a direct acknowledgment of the legacies of conquest. Further, *El Eco* remembered the US-Mexico War as an expansionist project resulting in a large loss of Mexico's territory. The country was again being threatened, the editors asserted, because US "scandal newspapers" were using the pretext of the Mexican Revolution (in 1911) to threaten further expansion into Mexico.[135]

A portion of *El Eco*'s article was reprinted in *La Crónica*, which made its readers aware of *La Crónica*'s international reach and demonstrated the transnational circulation of collective war memories. *El Eco* emphasized Mexican nationals' collective war memories by referring to the US Southwest as "our region" (acknowledging Mexico's previous claim to this territory) and justified its characterization because the United States had never respected the treaty. While the US government was selectively forgetting the treaty, *El Eco* was selectively remembering the US Southwest as a region that had previously belonged to Mexico. Such contrasting views demonstrated that memories of conquest were contingent and strategically used to advance political and social agendas.

Early Twentieth-Century New Mexico Statehood Campaign

Different historical interpretations and memories of the US-Mexico War also influenced New Mexico's decades-long statehood campaign. Its campaign began immediately after the US-Mexico War, and its popularity varied until New Mexico obtained statehood in 1912. The process was delayed for sixty-four years by Congress. Opponents of New Mexico statehood made three main arguments. First, Southern congressmen opposed statehood because some of New Mexico's leaders in the antebellum period had taken a stand against permitting slavery in the territory. Shortly after the US-Mexico War, a group of ten Nuevomexicanos and two European Americans authored a congressional petition requesting a territorial form of government to replace New Mexico's military government. Their petition raised the ire of Southerners, who objected to the petition's prohibition on slavery in New Mexico. Subsequent statehood efforts met consistent opposition from Southerners, who sought to expand slavery in the western territories. Southerners objected to the admission of New Mexico as a free state because they feared tilting the balance of power further against slave states.[136] Northerners also found reason to suspect the slavery views of New Mexico's residents due to the passage of several anti-Black laws in the 1850s prohibiting interactions between local residents and African Americans. Although chattel slavery was not significant in New Mexico, territorial legislators passed an 1859 Slave Code that prohibited assistance to runaway slaves, imposed harsh penalties for anyone assisting runaways, and forbade the emancipation of slaves within the territory.[137]

The second and third objections lingered throughout the nineteenth century and centered on the supposed characteristics of New Mexico's population. According to some opponents of statehood, New Mexico did not contain a sufficient white population to become a state. Opponents routinely characterized the territory's Mexican Americans as "nonwhite" despite the protests of New Mexico's Hispanos and European Americans. Several congressmen and the press remained wary of New Mexico's large Pueblo Indian population, who were also seen as nonwhite. Although Mexico had considered Pueblo Indians to be citizens, and Article 9 of the Treaty of Guadalupe technically allowed Pueblo Indians (as former citizens of Mexico) to choose US citizenship, various territorial and federal laws disenfranchised the Pueblo Indians. The Organic Act of 1850 required territorial authorities to make a clear "political and ethnic division between Indians and non-Indians."[138] Not surprisingly, territorial and federal officials ensured the persistent legal subordination of Pueblo Indians and their exclusion from the political process.

Additionally, the continued existence of peonage and Native American slavery in territorial New Mexico served to strengthen opposition to statehood among Northerners.[139] The drive for statehood was undercut by the death of Zachary Taylor, a proponent of New Mexico's statehood, in July 1850 and by an enduring boundary dispute with Texas.[140] Congressional opponents raised a third objection by claiming that New Mexicans (primarily its non-white population) were incapable of self-government. These arguments revolved around opponents' fears of including a state with a majority Hispano and Catholic population that might exhibit "undemocratic" and "hierarchical" values (referred to as "anti-Popery" fears).[141]

During the last intense period of the statehood campaign (1888–1912), news articles on the subject frequently reminded residents of the war of conquest, the promises of self-government contained in the treaty, and the war's long-term consequences. Editorials evaluated the merits of statehood, including the territory's wealth, a sufficient "white" population, and a stable, efficient government to warrant admission into the Union.[142] Several newspapers cited the treaty's Article 9 as guaranteeing self-government to the residents incorporated into the United States after the war. The New Mexico press closely watched statehood discussions in Congress, and whenever legislators debated the merits of statehood, the territory's newspapers reprinted their speeches. In these speeches, Congressmen spewed their racist views about Nuevomexicanos and Native Americans, which partially explained US officials' opposition to statehood.[143] These discourses brought up the treaty's guarantees for self-government and US citizenship. They also referred to territorial residents' second-class citizenship, with no congressional representation or right to elect their own governor. Consistent congressional opposition reminded Nuevomexicanos of the legacies of conquest and of the nation's strategic amnesia of its citizenship promises to Mexican Americans.

In the early 1900s, the congressional statehood debates addressed conquest, whiteness, and citizenship. In deliberations about the acquisition of New Mexico territory, some senators mischaracterized the United States' goals in the US-Mexico War as expanding "freedom and democracy," but others dismissed this anodyne view by correctly identifying the nation's goals as enlarging its territory and expanding slavery.[144] Several pro-statehood senators praised the character of New Mexico's residents: their loyalty, war service, and active participation in local government. One supporter, West Virginia's Stephen Elkins, accused the United States of violating Article 9 of the treaty by repeatedly denying statehood to the Mexicans of New Mexico and Arizona.[145] This characterization acknowledged the adverse consequences for Hispanos, who most stood to benefit from statehood. Opponents made their racist views explicit by criticizing the region's Spanish-speaking population as uneducated, illiterate in the English language, irredeemably Catholic, incapable of self-government, and most definitely not European American.[146] The articles on statehood campaigns effectively summarized the US-Mexico War's long-term consequences for New Mexico by ascribing US congressmen's continuing opposition to statehood to their views of Nuevomexicanos as "nonwhite." Due to these biased views, Arizona and New Mexico remained territories, and their residents continued to lack full citizenship rights throughout the nineteenth century. The newspapers reinforced residents' collective memories of conquest by reviewing the outcomes of the war and propagated these memories to younger generations, who would continue to push for full citizenship rights and statehood.

The intransigence of statehood opponents led Nuevomexicanos to employ collective memories of conquest selectively by claiming native status and by emphasizing their Spanish ancestry. To counter the derogatory characterizations of New Mexico residents as "mongrels" and "greasers" in eastern and midwestern newspapers, the territory's politicians and newspapers promoted the native status of Nuevomexicanos. Their ancestors were the region's first "colonizers," they claimed, so Hispanos held more "authority" to speak for the region than did European Americans. This logic posited Nuevomexicanos as the region's "legitimate settlers" while casting European Americans as the real "foreigners" and "immigrants" to New Mexico.[147] By making this distinction, residents recalled and promoted collective memories of Spanish (but not Mexican) jurisdiction over the region. Yet these selective memories along with Nuevomexicanos' appropriation of the term "native" ignored Indigenous people's long history as the region's original settlers.

Such collective memories also indirectly reminded residents that a war of conquest had led to the region's incorporation into the United States. In 1900, the territory's first Nuevomexicano governor, Miguel Otero, made a similar allusion to collective memories of Spanish colonization by reminding an audience gathered to celebrate the White House's centennial that New Mexico's governor's palace had "been occupied longer than any other building in America [meaning the United States] as the seat of government."[148] New Mexico held an older and richer colonial history, Otero asserted, than the original thirteen British American colonies. While his comments were meant to counter statehood opponents' claims that Nuevomexicanos were not capable of self-government, his contention also conveniently "forgot" the war of conquest that converted New Mexico's first "colonizers" into second-class citizens. Like other prominent Nuevomexicanos, Otero strategically remembered their Spanish colonial past while forgetting Hispanos' ties to the Mexican nation.[149]

Several politicians adopted this "native" Nuevomexicano identity to buttress their selective memories of conquest. Otero proudly self-identified as the "first native[-]born Governor of New Mexico," promoting his ancestry as a descendant of the territory's Spanish colonial settlers.[150] He hailed from a wealthy landed family who traced their ancestry to the Spanish colonial period on his father's side, but his mother was a European American. He was born in St. Louis, Missouri, and educated on the East Coast, where he spent his early years. But his supporters and the territory's newspapers nevertheless claimed him as a "quintessential native New Mexican."[151] As a way of establishing his ancestral roots, he and his supporters emphasized his links to New Mexico's Spanish colonial administrators. According to historian Anthony Mora, these public relations efforts to invoke "New Mexico's colonial past became a common means by which elite Mexicans could upgrade their racial and social status."[152] During his tenure as governor, Otero forcefully argued on behalf of New Mexico's Hispanos and characterized them as "Americans" worthy of all the rights of US citizenship. But his advocacy did not extend to the territory's Native Americans, whom he disparaged as undeserving "brutal savages."[153] Otero's strategy of characterizing himself as the embodiment of a "native New Mexican" was highly successful, as this identity was popular both in the territory and across the country and allowed him to obtain three appointments as the territory's governor.[154]

Another ethnic Mexican governor adopted a similar strategy of promoting his own "native" status and equating Nuevomexicanos with Americans. Born in Chihuahua, Octaviano Ambrosio Larrazolo immigrated to Arizona and eventually to New Mexico, where he became governor in 1918, after New Mexico had obtained statehood. Larrazolo adopted a fictive "native New Mexican" identity and promoted the links between Hispanos and Spanish colonial authorities. In the early twentieth century, officials began extolling the Spanish conquistadores of the territory's early history, and Larrazolo enthusiastically embraced such celebrations. He also promoted an image of Nuevomexicanos as patriotic Americans who had participated in the Spanish-American War, supported US territorial expansion, and strongly believed in nationalism.[155]

In their campaigns for statehood, for full citizenship rights, and against public segregation, Nuevomexicanos asserted their native status, recalled war memories, and alluded to the promises of citizenship in the Treaty of Guadalupe Hidalgo. Spanish-language journalists in New Mexico made similar arguments as those by activists in other states when advocating on behalf of Mexican Americans who were excluded from public services. Newspaper editors advocated for Mexican Americans' full citizenship rights by decrying segregated schools in New Mexico and Texas. Their arguments acknowledged a shared struggle among Mexican Americans throughout the Southwest who continued to be denied citizenship rights despite the treaty's promises. Moreover, to promote civil rights struggles, New Mexico's politicians and journalists highlighted *hispano-americanos'* military service and patriotism. Like Mexican Americans elsewhere, they presented their military service in the US Civil War and the Spanish-American War as proof of their loyalty.[156]

By recalling Mexican Americans' military service on behalf of the United States, Nuevomexicanos addressed European Americans' suspicions that ethnic Mexicans were disloyal and untrustworthy. Through their emphasis on Mexican Americans' military service, they echoed arguments made by African American veterans, who similarly touted their military credentials in their civil rights struggles.

México de Afuera and Memories of Conquest

Memories of conquest were also disseminated by the Spanish-language press elsewhere in the US Southwest, which had long served as a vehicle for cultural retention by promoting Spanish-language literacy as well as Mexican traditional celebrations. These newspapers defended Mexican American communities, promoted regional identities, and informed their readers about civil rights issues. They also served as vehicles for social and cultural exchange with Mexican newspapers, especially along the border.[157] In addition to publishing in Spanish, these newspapers covered local community events, both civil and religious, that emphasized Mexican cultural traditions, such as celebrations for *fiestas patrias* and saint's days. The readers were a mix of Mexican Americans and Mexican immigrants, with the latter being more numerous for newspapers published by Mexican exiles. Moreover, many Spanish-language newspapers carried articles about news and events in Mexico, helping recent immigrants maintain ties there. News about the homeland combined with articles reminding readers about Mexican cultural practices helped halt "Americanization" among Mexican immigrants, which was especially important for exiles whose long-term goal was to return to Mexico.[158]

Spanish-language newspapers spread a Mexican exile version of history among Mexican Americans and led efforts to sustain this sentiment among

Mexican immigrants. Influenced by Mexican nationalism and by Mexico's public education system, the exile perspective offered Mexican Americans a counterhistory of the US-Mexico War. Mexico's official view of the war blamed the United States for launching a military conquest to obtain additional territory. A desire to expand slavery and racism toward Mexicans, according to Mexico's view, also motivated the United States to instigate the war.[159] Mexican American readers of Spanish-language newspapers became aware of this history in news stories that reviewed Mexico's land loss through a war of conquest. Such articles also complemented information about the war's history shared through word of mouth by Mexican immigrants with their Mexican American neighbors, coworkers, and family members.[160]

The massive immigration of Mexicans in the early twentieth century inspired Rodolfo Uranga, a Mexican exile journalist, to coin the term "*México de afuera*" (literally, "Mexico of the outside") to refer to the "Mexican colony existing outside of Mexico," or specifically in the United States. To some scholars, this exile group consisted solely of the intellectual and financial elite, while others included all exiles (regardless of class and education). Mexican Americans, according to a few exiled writers and journalists, were also part of *México de afuera*.[161] While some Mexican Americans might have agreed with the goals of the *México de afuera* group, such as continuing Mexican traditions, maintaining the Spanish language, and retaining the Catholic faith, few wanted to return to Mexico, as did many Mexican exiles and immigrants fleeing the Mexican Revolution. Instead, most residents raised and educated in the United States believed in "permanency," the concept that Mexican Americans' future was as "Americanized" and integrated US citizens.

In contrast, the Mexican nationals in this group, contended historian Mario García, held on to a "Mexican dream, not an American dream," because they sought to return to Mexico.[162] Although some Mexican Americans might have shared the exiles' and immigrants' Mexican nationalism, many Mexican Americans did not. Instead, some Mexican Americans, especially members of the League of United Latin American Citizens, tended to promote US nationalism as a way to prove their loyalty to the United States, which they hoped would ensure the enjoyment of full citizenship rights.[163] Moreover, a significant number of influential Mexican Americans, like the Idars of Laredo, were former Mexican immigrants who spent time in both countries, held on to their transnational identity, and remained conversant with US and Mexican nationalism.

The differences between the goals of Mexican immigrants and those of Mexican Americans notwithstanding, both groups influenced each other.

Mexican exiles published and edited several US-based Spanish-language newspapers. Through this mass media, Mexican exiles disseminated the goals of *México de afuera* and influenced Mexican Americans' understanding of Mexican culture and history from an exile and immigrant perspective. Spanish-language newspapers published news about Mexico's political and economic developments, the ethnic Mexican community in the United States, US-Mexico relations, world events, and various social and cultural issues.[164] Some exile-owned newspapers, like *La Prensa* and *La Opinión*, devoted most of their news coverage and editorials to events in Mexico, limiting their coverage of issues about Mexican immigrants living in the United States.[165] For Mexican exile and transnational journalists, the progress of the Mexican Revolution and the status of Mexican immigrants in the United States remained of particular concern.

Spanish-language newspapers also published ephemera on Mexican history, including accounts of the US-Mexico War and the repercussions of the Treaty of Guadalupe Hidalgo on current events. The impact of Mexican exiles and immigrants on Mexican Americans was quite extensive in the news media and cultural productions. Such influence led Federico Allen Hinojosa, an immigrant and the former editor of San Antonio's *La Prensa* newspaper, to contend in 1940 that Mexican exiles and immigrants were in the process of "reconquering the lands lost during Mexico's dismemberment in 1837 and 1847."[166] Hinojosa's phrasing invoked collective memories of conquest by referring to Mexico's land loss after the Texas rebellion and the US-Mexico War. He was not referring to a territorial reconquest but rather to a social and cultural reconquest of Mexico's lands by the increasing number of immigrants. This influx and other references to the repopulation of Mexico's former lands by Mexican immigrants reminded Mexican Americans not only of the war's tragic consequences (the literal dismemberment of the Mexican nation) but also of the positive impact of immigration and the long-term effects of demographic change. Such a social and cultural reconquest of Mexico's far north appealed to both Mexican immigrants and Mexican Americans, as it posited a future ideal in which the US Southwest would predominantly be socially and culturally Mexican.

A River Changes Course, a Boundary Moves

Boundary disputes between both nations during the first decades of the twentieth century demonstrated the war's continuing legacies and the importance of the Treaty of Guadalupe Hidalgo in shaping binational relations. In

1848, each country's treaty negotiators agreed to use the Rio Grande to establish the limits of the eastern part of the international boundary. This redrawing of the international boundary indicated that borders are social constructs that rarely make sharp distinctions between people or geography. As an arbitrary demarcation, the US-Mexico border in Texas was placed at the Rio Grande—a river that for centuries had served to unite (rather than divide) people and that had ethnically similar populations on either side. Unfortunately for both nations, the Rio Grande was not part of the agreement. Less than sixteen years later, the river changed course due to the first of several floods, altering the land in the El Paso–Ciudad Juárez area. By the turn of the twentieth century, the changes in the river's course had transferred some 600 acres of land previously belonging to Mexico to the United States.[167] This land, known as El Chamizal for the brush that grew there, became a subject of controversy because it was claimed by both countries. Despite the establishment of a bilateral International Boundary Commission in 1889, the ownership of El Chamizal continued to be disputed throughout most of the twentieth century.[168]

Both governments agreed to submit their claims to international arbitration. In 1911, a three-member arbitration board decided to divide the disputed land between Mexico and the United States, but the United States refused to abide by this ruling, citing technicalities.[169] The decision to reject the arbitration seriously impeded future negotiations over El Chamizal, as Mexico's officials and press repeatedly reminded the United States of its failure to abide by the 1911 decision.[170] Mexican Americans reading about the United States' rejection of this international arbitration likely remembered its previous refusal to enforce another international agreement—the Treaty of Guadalupe Hidalgo. The refusal to accept this arbitration also reminded Mexican Americans and Mexican immigrants of the unequal power dynamics that had long shaped diplomatic relations between the two nations and influenced domestic policies, including the United States' lack of enforcement of the treaty's citizenship guarantees. The refusal to abide by the 1911 arbitration also influenced US-Mexico diplomatic relations for the next fifty years, as observers in Mexico and elsewhere in Latin America viewed the El Chamizal dispute as another example of "American imperialism."[171]

At the turn of the century, Spanish- and English-language newspapers in the Southwest carried occasional stories on claims by Mexican nationals over El Chamizal and the binational boundary talks. The International Boundary Commission reviewed these claims to adjudicate disputes over the river's changing course. This commission had heard some 700 claims over land title

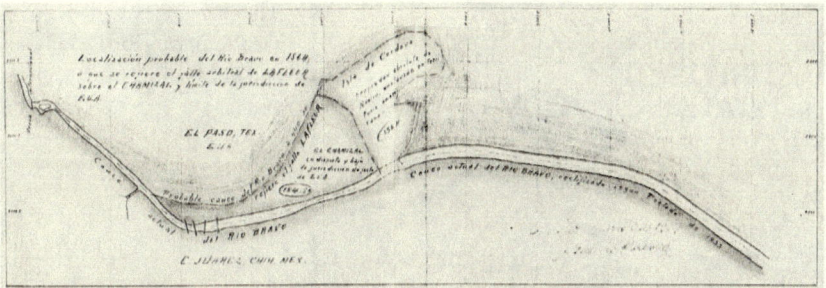

Drawing showing the likely 1864 channel of the Río Bravo (Rio Grande) with the locations of El Chamizal and Cordova Island. International Boundary and Water Commission, Mexican Section.

disputes by the early twentieth century.[172] After the failure of arbitration in 1911, El Chamizal became a nationalist rallying cause in Mexico as well as an issue that symbolized the territorial ambitions and conceit of the United States.[173] Articles about ongoing disputes over El Chamizal and Mexican nationals' claims often referred to the Treaty of Guadalupe Hidalgo as establishing the international boundary after the war.[174] While such stories were probably most relevant to each country's diplomats and to local border residents, the articles nevertheless disseminated information about the border controversy and the treaty's continuing relevance to readers throughout the US Southwest. Spanish-language newspapers usually referred to the war of conquest, while the English-language press rarely mentioned the US-Mexico War.[175] The former selectively remembered the US-Mexico War, while the latter strategically forgot the conflict.

The news coverage indicated how regional issues could bear international implications, providing an opportunity for journalists and politicians to offer alternative views of the war and the treaty. Such views undoubtedly reinforced Mexican Americans' collective war memories of land loss and the treaty's unfulfilled promises of full citizenship. The controversy over El Chamizal continued to invoke memories of conquest and generated occasional news stories into the mid-twentieth century. The United States and Mexico did not resolve the El Chamizal controversy until 1963, when they signed a binational agreement that returned some land to both nations, razed most structures in El Chamizal, and displaced the residents there.[176]

Another territorial dispute concerning the treaty emerged in the late 1910s. As the Mexican Revolution (1910–20) drew to a close, Mexico and the United States began negotiations over land and property owned by US citizens and corporations in Mexico. US negotiators asked Mexican officials for guarantees

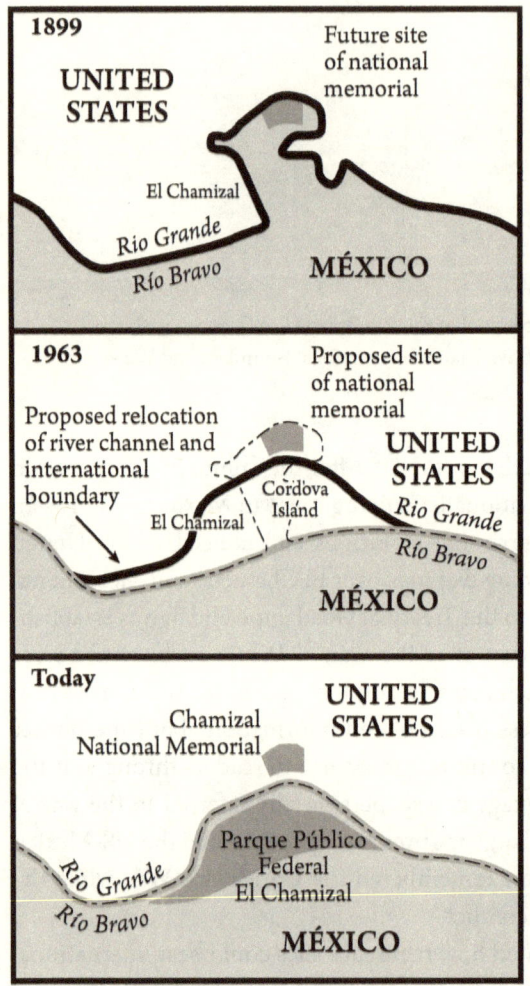

The changing boundaries of the Río Bravo (Rio Grande) and El Chamizal in 1899, 1963, and 1980

that no property owned by Americans would be confiscated by Mexico's government. US officials brazenly and falsely claimed that the federal government had committed itself to protecting the property rights of Mexicans incorporated into the United States after the US-Mexico War. The Spanish-language newspaper articles covering these new negotiations highlighted the property rights of Mexicans in the ceded territories stipulated in Articles 8 and 10 of the treaty. The US Senate, the articles noted, had eliminated Article 10 (which provided protection for Mexican land grant holders) from the final treaty during negotiations under the excuse that it was superfluous due to the rights guaranteed under the Treaty of Louisiana. Moreover, one article stressed that the guarantees regarding the private property rights of US citizens in Mexico requested by the United States (in the 1920s) were actually similar to the guarantees that Mexico requested for its former citizens in the Treaty of Guadalupe Hidalgo.[177]

During the late 1910s, some Mexican government officials suggested that the United States should pay for the territory of El Chamizal that it now claimed.[178] General Amado Aguirre, the subsecretary of agriculture and public works, devised a more creative formulation based on his interpretation of the Treaty of Guadalupe Hidalgo. Aguirre's reasoning appeared in newspapers in Mexico and the United States, which disseminated his views and Mexican officials' collective memories of conquest to a wide audience.[179] According to Aguirre, the treaty did not give the United States jurisdiction over the nine Channel Islands off the coast of California, which had previously belonged to Spain and subsequently to Mexico.[180] Aguirre was undoubtedly aware of the 1894 Mexican newspaper stories, which made a similar case.[181] Since the United States had assumed jurisdiction over these islands without official title to them, Aguirre maintained that the United States should pay Mexico indemnification for their use and for El Chamizal. In turn, Aguirre reasoned, Mexico could use the indemnification to pay its foreign debt.[182] Mexican officials in Washington, D.C., offered a slightly different view by stating that the compensation money could be applied against claims for damages to US-owned property in Mexico during the Mexican Revolution.[183]

Although Mexico's government never officially submitted the claim for California's islands to the US government, the articles demonstrated the lingering effects of the war of conquest. Such collective memories illustrated that some Mexican nationals continued to mourn the loss of their nation's vast northern territory. Moreover, the transnational circulation of a claim to Mexican ownership of California's islands informed Mexican Americans of the treaty's ongoing relevance. This claim also illustrates how contemporary issues (binational negotiations over damages during the Mexican Revolution) could affect the transmission (via newspapers in the United States and Mexico) of collective war memories. The newspaper coverage provided an alternative view of the treaty's provisions and informed readers of the collective memories of conquest of Mexican nationals and Mexican Americans.

During the 1920s, Spanish-language newspapers brought up various tense episodes in US-Mexico relations, including the US-Mexico War. For example, the United States' continued interest in acquiring more territory from Mexico was the subject of a 1920 editorial that described US diplomatic and military efforts to wrestle Baja California from Mexico. The essay delved into several filibustering expeditions (including those of William Walker) into Baja California. It linked these nineteenth-century incursions to the earlier US-Mexico War by contending that US greed motivated these expeditions. The Treaty of Guadalupe Hidalgo, the author observed, had not provided Mexico with sufficient protection to prevent Walker's filibustering in 1852. The treaty had obligated both nations to respect their shared international boundary. However, by neglecting to stop Walker's filibustering expedition into Mexico, the author maintained, the United States failed to enforce the treaty and respect Mexico's sovereignty. The editorial closed by reminding readers that similar unsuccessful expeditions into Mexico continued into the present.[184] For Mexican American readers, the article recalled the US-Mexico War and informed them of the long history of US intervention in Mexico.

Ephemera on Mexican history appeared repeatedly in Spanish-language newspapers, occasionally referring to memories of conquest. Another reminder of the war appeared in 1921, on the anniversary of the Treaty of Guadalupe Hidalgo, when the editors of *La Prensa* reprinted an article from May 1848 describing the Mexican congress' treaty ratification. Mexican government officials, the article explained, had met in Queretaro in 1848 because US troops had occupied Mexico City and remained there until Mexican officials ratified the treaty. At the ratification meeting of Mexican senators and deputies, Luis de la Rosa, Mexico's minister of foreign relations, gave an impassioned speech explaining why Mexico needed to cede part of its national territory for peace. Other countries facing defeat in a war, de la Rosa argued, had fared worse than Mexico.[185] These articles reminded readers of the tragic loss of Mexico's northern territories, the treaty's signing while Mexico remained occupied by US forces, the United States' tacit lack of respect for international boundaries, and the lingering effects of conquest.

New Mexico's Native Son Defends His "Race"

Conquest memories, the struggle over statehood, and racial perceptions of Nuevomexicanos were major influences on Benjamin Maurice Read, who promoted Nuevomexicano identity through his published history books. Born into a prominent family in Las Cruces, New Mexico, in 1853, he was the oldest son of Benjamin Franklin Read, a European American newcomer to New Mexico, and Ignacia Cano, a Nuevomexicana born to Mexican immigrant parents. Originally from Delaware, Benjamin Sr. was a direct descendant of George Read, a signer of the Declaration of Independence. He had arrived in New Mexico in 1846 as a US Army officer during the US-Mexico

War.[186] Benjamin Jr.'s maternal grandfather, Ignacio Cano had reached New Mexico from Sonora in the early nineteenth century, achieving renown and wealth through his co-discovery of the Ortiz gold mine (also known as the Dolores Placer) in southern Santa Fe County in 1833.[187] Benjamin Jr. was part of the first generation of Mexican Americans born and raised in the United States. His father's death at an early age left his mother struggling. She moved her family to Santa Fe, where Archbishop Jean-Baptiste Lamy helped the Read siblings obtain textbooks and enroll in Catholic schools. Impoverished by years of litigation over the Dolores Placer mine, Cano nevertheless managed to educate her three sons, who all became attorneys. After his father's death, Read began to identify more with his mother's family and with the larger Nuevomexicano community. His mother's subsequent remarriage to Mateo Ortiz further immersed Read and his siblings within Hispano society. His embrace of Nuevomexicano culture, according to literary scholar A. Gabriel Meléndez, was further motivated by being "estranged from Anglo society because he was of mixed parentage."[188] Read overcame this obstacle through his academic preparation and extensive social networks.[189]

Read's education and ties to Nuevomexicano and European American society allowed him to obtain prominent positions in local and territorial governments. At sixteen, he began working as a railroad section hand, rose to become a conductor, and subsequently assumed a series of appointed and elected government positions. Read's bilingual ability and social connections earned him appointments as secretary for two territorial governors in 1871 and 1881. Between his two stints as the governor's secretary, he became preceptor of St. Michael's College while also superintendent of Santa Fe's public schools. After obtaining his legal license in 1885, he established a successful private law practice. Subsequently, Read helped organize the New Mexico Bar Association and revise the state's legal statutes. After serving as a translator in the legislative assembly and chief clerk of the legislative council, he won elected office three times, serving in the assembly in the 1890s and as Speaker of the House in 1901. As a translator, he realized the importance of correct translations of Spanish-language documents in legal cases, as errors could present significant problems for Hispano litigants. This experience shaped his books, articles, and Spanish-language newspaper essays, which reached broad audiences. His books are credited as the first to present history from a Nuevomexicano perspective. Moreover, Read's *Guerra México-Americana* (1910) was among the first books published in the United States to challenge dominant US perspectives of the US-Mexico War and to incorporate the interpretations of Mexico's historians.[190]

Benjamin Maurice Read, who became a lawyer, elected official, and author of *Guerra México-Americana* and *Illustrated History of New Mexico*. *Guerra México-Americana*.

In the introduction to *Guerra México-Americana*, Read summarized his arguments and contributions to historical scholarship. He characterized the war as resulting from the US *invasion* of Mexico, which forced the latter into a defensive war. By using "invasion," Read challenged previous US interpretations that blamed Mexico for the war by refusing to negotiate over Texas's independence and attempting to keep the separatist republic within its jurisdiction.[191] Moreover, he subverted dominant perceptions of Mexicans as "foreigners" by identifying westward-moving European Americans as the most recent newcomers and the real "foreigners" in New Mexico, thereby reinforcing Nuevomexicanos' "native" status.[192] Read's sharp criticism of the US invasion was evident in his deeming the war "unequal, unjust, unprovoked, and inexcusable." His family's collective memories, passed down by his mother's and stepfather's ancestors, probably shaped his interpretation of the war. Read consulted scholarship by North American (whom he identified as Anglo-Saxon) and Mexican historians, and found, to his surprise, that many agreed on the war's causes and consequences. Nevertheless, he characterized previous interpretations of the US-Mexico War as incomplete because some North American and many Mexican historians had attributed the outbreak of the conflict to US expansionism and the South's goal of expanding slavery. He posited that the war was the "culmination of the antipathies and discords among the two races, Anglo-Saxon and Latin," instigated much earlier. Believing previous explanations insufficient, Read contended that historians must examine the nation's earlier history to understand the war's true origins.[193]

According to Read, the war resulted from racial hatred caused by two countries' competing territorial ambitions. Previous historical interpretations had identified increased tensions after the 1819 Adams-Onís Treaty transferred jurisdiction over Florida from Spain to the United States. Yet, he proffered, the war's origins predated 1819. Characterizing the United States as gripped by expansionist fever since its earliest days as a nation, as was Spain after the "discovery of América," he did not fault the role of conquest but rather the resulting racial antagonism (anti-Spanish and anti-Mexican).[194] The Florida and Louisiana Territories (held by Spain, France, and England) had served as a barrier, he expounded, for US commercial expansion. This barrier prevented US access to the Gulf of Mexico through the Mississippi River, which frustrated European Americans and fed their racial hatred. He concentrated on the tensions between the two "races," perceived as Anglo-Saxon and Latin (*raza latina*). In Read's view, the earliest territorial and commercial competition between the United States and Spain incited racial acrimony, which were the true origins of the US-Mexico War.[195]

Read's premise about the war connected to his claims about the book's unique perspective. The introduction to *Guerra México-Americana* ends with an explanation of the author's subject position and ultimate goal. Calling his book an impartial interpretation of the war, his stated objective was to be fair to both countries. Declaring his book as the first written by a native son of New Mexico, he identified as a descendant of both races: "Anglo-Saxon and Latin."[196] Given his subject position, Read claimed authority to describe the war between the two countries. European American historians' incomplete knowledge of the Spanish language created "inaccuracies" and "striking contradictions" in their scholarship. These errors resulted from their incorrect translations of colonial-era Spanish documents and frequent plagiarism of other English-language works without consulting the original Spanish-language documents.

Read claimed to be "better equipped" (presumably as a native Spanish speaker) to translate and interpret colonial-era documents than European

American historians. Moreover, he accused European American historians of bias toward Hispanos and their ancestors, challenging their misrepresentations of Nuevomexicanos' culture and society.[197] Here again, Read's account was shaped by his lifetime immersion in Hispano culture and the collective conquest memories from his family and the greater Nuevomexicano community. Read collected oral history interviews with older Hispanos as well as written testimonies from Hispano elders to incorporate their collective memories into his scholarship.[198]

Casting *Guerra México-Americana* as a precursor to his *Illustrated History of New Mexico*, Read regarded both as attempts to stress the unjust treatment experienced and endured by the Latin race. Read considered his book not only as a corrective to previous histories but also as a protest against Nuevomexicanos' unjust treatment. If his writings restored the honor of the sons of New Mexico, Read concluded, his efforts would have been generously compensated.[199]

Read's identity as a Nuevomexicano hinged on competing colonial and national projects, US territorial expansion, and the postwar struggle for New Mexico statehood. The territorial expansion of Mexico and the United States influenced Read's identity, as his ancestry was a product of the migration of colonial and national agents in the service of opposing agendas. His maternal grandfather was one of the Spanish immigrants who migrated to Mexico's far north in search of economic opportunities, while Read's father was a soldier in the US Army sent to conquer New Mexico in the mid-nineteenth century. According to Read, the racial tensions that caused the US-Mexico War lingered in the postwar period and led him to shun the "Mexican" label, which carried a negative racialized connotation after 1848. Instead, he considered himself a Nuevomexicano or *neo-mejicano*, as did other elite New Mexicans, who claimed whiteness in their campaigns for statehood.

Read's childhood and family experiences deeply shaped his historical interpretations. He had grown up immersed in the culture of Nuevomexicanos after his mother remarried (when he was three years old) and he became part of his stepfather's Hispano extended family.[200] While he identified as a native son of New Mexico, his claim was tenuous but undisputed by fellow Nuevomexicanos during his lifetime. His assertion of roots in New Mexico teetered on his family's relatively recent arrival, because his European American father was born in Delaware and his maternal grandfather was an immigrant from Spain.[201] Yet he readily adopted a Nuevomexicano identity. In his *Guerra México-Americana*, Read avoided using the "Mexican" label to refer to New Mexicans of Mexican descent. Instead, he used "*neo-mejicanos*," "*los habitan-*

tes de Nuevo México," and other labels, yet referred to Mexican American residents of Texas as "*mexicanos.*" Like other elite Nuevomexicanos, Read strategically chose these labels, according to historian Anthony Mora, to denote "ownership and hereditary entitlement to the territory."[202]

In the 1890s, New Mexico's Spanish-language newspapers had begun employing the term "*hispano-americanos*" (Hispanic Americans or Spanish Americans) to refer to Nuevomexicanos. These labels implied that *hispano-americanos* shared certain positive racial traits as direct descendants from "Spanish" ancestors, while also highlighting their "American" national allegiance. According to historian Nieto-Phillips, these newspapers' use of "*hispano-americanos*" occurred in the context of Nuevomexicanos' racist exclusion from national politics. By using "*hispano-americanos,*" they were "redefining their identity in new ethnic, historical, and racial terms" instead of letting European Americans construe them as "Mexicans," which had become a term of disparagement.[203] Like many of his contemporaries, Read identified solely with the Spanish conquerors, not with Indigenous people.[204]

For Read and others in New Mexico, *hispano-americano* and *neo-mejicano* denoted an ethnic identity tied to their Spanish ancestry and a political identity associated with their region. Mexican Americans elsewhere in the US Southwest also claimed Spanish ancestors, but New Mexico residents insisted on such ancestry as they struggled for New Mexico statehood.[205] By claiming Spanish ancestry, *hispano-americanos* also claimed "whiteness" at a time when US politicians and the eastern press heavily criticized the territory for its nonwhite population.[206] The promoters of Nuevomexicano identity (including Read) viewed themselves as descendants of colonizers who had brought "civilization" and "Christianity" to the region. Ultimately, their use of "*hispano-americano*" and "*neo-mejicano*" alluded to the "language of blood," which they associated with superior Spanish ancestry.[207]

As a Nuevomexicano of mixed ancestry, Read was intimately aware of the enduring racial tensions instigated by the US-Mexico War and, more importantly, believed a response to these tensions was necessary. He acknowledged the role of US territorial expansion and the US South's desire to expand slavery in provoking the war, but he believed that these reasons were insufficient. By citing the racial antagonism between Anglo-Saxon and Latin "races" as the origins of the war, Read established a link between the causes of the war and its long-term consequences on Nuevomexicanos and Mexican Americans elsewhere. As statehood proponents continued their campaign in the early 1900s, the eastern press published an endless litany of derogatory articles against New Mexico statehood due to its "unfit" Spanish-speaking Catholic population. In response to these attacks and to a critical congressional committee report, Read wrote, "Our people have been so vilely treated since the territory became part of the American nation that since that time we and those who preceded us have been constantly busy refuting unmotivated, unjust, cruel[,] and cowardly attacks."[208]

Read's book was unique in countering the interpretations of mainstream historians and because his target audience was Nuevomexicanos. He was the first historian to link the war's causes and the prolonged racial tensions experienced by Mexicans. Historians of Mexico and the United States offered interpretations that focused on national issues and government relations, while Read emphasized relations between people. Significantly, this distinction suggests that Read's subject position, as a descendant of Spanish Mexicans and European Americans, influenced his views and his book's goal. While he claimed objectivity, he also sought to restore honor to *hispano-americanos* whose history, he posited, was ignored by previous historians.

His decision to write the book in Spanish revealed that his intended audience was Spanish-speaking Nuevomexicanos. While Read sought to contest prevailing interpretations of the war, he took more interest in presenting his account to his fellow *hispano-americanos* than to English-speaking European Americans. Some of his contemporaries believed this decision hampered Read's success. In the *New Mexico Historical Review*, Read's obituary claimed that he had failed as a historian precisely because he wrote in Spanish and practically ignored English-speaking audiences. However, Read's ideological goal was "to denounce Anglo Americans' prejudice and encourage Nuevomexicanos to take pride in their own conquistadorial past," so his decision to publish in Spanish made sense.[209]

Read's chosen audience and his book's goal emphasize the transmission and strategic deployment of collective memories. As a Nuevomexicano, he had absorbed war memories from his family and community.[210] He interviewed older *hispano-americanos* to incorporate their memories into his historical interpretations. Occasionally, Read asked Hispano elders to record their recollections of life before the US takeover. Don Demetrio Pérez of Santa Fe wrote such an account of his experiences under Mexican rule, including a photograph of himself in military uniform.[211]

Aware that Nuevomexicano voices might not be found in the territory's libraries, Read preserved their recollections in local archives. His efforts acknowledged that one legacy of conquest was the silencing of alternative histories. Read grasped the power of archives. As archivists Joan Schwartz and

Terry Cook posit, "Archives—as records—wield power over the shape and direction of historical scholarship, collective memory, and national identity, over how we know ourselves as individuals, groups, and societies."[212] Lamenting in a letter to an editor the lack of historical accounts written by Nuevomexicano ancestors, Read advocated the use of "unpublished written documents of those turbulent times, in order to vindicate the memory, reputation, and good name of our ancestors."[213] His recollection of his family and community's collective memories influenced his goal for *Guerra México-Americana*. Read wanted to "invigorate the historical memory of his Spanish-speaking audience," contended historian Nieto-Phillips, "and to foment among Nuevomexicanos a pride in their Spanish past."[214] In addition to countering previous war interpretations, Read sought to propagate *hispano-americanos'* collective memories among future generations.

The receptions to *Guerra México-Americana* and his other books demonstrate that Read accomplished his goal of re-instilling pride among Nuevomexicanos. New Mexico's Spanish-language press enthusiastically praised the book. The editors of *El Neomexicano* urged him to publish an English-language version, concluding that the book "should have a place in every historical collection and in every Spanish American family in the Southwest."[215] An indication of his popularity appeared in a circular for his *Historia ilustrada de Nuevo Mexico* (1910), whose publisher noted that his first edition had sold out soon after its publication.[216]

Several native New Mexicans praised his book's "impartiality" and its description of the war's "true origins." Among several items that *hispano-americanos* highlighted were the way *Guerra* avoided the exaggeration in previous histories of the US Southwest by European American historians. Various letters recognized the book's importance in contradicting the prevailing interpretations in US history books. *Guerra*, some believed, would lead Nuevomexicanos to take pride in their history and confirm their beliefs about the "gross injustice on the part of the United States" in attacking Mexico. Others anticipated that *Guerra* would be very useful "for our children" and "especially for those Americans who ignore our history." The references to the book's impact on "our children" demonstrated that *hispano-americanos* realized *Guerra*'s value in disseminating their collective war memories and promoting pride among their children.[217] Undoubtedly, Read's earlier stint as a school superintendent had convinced him of the significance of presenting the state's history from a Hispano viewpoint. Read recognized the importance of sharing collective memories with future generations by publishing a condensed version of his *Historia illustrada de Nuevo México* to enable "the poor and the children" of New Mexico to learn about the region's Spanish ancestors.[218]

WORKERS, NEWSPAPERS, AND ORGANIZATIONS invoked collective memories of the war and treaty to pursue civil rights reforms and diplomatic objectives. *Mutualistas*, whose origins and goals were explicitly tied to the long-term effects of the US conquest, sought to protect Mexican immigrants and help them adjust to US society. Popular across the US Southwest, these mutual aid societies informed rural and urban workers of their citizenship rights and promoted cooperation among immigrants and Mexican Americans. These mutual aid societies and fraternal organizations reinforced Mexican culture through various celebrations and remembered a preconquest past in the names for their organizations. Urban and rural parents in San Angelo, Texas, cited the treaty's citizenship promises to protest school segregation. Their school boycott, their appeal to a Mexican consul for assistance to end segregation, and newspaper coverage of their direct actions propagated awareness of the treaty and collective memories of conquest.

Spanish-language newspapers published articles on discrimination and Mexican Americans' civil rights campaigns. These articles disseminated collective memories on both sides of the border and allowed for the transnational circulation of memories as Mexican Americans learned of Mexican nationals' views through the press and vice versa. Journalists cited the treaty in stories on working-class lynching victims and to draw attention to poll taxes, segregated public places, and the criminalization of laborers. Mexican diplomats recalled the treaty to assert the rights of Mexican immigrants and to dispute boundary issues in El Chamizal, home to poor workers. By citing the war and treaty, their efforts demonstrated the treaty's continued relevance, reinforced Mexican Americans' collective memories, and informed them of the civil rights guaranteed by the treaty. Newspaper coverage of these diplomatic efforts also contributed to the transnational circulation of each country's official collective war memories. The campaign for New Mexico statehood continued to reveal regional differences in war memories as Hispanos asserted a "native" status, remembered their loyal Civil War military service, and foregrounded their claim to whiteness. The scholarship of Benjamin Read offered a Hispano reinterpretation of the US-Mexico War, and his archival preservation efforts documented the collective memories of Hispano elders. Finally, contemporary civil rights issues and diplomatic concerns continued to shape the politics of collective memories.

CHAPTER FIVE

Patriotism and Legacies of Conquest
Segregation, Electoral Politics, and Jury Representation

In August 1927, Tejanos and Mexican immigrants gathered in Harlingen, Texas, to create a new civil rights organization. After electing a presiding officer, the attendees discussed membership qualifications, sparking a heated debate. Several Mexican Texan leaders urged participants to exclude Mexican immigrants from membership. Frustrated with the resistance to a wider membership base, 75 percent of attendees walked out. The organization that resulted, the League of Latin American Citizens, would join three other organizations (the Order Sons of America, the Order Sons of Texas, and the Order Knights of America) to establish the League of United Latin American Citizens (LULAC) in Corpus Christi in February 1929. In addition to emphasizing patriotism and civic duty, the new organization excluded Mexican nationals from membership.[1]

For LULAC's leaders, it was a pragmatic choice: focus solely on defending Mexican American civil rights but exclude the struggles of Mexican nationals. Most did not believe the organization could effectively defend both Mexican Americans and Mexican nationals. Past efforts to fight discrimination by mutual aid societies and the Mexican consulate, contended LULAC's cofounder Alonso Perales, failed because government officials did not respect organizations of noncitizens.[2] According to LULAC's leaders, Mexican Americans and Mexican immigrants shared similarities but ultimately held different goals. This view assumed Mexican nationals eventually sought to return to Mexico, while Mexican Americans strove for political integration in the United States.[3] Several LULAC members prioritized rights for Mexican Americans before assisting Mexican immigrants.[4] "The day that the Mexican American betters his condition and finds himself in a position of being able to make useful his rights of citizenship," Perales wrote, "that day he will be in a position to aid the Mexican citizen to [gain] his rights, and to collaborate with him all that goes to assure his welfare and happiness."[5] The organization must have received consistent criticism over their strategy of excluding Mexican immigrants because spokespersons spent considerable time "explaining and refining their position" in their writings over the years.[6]

Increasing anti-Mexican sentiments throughout the 1920s led some LULAC members to blame unrestricted Mexican immigration for European Americans' racism. Perales believed the presence of numerous poor Mexican immigrants had solidified negative stereotypes of Mexicans.[7] According to others, Mexican immigrants' social conditions, cultural practices, and lack of English-language proficiency reflected poorly on all Mexicans. European Americans' inability to differentiate between Mexican nationals and Mexican Americans motivated LULAC members to distance themselves from Mexican immigrants and to present themselves as more respectable. However, members were conscious that efforts to separate themselves from Mexican nationals implied that Mexican Americans were embarrassed about their ethnic origins.[8] Therefore, members sought to reassure Mexico and Mexican nationals that they respected their ancestors' native country and their origins. Such criticism of LULAC's apparent discomfort with their ethnic origins would reoccur in subsequent years. Continuous Mexican immigration led LULAC and other civil rights organizations to invoke collective war memories but often for distinct political purposes.

LULAC, Whiteness, and Tejano History

Conquest memories about the 1836 Texas secessionist rebellion were the subject of an exchange of letters between Carlos E. Castañeda and José T. Canales. In 1935, they discussed correcting the omission of Tejanos from public school history textbooks. Castañeda worked as an archivist but would become a distinguished professor of history at the University of Texas at Austin (UT Austin), while Canales was a civil rights activist and former state legislator. A lawyer by training, Canales was an avid lay historian who wrote scholarly essays and engaged in spirited debates with academics. Both believed in preserving Mexican Texan archives, so Canales asked Castañeda to deposit various items in the university's Genaro García Collection, which Castañeda supervised. The documents included primary sources and articles about Tejanos' role in the state's separatist struggle and a rebellion led by Juan Cortina (a great uncle of Canales), as well as the legislative report from the Canales-initiated Texas Ranger investigation in 1919.[9] In one letter, Canales optimistically wrote, "I assure you Doctor, that public opinion will change within five years and a new Texas History will be written wherein acknowledgment will be made for the services rendered by the Mexican Texans in behalf of Texas Independence."[10] He and Castañeda probably could not imagine that the role

Portrait of José T. Canales, c. 1909–10. A lawyer, Canales became a legislator and prominent civil rights activist. The State Preservation Board, Austin, Texas.

of Mexican Texans in Texas history would continue to be debated in the twenty-first century.

Collective memories of conquest and family histories led to early challenges to the omissions and disparagement of Tejanos in the state's history and in public school textbooks. Several intellectuals and organizations engaged in these efforts during the 1930s, when the economic stress of the Great Depression exacerbated xenophobia. Anti-immigrant sentiment targeted all ethnic Mexicans, as Anglo-Americans failed to distinguish between Mexican Americans and Mexican immigrants.[11] These tensions led LULAC to distance itself from Mexican immigrants while emphasizing its members' US citizenship and loyalty as it pursued civil rights reforms.[12] One of its campaigns focused on revising Texas history textbooks. LULAC blamed the state's textbooks for distorting Mexican Texan history by mischaracterizing the Texas Revolution as a racial conflict between Anglo-Texans and Mexicans without acknowledging Mexican Texans who participated in the separatist rebellion. In LULAC's view, the state's Anglo-centric history textbooks helped justify discrimination against Mexican Texans.[13] Historians have confirmed LULAC's characterization that early twentieth-century history books on Texas perpetuated Anglo-centric myths instead of reflecting the diversity of the state's residents.[14] The writings and correspondence of Castañeda, Canales, Adina Emilia De Zavala, and Elena Zamora O'Shea illustrate their pursuit of LULAC's goal to revise the state's history of Tejanos. Canales was one of LULAC's founders, Zamora O'Shea and Castañeda were members, and De Zavala was in frequent contact with LULAC members.[15] Mexican Texans' derogatory representation in the state's textbooks, they reasoned, contributed to their second-class citizenship. They held direct knowledge of the state textbooks' harmful effects on schoolchildren because all four had worked in the state's public school system: Castañeda, De Zavala, and Zamora O'Shea had been schoolteachers, Zamora O'Shea had been a school principal, and Canales and Castañeda had been school superintendents.

These four intellectuals' conquest memories challenged dominant versions of the Texas separatist rebellion, motivating them to correct negative textbook interpretations and preserve primary sources about Mexican Texan history. Their efforts represent a generation that endeavored to avoid the racial animosity against Mexican immigrants. They claimed whiteness to varying degrees, as did some LULAC members, in order to exercise their citizenship rights, while extolling their Tejano ancestors as patriotic to disprove the historical distortions of their forebears as disloyal.[16] Like African American scholars of the same period, these intellectuals sought to create a new narrative of the past, or a "counter-memory," that included Mexican Texans.[17] Their efforts to create an inclusive history and preserve Tejano historical sources supported their struggle to advance civil rights reforms.[18] While they shared ideological goals to refute negative stereotypes of Mexican Texans, their efforts were not always coordinated because they operated in different arenas. Castañeda was an academic whose publications challenged adverse portrayals of Spanish colonists, while Canales was more directly involved in civil rights campaigns. De Zavala and Zamora O'Shea sought reform through historical preservation and lay history publications. Yet each intellectual shared a commitment to preserve Tejano archives and often coordinated their preservation efforts.

During the 1930s, ethnic Mexicans throughout the United States experienced significant tensions as the Great Depression gripped the nation, joblessness rose, and nativism worsened. In the previous two decades, the number of Mexican immigrants had swelled as the Mexican Revolution (1910–20) pushed them out of Mexico and the increasing employment opportunities created by the United States' entry into World War I pulled them north. They also filled a labor need caused by a decrease in the availability of southern and eastern European immigrants, who became subject to quotas beginning in the 1920s.[19] The arrival of numerous Mexican immigrants exacerbated racial tensions by contributing to the immigration debate over origins quotas. Blaming immigrants for lowering wages and working as strikebreakers, many labor unions sought to curtail immigration. They joined restrictionists who successfully lobbied to pass the so-called quota laws of the 1920s, which restricted European immigration and excluded immigrants from Asia. The country faced a "Mexican problem," claimed some restrictionists, caused by immigrants who fueled an increase in disease, crime, and illiteracy while they replaced native-born workers in the nation's agricultural fields. The restrictionists failed to obtain a similar quota on Mexican immigrants due to the efforts of the agricultural industry, which lobbied Congress to exempt immigrants from the Western Hemisphere. This exemption allowed the agricultural industry to continue to hire Mexican immigrants for jobs few US citizens were willing to accept.[20]

Mexican Americans throughout the country were troubled that many European Americans made no distinction between immigrants who remained Mexican nationals and Mexican Americans with US citizenship. Stymied by the legacies of conquest, Mexican Americans had struggled to exercise their rights as US citizens since 1848.[21] Although promised full citizenship rights by the Treaty of Guadalupe Hidalgo, most Mexican Americans could not exercise those rights due to European Americans' dominant racial views. The surge in Mexican immigration in the early twentieth century clearly exposed the contradictions between the promises of full citizenship and Mexican Americans' second-class status. Mexican Americans held mixed reactions to the large influx of Mexican immigrants. While some welcomed the new arrivals, others were hostile to immigrants with whom they competed for jobs and housing.[22] Moreover, as the nation's economy deteriorated with the onset of the Great Depression, local and federal government agencies began targeting Mexicans for deportation. In December 1930, the secretary of labor ordered agents of the Immigration Bureau to identify and deport undocumented workers, beginning with striking workers. In response to harassment and intimidation, some Mexican immigrants "voluntarily" returned to Mexico. From 1929 to 1937, between 350,000 and 1 million people left the United States for Mexico, including US-born children of immigrant parents.[23]

In addition to external tensions over Mexican immigrants, the Tejano community's internal disagreements provided the context for the efforts of intellectuals who sought to correct the state's official history of Mexican Texans. As part of the so-called Mexican American generation, whose members became politically active in the 1930s, they entered politics determined to forge "a new consciousness among Mexican Americans."[24] According to historian Carlos Blanton, the Mexican American generation were "often the children of immigrants, [who] emphasized US citizenship, civic equality, and cultural pluralism while de-emphasizing Mexico-centered cultural nationalism."[25] This generation viewed the United States, and not Mexico, as their permanent future and emphasized obtaining "first-class citizenship."[26] Some middle-class activists of this cohort, like LULAC, sought to establish civil and political organizations apart from those groups that welcomed Mexican immigrants.[27] Meanwhile, others, like the working-class union laborers who established the Asociación Nacional México-Americana (ANMA), endeavored to establish alliances among Mexican Americans and Mexican immigrants. The Mexican American generation was not monolithic, as it included both radical workers and middle-class assimilationists. Accommodationist goals had motivated activists (like Canales) to establish LULAC and support immigration restrictions.[28] The organization's founders justified this exclusion by insisting that a Mexican American organization would make more progress than one including immigrants (non-US citizens) because US citizens held specific rights (e.g., the right to vote and sit on juries) to advance their goals that Mexican immigrants did not. Moreover, they reasoned, Mexican immigrants could appeal to the Mexican consulate for assistance, while Mexican Americans relied on the US government.[29]

Using a strategy known as the "citizenship sacrifice," some activists endorsed immigration restrictions as a way to obtain civil and economic rights. Distancing themselves from Mexican immigrants, LULAC members affirmed, would help convince Anglo-Americans to accept them as US citizens, stop grouping Mexican Americans with Mexican immigrants, and halt the labeling of Mexican Americans as "foreigners."[30] LULAC promoted US citizenship and encouraged members to become politically involved in fighting against discrimination.[31] While distancing themselves from Mexico and Mexican immigrants, LULAC members remained proud of their ethnic roots. "Being a Mexican by blood and being just as proud of my racial extraction as I am of my American citizenship," wrote LULAC cofounder and San Antonio lawyer Perales, "I feel it my duty to deny most emphatically that the Mexican race is inferior to any other race."[32] Not all LULAC chapters, however, distanced themselves from immigrants. Some chapters reached out to Mexican immigrants, and a few ladies' auxiliaries worked with immigrant women.[33]

Castañeda overcame several personal and financial challenges to obtain a doctorate in history and write about Spanish and Mexican colonists in Texas. Unlike De Zavala, Canales, and Zamora O'Shea, who hailed from illustrious colonial Texas roots, Castañeda came from humble immigrant origins in northeastern Mexico.[34] After his family moved to Brownsville, Texas, his parents died, so Castañeda began working part-time at a grocery store and as a math and Spanish-language tutor while attending high school to help support three sisters, with whom he lived. Since he received his early primary school education in Mexico, Castañeda learned Mexico's side of the US-Mexico War before entering school in Texas as a ten-year-old. While pursuing his undergraduate and graduate studies, Castañeda worked as a translator, engineering aide, highway supervisor, and Spanish tutor, and he later volunteered for the army (before becoming a US citizen) to continue supporting his sisters.[35]

As his financial and personal challenges continued, Castañeda accepted academic positions that introduced him to Tejano scholars and activists. While pursuing his doctorate in the 1920s, Castañeda taught at William and Mary College before returning to Texas to become a librarian at UT Austin. Castañeda taught university courses in summer, continued publishing journal articles, and made several research trips to Mexico.[36] As supervisor of the Genaro García Collection, Castañeda met LULAC activists through Canales, his lifelong friend, and began corresponding with De Zavala and Zamora O'Shea, who were involved in historical preservation. Although Castañeda sympathized with LULAC's goals, he distanced himself from the organization's ideological debates because he was a state employee and remained a Mexican national until 1936.[37] After becoming a naturalized US citizen, Castañeda grew more outspoken. In the early 1940s, he took a leave of absence from his academic post to become associate director of the Dallas Regional Office of the Fair Employment Practice Committee, where he investigated discriminatory practices in companies and unions involved in federal defense contracts. While there, Castañeda became more vocal in disputing discrimination against ethnic Mexicans, African Americans, and Native Americans. According to historian Mario García, Castañeda also recognized the link between workers' economic exploitation and racism.[38]

Memories of conquest and the treaty's citizenship promise shaped several of LULAC's political views, from its chosen name to the organization's attachment to whiteness. The anti-Mexican environment that festered after the

Carlos E. Castañeda, an archivist and history professor at the University of Texas at Austin. Alonso S. Perales Papers, reprinted with permission from the publisher, Arte Público Press, University of Houston.

Texas separatist revolt and the US-Mexico War led to charges of disloyalty against Tejanos, with long-term outcomes. One consequence influenced LULAC's strategy of promoting loyalty and emphasizing citizenship, which scholars characterize as assimilationist. However, LULAC members held contradictory views of the relationship between their ethnicity and citizenship. The organization's strategy to distance itself from Mexican immigrants partially explains its name, as the organization's founders chose "Latin American" to avoid the negative associations with "Mexican."[39] As political scientist Benjamin Márquez and historian Cynthia Orozco show, LULAC activists pledged loyalty to the United States in order to further their claim of being "100% Americans" and attempt to reap the full benefits of US citizenship.[40] Yet LULAC's political views cannot be characterized as exclusively assimilationist. In a *LULAC News* editorial titled "Are Texas-Mexicans 'Americans'?," the editor, F. Valencia, portrayed Mexican Texans as the original "white" settlers of Texas while casting Anglo-American colonists as "foreigners."[41] However, Valencia and other LULAC members did not equate Mexican Americans with Anglo-Americans, and were not entirely supportive of complete assimilation. His appeal to whiteness was based on the citizenship rights granted by the Treaty of Guadalupe Hidalgo. Like Nuevomexicanos, Valencia also claimed a native status by casting Tejanos' ancestors as the region's first settler-colonists.

Valencia's view of Mexican Texans as the region's original "white" settlers remained consistent with LULAC's emphasis on whiteness. To understand LULAC members' claims to whiteness, it is important to consider the 1930s political environment in which the organization was operating. Members understood that the Treaty of Guadalupe Hidalgo guaranteed Mexican Americans US citizenship rights. Because white Americans were the only group who could legally exercise full citizenship rights in the mid-nineteenth century, the treaty legally equated Mexican Americans with white Americans. However, many Anglo-Americans considered Mexicans to be nonwhite due to their racially mixed ancestry. Their classification as nonwhite angered many Mexican Americans, such as LULAC president Perales, who wrote, "We are very proud of our racial origins and do not wish to give the impression that we are ashamed of being called 'Mexicans.' Nevertheless, we have always resented the inference that we are not white."[42] In the view of most Anglo-Americans, Mexicans' Spanish, African, and Indigenous ancestors made them an inferior "mongrel" people. Legal scholar Laura Goméz frames Mexican Americans' conflicting legal and social status succinctly: "Tensions around Mexican Americans' racial status arose because this legal whiteness contradicted the *social* definition of Mexicans as non-white."[43]

Perales led LULAC in opposing the separate "Mexican" category in the 1930 US census because this category would further stigmatize Mexican Americans. Census officials had categorized Mexican Americans as "white" on previous censuses but chose the new category for 1930. After vigorous protest from many Mexican Americans, elected officials, and the Mexican government, the US government abandoned the category for the 1940 census.[44] White Americans remained the only citizens who could fully exercise rights in the 1930s, so LULAC members claimed whiteness because they too wanted to exercise full citizenship rights.[45] The organization's members particularly opposed the federal and state governments' attempts to classify Mexicans as nonwhite, because they wanted to avoid the adverse repercussions on their voting rights, educational opportunities, and access to public places.[46] As historian Neil Foley explained, "They understood that basic citizenship rights—such as the right to vote, sit on juries, hold public office, and so forth—depended less on their citizenship status than on their right to claim status as white citizens of the United States."[47] Rather than directly criticizing the nation's racial hierarchy, LULAC members claimed a white status to exercise the privileges of whiteness and citizenship. This strategy also led the organization to distance itself from African Americans as potential allies in civil rights struggles.[48]

LULAC members' claims to whiteness complicate the organization's record of civil rights struggles. Several scholars criticize them for claiming "whiteness" and distancing themselves from African Americans.[49] Foley argues that LULAC members made a "Faustian pact with whiteness" by equating Americanness with whiteness and avoiding alliances with African American civil rights activists.[50] This critique partly applies to the national organization's strategy, but as historians Carlos Blanton, Benjamin Johnson, and others note, such criticism does not take into account the variety of racial identities and political strategies among LULAC members.[51] By "establishing a tradition of avoiding an association with [B]lack politics," reflects political scientist Benjamin Márquez, "LULAC maintained that Mexican Americans were white, and therefore had privileges coming to them such as admission to white schools and public places."[52] Granted, some members held anti-Black views and opposed building alliances with African American political organizations.[53] In the 1930s, for example, LULAC officials in Corpus Christi objected when African American musicians, who had been hired to play at public dances, began intermingling with young Mexican American women. These actions, the officials warned, were a threat to "our manhood and womanhood to mingle with them on an equal social basis."[54] Other members acknowledged the injustice of African Americans' second-class citizenship but deliberately avoided alliances with them because they feared losing their claim to whiteness. Perales argued that an African American was "entitled to JUSTICE, but if we champion his cause, we are doomed."[55] According to historian Max Krochmal, members held diverse opinions about alliances with African Americans as exemplified by John J. Herrera, who worked in coalitions with African Americans, unionized workers, and white liberals.[56]

LULAC members did not hold monolithic view of whiteness. Instead, they expressed multiple positions that reflected their varied ancestry and ideological influences. Canales believed that Mexicans had a "Latin" background linking them to the great Roman civilization. Individuals of this Latin race, posited Canales, had become great musicians, artists, and political leaders. Moreover, he maintained that Anglo-Americans and Mexican Americans shared a Latin background.[57] While Canales's views were not unique, some

LULAC members' views about whiteness were more complicated. Among the most vigorous defenders of Mexicans' "whiteness" claims were several members who proudly proclaimed their own Indigenous ancestry. Alberto García, a member from Austin, highlighted Mexicans' Indigenous ancestors by emphasizing their racial intermixture with Aztec and Mayan Indians.[58] José de la Luz Sáenz, a schoolteacher and activist, went a step further by claiming an Indigenous ancestry and self-identifying as an Aztec.[59] These claims to Indigenous ancestry coincided with the racial views dominant in Mexico but contradicted US racial views steeped in the nation's racial binary. Mexican Americans were Caucasians, insisted Perales, "who have Indian blood"—a statement that did not make sense in the US context, in which Anglo-Americans believed in their racial purity.[60] Perales's views were common among LULAC members, demonstrating the influence of Mexico's early twentieth-century racial ideology. According to Mexican philosopher and politician José Vasconcelos, Mexicans were a "cosmic race" due to their racial ancestry. Unlike Anglo-Americans' negative perceptions of racial mixture, Vasconcelos and other Mexican intellectuals offered a positive view of racial fusion. They believed that mestizos were a superior race due to their racial fusion, as opposed to eugenicists' beliefs that racial mixture degraded the "white" race.[61] Vasconcelos's premise, indicates historian Benjamin Johnson, influenced many LULAC members. Some aspects of the "cosmic race" concept emerged in members' pride in their Indigenous and Spanish ancestries, their insistence on Mexican Americans' white status, and their belief that Mexicans were a separate race.[62]

LULAC members' claims to whiteness did not equate to support for white supremacy. Scholars criticize the strategy of claiming whiteness and some members' racist views toward African Americans, but these ideas were far from universally accepted due to large variations in members' racial views. Historians Patrick Lukens, Carlos Blanton, and others deem the organization's strategy as pragmatic, albeit misguided, "legal opportunism," which did not support white supremacy or the concept of racial purity for Mexican Americans.[63] Several LULAC members denounced Anglo-Americans' practice of racial segregation and racial classification. Although they sought to obtain white status, members did not believe in their own racial purity and criticized Anglo-Americans' purity claims. Perales's racial views exemplified members who were proud of their mixed racial ancestry but also claimed whiteness. According to Márquez, Perales "never argued that Mexican Americans were racially identical or culturally similar to Anglos nor did he believe that cultural assimilation was a desirable goal."[64] Moreover, several LULAC members supported multiracial coalitions, condemned white supremacy, and linked the discrimination experienced by African Americans, Mexican Americans, and Native Americans.[65]

Correcting History in Texas

De Zavala's goals were also shaped by the legacies of the Texas separatist rebellion and the US-Mexico War. Although De Zavala did not refer to whiteness in her correspondence or scholarship, she supported LULAC's goals of claiming citizenship and a role for Tejanos in the state's history. The state's official historical interpretation of its early settlements and the Texas Revolution inspired De Zavala to challenge the state's neglect of Spanish and Mexican contributions. She came from a well-known family involved in politics in Mexico and Texas. Her grandfather was Lorenzo de Zavala, the first vice president of the Texas Republic and one of the framers of its constitution. He had been a former governor of the state of Mexico, a congressional representative and senator for his native state of Yucatán, a contributor to Mexico's constitution of 1824, and an empresario in Texas.[66] Born in 1861 near the historic San Jacinto battlefield, Adina De Zavala grew up in Galveston and San Antonio and obtained a college education before working as a schoolteacher for several years.[67] Her father, Augustín, was the son of Lorenzo de Zavala and his second wife, Emily West de Zavala, an Irish American from New York. De Zavala also inherited Irish ancestry from her mother, Julia Tyrrell, whose parents were Irish immigrants. Although scholars suggest that De Zavala did not identify as a Tejana, she felt proud of her Mexican ancestors and shared alliances with Mexican Texan activists and scholars.[68] De Zavala empathized with Mexicans, anthropologist Richard Flores contends, while "celebrating Americanism" in her efforts to preserve and highlight the state's Spanish and Mexican pasts.[69] These goals led De Zavala to engage in frequent communications with Castañeda, who shared her interest in revising the state's public history to highlight the role of Tejanos. Best known for her efforts to rescue the Alamo mission complex from developers in the 1900s, De Zavala was also active in promoting Texas history through publications and various conservation efforts. In the late 1880s, she began meeting with other San Antonio women to discuss the state's founders. This women's society group eventually joined the Daughters of the Republic of Texas (DRT) as the De Zavala chapter, in honor of Lorenzo de Zavala, and was chiefly responsible for preventing the destruction of the Alamo by real estate developers.[70]

Adina Emilia De Zavala, c. 1908. She was active in the Daughters of the Republic of Texas and wrote *History and Legends of the Alamo and Other Missions in and around San Antonio*. Courtesy of the Sister of Charity of the Incarnate Word Archives and the University of the Incarnate Word.

De Zavala and Castañeda cooperated to preserve Mexican Texan sources and recover Tejano history from the margins. In the early 1930s, De Zavala corresponded with Castañeda to offer her historical interpretations and to ask for his essays about her grandfather, Lorenzo de Zavala, and for information on various Texas missions.[71] Her exchanges with Castañeda demonstrated De Zavala's confidence in offering her judgment about historical issues to a fellow historian with more academic training.[72] While De Zavala often obtained research assistance from Castañeda, the friendship was mutually beneficial. In 1940, Castañeda wrote De Zavala to inquire about a collection of papers belonging to Lorenzo de Zavala that her father had deposited at the Galveston Historical Society (GHS) in 1874 but which had been withdrawn in 1889. Spurred by a fellow doctoral student who had begun a dissertation on Lorenzo de Zavala, Castañeda sought access because he considered her grandfather's sources valuable. De Zavala replied that she possessed her grandfather's papers and would permit the student to review them.[73] While she did not indicate why her family removed the collection from GHS, she wanted the sources made available to fellow researchers. Like Canales, De Zavala recognized the importance of preserving historical sources and ensuring access to future researchers.

De Zavala absorbed collective memories of conquest from her ancestors, which she promoted through her publications and public history projects. De Zavala and Castañeda often asked each other for feedback on their essays and research. While Castañeda wrote his multivolume *Our Catholic Heritage in Texas*, De Zavala urged him to use the term "the Alamo" to describe the fort and mission complex and not simply to allude to the mission. To support her argument, De Zavala referred Castañeda to her book *History and Legends of the Alamo* and warned him to avoid the mistakes of other contemporary scholars. Her expertise in historical preservation motivated De Zavala to emphasize a certain account of and terminology for the Alamo.

Indisputably, De Zavala had shared her struggles with Clara Driscoll over control of the DRT. In at least two letters, De Zavala confided in Castañeda her difficulties in convincing "our friends—the enemy—(yours and mine)" about the physical description of the Alamo based on primary sources and its current state of disrepair.[74] Her reference to their shared enemies pointed to Driscoll and her associates. Besides disagreeing on the historical aspect of the Alamo complex, De Zavala and Driscoll differed on Mexicans' role in the state's history. According to anthropologist Richard Flores, Driscoll construed Mexicans as "deeply flawed" and responsible for their own lower socioeconomic status in Texas.[75] In contrast, De Zavala highlighted the contributions of Spanish and Mexican settlers. De Zavala shared goals and created an ideological alliance with Castañeda and others to revise the state's history.

His family's collective memories of conquest also influenced Canales to contribute to an alternative history of the state. Born on his maternal great-grandfather's ranch near Corpus Christi, he received his early education in Tamaulipas and Texas before attending a business college in Austin, subsequently obtaining his law degree from the University of Michigan. Canales practiced law in South Texas and became a representative to the Texas House, serving five terms between 1905 and 1920.[76] While out of office from 1912 to 1914, he became the elected superintendent for Cameron County schools. His legislative proposals and his educational reform efforts were shaped by his family's long history in colonial Texas and by the discrimination endured by Tejanos. Beyond his duties as an elected official, Canales sought to mitigate racial tensions and protect the Mexican Texan community. During the Border War caused by the Plan de San Diego uprising in 1915–16, Canales organized the Canales Scouts to stop the cross-border raids and urged the military to reduce their repression of local Mexican Americans.[77] The experience of Mexican Texans during the Border War demonstrated their tragic in-between status. They were not fully accepted as US citizens, and they did not hold Mexican citizenship. According to literary scholar John Morán González, this border conflict convinced many Mexican American activists of the Mexican government's unwillingness to protect their community despite Tejanos' strong political and cultural identification with Mexico. Neither did the US federal government intervene to protect a Mexican Texan community under assault.[78]

Motivated by the Rangers' abuses and by his family's memories of conquest, state representative Canales launched a legislative investigation into the misconduct of the Texas Rangers during the previous five years and filed nineteen charges against the force in 1919. Since the early nineteenth century, the Rangers had kept ethnic Mexicans subordinate by terrorizing the community and intimidating voters. The Rangers had exacerbated racial tensions along the US-Mexican border beginning with their involvement in the struggle for Texas's independence and later the US-Mexico War, but their abuses escalated during the Border War of 1915–16. In twelve days of hearings, during which eighty witnesses contributed some 1,400 pages of testimony, Canales sought to convince fellow legislators to reform the Rangers by limiting their number, holding the force accountable to local officials, and making them liable to civil suits. Unfortunately, the governor and other legislators stymied many of his proposed reforms, but the investigation led to the cancellation of special Rangers' appointments, the dissolution of several companies, and the dissemination of detailed evidence of the Rangers' widespread abuse of Tejanos.[79] Due to his background as a lawyer and his ancestors' struggle to obtain the proper documentation to certify their Spanish and Mexican land grants, Canales was well aware of the importance of preserving official documents.[80]

Canales sought to protect a copy of the 1919 legislative testimony. In July 1919, his last legislative act transferred a copy of the proceedings to the State Library. "Perhaps aware of the possibility that the copy might disappear," infers historian Robert Ribb, "Canales included in his resolution [which directed officials to deposit the testimony in the archives] the necessity for obtaining a receipt from the State Librarian."[81] Canales's suspicions proved well founded. Writing to Castañeda in 1930, Canales offered a copy of the investigation to deposit in the archives at the University of Texas. By this time (only eleven years after the investigation), the copy that Canales had deposited at the state's General Library (later known as the Texas State Archives

[TSA]) had already been misplaced, or so it seemed. Significantly, Canales chose not to deposit another copy with the General Library. Instead, he found a way around the General Library's hold on official records by depositing a copy with a friendly archivist at an alternative location. The TSA's copy of the Ranger investigation testimony remained inaccessible until historian James Sandos gained access to it in the mid-1970s as a doctoral student through sheer persistence.[82] The one individual who had gained access in the previous five decades reveals much about the politics of the TSA administration. That individual was historian Walter Prescott Webb, who published a glowing portrayal of the infamous law enforcement force.[83] Canales understood that the "archives [are] never a neutral space," as his suspicions (along with the experience of researchers at the TSA) confirmed archivist Alex Poole's point that "second-class citizenship thrived in the archives."[84]

Given the TSA's tendency to grant preferential access to the 1919 legislative testimony, Canales correctly deposited a copy of the proceedings at UT Austin's Genaro García Collection. In a letter to Castañeda, Canales wrote, "I want you to take and place it [the Ranger investigation testimony] where it shall be preserved as it may become very important in the future."[85] His prescient remarks alluded to the importance of archive preservation as well as to safeguarding official testimony of state-sponsored abuses of Tejanos. Canales's actions underscore his recognition of the power of archives in shaping history. As archivists Joan Schwartz and Terry Cook explain, "Archives—as records—wield power over the shape and direction of historical scholarship, collective memory, and national identity, over how we know ourselves as individuals, groups, and societies."[86] Castañeda's response to Canales recognized the importance of the Ranger investigation proceedings, providing assurances that state archivists were unable to offer. "Let me assure you that I shall be delighted to get that copy of the Ranger investigation," Castañeda wrote. "I will see to it that it is not lost or misplaced, for as you say it is a most interesting incident whose permanent record should be safeguarded for future generations."[87] Canales and Castañeda grasped that future revisionist histories would depend on access to such records.[88]

Canales endeavored to revise the state's history to highlight Mexican Texans' loyalty in order to counter the legacies of conquest that cast them as unpatriotic. As president of LULAC in 1932–33, Canales sought to fulfill one of the organization's goals by highlighting nineteenth-century Tejanos' loyalty.[89] LULAC wanted "to honor the memory of Texas Mexicans and the other Latin American patriots who fought for the independence of Texas," according to its official letterhead. As a member of LULAC's centennial committee, Canales helped publish a pamphlet in time for the Texas Centennial (1936) celebration.[90] Presenting a "counter history" of the Texas Revolution, the pamphlet was part of LULAC's detailed plan to refute the derogatory depictions of Mexican Texans in published historical scholarship and at public history sites. LULAC pursued this campaign because many members blamed the state's history textbooks for "exacerbating Texas-Mexican alienation from the US polity" by portraying all Tejanos as "foreigners" who had not supported the Texas Revolution.[91] Like the National Association for the Advancement of Colored People, which sought to revise history textbooks' depictions of African Americans in the 1930s, LULAC understood how textbooks' harsh characterizations of Mexican Texans shaped public opinion.[92] Canales believed that publishing an inexpensive pamphlet with an alternative narrative would reach a broad audience and improve the public view of Tejanos.[93] Published as *Viva Tejas: The Story of the Mexican-Born Patriots of the Republic of Texas* in 1936, the pamphlet highlighted Mexican Texans' significant roles in the state's independence struggle and in the commemoration of its fallen heroes.[94] To correct negative characterizations through public history, LULAC suggested that a portrait of Juan Seguín be placed inside the Alamo and that Tejano Boy Scouts lead tours of the San Antonio missions.[95]

Canales's efforts to create a counterhistory buoyed his attempts to revise the official view of his great uncle Juan N. Cortina. Cortina was a land grant heir who lived in Brownsville, Texas, where he led a six-month rebellion in 1859. Attempting to stop police brutality against a Mexican worker, Cortina shot local marshal Robert Shears and rescued the laborer. This incident sparked the rebellion, which exposed long-simmering tensions resulting from the aftermath of the US-Mexico War. Cortina's forces eventually numbered some 400 men, who fought local authorities, Texas Rangers, and federal troops. The Cortinistas published proclamations declaring their motivations for the rebellion, including Mexican Texans' increasing land loss, criminalization, and denial of citizenship rights.[96] A combined force of Texas Rangers and federal troops eventually suppressed the rebellion, but not before the conflict caused widespread devastation and the abandonment of many ranches in the region. Tracing this unjust treatment to US annexation, the Cortinistas accused the United States of failing to uphold Tejanos' citizenship rights.[97]

By the 1930s, several historians had published negative portrayals of Cortina, construing him as a cattle thief, bandit, and scourge. Among these scholars were Webb and J. Frank Dobie, whose influence helped shape public opinion. Canales believed that the views of Cortina were not only mistaken but also harmful because they led to adverse perceptions of Mexican Texans. As part of the effort to rehabilitate the academic interpretation of Cortina, Canales helped his son-in-law, Charles Goldfinch, obtain primary sources not previously consulted by scholars. Goldfinch's master's thesis posited that neither Cortina nor his followers stole any property during their rebellion. Goldfinch contended that Cortina held legitimate reasons, including Tejanos' land loss and increasing criminalization, for launching the rebellion.[98] Canales also helped published Goldfinch's thesis as a book.

Canales subsequently published an essay suggesting that Cortina had not been given an "impartial trial" by historians who misconstrued his actions. He decried historians' distortion of Cortina as "'a bandit' and 'a thief'; as 'the red robber of the Rio Grande'; as 'the black sheep of his Mother's otherwise commendable flock'; and as 'The Rogue of the Rio Grande.'"[99] These epithets "like labels on bottles, are of easy manufacture," Canales contended, but they do not reveal a man's true character. Canales presented a detailed defense by concluding that Cortina was a diplomat and a good patriotic soldier who opposed slavery in the United States and the French intervention in Mexico.[100] This reinterpretation of Cortina was necessary for Canales for personal reasons (Cortina was his ancestor) and due to the Cortinistas' goal: they demanded that the United States respect Mexican Americans' citizenship rights and honor the Treaty of Guadalupe Hidalgo. In effect, the Cortinistas were predecessors to LULAC, which Canales had helped found.

Canales also sought to disseminate new scholarly interpretations to academics whose publications cast Cortina in a negative light. In December 1949, Canales wrote Castañeda, asking for Dobie's and Webb's mailing addresses to send them a copy of Goldfinch's thesis. Both Dobie and Webb excused the Texas Rangers' violence and their indiscriminate destruction of Tejano ranches during Cortina's uprising. Moreover, both scholars depicted Cortina as a "black sheep" and a "bandit" who was responsible for a "reign of terror."[101] Castañeda provided the scholars' mailing addresses and acknowledged that the thesis would gain a wider audience through publication.[102] Believing that Goldfinch's thesis offered a significant contribution, Castañeda deposited a copy in the UT Austin library's Texas Collection.[103] Webb and Dobie thanked Canales for copies of Goldfinch's thesis. Webb replied, "It is too bad that I did not have access to the other side of the story," making the excuse that "the limitation[s of] time, energy[,] and money" led to the one-sided slant of his book *The Texas Rangers*.[104] Despite his protestations, Webb could have consulted various primary sources that proved the Rangers' abuses, which he cavalierly ignored, according to historian Robert Ribb. Dismissing the evidence of Ranger abuses, Webb had exonerated "the Rangers as he [vilified] the Border Mexicans."[105]

The legacies of the US-Mexico War motivated Canales to engage historians to correct negative depictions in their scholarship. Webb had written the Ranger book in response to the Canales-led 1919 Ranger investigation. Significantly, his book defended Texas Ranger abuses, a thinly veiled apology justifying their white supremacy.[106] Nevertheless, he appreciated Canales's and Goldfinch's historical contributions.[107] Webb personally assured Canales that "a new appraisal will be made on Cortina" in a revised textbook.[108] Dobie also harbored misgivings about his published interpretation of Cortina and acknowledged that the truth appeared more difficult to comprehend as he grew older. If he rewrote his coauthored *A Vaquero of the Brush Country*, Dobie maintained, he would "revise some things said about Juan N. Cortina." Dobie also thanked Canales for copies of a pamphlet on the US-Mexico War that reinterpreted Antonio López de Santa Anna's role in the conflict.[109]

Canales's correspondence with various scholars and activists demonstrated his attempts to improve the dominant views of Mexican Texans, creating a counter-memory of Tejanos in the state's history. In a March 1950 letter to Castañeda, Canales outlined three life aims. The first was to "do away with Pennybacker's *History of Texas*, which spawned a great deal of prejudice against our people."[110] Anna J. Hardwicke Pennybacker published *A New History of Texas* in 1888, and it quickly became the textbook most widely used to teach Texas history in the state's public schools. Although revised several times, her textbook still presented decidedly anti-Mexican views. These negative distortions appeared in a passage about land grant disputes between empresario Hayden Edwards and various nonwhite settlers in East Texas. "It happened that, scattered here and there over Edwards' land, were settlers who had come before he received his grant; these parties claimed immense tracts of land. Some of them were lazy, insolent Mexicans, while many others were criminals from the Neutral Ground."[111] According to literary scholar John Morán González, Pennybacker's textbook portrayed Anglo-Americans as the first settlers of Texas and thereby ignored various Native American nations and Spanish colonists who were living in Texas when the Anglo-American arrivistes arrived in the region.[112]

Canales recalled that the textbook's interpretation of Texas history exacerbated racial tensions in public schools. Pennybacker's textbook, Canales maintained, helped Anglo-Texan teachers and students construe Tejanos as foreigners and enemies of the "state's true founders." As a teenager, Canales moved from Corpus Christi's environs to Austin because he grew tired of a local teacher's overreliance on Pennybacker's textbook, which "failed to recognize Mexican Texan contributions to political and economic development."[113] According to sociologist Paul S. Taylor, the antagonistic views about Mexicans in Texas history were so pervasive among Anglo-American teachers and students that some Tejano students dropped out of school due to their distress.[114]

Canales's second life goal aimed to vindicate "the memory of [General] Cortina from the charges of being a 'bandit' and a 'cattle thief.'" His assistance to Goldfinch to complete and disseminate his master's thesis certainly fulfilled this goal. Finally, Canales's third goal was to publish a book with "historical facts, which have been ignored in Texas, and which prove that the Mexican people are not only loyal but generous and above all, they behave like good Christians."[115] Canales published *Bits of Texas History in the Melting Pot of America* in two parts, the first in 1950 and the second in 1957.[116] His two-part anthology contained essays that highlighted the compassion by Mexican civilians toward Anglo-Texan prisoners during the Texas Revolution, and the contributions of various Mexican Texans to the cause of Texas Independence.[117]

Like Canales, Zamora O'Shea was a lay historian who often communicated with Castañeda about historical sources and interpretations as she sought to create a counter-memory. Born on a ranch in Hidalgo County, Zamora O'Shea was a descendant of land grant heirs who helped established the *villas del norte* (northern towns) of Nuevo Santander along the Río Bravo (Rio Grande) in the mid-eighteenth century.[118] She absorbed collective memories of conquest from her family and learned the value of primary sources from her ancestors' experience proving property ownership in the state's courts after the US-Mexico War. Her family's ties to Mexico remained strong after the war.[119] After learning English at Laredo's Ursuline Convent in the late 1880s, she began her teaching career at Palito Blanco, a ranch school in Jim Wells County, when she was only fifteen years old, and would later teach at a school on the King Ranch. Subsequently, Zamora O'Shea furthered her education by attending several universities in Mexico and Texas, and eventually graduated from Southwest Texas State Normal School in San Marcos, Texas, with a teacher's certificate.[120] She devoted herself to education and resented Tejanos' underfunded schools due to the state's classification of Mexican Texans as nonwhite, as did LULAC members, and, unsurprisingly, "insisted that she was Caucasian, a white."[121]

Zamora O'Shea and Castañeda shared several goals, including preserving primary sources about Tejanos' ancestors and correcting the state's

María Elena Zamora (at the end of the fourth row on the right) pictured in the 1906 *Pedagogue* yearbook of Texas State University. Zamora O'Shea became a schoolteacher and lay historian and wrote the historical novel *El Mesquite*. University Archives, Texas State University, San Marcos, Texas.

historical omissions. As an archivist and historian, Castañeda repeatedly asked Zamora O'Shea about acquiring the personal papers of her father, who had served in Mexico's Republican forces against the French invaders at Puebla and been the personal secretary of Juan N. Cortina from 1865 to 1872, when the latter was a general in Mexico's military.[122] Her father had formed ties to political and military leaders in Mexico and to Canales's family. Although Zamora O'Shea understood the importance of depositing her father's personal papers (held by her siblings) at a university archive, she struggled to convince her brother and sister to preserve such documents.[123] Zamora O'Shea and Castañeda believed it was important to demonstrate Mexican Texans' early literacy and knowledge of history. In the course of their communication, Castañeda learned about her famous ancestor: her maternal grandmother, Concepción García de Moreno, was related to Genaro García, the Mexican historian and politician whose vast collection of books and primary sources Castañeda oversaw at UT Austin. Ultimately, Castañeda convinced Zamora O'Shea to share family documents that established the connection to Genaro García and offered payment from the university for such a collection.[124]

Zamora O'Shea worked tirelessly to correct the state history's omission of Spanish and Tejano colonists' contributions through her work as a schoolteacher, school principal, lay historian, and public intellectual. She forwarded a draft essay on Cortina (and offered a photograph of her father with Cortina) to Castañeda for his suggestions.[125] Both Zamora O'Shea and Castañeda believed that its publication would refute the nasty impressions in Pennybacker's "imaginary history of Texas," which contained "history fables."[126] In turn, Canales shared his writings on Cortina with Zamora O'Shea and sent her copies of his legislative resolutions on Cortina.[127] Canales, Zamora O'Shea, and Castañeda shared a goal of portraying Cortina (and Zamora O'Shea's father) in a positive light and emphasizing their contributions to the state's early history. Zamora O'Shea agreed with Canales that Pennybacker's textbook was extremely biased against the state's early Mexican colonists and detrimental to Mexican Texan students' education. She had taught school for twenty-three years and understood these detrimental effects.[128] As a schoolteacher in South Texas, Zamora O'Shea witnessed the damage of Pennybacker's textbook on her students, who stiffened at their desks when she discussed the Battle of Goliad in which Anglo-Texan prisoners of war were executed on the orders of General Santa Anna. In her historical novel *El Mesquite*, she described her goal of placing Tejanos back into textbooks: "Sometimes I have wondered why it is that our forefathers who helped with their money, their supplies, and their own energies have been entirely forgotten. History should be told as fact, pleasant or unpleasant."[129]

Zamora O'Shea often sought Castañeda's expertise in answering her historical queries. She asked about the chronology of the Spanish colonization, about the history of Tamaulipas, and for confirmation of her father's collective memories. According to her father, the Spanish established towns in Texas before they created Spanish settlements in California, which Castañeda confirmed.[130] She made a convincing case for the founding of *ranchos* in Nuevo Santander before establishment of the region's missions. In making this argument, Zamora O'Shea mentioned several local Indigenous groups (Tampacuas, Carrizos, and Tejones) but concluded that the Spanish owners of *ranchos* in northern Nuevo Santander were the region's true "pioneers." Zamora O'Shea argued that these Spanish colonists introduced the horses to the Nueces Strip.[131] She also expressed the desire to prove that the Spanish had settled Texas before the arrival of French explorer René-Robert Cavelier in the 1680s, which was the popular claim in Anglo-Texan history books. Zamora O'Shea's determination to refute that La Salle was the first European to arrive in Texas was partly motivated by the collective memories absorbed from her father and grandmother.[132] This goal was part of her efforts to correct the state's omission of the role of Spanish Mexican colonists and Tejanos' ancestors in establishing early settlements in Texas.

Aware of the varied ways that historical interpretations were disseminated, Zamora O'Shea dreaded that a forthcoming book and proposed film based on another flawed history of Texas might depict the Mexican population as debased and uncultured. In 1929, she informed Castañeda about a forthcoming book titled "The Birth of Texas" that ignored Mexican Texans' contributions, and urged him to intervene.[133] Worried that a film based on the aforementioned book would likely perpetuate the myth that "our ancestors were truly brutish," Zamora O'Shea contended that the Tejano "descendants of the first colonists should do something to stop the continuous offenses that they give us in their history books."[134] Her concerns were justified given a previous notorious depiction of the state's independence struggle in *Martyrs of the Alamo, or the Birth of Texas* (1915), which perpetuated horrible stereotypes of Mexicans. According to anthropologist Richard Flores, *Martyrs of the Alamo* was supervised by D. W. Griffith and clearly inspired by his explicitly racist film *Birth of a Nation* (1915). *Martyrs of the Alamo* depicts the Mexican population as drunks, lazy, and lustful of Anglo-American women. The film played into Anglo-Americans' fears and supported the state's official caricatures of Mexican soldiers and civilians as treasonous, inept, and corrupt. Flores indicates that *Martyrs of the Alamo* and *Birth of a Nation* spewed similar depictions of Mexicans and African Americans as morally reprehensible, disrespectful, and sexually promiscuous.[135]

Collective memories of conquest played a significant role in efforts to change school textbooks in Texas. The efforts of Castañeda, De Zavala, Canales, and Zamora O'Shea to revise offensive historical distortions and offer a counter-memory, or alternative narrative, that included Tejanos were part of a broad civil rights campaign to obtain full citizenship. These intellectuals deserve more recognition for their attempt to preserve archives about Mexican Texan history, create a counter-memory that included Mexican Texans, and promote their ancestors' significant role in the state's history. Although their activities and pursuits varied, these scholars shared a commitment to social justice for Tejanos. They believed in the significance of Spanish and Mexican contributions, the importance of public education, and the value of preserving archives and historical sites about Mexican Texans.

These early scholars were immersed in a binational experience that included traveling to Mexico, learning about Mexican history, and interacting with scholars from Mexico. They also felt proud of their bicultural background and resisted Anglo-American efforts to describe Mexican culture as inferior. These intellectuals' correspondence demonstrates their significant role in challenging the state history's omission of Tejanos and their strong belief that this exclusion was damaging schoolchildren's education. Their efforts confirm that the struggle against harsh portrayals of Mexican Americans in the state's textbooks has been a long process, one that continues to the present day.[136]

The Great Depression and Repatriation Campaigns

The xenophobia unleased during the Great Depression harmed the US public's view of ethnic Mexicans and motivated activists to invoke conquest memories. A legacy of conquest, this xenophobia construed ethnic Mexicans as stubbornly disloyal and perpetual foreigners.[137] The Great Depression witnessed the deportation of thousands of Mexicans and a surge in anti-Mexican sentiments, which severely tested LULAC's stance on immigration. It faced intense political pressure in one of its first public stands on immigration. Within a year of LULAC's founding, the organization's leaders went on record to offer qualified support for pending US Congressional legislation to restrict immigration.[138] The organization's view of immigration seemed to harden during the Great Depression due to extensive forced deportations.[139] LULAC did little to stop the deportations and even viewed repatriations as an opportunity.[140] In October 1931, M. C. Gonzales, a founder of LULAC, published an editorial titled "What Is Our Duty?" on forced deportations.[141] Gonzales witnessed the deportation of 3,000 Mexican nationals through San Antonio. Instead of portraying this episode as tragic, Gonzales offered an incredibly optimistic account of hardworking laborers as "happy" to return to their native land to escape the economic crisis and sparse work opportunities in Texas. He painted a rosy picture of Mexico as a place "where their [the deportees'] language is spoken, where there are no distinctions, not in schools, not in restaurants, not in any other place, where justice is administered equally to the native as to the foreigner, and where the school program is administered without using ridiculous pedagogical theories to favor members of one race to the exclusion of another."[142] With this overly positive portrayal of Mexico, Gonzales clearly exposed one of the legacies of conquest: existing discrimination against immigrants..

His idealization of Mexico assuaged his conscience (and that of other LULAC members) for not opposing the forced deportations. Gonzales called for other Mexican Americans to take advantage of the unique opportunity offered by the rapid exodus of Mexican laborers. He believed the large departure of Mexican nationals would change the sociological, political, and economic situation that had previously hindered Mexican Americans. The implication was clear: the presence of large numbers of Mexican immigrants in the United States had curtailed the advancement of Mexican Americans. Gonzales posed several questions to emphasize this unique opportunity: What was Mexican Americans' duty? What was their opportunity? Rather than encouraging protests against the ongoing forced deportations (which had already affected at least 100,000 Mexican nationals), Gonzales urged Mexican Americans to "work intelligently, united, and with energy" because "now, more than ever, is the best opportunity" to ensure their legal rights. Gonzales suggested that the forced removal of Mexican nationals would help Mexican Americans pursue their civil rights—perhaps by removing the stigma (i.e., diseased, poor, and criminal) of poor Mexican immigrants that was often associated with all ethnic Mexicans.[143] This extraordinary statement revealed his (as well as LULAC's) callousness to the plight of poor Mexican immigrants whom federal and state governments were targeting for deportation.

LULAC's acculturation goals combined with its stance on immigration led some to selectively forget memories of conquest. As they witnessed the rise of anti-Mexican sentiment and the forced deportations of Mexican immigrants during the Great Depression, some LULAC members relied on historical distortions and creative explanations for these events. In a 1932 essay, LULAC member Andrés Hernández claimed that Anglo-Texans and Mexican Texans lived in harmony prior to the most recent wave of Mexican immigration: "There had never been any difference or distinctions between the old Texas of Anglo-Saxon descent and the old Texas of Latin American descent" until European American newcomers to Texas began encountering poor Mexican immigrants earlier in the twentieth century. As a result, Hernández maintained, "a different attitude developed from newcomers to Texas toward the laboring class of Mexicans who came from Mexico to work." Unsurprisingly, Hernández seemed unconcerned about the discrimination against Mexican immigrants but objected to bias against Mexican Americans. He contended, "This attitude has not been limited to alien laborers but has extended to United States Citizens [meaning Mexican Americans]."[144] He distorted history in several ways: by blaming recent Mexican immigrants for inciting

European American newcomers' racism and by implying that longtime European American residents of Texas did not exhibit such racism. Hernández selectively forgot the legacies of the US-Mexico War, which resulted in land loss, violence, political disenfranchisement, and criminalization for Mexican Americans. Such selective memory of conquest allowed the author to imply falsely that Tejanos' patriotism and acculturation during the 1800s gained them acceptance as equal citizens. His argument conveniently omitted the violent legacies of conquest to advance a fictive equality among the state's early Mexican and European American colonists.[145] Hernández's selective remembering illustrates how "the arts of memory are shaped by the world and shape it in turn."[146] His need to gain acceptance from European Americans led him to contrive a fictive past, which in turn influenced how he viewed his contemporaries—both European Americans and Mexican immigrants.

LULAC's members desperately hoped that their patriotism would result in their acceptance as equal citizens by European Americans. Their faith in democracy led members to emphasize their patriotism repeatedly and to remind European Americans that Mexican Americans were US citizens. LULAC members (and other Mexican Americans) chafed when European Americans lumped Mexican nationals together with Mexican Americans. Not surprisingly, Hernández lamented that European Americans' negative perception of Mexican immigrants harmed Mexican Americans because most European Americans could not distinguish between the two groups.[147] "There have been raised veritable barriers against Latin Americans," Hernández complained, "indiscriminately and regardless of whether they are American citizens or not." He then listed public places where ethnic Mexicans encountered discrimination "because they belong to another race."[148]

Citizenship and Mexican Americans' status within the state were the subjects of another editorial, which also selectively forgot the legacies of conquest. F. Valencia's editorial touched on citizenship, patriotism, and whiteness. It identified Mexicans as settlers who "first braved and tamed the Texas wilderness." While such an argument discounted Indigenous settlement in Texas, Valencia clarified that Mexicans were the "first white race to inhabit this vast empire of ours."[149] This assertion coincided with LULAC's general view that Mexican Americans were entitled to US citizenship and whiteness. The Treaty of Guadalupe Hidalgo (1848) was central to these beliefs because it bestowed US citizenship on Mexican Americans at a time when the law recognized only whites as citizens. Valencia and other LULAC members understood the importance of claiming whiteness to exercise their citizenship rights. According to historian Foley, Mexican Americans (including LULAC's members) in the

1930s "came to the realization that being a US citizen did not count nearly as much as being white, the racial sine qua non of Americanness."[150] Texas was a province of Mexico, Valencia explained, for one hundred years before the arrival of Anglo-Americans. Therefore, when Anglo-Americans began to settle and colonize Texas, they were "recognized and admitted as foreigners" by Mexicans who "owned and ruled Texas." This argument echoed early twentieth-century Hispanos who claimed "native" status as New Mexico's first colonizers.[151] In this case, Valencia correctly deemed Anglo-Americans as "foreigners" (inverting the contemporary view of Mexicans as "foreigners") but conveniently forgot that much of Texas was controlled (and some would argue "owned and ruled") by Native Americans in the early nineteenth century.[152]

Describing the treaty's guarantees, Valencia stressed the US failure to keep these promises. He directly linked Tejanos' second-class citizenship to several of the civil rights issues facing them, including the denial of suffrage, nonrepresentative jury service, the lack of Mexican Texan elected officials, segregated schools, and limited access to public places. Valencia linked the consequences of Tejanos' second-class citizenship to the omissions and stereotypes of Mexican Texans in the state's history textbooks. Correcting the 1930s version of early Texas history, the editorial deems Mexican Texans as patriots, participants, and survivors of the battle of the Alamo and signers of the state's declaration of independence. By highlighting Tejanos' contributions to the state's independence struggle, Valencia restored Mexican Texans back into Texas history to conclude that "Texas-Mexicans are <u>emphatically</u> real Americans."[153]

Valencia explained how the treaty granted US citizenship to Mexicans who resided in the acquired territory. Further, the US Constitution granted citizenship to all those born or naturalized in the United States. Then he added, "Latin Americans [meaning Mexicans] have a double reason to say that they are Americans"—by the treaty and by the federal Constitution. Indeed, both the Treaty of Guadalupe Hidalgo and the US Constitution did grant citizenship to Mexicans living in the annexed territories in 1848 and to ethnic Mexicans born in the United States after 1868 (when the Fourteenth Amendment provided for birthright citizenship).[154] Unfortunately, he buttressed his claims with a distorted account of Tejanos' past treatment. In addition to erasing Indigenous claims to Texas, Valencia misrepresented history: "Texas-Mexicans never have been considered as foreigners, and so far as the great State of Texas is concerned[,] the real, true-blue 'Americans' are native citizens of this State of Latin extraction."[155] This claim was far from the reality experienced by most Tejanos, in that state officials and Anglo-American residents often treated Mexican Texans as "foreigners in their native land."[156] By publishing this editorial, Valencia admitted that some Anglo-Americans did not treat Tejanos as US citizens. He concluded, "The greatest care should be exercised to distinguish between this character of citizen [Tejano] and the alien of Latin-extraction."[157] Valencia believed that Mexican Texans' citizenship claims were hampered by the presence of Mexican immigrants, whom Anglo-Americans confused with Tejanos.

According to Valencia, indifference, rather than racial hostility, led to discrimination against Mexican Texans. He wrote, "Indifference on the part of our fellow Americans of other racial extractions to accord to them [400,000 Tejanos] the rights and privileges that the law gives them" had produced discriminatory practices. As a result, Mexican Texans had been denied the right to vote, serve on juries, and hold political office. They also confronted segregation in public schools and public places. This discrimination led Tejanos to be "rendered practically social outcasts." Valencia chose a somewhat neutral term ("indifference"), which ignored the racism and violent suppression directed at Mexican Texans in the aftermath of Texas independence and US annexation. Such selective forgetting of the legacies of conquest portrayed discrimination as a result of European Americans' benign "choice" rather than a fundamental tool of oppression.

Patriotism and loyalty figured prominently in Valencia's editorial. Some 400,000 Tejanos, he contended, "believe in the United States of America as a government of, by[,] and for the people, whose powers are derived from the consent of the governed." They believed the US government was established on the principles of freedom, equality, justice, and humanity. Moreover, Mexican Texans believed in the duty to love "our country," support its Constitution, respect its flag, and defend the nation against all enemies. He concluded by reminding readers that LULAC was established to foster among "our race" the "best purest and most perfect type of a true and loyal citizen of the United States." To document Tejanos' patriotism, Valencia noted that the struggle for Texas independence was not solely an Anglo-American affair but also involved Mexican Texans, like Juan Seguín, José Antonio Navarro, and Lorenzo de Zavala. He followed Navarro's earlier efforts to shape the state's collective memory "by drawing parallels between Anglo-Texans and the revolutionary struggles of the Mexican Texans of San Antonio."[158] Valencia linked Tejanos' past patriotism with contemporary efforts: LULAC "is laboring to redeem and place on equality before the law and before God, not Mexicans, nor aliens, but bona fide descendents of Texas Patriots and also descendents of Latin-American citizens" who served in World War I and received full military honors when buried in "Flanders' field."[159] Military service on behalf of the Texas Republic in 1836 or on behalf of the United States during World War I, Valencia suggested, distinguished Mexican Texans from Mexican immigrants. Such military service provided "indisputable evidence of their devotion and loyalty to the flag and our native country."[160]

Valencia's expression of patriotism, despite his acknowledgment of discrimination against Mexican Americans, supported LULAC's goals for members to acculturate to US society and obtain an education to combat discrimination. An earlier *LULAC News* editorial stressed this point: "Education, union[,] and quick adaptation to the prevailing customs and usages of the best citizenry of this country will steer us safely over the sea of racial discrimination and injustice to our proper place as citizens of this country."[161] Depending on the misguided belief that acculturation and loyalty would ultimately result in acceptance, Valencia's hyperpatriotism required the selective remembering and forgetting of conquest memories.

M. C. Gonzales and Educational Reforms

Collective war memories also motivated M. C. Gonzales to struggle against educational discrimination resulting from the legacies of conquest. According to Gonzales, Mexicans in Texas faced five types of discrimination: segregation of public schools; "white man's primaries," which prevented Mexican Americans and African Americans from voting; segregation of public facilities (e.g., swimming pools, theaters, and restaurants); housing discrimination; and unjust jury selection.[162] LULAC promoted quality education to provide Mexican Americans with the tools and opportunities to fight discrimination. Education helped cultivate an informed group of members who actively exercised and defended their citizenship rights.[163] LULAC, according to Gonzales, supported "education, rather than political agitation, as the avenue to progress."[164] "Political agitation" indirectly referred to labor strikes, which LULAC did not support. Instead, LULAC promoted education as a practical tool for upward mobility. According to historian Richard García, while elite Mexican exiles believed that education provided status and culture, middle-class LULAC members stressed functional and pragmatic education to obtain jobs and careers.[165] To end school segregation, LULAC undertook a dual strategy. First, it sought to convince school officials to end segregated schools through negotiations, protests, and community pressure. When this strategy proved ineffective, LULAC pursued litigation to end segregationist policies.[166] Although not an official LULAC strategy, several LULAC members (including Manuel C. Gonzales and John J. Herrera) endeavored to change the public school curriculum.

Manuel Carvajal Gonzales's family and education made him uniquely qualified to lead LULAC and promote its goals. Born in Hidalgo County, he was a descendant of José María Jesús Carbajal, a nineteenth-century political leader who had supported the state's secessionist campaign against Mexico and later allied with European Americans in an unsuccessful attempt to establish another independent republic along the border.[167] After moving to San Antonio, Gonzales attended business school, where he obtained skills to secure secretarial jobs at a law firm and a courthouse. He helped establish a workers' organization and a legal association for Mexican Americans. Upon his return to the states after his army service in Spain, he became a secretary for a Missouri senator before attending law school. He also became involved in San Antonio politics by urging Tejanos to abandon the local political machine and support "better government" candidates.[168] He began a bilingual newspaper, *El Luchador*, which carried articles urging Mexican Texans to unite, fight discrimination, and defend their rights. He also helped organize the Mexican Chamber of Commerce, became a cofounder of LULAC, and served as its second national president.[169]

Gonzales promoted LULAC's educational agenda and urged the organization to fight various discriminatory practices. As a lawyer, he worked for the Mexican consulate in San Antonio and for the Guatemalan government. Advocating educational reform, he protested unjust public school policies, organized a parent-teacher association for Tejanos, and ran for local and state office. Gonzales also filed various lawsuits against San Antonio's segregated public schools and took on individual legal cases.[170] He led LULAC in raising funds for appeals to the 1930 class-action lawsuit *Del Rio ISD v. Salvatierra*, in which Mexican Texan parents sued the Del Rio school district for maintaining segregated schools, the first case in which Texas courts used judicial review to determine the constitutionality of a school board's policy toward Mexican American students.[171] Gonzales's advocacy efforts included writing letters to newspapers to correct bias and condemn law enforcement officials when they failed to protect ethnic Mexicans from direct threats.[172]

In 1931, Gonzales gave a speech to a group of public school teachers in which he addressed racial prejudice against Tejanos at San Marcos Normal School. Professor J. O. Loftin had asked him to speak to his class of public school teachers, who were scheduled to teach ethnic Mexican students.[173] Gonzales focused on the inadequacies of public education and rampant discrimination in the state. Citing LULAC's founding principles, he characterized the organization as seeking to "foster progress and education" and as a group of "genuine, active, [and] patriotic" US citizens. While expressing loyalty to the nation, he discussed the rights of Mexican Americans, who were "legally and morally entitled to all the privileges and prerogatives of any other citizen."[174] His military service influenced his argument that because Mexican Americans were willing to make the ultimate sacrifice for the United States abroad, the government should ensure that they had the same citizenship rights as European Americans. However, Gonzales then admitted the sad reality of European Americans viewing Mexican Americans as foreigners.[175] He asked rhetorically, "Why are we, because of our racial extraction[,] classed as foreigners[?] [W]hy won't you accept us as Americans, just like you do other American citizens of German, Irish, French, English, and other extractions?"[176] Gonzales cited specific instances of discrimination by listing restaurants, barber shops, theaters, swimming pools, and hotels as public places that segregated Mexican Americans. He believed that racism against people of Mexican ancestry explained European Americans' treatment of Mexican Americans despite their US citizenship, social standing, and economic status.

Gonzales invoked collective memories of conquest to address the common mischaracterization of Mexicans as newcomers to Texas and as "aliens." Relying on the collective memory of Spanish colonization in Texas, he reminded the audience, "As you are aware, Mexican and Spanish speaking people are not newcomers to Texas."[177] Gonzales recalled that Mexicans had been living in Texas continuously since before the signing of the Treaty of Guadalupe Hidalgo in 1848. As a descendant of Carbajal, who welcomed European American "newcomers" like Stephen F. Austin to Texas, Gonzales was well aware of the Spanish and Mexican claims to the region. The collective memory of Mexican Texans' colonial roots motivated LULAC's founding. "One of the principal reasons that gave rise" to LULAC, according to Gonzales, was the perception of all Mexicans as "aliens" and as "sojourning in this country."[178] To emphasize Mexicans' long Texas residency, he asserted, "Now we as native Americans have every right to live here."[179] His phrase echoed the beliefs of Nuevomexicanos, who identified their long presence in New Mexico to claim citizenship and community membership. Gonzales's assertion helped LULAC's members underscore their "authenticity" as long residents of Texas and distinguish Tejanos from Mexican immigrants.

He identified education as key to changing European American perceptions of Mexican Americans as foreigners. Blaming schoolteachers and history textbooks for omitting a true account of Mexican Texans' contributions to the state's independence, he exposed egregious examples of anti-Mexican bias in public education. The textbooks characterized a Mexican as "a bloodthirsty individual who assassinated Americans, Texas heroes."[180] He contended that textbooks cast the Alamo battle in 1836 as the place where "American blood ran like water" at the hands of "brutal degenerate assassins," putting the blame on Mexicans. These characterizations damaged schoolchildren of any ancestry and did not foster friendly feelings. Comparing the Alamo to the atrocities committed by German soldiers during World War I, he asked why German brutality had not led to the type of racial prejudice experienced by Mexican Americans.

Quoting Anna Pennybacker's *History of Texas*, Gonzales underscored the textbook's bias against Mexicans. He faulted teachers and textbooks for omitting the roles of Seguín, Navarro, de Zavala, and Francisco Ruiz in the state's independence struggle. Gonzales blamed both the negative portrayal of Mexicans during the state's secessionist rebellion and the absence of Tejano pro-independence figures from textbooks for the pervasive racial hostility against Mexicans in Texas. He delivered a potent argument for including Mexican Texans in this history. Concluding his speech, Gonzales implored schoolteachers to foster good relations between "our fellow-citizens" and the "good people of Mexico." With their help, he reasoned, LULAC could promote citizenship and brotherhood in the state and ultimately eliminate racial prejudice.[181] Gonzales urged public school teachers to include more Tejano history in their curriculum to combat European Americans' misperceptions of Mexican Americans. As these teachers were scheduled to teach ethnic Mexicans, his arguments might qualify as an early example of advocating the teaching of Mexican Texan history to help Mexican American students succeed academically.

Loyalty and Fighting Discrimination

Another LULAC leader with family roots in colonial Spanish Texas was John J. Herrera, whose paternal and maternal ancestors had arrived in colonial Texas in the 1730s to help establish the town of San Antonio de Béxar, while several other family members held significant roles in the state's independence struggle from Mexico.[182] Among Herrera's ancestors were José Francisco Ruiz, who held several military and civilian posts, including lieutenant colonel, Texas senator, and member of Mexico's Boundary Commission, and was one of two Tejanos who signed the Texas Declaration of Independence. Ruiz was related by marriage to the renowned Navarro family.

In addition to Ruiz, several of Herrera's ancestors played prominent roles in Texas's secessionist struggle, including a mayor of San Antonio who helped identify the dead after the Battle of the Alamo and a soldier who fought in Seguín's company at the Battle of San Jacinto.[183]

Despite his lauded ties to early Mexican Texan leaders, Herrera led a humble life before his college education helped propel him to political prominence and middle-class status. Herrera paid his way through law school as a taxi driver and as a ditch digger for Houston's water department. After joining the Latin American Club of Harris County, Herrera participated in the group's protest against police violence and pay inequities within the city.[184] At only twenty-six years old, Herrera wrote a letter to the *Houston Post*: he denounced a city councilman who argued that Tejano workers in the water department should not be paid on San Jacinto Day, since the Mexican army was defeated on that day—falsely implying that Mexican Texans maintained a greater allegiance to Mexico than to Texas. Herrera also asserted Tejanos' historical presence in the city and the state. The water department workers, according to Herrera, included Mexican Texans who could document their ancestry "10 generations back on Texas soil, and one whose direct forefather signed the Texas Declaration of Independence."[185]

As a lawyer, Herrera was involved in two path-breaking civil rights lawsuits. Along with his good friend Gus García, Herrera successfully litigated the landmark *Delgado v. Bastrop Independent School District* (1948) lawsuit, which challenged the segregation of Mexican schoolchildren. He also worked with García on *Hernández v. the State of Texas* (1954), a case decided by the US Supreme Court that prohibited the exclusion of Mexican Americans from juries and defined Mexican Americans as a "class apart." After many years of active membership in LULAC, Herrera served as its national president from 1952 to 1953. As president, he advanced the organization's school desegregation efforts and increased its councils in Texas and New Mexico. He also helped LULAC begin coordinating policy with the American GI Forum.[186]

In 1941, Herrera responded to a business speech on improving US ties to Latin America by writing a letter to the editor in which he offered several arguments about eliminating domestic discrimination against Latin Americans as a necessary first step. In a critical speech before the Rotary Club, T. L. Evans, a member of Houston's Chamber of Commerce, inverted a question about whether the United States could depend on Latin American countries during the war by asking whether these countries could depend on the United States. Evans also referred to discrimination against Latin Americans in Texas, which Herrera characterized as covering "a multitude of sins." In his letter to the *Houston Press*, he identified himself as part of a "Latin American family" who had lived in Texas for over eight generations and had fought against discrimination since Seguín's time. Herrera was not only claiming legitimacy as an eight-generation Texas native but also reminding readers about the long history of discrimination against Tejanos. He extolled Seguín as a "Texas Revolutionary War hero" who, along with other loyal Mexican Texans, had been driven into poverty and exile by "overzealous discriminators." Seguín explained his reasons for leaving Texas in a pamphlet, which stood "as an indictment of intolerance and prejudice." Herrera characterized prejudice and discrimination as "un-American" traits. By tracing the origins of current discriminatory practices to the Republic period, he signaled to Tejanos' collective memories of nineteenth-century conquest. Unlike Valencia, Herrera acknowledged that loyalty to Texas was no antidote against discrimination for Mexican Texans.[187]

Hererra cited local examples of the "multitude of sins" from discrimination and legacies of conquest. He included towns within 100 miles of Houston where Mexican Texans were denied access to public places, various Houston businesses that refused to hire Tejanos or promote them above janitor, and even a city councilman who refused to pay Mexican American workers the same wage as European American laborers. When visitors from Latin America observed blatant acts of discrimination, Herrera reflected, they returned to inform their country, which soured relations with the United States. Moreover, Nazi propagandists publicized these blatant acts of discrimination to turn Latin American nations against the United States. The United States could foster more cooperation with Latin American nations, reasoned Herrera, not by sponsoring more goodwill tours of Latin America but by "cleaning house" domestically. This goal could be accomplished by eliminating discrimination against US citizens of Latin American ancestry. To stamp out "the un-American practices of prejudice and discrimination indulged in by small time would-be-Hitlers," Herrera called for a "complete and united front" to show the world that the "greatest democracy composed of a melting pot of races and nationalities will and can survive." He concluded his letter with a reminder that every US citizen held a right to life, liberty, and the pursuit of happiness regardless of their descent or ancestry.[188]

Herrera remembered Tejanos' long residence in the state, rendered visible their history and loyalty, and advanced their civil rights. By referring to his family's eight generations in Texas, he recalled the legacy of Spanish Mexican colonization and conquest. Herrera's father had passed along memories of their family's colonial roots in San Antonio and their role in securing the independence of Texas.[189] The recollections of his family and other LULAC members combined to create collective memories of conquest, with Spanish Mexican colonists as the first non-Indigenous settlers of Texas. Such memories served the political purpose of refuting the US public's "foreigner" label for Mexican Americans. Reflecting on his familial collective memories, he recognized their influence in shaping his civil rights activism. In 1940, while attending his father's funeral at a San Antonio cemetery where illustrious Herrera and Ruiz ancestors were buried, Herrera experienced an epiphany about his family's role in the state's history. His father's stories about "the glory that was early Texas" placed his ancestors among the leaders of the state's independence struggle and early history, which made Herrera realize "what my heritage was, and that I was [now] sitting on a powder keg of injustice and prejudice."[190]

While LULAC did not emphasize memories of conquest as a motivation for its civil rights activism, these memories clearly influenced the activism of several of its members, including Herrera, Gonzales, and Canales. These leaders' writings and speeches disseminated their collective memories, supporting LULAC's goals of emphasizing Mexican Americans' loyalty and dispelling the "foreigner" label. Herrera reinforced these goals with references to Seguín's forced exile from Texas after his support for its independence. Moreover, Herrera's reference to Seguín's memoirs rendered visible Tejanos' history and their long struggle for civil rights to a newspaper audience likely unfamiliar with Seguín's memoirs. Herrera's skillful argument about advancing US–Latin American relations by improving domestic race relations demonstrates the common civil rights belief that democracy begins at home. Influenced by contemporary political rhetoric, he cited President Franklin Delano Roosevelt's Good Neighbor policy and contemporary politicians' preoccupation with "un-American" activities to challenge US foreign policy toward Latin America. Finally, Herrera's litany of examples of discrimination mirrored LULAC's civil rights campaigns to guarantee access to public places, end job discrimination, and eliminate wage differentials based on race or ethnicity.

The long history of Mexican settlement in Texas was the subject of another letter in which Herrera also invoked his family's collective memories of conquest. In 1950, he replied to a woman who had written a letter to the editor complaining about the FCC's decision to "ban" the *Czech Hour*, a radio show on a local Fort Worth, Texas, station. In her letter, the woman opposed the banning on free speech grounds but also wondered why the FCC did not eliminate Spanish-language broadcasts. She then accused Latin Americans (i.e., Mexican Americans) in Fort Bend County of being "Communists." On behalf of the county's Latin Americans, Herrera lauded the Czech contributions to Texas but objected to her characterization of Mexican Americans as communists. Citing Mexican Americans' long residence and loyalty, Herrera contended that Mexicans had lived in Texas long before "Czech people" arrived from "thousands of miles away." Recalling his family's memories of conquest and colonization, he explained that Spanish Mexican colonists "carved a civilization out of a wilderness," built roads, brought Catholicism to the region, and "converted the Indian."[191]

Like other LULAC members, Herrera claimed native status as a descendant of early Mexican Texan colonists and selectively remembered the Spanish conquest of Indigenous people while ignoring its brutality. His skewed memory of Tejanos' heroic past fits a pattern, noticed by writer Viet Thanh Nguyen: "those who see themselves as marginalized, dominated, excluded, exploited, or oppressed" and remember their past as "heroic" before they remember their "antiheroic past."[192] Thus, Herrera underscored Mexicans' long status as "Americans" by proclaiming that "we were American descendants of the Aztec who had organized on the American continent before the time of the Pharaohs in Egypt." By acknowledging his Indigenous roots, he broke with LULAC members who claimed only Spanish ancestry. Addressing Mexican Americans' loyalty, Herrera cited their military service and noted that Macario García was the only Fort Bend County serviceman to receive the nation's highest military honor. He also emphasized that the first US casualties from the US-Korean War included four Mexican Americans.[193]

Herrera's response reflected his view of Mexican Texans' native role in the region and the value LULAC placed on loyalty and military service. By rejecting the "communist" label for Tejanos with the rebuttal that they have been in Texas much longer than the Czechs, he associated "communists" with "foreigners," a common US belief during the Cold War. He implicitly suggested that the "foreigners" label was more applicable for the Czechs. Herrera was aware that European Americans had imposed the "foreigner" label on Mexican Texans since the conclusion of the Texas Revolution and the US-Mexico War.[194] By claiming "native" status, he was echoing LULAC's emphasis on Tejanos' long residence in the region and their entitlement to citizenship rights. LULAC members had gone to great efforts to distance themselves from Mexican immigrants partly to avoid the "foreigner" label. By describing Mexican Texans' ancestors as the Spanish colonists who brought "civilization" and "Catholicism" to the region, Herrera underscored their role as settler-colonists. Moreover, he went further than most members by tracing

Tejanos' Indigenous roots to Mexico (while eliding roots to Indigenous groups in Texas). By identifying Mexican Texans' pre-Hispanic roots in the Western Hemisphere with ancestors as "American descendants of the Aztec(s)," Herrera conferred more legitimacy on Tejanos than on recent European immigrants.[195]

In another letter to the editor, Herrera recalled the legacies of conquest in the aftermath of the Texas Revolution and the US-Mexico War. In 1964, he responded to an Ed Syers editorial, "The Man of Cinco de Mayo," which focused on Ignacio Zaragoza, a Mexican Texan who became a general in Mexico's army and led his men to victory against French troops in Puebla on May 5, 1862.[196] Herrera agreed with Syers that a shrine be built to honor Goliad-born Zaragoza, whom he characterized as a Tejano whose cowboy skills helped Mexico defeat the French. Prompted by Syers's comment that Zaragoza's family, "like many a South Texas Mexican—recrossed the Rio Grande," Herrera explained that Zaragoza's and Seguín's families fled to Mexico to escape violent reprisals.[197] Herrera deemed the area between the Rio Grande and the Nueces River a disputed "no-man's land," claimed by both Mexico and the Republic of Texas, where the US-Mexico War began. The war led to many "misunderstandings between the new Anglo-American settlers and the Mexican Texan supporters of Texas Independence." He noted that Zaragoza and Seguín were part of a large group of Tejano families who had lived in Texas for over a hundred years. This group had "carved out civilization out of a wilderness" but left the state in disgust after suffering numerous discriminatory acts. Regarding the resolution at LULAC's upcoming national convention to commemorate Zaragoza and Lorenzo de Zavala, the first vice president of the Republic of Texas, Herrera concluded, "These acts to perpetuate the memory of these Latin American heroes will do much to make sense to all freedom loving people of this hemisphere."[198] Like other LULAC leaders, Herrera planned commemorations to ensure the dissemination of collective memories to future generations.

Herrera's letter demonstrates his pride in Zaragoza's origins and role in the Battle of Cinco de Mayo. Elaborating on Zaragoza's cowboy skills illustrated Mexican Texans' pride about the Zaragoza family's origins in Texas, where those skills helped Spanish Mexican colonists make a living from livestock production. Such pride led Tejano border resident Onofre Cárdenas to compose a corrido, "A Zaragoza," in 1867 to honor his exploits. While Zaragoza's role in the Battle of Cinco de Mayo was absent from public school history textbooks, Mexican Texan families passed on their knowledge of Zaragoza across generations through songs, commemorations, and collective memories.[199]

Herrera portrayed Zaragoza as a "Mexican cowboy" whose troops referred to the general as "el Tejanito" (a diminutive of "Tejano" and a term of endearment). This collective memory of a Mexican Texan's military service in Mexico highlighted the shared ethnic ancestry and culture of Mexicanos and Tejanos, illustrating the transnational links that united them despite holding different citizenship. Recalling the military heroism also highlighted Zaragoza's loyalty (LULAC's common theme) to his adoptive nation after he was forced to flee.

In his letter, Herrera decried the discrimination experienced by Mexican Texans for over a century. Syers had made a passing reference to many ethnic Mexicans in South Texas leaving for Mexico after the Texas Revolution without explaining their departure. Herrera elaborated that these families' flight was due to "many misunderstandings" between "new Anglo-American settlers" and the "Texas Mexican patriots who had fought for Texas Independence." His wording cast Anglo-Americans as the actual newcomers to Texas while reinforcing Tejanos' native-born status. This characterization recalled Nuevomexicanos who asserted their claims to authority and community membership based on their long residence.[200] His euphemism "misunderstandings" to describe the anti-Mexican violence of the period was probably Herrera's way of not offending European Americans' sensibilities while signaling to Mexican Texans that he was aware of this tragic history.

Such claims to long residence in Texas reinforced LULAC's goal of refuting the "foreigners" label. Herrera connected Zaragoza's and Seguín's families' similar stories with the experiences of Mexican Texans who fled to Mexico due to racial violence. In referring to the Nueces Strip as "no-man's land," Herrera alluded to the devastation of the post–Texas Revolution period and explained that this territorial dispute led to the US-Mexico War. While Syers omitted the war, Herrera stressed that this war of conquest led to similar "misunderstandings" as the struggle for an independent Texas. He was probably aware that such violence was caused by European Americans' habit of confusing Tejanos' Mexican ancestry with loyalty to Mexico. Ultimately, Herrera recalled collective memories to forcefully rebut the history in the state's textbooks.

Herrera foregrounded commemorations as a means to preserve memories for posterity by supporting a shrine to Zaragoza and explaining LULAC's efforts to honor Zaragoza and de Zavala to "perpetuate" their legacy. Both efforts demonstrated the importance of disseminating collective memories, even when such remembrances included grim episodes in the state's history. Herrera put a positive spin on the commemorations by extolling both men as patriots who contributed to the "ultimate freedom" of both Mexico and Texas. He believed that the federal government's efforts to promote alliances with Latin American nations would be appreciated by "all freedom loving people of this hemisphere." With this premise, Herrera made the case for connecting Tejano history with the transnational history of the Americas.

Asociación Nacional México-Americana

While LULAC attracted a middle-class membership, the Asociación Nacional México-Americana (ANMA) was composed of working-class Mexican Americans. Begun in 1949 by workers from the International Union of Mine, Mill, and Smelter Workers and the Congress of Industrial Organizations, ANMA promoted a radical ideology as the mine union's political arm. The organization's founders participated in a campaign of the Independent Progressive Party to back former vice president Henry Wallace for president in 1948. ANMA's creation originated at an El Paso conference of Mexican American supporters of Wallace, who wanted a "strong, militant organization" that defended civil rights. Unlike LULAC, which restricted its membership to US citizens, ANMA welcomed people interested in furthering the organization's goals regardless of citizenship.[201]

ANMA diverged from LULAC in its view of history by emphasizing the legacies of conquest. While several LULAC members underscored Mexican Americans' roots in Spanish colonial society, highlighted their legal classification as white, and urged members to acculturate, ANMA believed its members should understand the history of their forced incorporation into the United States and did not embrace whiteness.[202] According to its official newspaper, *Progreso*, the organization thought it important "to understand the historical origins, reasons, and motives of current conditions of Mexican people in the US" to advance ANMA's goals of "improvement, advancement, and progress" of the Mexican people.[203] As part of its "Breve Historia del Pueblo Mexicano"—a series on the history of Mexicans in the United States—*Progreso* published an extract from Isabel González's *Step-Children of a Nation*. An activist from Denver, González led a social services agency for ethnic Mexicans and became ANMA's first vice president in 1949. The United States "has never recognized its responsibilities to the native people of the vast region it took from Mexico," has not recognized native people's distinct culture, González wrote, "and has not respected the Treaty of Guadalupe Hidalgo, which guaranteed to respect their language, customs, property."[204]

ANMA invoked collective memories of conquest to trace the historical origins for Mexican Americans' current conditions. It recalled the war and treaty to explain the "inferior" position of Mexicans. This view derived from ANMA's belief that "Mexican American history had commenced in violence, conquest, and the subjugation of the resident Mexican population."[205] It argued that the Mexican community in the Southwest began to lose political and economic power in 1848, when the government placed Mexicans in an inferior position. ANMA also described how European Americans' nineteenth-century arrival firmly established the conquest as ethnic Mexicans lost property in US courts and to squatters. By tracing Mexican Americans' subjugation to the mid-nineteenth-century conflict, the organization stressed the ongoing legacies of conquest as "poverty, segregation, poorly paid teachers, and inferior schools."[206]

In her "Breve Historia" essay, González provided an overview of discriminatory experiences from the nineteenth and early twentieth centuries. She explained how anti-Mexican violence increased during California's gold rush as the Foreign Miners' Tax was the first of a long campaign to target Mexicans, dispossess them of their gold placers, and drive them away through physical attacks. As the newcomer population increased, the use of the Spanish language, equality of justice in the courts, and limited political participation for Mexicans was gradually eliminated. In the early twentieth century, railroad companies, mining concerns, and large agricultural operations recruited Mexican immigrants with promises of good pay, good working conditions, and paid transport to their workplaces. But with the onset of the Great Depression, González contended, Mexican immigrants were the first to be considered superfluous. The same business interests that aggressively recruited them years earlier now urged the government to deport them. Families who received government support were given a choice: they could either accept their deportation or lose their social service aid.[207]

Deeming the farmworkers' economic plight another legacy of conquest, ANMA attributed these conditions to their children's poor educational opportunities. Without a union, farmworkers were subject to low wages, threats, long periods of unemployment, and squalor. These conditions led farmworkers to be easily intimidated and oppressed, exploitation that forced them to accept an inferior standard of living. Their children frequently changed schools as their families followed the harvests. As a result, children often transferred from a bad to a worse school, according to González, ultimately receiving poor education without health care.[208] In newspaper articles, ANMA lobbied for public education, criticized segregated schools, and promoted bilingual education. These positions coincided with the belief that access to an equal education was a goal of obtaining first-class citizenship.[209]

ANMA often cited the Treaty of Guadalupe Hidalgo to support its claims to citizenship rights. It believed housing discrimination was tied to the pervasive myth of Mexicans' inferiority, which limited Mexicans' housing choices to poor barrios. In turn, this prolonged residential segregation had convinced some Mexicans to believe in their own inferiority. This inferiority complex had led some to pass as "Spanish" or as "good Mexicans" while blaming fellow Mexicans for behaviors that appeared to confirm the belief in deficiency. At other times, these "good Mexicans" denied that discrimination existed.[210] While ANMA did not refer directly to LULAC, its criticisms obviously applied to some of LULAC's members.

According to ANMA, housing discrimination pervaded the country with long-term consequences. The organization denounced restrictive covenants that barred Mexican Americans from living outside poor neighborhoods. These covenants, while illegal in California, remained unofficially enforced, excluding Edward Roybal—the sole Mexican American city councilman in Los Angeles—from various neighborhoods despite his "intellectual and moral" status.[211] Unofficial covenants also barred Mexican American World War II veterans from white neighborhoods. According to an editorial in *Progreso*, these veterans were among the most "cultured, educated, and decent" people in the community and among the most assimilated, often not even able to speak Spanish, yet they were still subject to housing discrimination. "Despite the declarations in the US Constitution and the Treaty of Guadalupe Hidalgo," the editorial declared, "these US citizens are forbidden from living in many parts of the city."[212] Residential segregation paired with examples of discrimination illustrated two basic points: first, residential segregation had developed over a long period based on the perception of Mexican Americans' inferiority, and second, even the most assimilated, educated, and patriotic Mexican Americans were not able to overcome such long-standing discrimination. By citing the Constitution and the treaty, ANMA reminded readers that the federal government had failed to enforce the citizenship guarantees for Mexican Americans. Ultimately, ANMA cited residential segregation as another product of conquest that produced widespread negative ramifications.

ANMA often framed its civil rights activism as part of its goal to obtain "first-class citizenship." This goal, which echoed the principal aspiration of Mexican Americans, reflected ANMA's conviction that Mexican Americans had not been able to exercise full rights due to the legacies of conquest.[213] By urging members to vote and protest discriminatory practices, ANMA encouraged them to exercise their citizenship rights guaranteed by the treaty and the Constitution but long denied. An editorial in *Progreso* exalted the Constitution as a "ray of light" that "renews our motivation and strength to continue the struggle" against discrimination and segregation. It cited the "unalienable rights to life, liberty, and the pursuit of happiness" in the Declaration of Independence, but acknowledged these "pretty words [that] only in actions are made reality."[214] ANMA repeatedly reminded members that striving for "first-class citizenship" was tied to several civil rights goals, including the struggle for an equal education, to purchase homes in any neighborhood, to obtain decent jobs, and to travel freely without being suspected of criminal behavior.[215] The organization urged members to continue their campaigns for public housing, the right to protest, workers' rights, and public health.[216] Ultimately, the pursuit of "first-class citizenship" entailed a broad campaign to obtain rights previously guaranteed but not enforced.

The organization broadened its campaign by articulating a defense of Mexican American culture and by protesting police brutality. Like previous and future generations of activists, ANMA believed that the Treaty of Guadalupe Hidalgo guaranteed Mexican Americans' rights to continue speaking Spanish and maintain their culture.[217] To strengthen community ties and continue cultural traditions, ANMA promoted Mexican music, dance, and literature by encouraging members to attend cultural events (e.g., Cinco de Mayo celebrations) and motivating youth to enter cultural competitions.[218] Its support for Mexican culture promoted cultural pride and disputed the "inferiority complex" that it believed afflicted some Mexican Americans. The organization also denounced police brutality, including the targeting of civil rights activists, undocumented immigrants, and youth.[219] To curb these abuses, ANMA proposed specific reforms "to seek discipline of police responsible for acts of brutality."[220] It filed lawsuits on behalf of Mexican American victims of police abuse, attended court hearings, and issued press releases documenting the persistent violations of civil rights by law enforcement agencies. Highlighting success in their legal battles and mass demonstrations, ANMA urged those allies who wanted to stop police brutality to join their organization. The struggle against police abuse became central to its ultimate goal of obtaining first-class citizenship.[221]

The organization developed an antiwar position that grew out of its opposition to the Cold War and its anti-imperialist vision. In 1950, ANMA joined demonstrations in Los Angeles in support of the Stockholm Peace Appeal to end the Cold War. At least 20,000 Mexican Americans signed the Stockholm appeal, according to ANMA, confirming widespread community support. Its stance was motivated by a belief that the country's war preparations took money away from domestic programs.²²² Not only did nuclear weapons consume money better spent on domestic social services, but the organization believed the sacrifices of war fell disproportionately on Mexican Americans. "The biggest danger which exists today is the danger of another war," reflected Alfredo Montoya, ANMA's president. He focused on the casualties of World War II: "We, the Mexicans, recognize the sacrifices and horror of war. During the last war our people sacrificed more lives in proportion than any other group in the country."²²³

A 1952 *Progreso* editorial linked the human and economic sacrifices explicitly by opposing the Korean War. "The Mexican community has been forced to pay disproportionately for the excessive and unjust war costs," asserted the editorial, "in the form of higher taxes, higher prices, and lower wages." While LULAC emphasized loyalty, ANMA's anti-imperialist vision underscored the war's human costs: "In this war[,] not only have thousands of lives of Mexican youth been sacrificed uselessly, but also the well-being and the rights of the Mexican community."²²⁴ Like the US-Mexico War, the Korean War failed to improve Mexican Americans' civil rights. The Denver chapter's newsletter published various antiwar statements by community members, including criticism from a teenage woman who stated, "Many Mexican people are saying, we're good enough to fight and die in Korea for nothing, but not good enough to get jobs at home without discrimination and to be treated equal with respect and dignity."²²⁵ To explain the war's negative community impact, ANMA published a pamphlet about the disproportionate recruitment of Mexican American youth into the military, higher taxes, reductions in public housing, the loss of [economic] security for the elderly, and the decrease of public education.²²⁶

Highlighting a contradiction, ANMA emphasized that the nation loudly proclaimed its fight for democracy in other parts of the world while limiting democracy domestically. "While ours are fighting and sacrificing their lives in Korea to establish 'democracy,'" a 1950 editorial emphasized, "here in our country there are neighborhoods where African Americans and Mexican Americans cannot live."²²⁷ Like other civil rights organization, ANMA was well aware of the United States' failure to live up to its democratic ideals. Its disapproval of the war's disproportionate human and social costs borne by Mexican Americans established a precedent for Chicano organizations' similar criticisms of the US war against Vietnam. Its antiwar position followed from its view of the US-Mexico War as a conquest rather than an effort to spread democracy.

Its labor union origins and its attention to the legacies of conquest shaped ANMA's stance on mass deportations. By the 1950s, the Bracero Program—a program that brought guest workers from Mexico in order to offset the labor shortages caused by World War II—had been in effect for almost a decade. ANMA opposed the program because it exploited Mexican contract workers while displacing Mexican American agricultural laborers.[228] The Bracero Program increased undocumented immigration because Mexican nationals who were not selected for the program crossed the border illegally to obtain jobs. In response, the US government began a series of deportations that expelled some 2 million Mexicans between 1951 and 1953. In 1954, the government ramped up its deportations through Operation Wetback, which led to another 1 million expulsions. ANMA denounced this revolving-door process that exploited Mexicans as cheap, expendable laborers, who were considered "a beast of burden brought by enlistment from the Mexican countryside to work in the American fields and once completed they are again expelled to the other side of the border."[229]

ANMA condemned these deportations as attacks on the civil and labor rights of ethnic Mexicans. Mass deportations, it insisted, were a form of labor control similar to federal action during the Great Depression. The federal and state governments targeted union organizers under the antialien and antisubversive legislation passed during the McCarthy era.[230] The organization related the deportations to Mexicans' long-held subordinate position as exploited and disposable workers, which began in the mid-nineteenth century with the war of conquest.[231] The US-Mexico War remained in the minds of the organization's leaders when they charged that mass deportations violated the constitutional protections of the Treaty of Guadalupe Hidalgo.[232] The deportations had not only targeted undocumented Mexicans but often ensnared Mexican Americans as well. Further, the expulsions led to the separation of mixed-status families when undocumented relatives were expelled.

George I. Sánchez and *Forgotten People*

ANMA's view of Mexican Americans as a conquered people echoed the scholarship of educator and historian George I. Sánchez. Born in New Mexico into a working-class family with deep roots in Hispano society, Sánchez became interested in education after serving as a sixteen-year-old rural teacher.[233] After obtaining his PhD from the University of California, Berkeley, he worked for a variety of agencies and foundations, including the New Mexico State Department of Education, and eventually accepted a part-time position as a professor of education at the University of New Mexico (UNM). While at UNM, he wrote *Forgotten People*, which would become a classic early textbook for Chicano history.²³⁴ The book portrayed the US annexation of Mexico's northern territories as a war of conquest. "In the march of imperialism[,] a people were forgotten," he wrote, "cast aside as the byproduct of territorial aggrandizement."²³⁵ Sánchez considered the US takeover not as a blessing but as a conquest that caused long, adverse legacies for Mexican Americans.²³⁶ His book deeply influenced several of ANMA's leaders and was cited in *Progreso*'s "Breve Historia" series. Like previous Nuevomexicano activists, Sánchez contended that Mexican Americans were indigenous to the US Southwest, a claim repeated by future Chicano movement participants. His perspective on the US-Mexico War influenced Chicano historians who offered the "internal colonial" model to understand Mexican American history. Sánchez's emphasis on the US conquest also anticipated the new western history scholarship.²³⁷

Sánchez maintained that the US-Mexico War and the Treaty of Guadalupe Hidalgo had transformed Nuevomexicanos into a "forgotten people." Despite US democratic ideals, he contended, the war had led to second-class citizenship for Mexican Americans. "It was folly to expect that, by the magic stroke of a pen upon a treaty," he wrote, "the New Mexican should become an American citizen overnight."²³⁸ The treaty's citizenship guarantees were not sufficient because "no provisions were made to safeguard them in their rights as a society." He identified vast differences between New Mexicans' culture and US culture that prevented Nuevomexicanos from adapting to US society. He elaborated his criticism: the "treaty...failed to recognize the major issues involved in the incorporation of a people into a new culture."²³⁹ Tracing Nuevomexicanos' contemporary problems to the legacies of conquest, Sánchez stressed the neglect and isolation of the northern borderlands stemming from Spanish and Mexican rule, and the second-class citizenship resulting from US conquest.²⁴⁰

He believed the answer to Nuevomexicanos' second-class citizenship was integration and modernization. US annexation caused instability as Mexican Americans endured social and economic losses, Sánchez reckoned, due to differences in cultures. In the war's aftermath, European American politicians and merchants capitalized on Nuevomexicanos' lack of knowledge of US commerce and the legal system to acquire their land, livestock, and water rights. According to Sánchez, various Nuevomexicano politicians attempted to institute reforms to address Mexican Americans' lack of education. Unfortunately, the reforms did not improve public education. He faulted substandard schools for keeping Nuevomexicanos uneducated about US society and reinforcing their subjugation, a legacy of conquest that continued into the mid-twentieth century. "The New Mexican is not yet an American culturally," he wrote, "the Treaty of Guadalupe notwithstanding."[241] While *Forgotten People* tended to discount human agency and stressed victimization, it nevertheless offered hope that integration would allow Nuevomexicanos to exercise their citizenship rights. To compete with European Americans, Sánchez maintained, Nuevomexicanos needed to undertake modernization of their social, economic, and political practices. Ultimately, he blamed the US government for "forcibly" bringing Nuevomexicanos "into the American society" but neglecting its responsibility to properly educate them. "The legal right to 'life, liberty and the pursuit of happiness' is an empty privilege," he concluded, "when the bare essentials of Americanism and of social welfare are wanting."[242]

Like Castañeda, Sánchez embraced activism while remaining a prodigious scholar. His publications criticized IQ tests that faulted Mexican Americans for lower intelligence, opposed segregated schools, and promoted bilingual education.[243] Unlike Castañeda, who sought to emphasize harmony and progress in the Spanish borderlands, Sánchez underscored conflict in the same region, especially after US annexation. Sánchez's colonial roots in New Mexico and his family's history of activism influenced his political views, while Castañeda's humble immigrant roots, LULAC ties, and citizenship status shaped his moderate outlook. Sánchez insisted that Mexican Americans' contemporary problems were more the result of the US government's failure than of Mexican Americans' supposed inferiority. A prolific author, he continued his advocacy work by joining LULAC, helping with its lawsuits against segregated schools, and serving as its president in the early 1940s.[244] Ultimately, Sánchez's selective memory of conquest diverged from the collective memories of Castañeda and other LULAC members who chose to emphasize the "progress" achieved by their Spanish colonial ancestors while ignoring the ramifications of conquest on Native Americans and Mexican Americans.

WHILE MEMORIES OF CONQUEST motivated the civil rights activism of the Mexican American generation, its members did not hold a singular collective memory of conquest. Various scholars and activists, including those from LULAC and ANMA, selectively remembered the US-Mexico War to suit their political goals. This selective use confirms sociologist Maurice Halbwachs's argument that "just as people are members of many different groups at the same time, so the memory of the same fact can be placed within many frameworks, which result from distinct collective memories."[245] Even within LULAC, differences appeared, as some members from working-class backgrounds readily defended Mexican laborers' rights, while others focused on school and public segregation that affected the broader Mexican American community. Although some LULAC members emphasized the treaty's citizenship guarantees to claim whiteness, other members' racial views were more complicated as they simultaneously claimed Indigenous heritage. Individual activists and their civil rights organizations also differed in their view of interracial alliances and protection for Mexican immigrants. While some LULAC members chose to depoliticize the past to gain acceptance, other members (and most ANMA activists) remembered the ethnic conflict and discrimination resulting from the mid-nineteenth-century US conquest.[246]

ANMA also differed from LULAC in its strategic deployment of conquest memories on behalf of workers. Unlike LULAC, ANMA welcomed immigrants and cited the treaty's promises to protest issues pertinent to laborers, such as working conditions, housing discrimination, police brutality, and deportations. Rather than emphasizing its members' loyalty to the United States, as did LULAC, ANMA adopted an antiwar position that highlighted the nation's hypocrisy in proclaiming democracy abroad while allowing discrimination to persist domestically. While LULAC consisted of many university-educated members, ANMA members were mostly labor organizers who emphasized the legacies of conquest in their war memories. Ultimately, the activists and scholars of the Mexican American generation established several precedents that informed future Chicano movement organizers. These models emphasized poverty, substandard education, political disenfranchisement, and criminalization as persistent problems resulting from the "unending" US-Mexico War.

CHAPTER SIX

The Civil Rights and Antiwar Movements
Land Grants, Police Brutality, and the Draft

In December 1971, the Brown Berets arrived in Santa Fe, New Mexico, a stop along their Caravana de la Reconquista, a monthslong march through the US Southwest. From local residents, the Berets learned that General Stephen Kearny had raised the US flag in the town's main plaza on August 22, 1846, and declared New Mexico to be part of the United States. Kearny had led the US Army in capturing Las Vegas, New Mexico, at the inception of the US-Mexico War. One hundred and twenty-five years later, the Berets purposely traced part of the path of Kearny's troops through New Mexico, held rallies to demand better living conditions and civil rights for Mexican Americans, and raised Mexico's flag at various plazas. After experiencing threats, harassment, and arrests of several marchers, Brown Berets leader David Sánchez reflected on the long-term consequences of Kearny's campaign: "It was never clearer to me that we were the descendants of the Mexican inhabitants who had lived under the United States occupation, descendants who continue to live as a subordinate population to a white society which continues to destroy our culture, our health, and our existence."[1]

Like other Chicano civil rights organizations, the Brown Berets contested memories of conquest during their 1971–72 Caravana de la Reconquista. As they traveled from California across various states to Texas, the Berets collected, interpreted, and promoted collective memories. They visited various sites with ties to the US-Mexico War, invoking collective war memories to challenge the nation's dominant history. In addition to raising Mexico's flag at various stops to commemorate Mexico's previous jurisdiction, the Berets erected monuments to nineteenth-century Mexican rebels to remind local communities of their ancestors' resistance to the US invasion. According to the Berets, the war did not introduce democracy and civilization to the US West but instead led to the dispossession of Native Americans and Mexican Americans. This alternative view also addressed the war's legacies by tracing Mexican Americans' second-class citizenship to the broken promises of the Treaty of Guadalupe Hidalgo. The group's journey generated publicity but also reminded the nation that the US Southwest was a Native American and Chicano homeland. The Berets' symbolic reconquest of the region brought up the tragic consequences of the US conquest, challenged the "conquered" mentality among some Mexican Americans, and asserted Chicanos' claim to the land and to US citizenship. These Chicano civil rights activists strategically "remembered" the nineteenth-century conquest to raise awareness of Mexican Americans' contemporary poverty and disenfranchisement in the twentieth century.

This chapter will examine the multiple ways that civil rights organizations and activists employed memories of conquest during the 1970s to achieve their goals for better land rights, education, farmworkers' rights, and cultural pride. Inspired by the United Farm Workers union, students and youth created organizations that adopted more confrontational stances than the more accommodationist strategies of their predecessors. The burgeoning civil rights movements among other people of color became an additional inspiration and cross-cultural influence for Mexican American activists, who participated in and criticized the white middle-class focus of the antiwar and women's rights movements. As part of the Chicano movement, these activists celebrated their culture, discovered their Indigenous roots, and forcefully claimed their civil rights. Like previous generations of activists, they recalled conquest memories in their efforts not only to oppose the Vietnam War, condemn police brutality, and decry political disenfranchisement but also to claim their rights as US citizens and remind the nation of the unfulfilled promises enshrined in the Treaty of Guadalupe Hidalgo.

Reies López Tijerina and La Alianza

The civil rights activist most responsible for popularizing the treaty was Reies López Tijerina, whose background informed his interests and goals during the Chicano movement. Born near Falls City, Texas (southeast of San Antonio), in 1926, Tijerina was the fifth child of a poor migrant couple. His family endured a racist agricultural environment in which Mexican laborers earned low wages under harsh working conditions. According to his family's memories, the Texas Rangers killed his great-grandfather in the presence of his grandfather. Subsequently, European American vigilantes nearly lynched his paternal grandfather, while his father suffered a debilitating injury when European Americans dragged him off his land in Laredo.[2] Both of his parents labored in the agricultural fields. By the family's memory, his mother possessed such great stamina that she worked through her pregnancies and gave birth to Tijerina in the cotton fields. Victims of wage theft, the family lost their entire seasonal earnings more than once and often needed to hunt to eat. His mother was a devout Catholic, but his father had converted to Protestantism due to fear of anti-Catholic violence in Texas. After his mother died when Tijerina was not yet a teenager, the family increasingly turned to migrant work. They relied on the labor of Tijerina and his brothers as they migrated to West Texas, Arizona, and the Midwest in search of a livelihood. Not surprisingly, Tijerina and his brothers suffered through numerous school interruptions as the family followed the harvests. Forced to drop out in third grade, he became an autodidact through his voracious reading in English and Spanish.[3]

Tijerina's religious convictions formed early in life. While working in Michigan's sugar-beet fields, he met a Baptist minister whom he admired. Fifteen years old at the time, he converted, became baptized, and began reading the Bible. Eventually, Tijerina attended an Assemblies of God seminary near San Antonio and became an itinerant minister on both sides of the US-Mexico border.[4] In 1955, Tijerina, along with some ten families, established a religious commune (the "only known Mexican American religious utopian experiment in North America") on 160 acres in the Arizona desert called the Valle de Paz.[5] Tijerina's religious convictions, his desire to separate himself from the world, and his goal to leave organized religion led him to establish this commune.[6]

Moreover, the instability in his family's life as migrant laborers (as well as in the lives of other commune members) undoubtedly motivated them to acquire some land for self-reliance. His first wife, Mary Escobar, remembered their time at the commune fondly because her family held a permanent home, though humble, and did not need to rely on charity.[7] The adults worked in nearby agricultural fields, and food was shared among the commune members.[8] However, life in the commune was very difficult in the desert. The families confronted problems with Arizona education officials who wanted their children to attend public schools, neighbors who resented the commune's privacy and role as a refuge for other poor people (Native Americans and African Americans), and vandals who often destroyed the residents' living quarters.[9] Adding to the commune's problems was a torrential rain that flooded their living quarters and swept away their meager possessions within months of their arrival. Tensions between the religious commune and local European American landowners in Arizona resulted in a criminal charge against Tijerina, which he escaped by fleeing to northern New Mexico. His arrival in northern New Mexico led to his deeper involvement in the land grant movement.[10]

Tijerina's convictions and travels throughout northern New Mexico led him to conduct research on the Treaty of Guadalupe Hidalgo as the basis for land rights claims. The land grant movement had continued for several decades in New Mexico and elsewhere in the Southwest before its popularity increased through Tijerina's involvement.[11] Hispano landowners had lost land after the war and at various times during the twentieth century. During the Great Depression, the loss of land accelerated in northern New Mexico as the market for beef and mutton decreased and supplementary work (mines and construction) vanished, which forced small landowners to sell their property. In response to their dispossession, villagers engaged in fence cutting, arson, and livestock killing that targeted large European American landowners.[12] To stem additional economic losses and claim their communal land rights, descendants of the Tierra Amarilla land grant in northern New Mexico established the Abiquiú Corporation in the 1930s.[13] Poor villagers throughout the US Southwest had grown resentful of their land losses to the federal government, developers, and wealthy European American landowners. In northern New Mexico, the 1950s witnessed increased militancy and activism among Hispano villagers who resented new restrictions by the US Forest Service targeting water use, wood cutting, and grazing on forest land—common practices among Hispano villagers.[14]

Into this explosive situation arrived Tijerina, who began traveling across northern New Mexico as a fugitive, working odd jobs, and relying on his wife to support their family. Through his travels, Tijerina became more knowledgeable about the land grant movement and keenly aware of the deep resentment among Hispano villagers.[15] He was sympathetic to these villagers due to his wife's roots in the region and to his own background as a descendant of Tejano small property holders who had lost land due to European American violence. After losing the religious commune's land in Arizona, Tijerina had traveled to Mexico to research land grants and the Treaty of Guadalupe Hidalgo. He pored over books on Spanish law and the history of land grants, concluding that the United States had repeatedly violated the treaty by failing to enforce citizenship rights for Mexican Americans, especially their property rights. He characterized the US-Mexico War as an "act of aggression," whose cessation converted Mexican Americans into a "conquered people."[16] In the early 1960s, as Tijerina began advocating on behalf of land grant claimants, he founded La Alianza Federal de las Mercedes (the Federal Land Grant Alliance) in Albuquerque, an organization modeled after the Abiquiú Corporation.[17]

La Alianza's goals hinged on the unfulfilled promises in the treaty. Like the Abiquiú Corporation, La Alianza's priority was the restitution of land grants, but it broadened Abiquiu's focus beyond New Mexico to include the entire Southwest.[18] In a bid to expand its membership, La Alianza added bilingual education, economic equality, and civil rights as long-term goals. Nevertheless, these broader objectives were based on the guarantees in the Treaty of Guadalupe Hidalgo, which La Alianza members believed the United States had not enforced. Tijerina and other members began traveling across New Mexico encouraging villagers to join their organization. At this point, Tijerina borrowed a strategy from the African American civil rights movement by holding rallies in support of broad reform instead of solely focusing on the land grant issue. This strategy broadened La Alianza's appeal beyond Mexican American rural residents to include urban dwellers as well as African Americans, Native Americans, and sympathetic European Americans. As part of an outreach effort, Tijerina began hosting a radio show in 1965 describing the abuses endured by Hispanos and highlighting La Alianza as a civil rights organization.[19] His message was well received among a poor population with collective memories of land loss. Tijerina had tapped into their resentment, creating a groundswell of support that brought new energy into the land grant movement. Tijerina's popularity harnessed collective memories of loss to motivate activism. As writer and poet Sabine Ulibarri explained, Tijerina "was speaking the magic words.... The struggle had been alive for all these generations and here was a man on a white horse, a man with tremendous charisma, who plugged into deep-felt passion."[20]

La Alianza's confrontational tactics in the late 1960s earned the organization national prominence, catapulting Tijerina into the limelight of the Chicano movement. Beginning in 1966, La Alianza initiated occupations of land grants (some on forest land and some on private property) that led to disputes with park rangers and law enforcement officials. Federal and county officials arrested La Alianza members and charged them with various infractions, including obstruction of park rangers and unlawful assembly. One of the most vocal critics was Tierra Amarilla County's attorney, Alfonso Sánchez, who jailed eight members for unlawful assembly after they attempted to occupy the San Joaquín del Río de Chama land grant. In response, La Alianza members attempted to free their fellow members and conduct a citizens' arrest on Sánchez by attacking Tierra Amarilla's courthouse on June 5, 1967. The raiders' immediate goals were thwarted when neither Sánchez nor the eight jailed comrades were found at the courthouse. They shot and injured two law enforcement officials and took two hostages before releasing them unharmed.

While the raid led to a series of court cases for members, it also made Tijerina widely known to Chicano movement activists who admired the bold, radical actions of the land grant movement.[21] His prominence within the Chicano movement and the US civil rights movement grew. Urban Chicano movement activists became aware of the land grant movement and began inviting Tijerina and La Alianza to a series of conferences. Martin Luther King Jr. would even invite Tijerina and La Alianza to participate in the Poor People's March in Washington, D.C., in 1968. According to Tijerina, "Dr. King invited me to participate in the Poor People's March, and I agreed on one condition, that the treaty of Guadalupe Hidalgo be used and mentioned."[22]

During this visit to Washington, Tijerina attempted a citizens' arrest of Supreme Court chief justice Earl Warren for "committing crimes against the people." In addition to these publicity-grabbing events, La Alianza members continued confronting forest officials and attempted to set fire to National Forest signs. Eventually, federal officials sentenced Tijerina to five years in prison, which he began serving in 1969.[23] Upon his release in 1971 (he served his two- and three-year sentences concurrently and reduced his prison time with good behavior), Tijerina adopted a new tactic by espousing "brotherly love" among all races and ethnicities and more peaceful relations with the police. Due to a more accommodationist approach, Tijerina's role as a leader of the land grant struggle decreased and led to several defections from La Alianza and eventually to the organization's demise.[24]

Tijerina helped popularized the Treaty of Guadalupe Hidalgo and use it to advocate for cultural and language rights. La Alianza's attention-seeking actions and Tijerina's forceful arguments based on the treaty led national newspapers to describe the treaty as the basis for Tijerina's perspective, which likely introduced the treaty to many readers for the first time.[25] In addition to the mainstream press, Chicano movement newspapers provided detailed explanations of the war and treaty, which helped increase awareness of the rights guaranteed among Chicanos.[26] Tijerina claimed that the treaty included protections for the language and cultural rights of Mexican Americans.[27] Based on this interpretation, Tijerina advocated for changes to New Mexico's public schools in 1969 by reapportioning school boards and requiring that all subjects be taught in English and Spanish.[28] While visiting other Southwestern states, he asserted that the treaty guaranteed "bilingual schooling" in public schools.[29] The federal trials for La Alianza members led journalists to admit inconvenient truths long known to Mexican Americans but rarely acknowledged by the news media and politicians. For example, opponents' assumption of land grant activists as outsiders and recent immigrants compelled one journalist to refute these charges: "The Spanish-Americans involved in the land-grant controversy are not recent immigrants from Mexico, but descendants of Spanish settlers who changed from Mexican to American citizenship after the Mexican War in 1848."[30] Such discussions of the treaty and its repercussions on citizenship were rare in the mainstream news media prior to Tijerina's rise and helped promote knowledge of the treaty among the US public and especially among Mexican Americans.

In addition to language and cultural rights, Tijerina cited the treaty as a justification to pursue civil rights and self-determination for Mexican Americans. Tijerina's advocacy and media-capturing events led activists and observers to analyze the treaty and its consequences. After La Alianza seized forest land and executed the Tierra Amarilla courthouse raid, several observers recognized these actions as not limited to land grant goals but rather part of a larger civil rights struggle. Tijerina admitted that the takeover of forest land was a publicity ploy to force the federal government and the public to reconsider La Alianza's land grant claims. The group did not expect to obtain all the land grants its members claimed but rather to use the land grant issue to advocate for broader civil rights. "If through this land fight," he maintained, "we protect our civil rights, that's our goal."[31] La Alianza's ultimate motives became clear during the federal trial for the group's takeover of forest campgrounds when Tijerina maintained that land grants were not a singular goal but rather "our civil rights, our culture, our language of which we have been deprived—those are our goals."[32]

His alliance with the Black Panthers, the Student Nonviolent Coordinating Committee (SNCC), and other African American organizations confirmed the greater objective of wider civil rights reforms. During the forest takeover trial, New Mexico's Republican governor understood that the land grant issue was part of a larger set of grievances, including water rights, poor education and roads, and grazing rights. After years of speaking with the state's rural residents, Governor David Cargo admitted that their resentments were justified and the land grant issue had "become a symbol of their problems."[33]

Like other Mexican American civil rights leaders, Tijerina publicly voiced his opposition to the Vietnam War. The struggles of Chicanos and the Vietnamese, he suggested, were linked by a desire of each group for self-determination.[34] In a speech at a La Alianza protest in Albuquerque, Tijerina cited a recent news article about the disproportionate deaths of Mexican Americans in Vietnam. "They are sending your children to die in Vietnam," he attested, "and won't give you a decent living here." He elaborated his anticolonial position: "They are not satisfied with having stolen all the land from us here, they send your boys to a bloody death so that they can take more land away from the poor people over there."[35]

Enriqueta Vasquez and *El Grito del Norte*

Opposition to the war in Vietnam was prominent in several articles and opinion columns of *El Grito del Norte*. Elizabeth "Betita" Martínez, a SNCC member originally from New York, and Beverly Axelrod, a lawyer who had advised Tijerina, founded this newspaper in Española, New Mexico, in 1968.[36] Among the newspaper's staff were several La Alianza members, local journalists, and writers who had moved to New Mexico from other states. The newspaper's articles and columns focused on local events, the Chicano movement throughout the US Southwest, progressive activism, and international political developments.[37] One of the most prominent staff writers was Enriqueta Vasquez, whose column ¡Despierten Hermanos! became a regular feature after appearing in its inaugural issue. In a November 1968 column, Vasquez voiced her strong opposition to the war in Vietnam, urging her readers to question the US government's reasons for waging the war. She deemed the conflict as a rich man's war fought by poor soldiers, resulting in excessive casualties who were disproportionately ethnic minorities. "When are we going to realize that we are raising kids," Vasquez implored, "to fight the wars for big power?" Like Tijerina, Vasquez condemned the war in Vietnam as another manifestation of US imperialism, questioning whether Chicanos would be willing to fight against "our brothers" in wars in Latin America as well.[38] Beyond opposition to the war, her columns probed a variety of civil rights issues, which she linked to the legacies of conquest and the US-Mexico War.

Vasquez repeatedly emphasized the importance of knowing Chicano history to foster a positive self-identity among Mexican Americans. She often urged readers to remind others, especially children, that Chicanos were among the "founders" of the Southwest. In one column, she questioned the public's close association of Kit Carson with Taos. Rather than celebrate Carson as an early settler, Vasquez asserted, Mexican Americans should remember him as "the biggest Indian and Mexican killer" and celebrate their Hispano ancestors as the original settlers.[39] Through this column and several others, she challenged dominant public history and urged her readers to recall their memories of conquest. Vasquez believed that public schools were failing Chicanos by not teaching the history of Mexican Americans. Her columns aimed to instill pride by reminding Mexican Americans that their ancestors had been among the founders of towns throughout the Southwest. Like other Chicano movement activists, Vasquez felt proud of her Indigenous roots and about Spanish colonists' presence in the Southwest before European Americans' arrival.[40] She believed that public schools were responsible for Chicanos' negative self-worth and lack of knowledge about their own culture.

In a column devoted to education, Vasquez excoriated public schools for teaching children a history with which they could not identify, omitting Mexicans' role in the Southwest, and whitewashing the enslavement of Africans while downplaying the contradictions of the "ideals" in the US Constitution. She blamed the schools' role in shaping Chicanos' perception of their citizenship: "Don't let the schools *un*-educate you into thinking that you are a second-class citizen."[41] According to Vasquez, parents should teach their children critical thinking by not passively accepting school lessons. She highlighted education but wanted Mexican American students to remain critically engaged. Vasquez recommended that parents encourage their children "to speak up and question and discuss issues in the classrooms. Only in thinking and speaking up can they learn from each other."[42] In addition to questioning schools' history textbooks, she urged Chicanos to write their own books, which would correct the official history and oppose distortions of Mexican Americans in textbooks.[43] Heeding her own advice, Vasquez and Martínez wrote a history textbook, *Viva la Raza!*, several years later.[44]

Recognition of the US-Mexico War as a war of conquest was central to Vasquez's views about Mexican Americans' place in the Southwest. She repeatedly brought up that Spain and Mexico had claimed the Southwest before the arrival of European Americans and that Mexicans had Indigenous origins. Yet Vasquez failed to note the roles of Spanish and Mexicans as settler-colonists and as agents of colonialism. This omission was not unusual at the time, as various Chicano movement activists conveniently "forgot" the memories of the Spanish Mexican conquest of Native Americans and the appropriation of Indigenous lands. Vasquez admitted that Mexico was too weak after its long independence war with Spain to defend its northern territories against US aggression.[45] Casting the US-Mexico War as an invasion of Mexican territory, she identified the causes as based on the nation's belief in "manifest destiny" and in fulfilling European Americans' "land rush." Her criticism of the war led Vasquez to conclude that "the US stole the Southwest from Mexico."[46] She informed readers of the long history of US intervention in Mexico by noting that the US Army had invaded Mexico without congressional approval at least eleven times. Her comments were prompted by the publication of a long list of US interventions worldwide in the *Congressional*

Record in June 1969. Although the Republican representative who introduced this list into the *Congressional Record* intended to prove that interventions were part of US tradition, critics were quick to use the list to denounce US imperialistic aggression. *El Grito del Norte* not only published the list but highlighted the entry for the US-Mexico War, which correctly indicated that "President Polk's occupation of disputed territory precipitated it [the war]."[47]

Vasquez, like other activists, linked the US-Mexico War with the Vietnam War by noting the similar roles of several European nations and the United States as colonizers. Describing these similarities, she wrote, "They [Vietnam], too, have had French, English, Spanish, and US troops on their soil."[48] Vasquez also reported on the increasing sentiments against the Vietnam War in the Chicano movement, such as the antiwar resolutions discussed at the second National Youth Conference in 1970 and the attendees' support for the Chicano Moratorium.[49] She acknowledged the long tradition of military service among Chicanos who sought to prove their patriotism, but she did not glorify this service. Instead, she urged Chicanos to grasp that the Vietnam War was unjustified and led to disproportionate deaths among Mexican American soldiers. She praised the increasing number of Chicano draft resisters, like Rosalío Muñoz, Manuel Gómez, and others from across the Southwest.[50] Vasquez artfully changed the traditional argument that used masculinity to justify military service: "Our *Soldado Razo* [common soldier] knows his Machismo belongs to his people, to be used for his people not against them, to be used right here in the heartland of mi Raza, in Aztlán."[51] This argument resonated with the popular rallying cry of "*la batalla está aquí*" and the goal of antiwar activists to challenge young Chicanos to exercise their masculinity by pushing for civil rights reforms at home.

Vasquez's discussion of the US-Mexico War and her advocacy of the Chicano movement led her to discuss the failures of the Treaty of Guadalupe Hidalgo. In a column on the cultural significance of Mexican Americans celebrating the 16th of September, Mexico's Independence Day, she posited that the treaty had merely justified the theft of over half of Mexico's territory and that, moreover, the United States had never honored the treaty.[52] She often referred to the Southwest as Aztlán (the Aztec term for their mythical homeland) and characterized the Southwest as "our land." For example, in a column on the importance of teaching values to children, Vasquez decried the content of history books that "are all slanted to glorify the Anglo and to make him look like a superior," but Mexican American children "don't even learn that they belong in this land."[53] Stressing the second-class citizenship status of Chicanos, she discussed its tragic consequences in education, employment, and health. The nation's denial of equal rights and citizenship to Mexican Americans led Vasquez to paraphrase Juan Seguín: "Here in Aztlán, we have been made to feel like strangers in our own homeland."[54]

Because she covered the Chicano movement and gatherings like the Chicano Youth Conference in Denver, Vasquez often invoked the term "Aztlán" in the manner in which Chicano movement activists deployed the term. When using "Aztlán," she often referred to respect for the land, the history of Mexican Americans in the Southwest, and the land grant struggle. Her discussions of the land grant movement, which was based in New Mexico, inevitably led her to highlight the role of Tijerina in popularizing the treaty and advocating on behalf of land grant heirs. She found Tijerina's advocacy compelling because it reinforced the collective memories passed on by her parents regarding Mexico's previous ownership of the Southwest.[55]

The Brown Berets' Genesis

Collective memories of conquest also figured prominently in the activism of the Brown Berets. The Berets began organizing in the Los Angeles area in the late 1960s and achieved prominence through their participation in a series of events, including the East Los Angeles Walkouts, the Chicano Moratorium, a march from Southern California to Sacramento, a monthslong "caravan" throughout the Southwest, and the occupation of Catalina Island. Scholars trace the origins of the Brown Berets to the Mexican American Youth Leadership Conference, a meeting for high school student leaders to explore values, identity, and the label "Mexican American" held in April 1966. The three-day conference included discussions of shared commonalities among high school student leaders with the goal of creating alliances to improve their schools and neighborhoods. As their conversations extended beyond the conference, a group of six attendees, including Brown Beret founder David Sánchez, created the Young Citizens for Community Action (YCCA) the next month. This group sought to reform the local educational system through political action and electoral participation. The YCCA's first successful effort was to support the electoral campaign of Julian Nava to Los Angeles's school board. Several founders eventually served on advisory boards for the Los Angeles mayor's office and California's governor.[56]

Various civil and religious organizations assisted the YCCA by providing training and encouragement to participate in neighborhood improvement and community participation projects. One of these groups, the Community Service Organization (CSO), introduced members to Richard Alatorre, who would become a state congressional aide and a state assembly member. Alatorre mentored the youth in community organizing and local politics and helped them meet farmworker leader Cesar Chavez. As they gained political knowledge and met more Mexican American political and civic leaders, the youths expressed pride in their ethnicity, which led them to change their organization's name to Young Chicanos for Community Action. With the support of Father John B. Luce of the Episcopal Church of the Epiphany, the YCCA opened a coffeehouse, La Piranya, in East Los Angeles. La Piranya became a meeting place for local youth and a platform for talks by regional and national civil rights leaders, such as Stokely Carmichael and Hubert "Rap" Brown of SNCC, Tijerina of New Mexico's La Alianza, and Chavez of the United Farm Workers (UFW) union. Such speakers increased the youths' awareness of issues affecting minority communities beyond East Los Angeles. The coffeehouse also hosted informational sessions to encourage local youth to attend college.

The YCCA evolved into the Brown Berets, a militant cultural nationalist organization that remained reformist despite its rhetoric. Unfortunately, the meetings at La Piranya also drew the attention of the Los Angeles County Sheriff's Department, whose officers began harassing the customers. In response, the YCCA organized several protests at the East Los Angeles Sheriff's Station. These protests marked a shift in leadership and strategy for the YCCA, as several members ended their participation to concentrate on their college studies, and the YCCA became more confrontational under the leadership of David Sánchez. In January 1968, Sánchez led the YCCA to change its name to the Brown Berets and to adopt khaki-colored military garb and distinctive brown berets.[57] Targeting high school students for recruitment, the group included mostly poor males with little formal education and some with gang ties. Although some members were well read, they criticized college students as being out of touch with their community. The Berets espoused a highly masculinist Chicano cultural nationalism, leveled militant rhetoric against police harassment, and advocated for better schools. Despite their militant rhetoric, the Berets remained a reformist organization that identified the US Constitution and the Treaty of Guadalupe Hidalgo as laws that the United States must enforce.[58]

Marcha de la Reconquista

Frustrations with police harassment and the challenges of organizing a movement in the city led Chicano activists to plan a march from Southern California to Sacramento, the state's capital. In response to the disproportionate Chicano casualties in the Vietnam War, Rosalío Muñoz, a recent UCLA graduate, and Sánchez established the Chicano Moratorium Committee to plan a series of protests against the war. The protests culminated in the National Chicano Moratorium on August 29, 1970, which drew some 20,000 to 30,000 participants to Laguna Park in East Los Angeles but was marred by police aggression, damaged buildings, and the deaths of several participants, including *Los Angeles Times* reporter Rubén Salazar.[59] Police harassment of Moratorium Committee members increased in the march's aftermath, which led the Moratorium Committee to protest against police brutality.[60]

Subsequently, the Chicano Moratorium Committee decided to launch La Marcha de la Reconquista (March of the Reconquest) in May 1971, to reach a larger audience and to gather information on broader problems confronting Chicano communities elsewhere in the state. Sánchez remembered fielding many telephone calls from activists throughout the nation and coordinating contact information prior to the march but also feeling frustrated at the slow pace of organizing while dealing with paperwork. Along with other activists, he wanted to learn firsthand about the problems facing Chicanos elsewhere. The activists also sought to escape the city, "with all its complexities and potential destructiveness." Particularly, they wanted to take a break from the constant police harassment, undercover surveillance, and frequent arrests of activists. The Berets had been forced to close their headquarters because they could not afford the rent, so the march was also a way to make their headquarters "mobile" and escape the police pressure simultaneously.[61]

The name given to the march recalled the mid-nineteenth-century conquest instigated by the US-Mexico War. The view of the US-Mexico War as a conflict that led to the conquest of Mexican Americans became widespread during the Chicano movement in the late 1960s. The United States, many Chicano activists affirmed, had not enforced the Treaty of Guadalupe Hidalgo with respect to Mexican Americans' citizenship rights. A few years before the Marcha de la Reconquista, Tijerina had risen to national prominence with the Tierra Amarilla courthouse raid in New Mexico in June 1967. Tijerina had started La Alianza, a land grants organization, in 1963, with the goal of helping Mexican American descendants of Spanish and Mexican land grantees reclaim their ancestors' property. In addition to deeming the US-Mexico War a war of conquest, Tijerina had declared that the country had not honored the treaty.[62] Through their public actions and interviews with the press, Tijerina's adherents had exposed many Chicano movement activists to the history of the war and the treaty. Some activists had learned that the US Southwest had been part of Mexico through public school education and sought more information in history books. According to Sánchez, he first

La Marcha de la Reconquista began in Calexico, California, in May 1971. As marchers passed through San Fernando, California, students and residents carried banners and Mexican flags. Pedro Arias, La Raza Photograph Collection (#1000), UCLA Chicano Studies Research Center.

learned that California had been part of Mexico in fifth grade, and this knowledge led him to question Mexican Americans' role and status in the US Southwest.[63] Other activists learned about the US-Mexico War in university courses and from textbooks. Central to these activists' understanding of the war was the belief that the United States had failed to enforce the citizenship rights of Mexican Americans as stipulated in the treaty. Some activists learned an alternative version of the war from Mexican immigrants, who viewed the conflict as it was presented in Mexico's history textbooks, which portrayed the unprovoked war as a blatant act of aggression to acquire Mexico's land. Among the marchers in La Marcha de le Reconquista, for example, were several young men who were recent Mexican immigrants.[64]

The use of "reconquest" in the name of the march also implied historical agency for a Chicano community long subordinated throughout the US Southwest. The term "reconquest" was consistent with the Brown Berets' belief that Mexican Americans' lands were "temporarily occupied."[65] Far from believing that Chicanos would retake control of the US Southwest, the Berets deployed the term to refer to an awareness of rights and history.[66] While they considered the US-Mexico War as a military conquest and Mexican Americans as a conquered people, many activists, including some of the Berets, asserted that they did not possess a conquered mentality. By focusing on a symbolic reconquest, these activists presented an alternative view of the war and claimed a right to self-determination consistent with their embrace of cultural nationalism. Several explained that a goal of La Marcha de la Reconquista was to "reconquer the rights and dignity of Chicanos" and to "reconquer [Chicanos'] rights to be treated like people, and not like second-class citizens."[67]

The three-month march to Sacramento allowed the activists to learn about issues in Chicano communities along their route but also exposed them to several organizational and logistical problems. Beginning at Calexico, a US-Mexico border town, the activists remained in high spirits as a large crowd from both sides of the border cheered them on. Twenty-five activists demonstrated their ethnic pride by carrying a Mexican flag and beginning their march on May 5, 1971, a symbolic day commemorating the Mexican army's defeat of French imperial troops at the Battle of Puebla in 1865. Among the marchers were Brown Berets, supporters of the Chicano Moratorium Committee, members of the United Farm Workers, and Chicanos from across the nation.[68]

Within a week, the marchers had covered sixty miles, approaching the Salton Sea, but had already confronted formidable obstacles, including threats posed by speeding vehicles along the road, hot desert weather, and occasional hostility from local residents.[69] Practical issues, such as securing food, water, and lodging for the marchers, as well as transportation for their supplies, became constant concerns. In the ensuing weeks, they would face roadblocks set up by the Immigration and Naturalization Service and by local police departments. The core marchers staged rallies at various towns along the route and met with residents to learn about the challenges facing local communities. Joining the core group of marchers were residents, students, and farmworkers, who often traveled with the group for a few days. Although these reinforcements helped buoy the spirit and determination of the core group of marchers, some volunteers also caused serious problems by encouraging drunkenness, drug use, and infighting among the participants.[70] Along the 800-mile march, the protesters promoted various issues in speeches at rallies and in interviews with news reporters. They sought to draw attention to police brutality, the farmworkers' struggle, Chicanos' claim to land, their ethnic pride, and their opposition to the policies of Ronald Reagan, the state's governor. When they arrived in Sacramento, the marchers held five days of rallies at various locations, including at Governor Reagan's house and on the capitol steps. By the march's last day, the protesters had added better education (and specifically more Chicano studies courses at universities), welfare rights, and prison reform to their agenda. Despite formidable obstacles (including exhaustion, threats, and internal divisions) along their route, the protesters completed the grueling march to Sacramento to present their demands to the state government and thus considered their primary goal accomplished.[71]

Caravana de la Reconquista

The success of La Marcha de la Reconquista led the activists to plan another march to other states, which they called La Caravana de la Reconquista (Caravan of the Reconquest). This caravan began in Southern California in fall 1971 and proceeded over the next year to Arizona, New Mexico, Colorado, and Texas, with a side trip to the Midwest. Like the California march, the yearlong Caravana de la Reconquista attracted various students, activists, and organizations, which helped increase the number of participants on weekends and in large cities. The Brown Berets believed that the movement was dwindling after the August 29, 1970, march and that the Chicano Moratorium Committee had lost influence. According to these activists, organizing a march throughout the US Southwest would continue the movement by promoting important issues for the Chicano community.[72] The Berets wanted to visit the region and meet activists in the Southwest, where they planned to launch organizing drives. La Marcha de la Reconquista had convinced the Berets of the utility of a mobile headquarters to avoid police harassment and surveillance, so despite the challenges, the group decided to extend the march across the Southwest. While various police departments and the FBI continued to harass the marchers during the Caravana, the police encountered obstacles because the Berets were always on the move. Nevertheless, an FBI infiltrator briefly joined the marchers, but he left after they confronted him.[73]

As they ventured outside California, the Berets confronted the larger logistical challenges of coordinating a long march. In response, they reached out to Beret chapters in states where they visited to provide food and water as well as additional marchers.[74] As the group traversed border states historically tied to Mexico, they capitalized on various opportunities to challenge public history about the US Southwest, learn about local issues, and promote their message of cultural nationalism.[75]

Contesting the History of US Westward Expansion

While traveling across the US Southwest, the group often spoke with local activists to learn about community issues. During their visit to Tucson,

The Brown Berets' newspaper, *La Causa*, reported on the progress of La Caravana de la Reconquista, alerting readers of the route and dates when the marchers would arrive in their communities. David Sánchez Papers, UCLA Chicano Studies Research Center.

Arizona, in November 1971, one of their local guides (Anna) explained community efforts to convert part of the city-run El Río Golf Course into a public park in Barrio El Río, a Chicano neighborhood.[76] The city had previously agreed to build a park after nine months of persistent demonstrations, but the park remained unnamed. The Chicano community wanted to name the park after Joaquín Murrieta, the nineteenth-century "social bandit" from California, so the Brown Berets decided to stage an unofficial christening ceremony for the park. They organized an "invasion," set up tents, took over a miniature children's castle in the middle of the park, and raised two flags (one for Mexico and one for the Berets) over the castle. The group then conducted a march through various Tucson neighborhoods to announce a rally on the following day to name the park. As they had done elsewhere along their march, the Berets created a small monument to commemorate the park's name, Parque Joaquín Murrieta. Prior to unveiling the monument, several speakers addressed the crowd, giving speeches about the significance of Murrieta, California's gold rush, and US westward expansion. After exalting the park's namesake as a great hero who "stole from the rich to give to the poor," one speaker claimed that Murrieta understood the severity of the destruction caused by the European American westward movement. The speaker closed by summarizing European Americans' persecution of Mexicans during the gold rush, outlining the environmental damage they unleashed, and affirming Murrieta's struggle for "our cultural survival."[77]

The visit to Tucson illustrated how the Brown Berets used collective memories to contest the official history of the US West and Chicanos. Beret leader Sánchez recalled that the toy castle in the middle of the park had intrigued the group and led them to organize the rally and unofficial christening. The castle was ten feet tall and built of sturdy concrete, with authentic-looking gun sights. Sánchez recalled the group's fascination with the castle: "The park struck us as having been designed for battle and the fact that it needed a name intrigued us."[78] The military aspects of the children's castle reminded the Berets that US westward expansion in the mid-nineteenth century was an armed conquest. As they had done elsewhere along the march, the group raised the Mexican flag as a reminder that Arizona had belonged to Mexico. While the Mexican flag served to prompt the collective memory of a pre-annexation period among some of Tucson's Mexican American residents, it also angered the local police and other residents without social or cultural ties to Mexico. Raising the Mexican flag also reminded residents that La Caravana de la Reconquista was meant to highlight the Chicano community's grievances, many of which began with the mid-nineteenth-century US conquest. While the

Berets surely knew that they could not physically reconquer the US Southwest, their caravan did spread their message of symbolically reconquering the region through Chicanos' self-determination and community control.

The Berets' symbolic reconquest of the region challenged the dominant narrative of US westward expansion and brought up the tragic consequences of the US conquest. For example, one of the rally speakers inverted the US claims to "pacifying the wild west" as a justification for expansion onto lands claimed by Mexico and Indigenous nations. "Today, this serves as a reminder," he asserted, "that the [W]est was not wild until the expansion of the United States boundaries."[79] By accusing the United States of making the West "wild," the speaker publicly contested a common narrative about the nation's westward expansion as being responsible for introducing progress. He also connected Murrieta with Mexican American resistance to US conquest. In this reinterpretation of Murrieta's role, the social bandit's efforts were equated with the larger Mexican community's goals of protecting their land and culture. For Chicano activists, it seemed fitting to name this park after a nineteenth-century Mexican American hero who had fought against US expansion. After all, the park, created through local community efforts, was located in a Mexican American neighborhood in the borderlands that once belonged to Mexico. Although the Berets' naming ceremony was unofficial and the monument was temporary, the ceremony was consequential in that it fulfilled the community's intent to pressure municipal officials, who acquiesced to naming the park after Murrieta.[80] The unofficial naming ceremony, the raising of the Mexican flag, and the speeches denouncing US westward expansion enabled the Berets to effectively contest official public history of the US West and propagate an alternative memory of the war's tragic consequences for Mexican Americans. Moreover, their unofficial naming ceremony undoubtedly motivated some attendees and onlookers to read more about the nineteenth-century conquest.

As La Caravana de la Reconquista passed through New Mexico and Texas, the Brown Berets often experienced the transmission, contestation, and strategic use of collective memories of conquest. While visiting Silver City, the Berets were forced to sleep in campsites after a local priest rescinded his initial offer to house them at the Catholic Youth Organization Center upon discovering that they were not students. The group split into three smaller units to camp and train in different parts of Silver City. The Berets named the first unit the Nepomucenos squad, after Juan Nepomuceno Cortina, the South Texas native who led a rebellion in 1859. They named the second squad Los Tigres, after what they believed was one of Pancho Villa's units during the Mexican Revolution in 1910.[81] The third group, composed of women, was named Las Juanitas, after a Mexican woman whom California vigilantes hanged during the gold rush.[82]

The appellations chosen for the three squads demonstrate how the Brown Berets harnessed collective memories of resistance to conquest for civil rights goals. The first two groups recall popular male rebels, one in Brownsville and the other in Mexico's northern states, who fought against injustice and for land reform, respectively. Sánchez identified Cortina as a "famous Mexican general ... who captured Brownsville, Texas[,] in 1859 to free twelve Chicano prisoners."[83] He implicitly linked Cortina's postconquest efforts to fight criminalization by freeing Mexican American prisoners in 1859 with the Berets' struggle against the increasing incarceration of Chicano youth in the 1970s. The reference to Villa's soldiers highlights the importance of the Mexican Revolution and Mexican history to the Chicano movement, exemplifying the transnational circulation of collective memories of struggle. The Berets' choice to name a squad after Villa's unit might have been an effort to link the contemporary land reform struggles in New Mexico with land issues of the Mexican Revolution. The Berets probably also knew of Villa's 1916 capture of Columbus, New Mexico, about 85 miles south of Silver City. Villa's daring capture of Columbus and ability to avoid General John J. Pershing's troops increased his popularity among ethnic Mexicans, who admired Villa's ingenuity and challenge to US forces. Finally, by choosing the name Las Juanitas for the all-female squad, the Berets recalled a Mexican American woman who was hanged in northern California after she defended herself from a white miner's attack in the aftermath of the US conquest.[84] The squads' names indicate the Berets' desire to commemorate Mexican and Mexican American heroes and offer a counterhistory to the official narrative of US westward expansion. The names served as reminders of previous struggles against injustice, promoting these collective memories among Mexican Americans unaware of this history. The monikers also symbolized the Berets' understanding of a transnational history of resistance.

During the Berets visit to Mesilla, New Mexico, they stressed the US failure to honor the Gadsden Treaty of 1853. The treaty, signed in Mesilla, completed the US purchase for the transfer of 29,670 square miles of land in present-day southern Arizona and southwestern New Mexico from Mexico to the United States. The Berets located the old town square at La Placita, where they believed the Gadsden Treaty had been signed.[85] There they met an elderly resident, Cruz Alvarez, who provided an alternative history of the Gadsden Purchase. According to Alvarez, Mexico initially refused to sell the land but acquiesced after the United States threatened to use military force.[86] The exchange with Alvarez disseminated a local resident's alternative collective conquest memory to the Berets. In turn, Sánchez wrote about this meeting and further propagated a collective memory that countered the official US narrative. Sánchez elaborated that the United States had failed to guarantee the civil rights of the Mexicans who remained in the territory covered by the Gadsden Purchase. Like the Treaty of Guadalupe Hidalgo, the Gadsden Treaty had guaranteed that Mexicans who remained in the ceded territories would receive full US citizenship rights. The United States, the Berets contended, had violated both treaties.

By using Mexican Americans' collective war memories to illustrate the US failure to enforce nineteenth-century treaties, the group linked these legacies of conquest to the contemporary denial of civil rights for Mexican Americans. Highlighting the "right to assemble" as one of the civil rights guaranteed to US citizens, Sánchez offered several recent examples of the nation's violation of this right, including the police killings of journalist Rubén Salazar and two others during the Chicano Moratorium, and the police shootings of demonstrators in January 1971.[87] To underscore their right to assemble and their goal of reminding local residents of Mexico's prior claim to the land, the Berets camped out in La Placita and raised the Mexican flag on the town square's sixty-foot flagpole. Sánchez reflected on the Berets' choice: "We felt proud that the Mexican flag was once again spreading its influence over these historical grounds." Their actions did not trigger an official response from the police, but some angry residents fired shots at the Berets. While no one was hurt, the violence demonstrated that some local residents did not appreciate reminders that the US conquest had displaced a nation to which many local residents still held cultural and social ties.[88]

The Berets' efforts to symbolically reconquer the US Southwest included challenging the narrative of a benign, unchallenged US conquest of New Mexico in the mid-nineteenth century. As the group entered Santa Fe, they learned that General Kearny had raised the US flag over the city's main plaza in 1846 and declared the territory under US control. In this example of the transmission of collective war memories, the Berets learned about Kearny's occupation of Santa Fe as they entered the city—most likely from local residents who gave the group car rides from Albuquerque to Santa Fe. Some of these residents warned the Berets of the local police's hostility. Undeterred, the group staged a march to the state capitol to demand "better living conditions" for Mexican Americans. The march led the police to arrest twenty-six Berets for supposedly violating a local ordinance prohibiting marches in the streets.[89] After their release, the Berets continued along part of the route

Kearny took as he led the forces of occupation into Mexico's far north in the mid-nineteenth century. Wherever they camped along the way, the Berets raised the Mexican flag, which angered some local residents. Such malice to their peaceful protest surely influenced Sánchez's interpretation of the links between Kearny's invasion and the post-annexation consequences.

From Santa Fe, the group continued to Las Vegas, New Mexico, where Kearny was believed to have begun his invasion of the US Southwest. In his memoir, Sánchez provided background on Kearny's nineteenth-century invasion of New Mexico and the refusal of New Mexico's governor, Manuel Armijo, to resist US aggression. Sánchez noted a few details about the unofficial resistance from Mexicans and Pueblo Indians (and their subsequent massacre). His decision to include these details (which were gleaned from historian Rodolfo Acuña's *Occupied America*) demonstrated the emerging influence of Chicano historiography in shaping Mexican Americans' perspectives. It also illustrates how the collective memories of New Mexicans combined with Acuña's counterhistory to shape an alternative narrative of the US conquest. After summarizing Acuña's interpretation, Sánchez contended that General Kearny's forces had seized the US Southwest by force, which introduced Mexican Americans' second-class citizenship. His conclusion about Kearny's significance clearly attributes Mexicans' initial subordination to the ramifications of US conquest and blames their continued subservience on the US failure to ensure full civil rights.

Visit to Texas—Memories of War and Cortina

The Brown Berets' visit to Texas provided several opportunities to comment on Tejanos' contemporary problems as well as to recall memories of conquest. As they approached El Paso, Sánchez identified the border city as the place "where the US Immigration Headquarters had the largest traffic of detention and deportation of Mexican undocumented persons."[90] The march to El Paso highlighted the group's demands to curb several unjust practices of the federal government.[91] The US Immigration Bureau, the Berets demanded, should stop detention camps, raids on homes of undocumented workers, illegal searches of Mexicans at border inspections, and secondary border examinations. According to the group, these practices led to the harassment of ethnic Mexicans and increased the possibilities of police brutality. The Berets believed in reforming the Immigration Bureau, so they called for the disarming and testing of immigration officers as well as the removal of racist officials. Like other Chicano movement activists, the majority of the Berets on La

Caravana were Mexican Americans, but a few were Mexican immigrants. The group strongly sympathized with undocumented workers, condemning the long-term sentences imposed for crossing the international border illegally. Like other civil rights groups, the Berets understood the immigration problems of mixed-status families, so they advocated for work permits for undocumented workers who were parents of US-born children.[92]

As they protested these contemporary immigration problems, the Berets recalled the atrocities committed by the Texas Rangers. Using the local common derogatory term *los Rinches* to label the Rangers, Sánchez acknowledged the law enforcement group's long history of harassing Mexicans in Texas. Such historical comparisons led him to mention that the Texas border region was the site of several battles of the US-Mexico War. The Berets probably learned about the collective war memories from local residents, linking the mid-nineteenth-century US conquest to contemporary problems. The Texas Rangers, Sánchez explained, continued to enforce the subjugation of Chicanos by instilling fear as a way to dissuade South Texas residents from joining the "social movement for civil and human rights."[93]

As the Berets traveled along the Rio Grande in South Texas, they discussed the US-Mexico War, which the United States had instigated near Brownsville. According to Sánchez, the Berets "learned that the southwest takeover started with the first Americans who began to lose their lives in violent clashes with Mexicans who resisted their invasion."[94] Sánchez's *Expedition through Aztlán* alludes to the transmission of collective memories from local residents to the Berets, who learned that the region's Mexicans had resisted the nineteenth-century US incursion. His choice of words underscores the Berets' view that the US troop movement beyond the Nueces River was an invasion of Mexico's territory and contradicted President James Polk's infamous excuse for starting the war. Sánchez wrote, "The Americans were claiming the loss of American blood on American soil, but Mexico was claiming the loss of American blood on Mexican territory since the southwest was part of the Republic of Mexico." Sánchez concluded by calling the Americans "exploiters" and accusing the United States of forcibly taking land from Mexico.

While the Berets held an overall understanding of the US-Mexico War before embarking on their Caravana, their interactions with Mexican American communities along their march allowed them to absorb local conquest memories. While such collective memories were passed from one generation to another by family members and neighbors, the Berets' visit to the region prompted local residents to spread such memories beyond their immediate community. Individual Berets surely shared this information on the war and the US conquest with their family members and friends, while others passed it to a wider audience through the Berets' newspaper, *La Causa*. Sánchez reached even more people by relaying this information through his book, published seven years after La Caravana. The Berets strategically deployed these newly acquired collective war memories to highlight the purpose of their trip—the symbolic reconquest of the US Southwest through reshaping community memories of conquest for contemporary political purposes.

The Berets' visit to Brownsville gave them an opportunity to discover more about Cortina from local residents and to honor his legacy. Many Brownsville residents, the group was surprised to learn, had not heard of Cortina, a nineteenth-century resident who had led a rebellion. This lack of knowledge of a famous Mexican American rebel illustrates the uneven spread of collective memories within a community.[95] It also confirms that the educational system had failed to inform them about an important episode of resistance to US westward expansion. The Berets were pleased to meet an older woman, Teresa Canales, who shared her family's collective memories of Cortina. Canales claimed to be the sister of J. T. Canales (a local lawyer and politician) and a descendant of Cortina's family. She explained how Mexicans who became US citizens after the war lost land because they lacked knowledge of US laws, failed to pay property taxes, and relied on European American lawyers and real estate agents who defrauded them. Canales also explained Cortina's 1859 shooting of a European American marshal to stop an incident of police brutality against a Mexican worker and his subsequent raid on Brownsville.

Canales underscored the US government's failure to enforce the Treaty of Guadalupe Hidalgo and protect Mexican Americans' property rights.[96] The Berets' criticism of the increasing incarceration of Chicano youth inspired their fascination with Cortina, who had freed ethnic Mexican prisoners from Brownsville's jail. Before leaving the city, the Berets held a rally to dedicate a monument to Cortina for his role in fighting "for justice for the Mexicans living in the US."[97] As they had done elsewhere on their march throughout the Southwest, the Berets sought not only to correct the historical narrative about Mexican Americans but also to create an alternative public history with monuments to Mexican American heroes. They wanted to "preserve the past in the present" by creating a physical form of their recently acquired collective memories.[98] While these monuments were temporary (local officials quickly tore them down), they served to commemorate the Mexican American historical figures that official US history forgot.

The Berets' construction of monuments to Mexican American historical figures encapsulated their response to the power struggle over public history, challenging local and state officials who had neglected the history of Mexican American communities. The Berets believed that historical monuments did not commemorate the history of Chicanos in a meaningful way. The dominant public history in the US Southwest "disremembered" Mexican Americans, or forgot them as actors and only remembered them as subjects of European American conquest. Thus, the Berets used their Caravana de la Reconquista to begin the process of "remembering, imagining, and narrating." To paraphrase writer Viet Thanh Nguyen, the Berets were not satisfied with being disremembered, so they adopted the view that "we who are others find that it is up to us to remember ourselves."[99]

By constructing monuments, the Berets were rendering in physical form the collective memories they had learned along their march throughout the US Southwest.[100] Their monument building was a kind of "strategic memory project" to commemorate not only local collective memories of Hispano ancestors but also memories of Mexican American resistance elsewhere in Aztlán, as with the California-based "social bandit" Murrieta, whom they memorialized in a park in Tucson, Arizona. The Berets' efforts to establish monuments and create new place names reinforced their goal to help Chicanos reclaim their place in the history of the US Southwest. On some level, the activists understood that their sense of place was shaped by their experiences, memories, and the wider culture (including historical markers and monuments).[101] They grasped the importance of passing on collective memories of conquest to future generations by creating monuments that reflected Chicanos' long presence in the Southwest.

Brown Berets' Takeover of Catalina Island

At the conclusion of their Caravana de la Reconquista, the Brown Berets made plans for another trek that would underscore the continuing significance of the Treaty of Guadalupe Hidalgo with an attention-grabbing occupation of Santa Catalina Island. Part of the Channel Islands off California's coast, Catalina Island is located some twenty-two miles southwest of Los Angeles. In 1972, the island was owned by the Santa Catalina Island Company and contained one major tourist town, Avalon. According to Sánchez, the Berets had been planning to occupy the island for two years prior to the arrival of twenty-six Brown Berets on the island in late August 1972. He and other Berets had visited Catalina Island several times to scout the environment and learn more about the island residents and security. As they camped at the Grand Canyon in Arizona, Sánchez briefed the Berets who had completed La Caravana de la Reconquista. At this meeting, Sánchez contended that Article 5 of the treaty did not include the Channel Islands within the new US boundaries.[102] As far back as the 1890s, several groups in Mexico had apparently made a similar claim that Mexico had not ceded the Channel Islands in the treaty. One version held that Mexico retained ownership of the islands, and President Benito Juárez had issued a ninety-nine-year lease to Catalina Island that was set to expire in 1970. While this claim was false, its circulation in Mexico and among Mexican Americans in the United States suggests, according to historian Richard Griswold del Castillo, "a need to keep alive the issue of the illegal seizure of community lands."[103] This interpretation alludes to the political uses of collective memories even when these recollections contain false elements. Recalling Mexico's jurisdiction over the Channel Islands became part of ethnic Mexicans' collective war memories, which spread across Mexico and within the United States through the transnational circulation of collective memories to inform the Berets, Avalon residents, and other Mexican Americans.[104]

In addition to transnational influences, the views and strategies of other civil rights activists affected the Berets. The plan to occupy Catalina Island, according to historian Ernesto Chávez, was likely inspired by the nineteen-month occupation of Alcatraz Island, located in the bay of San Francisco, by the American Indian Movement (AIM) in 1969–71. The AIM action was motivated by a reinterpretation of the Treaty of Fort Laramie (1868) that allowed for Indigenous people to reclaim abandoned federal land, which AIM activists asserted, applied to Alcatraz Island after the closing of the penitentiary there in March 1963.[105] Like AIM, the Berets also reinterpreted a long-standing US treaty with a sovereign nation to justify their occupation.

The Berets' peaceful occupation of Catalina Island lasted twenty-four days and garnered widespread attention. Twenty-six Berets traveled to the island by ferry and airplane in late August and set up a camp, christened Campo Tecolote (Owl Camp), on a hill overlooking Avalon, where they raised the Mexican flag. This action as well as the Berets' military uniforms (adorned with Mexico's flag) initially led tourists and local residents to believe that Mexico's military had invaded the island. The Berets met with local officials and the media to explain their purpose and reassure the public that they carried no weapons and were participating in a peaceful demonstration. The goal, Sánchez explained, was to obtain publicity for *la causa* and discuss problems confronting Mexican Americans.[106] During their stay, the activists issued press releases, held regular marches, and spoke with local residents. Initially, the Berets received food and drinks from the locals, including the vice president of

The Brown Berets during their takeover of Catalina Island. Maria Marquez Sanchez, La Raza Photograph Collection (#1000), UCLA Chicano Studies Research Center.

the Santa Catalina Island Company, a restaurant owner, and Chicano residents of Avalon.[107] Over time, however, some local European American residents grew weary of the activists' presence, while the management of the Santa Catalina Island Company allegedly pressured Avalon's Chicano community to stop their assistance. The occupation ended on September 22, after a Los Angeles municipal judge threatened the Berets with arrest for violating Avalon's camping ordinance. The activists broke down their camp and left peacefully without any charges. Their occupation of Catalina Island, according to Ernesto Chávez, was the group's last of several "attention-grabbing exploits," as they thereafter fell into disarray due to internal disputes, law enforcement harassment, and infiltration. The Berets disbanded gradually over the next year.[108]

The excursion to Catalina Island promoted the group's interpretation of the treaty and alternative collective memories of the US-Mexico War. In their media interviews and press releases, the Berets emphasized that their peaceful occupation was inspired by their belief that the treaty did not grant the United States jurisdiction over the nine Channel Islands. The group also denounced the US war against Mexico in the mid-nineteenth century as an illegal takeover that resulted in the forcible incorporation of ethnic Mexicans.[109] Their interpretation of the war and the treaty challenged the dominant view of the "winning" of the US West by condemning the US acquisition of territory as conquest and antithetical to democracy. While their occupation lasted less than a month, it bore far-reaching consequences as it helped publicize *la causa* and the Berets' collective war memories—namely their reinterpretation of the treaty and the enduring consequences of the US-Mexico War. News articles throughout the nation conveyed the Berets' reinterpretation of the treaty and their desire to address social problems (some of which began with the US-Mexico War) confronting the Chicano community.[110] The activists consistently promoted the belief that the US-Mexico War was a forceful conquest, the US Southwest was "stolen land," and the United States was an "occupying government." They also questioned the legitimacy of the Treaty of Guadalupe Hidalgo by pointing out that Mexico signed it under occupation.[111] While the group clarified that they did not represent the Mexican government, they continued to fly Mexico's flag, refer to Mexican ownership of the US Southwest, and commemorate Mexican Independence Day.[112]

The Berets' public actions highlighted the protracted consequences of the US-Mexico War as the cause of the continued subordination of Chicanos. In their organization's newsletter, press releases, and various writings, they contended that the US-Mexico War led directly to land theft and the denial of US citizenship despite the treaty's promises. According to Sánchez, the United States enforced Mexican Americans' subordination through Americanization programs that promoted forced acculturation through poor public education, leading to high dropout rates.[113] Their peaceful occupation of Catalina Island stressed the poor living conditions of Chicanos, the scourge of drugs afflicting the community, and the gang-related deaths of its youth.[114] In *La Causa*, the group decried the high incarceration rates of Mexican American youth and the police violence targeting their community.[115] Through the occupation of Catalina Island, the Berets promoted their ethnic identity by deeming Chicanos as "people of Mexican and Indian descent who need a place to live and to be free," which also emphasized their desire for self-determination.[116] Again, their rhetoric and tactics echoed AIM's, which revealed the interaction among distinct civil rights groups.

The Berets' Marcha de la Reconquista, Caravana de la Reconquista, and occupation of Catalina Island demonstrated the transmission, political use, and promotion of collective war memories. The group learned about collective war memories and interpretations of history from residents they encountered on their march throughout the Southwest, groups based in Mexico, and other activists. These collective memories led the Berets to reinterpret the Treaty of Guadalupe Hidalgo and challenge its legitimacy. By linking the long-term consequences of the US-Mexico War to the continued subordination of Mexican Americans, the activists strategically used war memories to advance their political agenda. They traced the origins of Chicanos' subordination to the aftermath of the US-Mexico War, documented problems facing the Chicano community, and challenged official public memories of US westward expansion. By contesting public memories and histories that excluded Mexican Americans, the Berets also advocated for the importance of Chicano studies. To challenge official memories, the activists created alternative monuments to Mexican Americans who had fought on Mexico's behalf during the US-Mexico War or who had defended Mexicans from European American attacks in the war's aftermath. They also raised the Mexican flag at war landmarks as a reminder of Mexico's former claim to the land. Through their marches, monuments, and occupation, the Berets were employing "a fusion of narrative and performance to give added meaning to the past."[117] Ultimately, these and other Chicano activists combined collective memories of conquest with myths to construct a view of the US Southwest as a Chicano homeland and promote entitlement among Mexican Americans who had been politically and socially marginalized.

As memory scholars remind us, the act of remembering is accompanied by the act of forgetting. While the official US history willfully remembered a "bloodless" conquest of the US Southwest, it deliberately forgot Mexican Americans' active resistance during and after the war. The dedication of monuments to Mexican American rebels like Murrieta and Cortina demonstrate the Brown Berets' attempt to forge a counternarrative to the nation's public history and propagate collective memories of these rebels as champions of civil rights. This activism illustrated the Berets' strategic use of conquest memories and the links between social and political uses of memory.[118] Each time activists recalled the war in their pamphlets, speeches, or media interviews, they reminded the country of the prolonged consequences of the US-Mexico War, the unfulfilled promises of the Treaty of Guadalupe Hidalgo, and the justifications for civil rights activism. Moreover, by recalling the war and the treaty's promises in their publications, campaigns, and community interactions, activists reinforced and shaped their communities' memories, thus transmitting conquest memories across several generations.

Parallels between the US-Mexico War and the Vietnam War

The Chicano movement's call for civil rights reform and the increasing Mexican American casualties in Vietnam led to the emergence of a Chicano antiwar movement. Several established Mexican American civil rights organizations, such as LULAC, the American GI Forum, and the Mexican American Political Association (MAPA), initially supported US involvement in Vietnam.[119] In their call for reforms, these organizations continued to extol the military service of Mexican Americans as a sign of patriotism as well as to tout the community's relative absence in antiwar protests. MAPA followed this tactic when it issued a resolution complaining about civil rights reforms focused on African Americans while the federal government ignored Mexican Americans' civil rights. The resolution, signed by the California branches of the American GI Forum, LULAC, and the CSO, recast Mexican Americans as defenders of the country since the early twentieth century. As historian Lorena Oropeza indicates, in rewriting borderland history, the resolution "forgot" the military conquest of the US-Mexico War by instead describing the "incorporation" (a more benign term) of Mexico's northern territories into the United States.[120] This statement was another example of a civil rights group strategically using collective memories of the war (and conveniently forgetting the US forced incorporation and dispossession of Mexicans) to advance their political agenda. It also illustrates historian Peter Novick's argument that "when a memory doesn't reflect our self-understanding (and how we want others to see us), we marginalize it."[121]

As the decade wore on and the war's resolution remained elusive, despite the government's substantial increases in money and troops, several of these organizations began questioning the impact of the draft on Mexican Americans. According to Oropeza, US involvement in the Vietnam War helped transform some Mexican Americans' strategy from the politics of supplication to the politics of confrontation.[122] As the country increased its troop commitments in Vietnam, scholars noticed the disproportionate casualty rates of people of color, specifically African Americans and Mexican Americans. Both groups had pursued a long history of military service as a quest to prove their patriotism, yet the nation continued to deny African Americans and Mexican Americans full citizenship in the 1960s. For Chicanos, this contradiction came into stark relief when Ralph Guzman, a UCLA political scientist, discovered that Mexican Americans made up 19.4 percent of the casualties in Vietnam but only 13.8 percent of the population of the US Southwest.[123] Placing his findings in unequivocal terms, Guzman concluded, "American servicemen of Mexican descent have a higher death rate in Vietnam than all other G.I.s."[124] Exposing the hypocrisy of the federal government in denying civil rights but expecting ethnic minorities to serve in the military, veteran Charley Trujillo minced no words: "They wanted us to come out here and work in the cotton fields and call us Mexicans," he maintained, "but as soon as there's a war, all of a sudden, we're American."[125]

The disproportionate casualties among Chicano soldiers led several civil rights organizations and activists to question the composition of the draft boards, the military enlistments of Mexican Americans, and the war itself. By 1967, a few prominent scholars, like George I. Sánchez, and politicians, such as Edward Roybal of Los Angeles, had become vocal critics of the nation's involvement in Vietnam.[126] Civil rights groups became more outspoken as the decade wore on. Chicano movement organizations, labor unions, and student groups were more willing to oppose the war than were the older Mexican American civil rights groups. In late 1967, activists at the La Raza Unida conference in El Paso criticized the federal government's priorities to spend millions on war in Vietnam while cutting domestic programs that would benefit Mexican Americans. Conference attendees issued a proclamation outlining their grievances, with reference to the treaty: "We demand the strong enforcement of all sections of the treaty of Guadalupe Hidalgo, particularly the sections dealing with land grants and bilingual guarantees."[127] The Crusade for Justice, based in Denver and led by Rodolfo "Corky" Gonzales, came out against the war in August 1966.[128] In an increasingly common critique about the war, Gonzales asserted that Chicanos should prove their masculinity by helping their communities at home rather than fighting in Vietnam.[129] The war's unpopularity also pushed mainstream Mexican American groups to voice their concerns. The American GI Forum began to ask government officials to include Mexican Americans on draft boards, which were overwhelmingly composed of middle-class European American men, because the boards were actively drafting working-class men of color while supplying deferments to middle-class European American men.[130]

The tragic injustice of US involvement in the Vietnam War led some young men, including Chicanos, to resist the draft and, in some cases, to publicly oppose their induction orders. When young men received their induction notices, they faced three basic choices: they could follow their orders by joining the army, go underground and possibly escape to another country, or publicly oppose their induction. Those youth who made the latter choice faced ostracism, persecution, government surveillance, and family turmoil. Among the brave young men who publicly refused induction were several

Latinos. For Mexican Americans and Puerto Ricans, the choice to resist the draft was harder to make than for young white men due to Latinos' status within US society, their desire to prove their patriotism, pressures to affirm their masculinity, and their duty to their families.

Most working-class Latinos did not hold the same opportunities to avoid the draft as did middle-class white men, who could apply for college deferments or obtain conscientious objector status. At the time, Latinos were not enrolled in college in large numbers, and few gained the knowledge or access to the resources to apply as conscientious objectors.[131] Moreover, some draft boards discouraged Chicanos from attending college by falsely claiming that student deferments were not available.[132] As literary critic George Mariscal explains, the invitation to refuse induction "offered to minority draftees by the relatively privileged student leaders of the campus anti-war movement wholly ignored the intense pressures and contradictions felt by members of working-class communities of color."[133]

Nevertheless, some Latino youth began resisting the draft. Ernesto Vigil became the first Chicano to publicly refuse induction into the armed forces.[134] From Denver, where he eventually joined the Crusade for Justice civil rights group, Vigil explained that he refused to join the army because he did not want to fight his "brown brothers in Vietnam."[135] Vigil was eventually joined by other Latinos, including Rosalío Muñoz (former UCLA student body president), Fred Aviles (a Puerto Rican who favored island independence), David Corona (son of labor activist Bert Corona), and Manuel Gómez (CSU Hayward student and poet).[136] In resisting the draft, a few young men began comparing the Vietnam War to the US-Mexico War as unjust military conflicts and decrying the failures of the Treaty of Guadalupe Hidalgo to ensure equal rights for Chicanos. Along with other antiwar activists, the draft resisters strategically invoked the collective memories of the US-Mexico War to oppose a contemporary war begun under similar false pretexts and for different but equally disingenuous goals.

In explaining their draft resistance, several Chicanos referred not only to the Vietnam War as unjust but also to the injustice in the nation's failure to ensure full rights for Mexican Americans. One of the most celebrated Chicano draft resisters was Rosalío Muñoz, who declared his "independence from the Selective Service System" on September 16, 1969, Mexican Independence Day and his induction date, upon outlining the reasons for his draft resistance. Modeled after Emile Zola's "J'accuse," Muñoz addressed a crowd of supporters outside downtown Los Angeles's induction center: "I accuse the draft, the entire social, political, and economic system of the United

States of America of creating a funnel which shoots Mexican youth into Viet Nam to be killed and to kill innocent men, women, and children."[137] He accused the United States of stripping Chicanos of their language and culture, providing poor education, offering few choices outside of military service, and persecuting Mexican Americans with police brutality. While Muñoz did not mention the US-Mexico War, he did describe many problems that civil rights activists had identified as resulting from the mid-nineteenth-century conquest and US failure to uphold the Treaty of Guadalupe Hidalgo. Other draft resisters similarly faulted the United States for its treatment of Chicanos. In January 1968, Vigil also described his reasons for refusing induction in a letter to the Selective Service mailed with his draft notice: "I will not fight the war of a power and system that I feel is unjust, hypocritical, deceitful, inadequate, and detrimental to the happiness and best interests of its own people and the people of the other nations of the world."[138]

Although his charges for refusing induction were dropped, Vigil was subsequently indicted for grabbing a marshal in a scuffle on the day of his rescheduled induction and sentenced to three years of federal probation. During his trial for assault, Vigil and his lawyers entered motions "based on the Treaty of Guadalupe Hidalgo, the treaty that finalized the invasion of Mexico by the United States, a Vietnam-style conflict of the preceding century."[139] Vigil considered the probation a victory, partly because his defense motions comparing the US-Mexico War to the Vietnam War and outlining the failures of the treaty were presented in court. The trial highlighted the illegality of the Vietnam War and allowed the public to hear arguments about the US failure to enforce the treaty. Corky Gonzales had declared his opposition to the Vietnam War several years prior, so he was an enthusiastic supporter and publicist of Vigil's draft resistance in 1968.[140] Vigil effectively deployed collective memories of the US-Mexico War to protest a contemporary war and propagated conquest memories to future generations.

While young men attracted much of the media's attention as draft resisters, Chicanas played a significant role in voicing their opposition to the war and in encouraging resistance to forced conscription. Motivated by the induction of their male relatives and the student antiwar movement, several Chicanas became draft counselors to inform their male counterparts about deferments and ways to resist conscription. One of the early draft opponents was Francisca Flores, the editor of *Carta Editorial*, who criticized the US role in Vietnam as supporting "a series of dictatorships" rather than a real democratic government. She urged Chicanos to support Mexican American soldiers by pressuring the United States to end the war and bring the soldiers home.[141]

Similarly, Enriqueta Vasquez published an antiwar column condemning the war as an unjust conflict fought by poor people of color on behalf of the nation's wealthy. Several Chicanas also encouraged Chicanos to resist conscription by handing out flyers at induction centers.[142]

In the Los Angeles area, Ramona Tovar, Irene Tovar, and Katarina Davila del Valle engaged in antiwar activism by serving as draft counselors and later joining the Chicano Moratorium Committee. Growing up hearing of the domestic mistreatment of Mexican American GIs upon their return home and convinced that the Vietnam conflict was a civil war, the Tovar sisters became draft counselors because they strongly opposed Chicanos dying in a foreign war unnecessarily while denied equal rights domestically.[143] By emphasizing Chicanos' unequal treatment and continued denial of civil rights, these assertions indirectly raised the Treaty of Guadalupe Hidalgo, which was widely discussed in Chicano movement newspapers and activities as guaranteeing full citizenship to Mexican Americans. Lea Ybarra and Nina Genera from the San Francisco Bay Area became involved in anti-draft efforts as students at UC Berkeley. Both held personal and ideological reasons for opposing the war. Ybarra's brother and eighteen cousins were serving in Vietnam, while Genera's younger brother had been drafted despite their family's attempt to secure deferment due to their mother's terminal illness.[144] Ybarra and Genera founded Chicano Draft Help, "one of the longest running counseling centers" advocating against the draft, and later coauthored *La batalla esta aquí*, a bilingual pamphlet that described the US involvement in Vietnam, military service among Mexican Americans, and, more importantly, legal avenues for obtaining deferments.[145] Influenced by the antiwar activism at UC Berkeley, Ybarra and Genera had developed strong sentiments against the war and were concerned that Chicanos were not aware of deferments.

Chicanas leveled several criticisms against the war that directly and indirectly invoked the US-Mexico War and the Treaty of Guadalupe Hidalgo. In *La batalla esta aquí*, Ybarra and Genera stressed the war's devastation on the Vietnamese community, the high Mexican American casualty rate, and the increasing anti-draft sentiment among Chicanos. They also drew parallels between the historical experience of the Vietnamese and Chicanos. Both groups were "oppressed by the same imperialist system" and had attempted to defend their communities against US foreign intervention. The media portrayed the North Vietnamese as "the enemy" simply for seeking their "own form of government," while "Chicanos in the US are equally portrayed when we make it known that we will attain our equal rights and justice through self-determination in all aspects of our life."[146] Moreover, the United States

Cover of *La batalla esta aquí* by Lea Ybarra and Nina Genera, a bilingual pamphlet containing arguments against the war in Vietnam and advice on military deferments.

promoted distorted depictions of both groups when it charged the North Vietnamese with invading their own country, while Chicanos, the writers contended, had long been "considered foreigners in our own country—the land that originally belonged to our own forefathers."¹⁴⁷ Like fellow activists who described the United States as the real invaders, Ybarra and Genera echoed Seguín's famous words about the US labeling Mexican Americans as foreigners in their native land. Activist María Varela expressed a similar sentiment in a stinging editorial accusing the United States of being the real "outside agitator" in Vietnam, the Southwest, and Latin America: "If the government is so concerned about 'outside agitators,' maybe they should pass a law against the [A]nglos who came into the Southwest and stole our land."[148] In addition to linking the struggles for self-determination of Chicanos and Vietnamese, this denunciation characterized the US-Mexico War as a war of conquest that resulted in land loss for Mexican Americans, implying that the Vietnam War might lead to similar consequences.[149]

According to these Chicana activists, the most significant battle for young Chicanos was promoting civil rights in the United States, not fighting an imperialist war in Vietnam. Antiwar activists reminded potential draftees of the contradiction between soldiers fighting for democracy abroad while the United States denied them full civil rights at home. Some draft counselors linked Chicanos struggle for civil rights with the poverty and lack of opportunities that forced men to enter the military.[150] The slogan "*La batalla está aquí*" became a popular rallying cry for antiwar protests because activists readily made the case that war expenditures were taking money away from domestic programs designed to help the poor and people of color. By educating Chicano draftees on legal ways to seek deferments, Chicana draft counselors sought to educate them about their rights. Many considered Mexican Americans' lack of knowledge about deferments as symptomatic of their inability to exercise full citizenship, which subtly referred to the rights guaranteed by the Treaty of Guadalupe Hidalgo. A corollary focused on dispelling the notion that military service was needed to prove Chicanos' masculinity or rights to citizenship. Several Chicana draft counselors sought to convince Chicanos to obtain deferments and express their masculinity not through military service but by defending their community.[151] Finally, some Chicana antiwar activists believed that US citizens held a right to criticize their nation's imperialist adventures, and that Chicanos must question their community's blind patriotism to truly exercise their citizenship.[152] Beyond their criticism of the war, Chicana draft counselors offered practical advice for young men facing the draft. In *La batalla esta aquí*, Ybarra and Genera provided detailed bilingual instructions on seeking deferments, the consequences of refusing induction, and suggestions on obtaining legal advice.[153]

Open Wound in the Souls of My People

One of the most eloquent Chicano draft resisters was Manuel Gómez. He grew up in the conservative environment of Orange County, California, as one of eight children of migrant parents. His parents had attended segregated schools but dropped out in elementary school. As a child in Colorado, Gómez had picked sugar beets and developed a strong compassion for farmworkers. He obtained his love of language by listening to his mother and her friends as they worked in the fields. An excellent student in high school, he became student body president, turned down a scholarship to Harvard University, and chose to attend CSU Hayward to remain closer to his parents.[154] Gómez remembered the politically progressive Bay Area as an "extraordinary amalgam of political ideologies, histories, protests, [and] activities that were going on at all levels of a cultural resistance in a sense, including music, drama, poetry."[155] In this new environment, he became intrigued by the politics of the student, antiwar, and Chicano movements. He remembered learning about the historical origins of the Vietnam War first from antiwar pamphlets and later from his own research. As a history major, Gómez also began learning about the US-Mexico War and was captivated by the parallels between President Polk's false claim that "American blood had been shed on American soil" and the Gulf of Tonkin Resolution's claim that the North Vietnamese had conducted unprovoked attacks against US ships.[156] His comparison led him to research both wars, concluding that "the Chicano plight was not unique but part of a bigger, systematic oppression by a brutal empire."[157]

Gómez also drew parallels between the disproportionate Chicano casualties in Vietnam and the Chicano deaths domestically due to police brutality. Influenced by antiwar activism, Gómez became a conscientious objector and a Quaker-trained counselor for youth opposed to the war.[158] Eventually, Santa Ana's draft board revoked his classification without any explanation and even sent him a draft call. In response, Gómez wrote an eloquent letter refusing induction and brought the letter to the Oakland induction station on December 8, 1969. After refusing his induction orders, he distributed the letter to fellow draftees, while his friends circulated the letter to the crowd gathered outside. Gómez recalled his decision to write this letter: at the time, he thought that officials would send him directly to jail, but he was released after a lengthy interrogation. Various newspapers reprinted his letter and promoted its message.[159]

In Gómez's letter, he cited the memory of the US-Mexico War and the broken promises of the Treaty of Guadalupe Hidalgo as motivation. While some political commentators and politicians had linked the Vietnam War to the US-Mexico War, Gómez made the comparison explicit. His vivid language gave the words poignancy for others facing the draft. The letter harshly denounces the nation's betrayal of its ideals and broken treaty promises. It illuminates both the inner turmoil within draftees and the anger of a young

Chicano who had discovered, through his own research, the inequality and lies upon which the US empire was built.[160] After declaring that Mexicans were "among the first victims" of the US empire, he wrote: "The memory of the Mexican-American War is still an open wound in the souls of my people."[161] By identifying Mexicans as the victims of the US empire, he directly linked the US-Mexico War to the Vietnam War. Although the US-Mexico War had ended over a century earlier, Gómez maintained that Mexican Americans continued to remember the war and its long-term consequences.

By referring to Mexican Americans' collective memory as an "open wound," Gómez acknowledged that time had not healed the disruption caused by the war, and its memory had long-term psychological ramifications. Recalling his poetic letter years later, Gómez explained his use of memory: "We had so much of our memory [that] had been erased or blurred, or distorted through the educational system."[162] He also identified the Treaty of Guadalupe Hidalgo as a "lie," similar to treaties signed by "our Indian brothers." Gómez not only cited the treaty's failed promises but also likened it to others signed by Native Americans and broken by the federal government. He believed these latter treaties had "been whitewashed and violated at will."[163] Calling Native Americans "brothers" alluded not only to Mexican Americans' claims to Indigenous ancestry but also to a shared experience as victims of the US empire. Gómez elaborated that the "war did not end" but rather continued in the "minds and hearts of the people of the Southwest." Here he was referring to the emotional and psychic toll of the continuing "legacies of conquest" for Mexican Americans and Native Americans. Stressing the impact of conquest as "strife and bloodshed," he blamed US society, with its "Texas Rangers and Green Berets" who "never allowed our people to live in peace."[164] These comments compare the consequences of a domestic colonial enforcement by Texas Rangers to the international colonial project enforced by the Green Berets in Vietnam. As a result, Gómez contended, the land was soaked in blood from the continuing repercussions of conquest. He ended the paragraph by calling "American Freedom" a lie for which too many of his "brothers" have died on both domestic and international battlefields.[165]

Gómez then expanded on the continued costs of the legacies of the US conquest and further compared the US war against Vietnam with its war against Mexico more than a century earlier. He accused US society of inflicting "racist tyranny and brutal oppression" on Mexican Americans as a result of the conquest. The ongoing legacies of conquest, he inveighed, were contemporary issues facing his community. He charged the US educational system with butchering minds, poisoning souls, prohibiting the speaking of the Spanish language, castrating "our culture," and "making us strangers in our own lands." This criticism reflected antiwar activists' belief in US secondary schools indoctrinating students with blind patriotism, and schoolteachers' and administrators' habit of devaluing Mexican culture, which resulted in students with conflicted ethnic and national identities. Gómez's use of "strangers in our own lands" echoed Seguín's famous phrase of feeling like a "foreigner in my own land" after the European American invasion of Texas. Like Seguín, Gómez referred to the sense of isolation among Mexican Americans. Gómez's criticisms of schools were meant to draw attention to the detrimental aspects of the US educational system's erasure of Chicano history.[166]

Years later, Gómez justified his choice of words by recalling that some Chicanos entered primary school fluent in Spanish and graduated from high school speaking little or no Spanish and with scant knowledge that the US Southwest had been part of Mexico.[167] He reminded the US public that Mexican agricultural workers had fed the nation and continued to do backbreaking work. Gómez also criticized the country's laws, which exacerbated injustice and increased the incarceration of Mexican Americans. Again referring to the US-Mexico War, he denounced the United States as an occupying power but refused to equate Mexican Americans with a conquered people. Instead, in a reference to the military draft, he asserted his agency by claiming freedom to choose his battles and declaring his preference to fight domestically rather than abroad. Gómez also accused the United States of fueling environmental degradation in the Southwest and converting lands previously held in common into private property. As historian Lorena Oropeza notes, this criticism reflected the counterculture's environmentalism and the Chicano movement's emphasis on land as significant for cultural retention and community control.[168] His letter blames the nation's leaders for basking in luxury while sending poor citizens to fight a war in which helpless and innocent people on both sides suffered. He also claimed a brotherhood with Vietnamese people who were not enemies but rather "brothers" struggling against a common enemy—the United States.[169]

This letter illustrates the relationships among memories within several communities. Gómez absorbed memories of the war from various groups to which he belonged, including academia, the antiwar movement, and Chicano activists. Years later, he recalled that he did not learn about the US-Mexico War from his family, who "didn't want to cultivate hatred within their children."[170] Neither did he learn about the war in school. Gómez learned about the war and about US conquest through self-directed research into the nation's wars and its treatment of Native Americans.[171] He began reading about the war and Joaquín Murrieta in the library, especially Carey McWilliams's *North from Mexico*, which became his "bible."[172] As a student, he recalled reading the Treaty of Guadalupe Hidalgo "thoroughly and completely," concluding that "that this treaty had been broken and violated."[173]

Moreover, Gómez absorbed the critiques of war, imperialism, and capitalism from the progressive and radical leaflets and newspapers easily available throughout the Bay area. He remembered the region as "ground zero of the beginning ideological opposition to American racism and American discrimination," where there was a "sophisticated distribution of material, Marxist material, socialist material, anarchist material, New Left material, Quaker, antiwar material, [and] newspapers galore."[174] Gómez also worked as a researcher for Professor Theodore Roszak, whose work on counterculture influenced him as a participant-observer of various activists, including the Black Panthers and the Peace and Freedom Party, whose founding convention he attended.[175]

But perhaps the largest influence on Gómez's views of the US-Mexico War was the Chicano movement. After helping establish CSU Hayward's Mexican American Student Confederation to urge the university to increase the numbers of Chicano faculty, staff, and students, he became involved in the UFW's grape boycott, lobbied against police brutality, and joined the Brown Berets.[176] In March 1969, he attended the Chicano Youth Liberation Conference in Denver, where the Plan Espiritual de Aztlán was issued and where he met Chicano activists from other states. Subsequently, Gómez invited Reies López Tijerina, as well as Corky Gonzales, to CSU Hayward and to the Bay Area.[177] He heard them discuss the failed promises of the Treaty of Guadalupe Hidalgo, and later described learning as much as possible about the land grant movement. Along with Cesar Chavez, Tijerina and Gonzales had declared their opposition to the Vietnam War by 1966.[178] Their antiwar pronouncements as well as the disproportionate Chicano casualties fueled antiwar sentiments among Mexican Americans. Throughout 1969, discussions of Chicanos' increasing war casualties and antiwar activism appeared in movement newspapers and were featured in a *Los Angeles Times*' article about former UCLA student body president, Rosalío Muñoz, refusing the draft.[179] Such discussions also occurred at conferences, including Denver's Chicano Youth Liberation Conference in March and CSU Hayward's Chicano Liberation symposium, which Gómez helped organize.[180]

Gómez's letter wonderfully illustrates the political uses of collective memory and its transformation to address contemporary issues. Convinced that the US-Mexico War had caused land loss and political disenfranchisement, he attested that the Chicano community continued to remember the war and its ongoing adverse consequences (e.g., "the war did not end"). His letter recalled the US-Mexico War and its devastating effects to oppose another war of conquest in the service of US empire. Reprinted in numerous Chicano movement letters and leaflets, including the San Quentin prison newspaper, *La Raza; El Grito del Pueblo*; and even several non-Chicano newspapers, his letter reached a wide audience in California and throughout the US Southwest.[181] Several textbooks on the Vietnam War and Chicano history books also reprinted Gómez's letter.[182] His actions and speech, along with those of other Chicanos who refused induction, helped popularize draft resistance among a community that held military service in high esteem and was suspicious of draft resisters. Its use by draft counselors indicated their hope that potential recruits would be swayed by its powerful critique and social analysis by a youth from their community.

Gómez's journey to draft resistance demonstrates the reception and transmission of war memories. Significantly, Gómez's collective memories, like those of other activists, did not stem from one source but multiple. He constructed his views about the Vietnam War and civil rights activism from his immigrant parents, university courses, other draft resisters, books, antiwar demonstrations, and even his research assignment for Professor Rozsak, and obtained his perspective on the US-Mexico War from books, community activists, newspapers, and his family and friends. The letter's popularity helped spread one Chicano's interpretation of the US-Mexico War and its parallels to the Vietnam War to a large audience. Readers learned of his antiwar stance and the continued multiple violations of the treaty. Although Gómez absorbed numerous influences that shaped his view of the war, he drew on the collective memories of Chicanos who still viewed the US-Mexico War as the inception of their community's struggles to obtain civil rights and the Treaty of Guadalupe Hidalgo as a promise that was never fulfilled.

THE TREATY OF GUADALUPE HIDALGO assumed greater significance for civil rights reform for the Chicano movement of the 1960s–70s. During a period of civil unrest and numerous protests across the United States, multiple influences affected the collective war memories of Mexican Americans. Through his speeches and writings on behalf of the land rights movement in New Mexico, autodidact Reies López Tijerina helped popularize the treaty and the collective memories of its failures. The domestic antiwar movement, wars of liberation across the world, and various civil rights struggles led Chicanos to link the US-Mexico War to the Vietnam War, call for self-determination, and seek multiethnic alliances. Various Chicano activists, students, and workers also recalled the collective memories of earlier generations who strategically remembered the war's consequences to press for various civil rights reforms. Chicano youth tied the underfunding of their schools, high dropout rates, and textbooks that omitted Chicano history to legacies of conquest as had Mexican American activists in the early twentieth century. Similarly, the Brown Berets' occupation of Catalina Island was motivated by the collective memories of Mexico's continued jurisdiction over the island based on a reinterpretation of the treaty promoted by nineteenth-century newspapers and officials in Mexico. Not only did antiwar activists draw parallels between the US expansionist projects of the US-Mexico War and the Vietnam War, but they also echoed ANMA's antiwar positions and its critique of the United States' promotion of democracy abroad while people of color could not exercise civil rights domestically. Yet not all Mexican American activists opposed the Vietnam War. Members of the American GI Forum, LULAC, and the CSO selectively used collective war memories to emphasize Mexican Americans' loyalty and to initially support US involvement in Vietnam.

The Chicano movement expanded the list of issues resulting from the US failure to enforce the treaty. Various organizations and activists compiled a long list of grievances—from land loss and political disenfranchisement to police brutality and discriminatory draft procedures—that resulted from the second-class citizenship of Mexican Americans. Chicano activists also echoed Nuevomexicano parents and politicians who reinterpreted the treaty in the early twentieth century as guaranteeing language and cultural rights. Perhaps the greatest contribution of this generation of activists was to recall, analyze, and publicize their thoughts on the US-Mexico War and its treaty. They strategically deployed collective memories to advance their varied and contradictory political goals. Their "strategic memory project" was not just to remember the war and its detrimental consequences but to highlight the failure of the United States to enforce the treaty and live up to the ideals enshrined therein.[183]

Conclusion

In spring 2006, thousands of Latinos, immigrant rights activists, and their supporters marched in the streets across the country to protest a proposed immigration reform bill. After rallies numbering 30,000 in Washington, D.C., and 100,000 in Chicago early in the spring, activists organized a national economic boycott—A Day without an Immigrant—on May 1. The boycott coincided with rallies in various cities that drew 500,000 supporters in Chicago; 1 million in Los Angeles; and hundreds of thousands in Houston, New York City, and Atlanta.[1] The large turnouts for these protests resulted from years of organizing by immigrant rights activists and the urgency about the bill's punitive measures. The rallies' attendance was also boosted by popular media that catered to Latino immigrants. Throughout the nation, Spanish-language newspapers and radio played a significant role in encouraging people to attend the protests. Spanish-language media outlets followed a long-standing pattern of journalists getting involved in civil rights struggles. Another persistent pattern was the role of collective memory of the US-Mexico War in inspiring activism. Among numerous protest signs carried by the marchers read several that proclaimed, "We didn't cross the border, the border crossed us"—a slogan that has been deployed by Mexican American activists since the 1960s to gain support for various civil rights campaigns.[2] Some forty years after the Chicano movement popularized the slogan, immigrant rights activists repurposed it and gave the phrase new meaning to claim the right to live in the United States.

The motto alludes to the redrawing of national borders, which occurred after the US-Mexico War and the Treaty of Guadalupe Hidalgo. As the phrase indicates, the nation's first Mexican Americans did not cross the international border as immigrants; rather, the international border moved to incorporate them as US citizens, as stipulated by the treaty. In addition to its use by activists and academics, the phrase had appeared in multiple popular media outlets, including songs and movies. The Grammy-winning Mexican Norteño band, Los Tigres del Norte, incorporated the slogan into its 2001 pro-immigrant rights song, "Somos más Americanos" (We are more Americans). This song challenges the media's depiction of immigrants as "invaders" by asking "Who is the real invader?" and directly invokes Mexico's previous claims to eight US Southwestern states that were taken by conquest. Subsequently, the phrase spread so widely that it appeared in the dialogue of the 2010 action movie *Machete*, written and directed by Mexican American filmmaker Robert Rodriguez.[3] Although the slogan's reception among the US public is not uniform, some Mexican Americans undoubtedly recognize the reference to the mid-nineteenth-century war of conquest. Its ubiquity suggests the dissemination of these collective memories to a younger generation. Moreover, the use of this phrase by activists and the popular media demonstrates the ongoing significance of the collective memory of the US-Mexico War to inspire civil rights movements.

The memory of the war endures in Mexico and often percolates to the surface during policy debates. At various times during national debates on immigration reform, the US press has carried articles or opinion essays that raise the war and treaty. Hardly anyone remembers the war in the United States, contends a 2004 opinion essay, while in "Mexico, almost no one has forgotten." In the essay, a Mexican historian opines that the war, known as "the American invasion," divided the country's territory and "the wound never really healed."[4] A more recent example was the reaction of some politicians and scholars to the 2016 election, during which one presidential candidate maligned Mexican immigrants as invaders and criminals while casting the United States as a victim. Such a derogatory portrayal is not new, but its xenophobic message and prominence during a national election led some Mexican intellectuals to remind the United States that Mexico was "the first victim of American imperialism."[5] In the aftermath of the election, one of the elder statesmen of the Mexican Left, Cuauhtémoc Cardenas, implored Mexico's government to support a lawsuit to nullify the Treaty of Guadalupe Hidalgo. The treaty violates international norms, Cardenas and others asserted, because the treaty was signed while the US Army occupied Mexico City.[6] Even if the treaty was declared valid, the lawsuit's proponents maintained, the United States had violated many of its articles, specifically the stipulations about Mexican Americans' citizenship rights. According to several experts in international law, the proposed lawsuit was unlikely to succeed due to several obstacles. But its political impact could be significant, posited historian Enrique Krauze in a *New York Times* editorial. He urged universities, school, museums, films, and television programs to reconsider the nation's "first imperial war" by focusing on "the aggression against Mexico and the plundering of its territory." Addressing himself to "us Mexicans," Krauze thought that the proposed lawsuit was an opportunity for a reconquest—not a physical one or reparations for "stolen land" but rather a "reconquest of the memory of that war so prodigal in atrocities inspired by racial prejudices and greed for territorial gain."

Immigration reform, he believed, was the best possible compensation for the "descendants of those Mexicans who suffered the unjust loss of half their territory."[7]

This editorial is a recent example of the long pattern of deploying memories of the US-Mexico War to advocate for civil rights reforms. Krauze urges Mexicans to "reconquer" the collective memory of the war by deploying it to promote immigration reform. His reference echoes historical "reconquest" antecedents for Mexico's lost northern territory, perhaps most famously inscribed in Mexican American history by the Brown Berets' Caravana de la Reconquista. Like the Berets, Krauze strategically harnessed collective memories for the political goal of reforming US immigration laws. His editorial also recalls the earlier transborder efforts of Mexico-based journalists to advocate for civil rights reforms on behalf of Mexican Americans. Krauze's essay demonstrates the transnational circulation of war memories, whereby collective memories of Mexican nationals affect Mexican Americans' war memories. As a historian, Krauze recognizes the power of education, popular culture, and public history to shape the US public's views of the war, and this potency explains his call for these avenues to reconsider the war's immediate effects and enduring legacies. His reference to museums was perhaps sparked by his knowledge of the National Museum of Interventions in Mexico City, which commemorates the foreign incursions by Spain, France, and the United States on Mexico's soil.[8] Opened in 1981, this museum remains housed in a former convent captured by US troops in 1847 and contains several exhibits on the Texas separatist struggle and the US-Mexico War.[9]

While no comparable US museum attends to the US-Mexico War, the Palo Alto Battlefield National Historical Park does engage the first official battle of the war. Efforts to create this park began in the 1970s, after the developers discovered a mass grave of Mexican soldiers at the site, north of Brownsville, Texas. Local historians and activists worked several years to obtain support from government officials and persuade the National Park Service to create the park. As the efforts expanded to include scholars and citizens of both nations, debates about the causes and effects of the war cropped up. Before Congress and the president approved funding for the park in 1992, the National Park Service commissioned a study to gauge local residents' support and obtain their suggestions for the park's interpretive narratives. The interviewees, from Matamoros and Brownsville, consisted of Mexican nationals, Mexican Americans, and European Americans.

While all seventy-six interviewees agreed on the importance of establishing the park and on the US and Mexican governments' collaboration on interpretations of the war, some differences emerged on how the park should portray the war. European American respondents worried that the United States might be portrayed as an expansionist power, wanting to emphasize peaceful relations between the two countries. Mexican nationals, concerned that the park's interpretation might not be fair to Mexico's viewpoint, cast the war as an invasion. Mexican American respondents hoped the park would help them understand their culture and identity without forgetting that the conflict was a war of conquest.[10] But the controversy continued. The president of the park committee, a European American Brownsville resident, hoped the park would convey the US view of the conflict instead of condemnation of the US role that he attributed to academic historians. His opinion clashed with those comments expressed by participants in a 2002 conference on the war. While a Mexican historian implored the United States to pay additional war reparations, some Mexican American conference attendees advocated for immigration reform.[11]

The goal for the park's interpretive center was to offer a balanced view of the war. In response to veterans and heritage organizations who wanted Congress to allocate funds to build a US-Mexico War monument, legislators designated funds to build an interpretive center at the Palo Alto National Park. While Congress asked the park's staff to consider the Mexican point of view, it did not formally ask the Mexican government for input. So the staff sought input from residents of Matamoros and Brownsville through surveys, community meetings, and binational conferences. They faced some opposition from some Mexican nationals from Matamoros, who feared the park would celebrate their nation's defeat. Ultimately, the park's staff created an interpretive center that attempted to initiate dialogue instead of supplying a uniform view of the war.[12]

Despite the park staff's attempts to offer a balanced view, the narratives on the interpretive center's displays and pathways' plaques were woefully lacking in 2019. While the displays and plaques inform visitors about US expansionism, manifest destiny, US war opponents, and Mexico's instability, the war's causes remain unclear, as the bilingual narratives try not to fault the United States for starting a war of conquest by annexing Texas and sending troops into the disputed territory below the Nueces River. Although one of the causes of the war is correctly identified as competition over territory, the explanation of this dispute obscures the expansionist motives of the United States. "In 1846, two presidents pushed this long-standing dispute towards war," reads a display that cites President James Polk's expansionist goals while construing Mexico's president Mariano Paredes of being guilty of defending "Mexico's vast territory." The initial battle, the Thornton Skirmish, is described in bland terms, without an explanation that US troops were trespassing on Mexican soil and without then general Ulysses S. Grant's admission that US soldiers had been sent into the region to provoke Mexico's military to attack first. Similarly, the vigorous opposition to the war is minimized with a display of a cartoon depicting Massachusetts senator Daniel Webster, but no mention of Abraham Lincoln's Spot Resolutions, the Whigs' vocal criticisms of "Mr. Polk's War," abolitionists' condemnation of the war as an avenue to expand slavery, or Henry David Thoreau's "Notes on Civil Disobedience."

The displays also fail to address the racist congressional debates that regarded Native Americans and Mexicans as mere obstacles to US expansion.[13] Park visitors unsatisfied with the interpretations at the displays and plaques might find more critical perspectives in various studies available in the interpretive center's bookstore. Visitors will find books offering overviews of the war, as well as monographs focusing on soldiers' letters, the San Patricios, war literature, specific battles, the role of Native Americans in the war, and the Treaty of Guadalupe Hidalgo. According to one historian whose book is available at the center, "Palo Alto is disputed territory—a battlefield of memory."[14] Yet this memory, like the battle that took place in 1846, heavily favors one side. While the books do not represent a monolithic view of the war, they decidedly derive from the perspective of US historians. All the books remain English-language titles, and none are written by historians of Mexico. Only a few titles are by Mexican American historians. Ultimately, the park squanders the opportunity to critically inform the public about the causes, effects, and long-term consequences of the US-Mexico War.

Some of these harmful consequences have recently been highlighted by Mexican American scholars and activists. Throughout the twentieth century, civil rights activists identified Mexican Americans' poverty, isolation, segregation, and political exclusion as lingering ramifications of the US-Mexico War. In addition to immigration reform, public history has again become a battleground for Mexican Americans. As recent protests against police brutality and racial injustice have gripped the nation, activists and government officials have begun removing Confederate monuments from public venues.[15] Efforts to remove these monuments to white supremacy have been spearheaded by Black Lives Matter activists. These efforts have led people to question other commemorations to white supremacy, including the names of public buildings, schools, and sports mascots.

In a related development, recent scholarship on the Texas Rangers has exposed the pervasive history of this law enforcement agency's violation of African Americans' and Mexican Americans' civil rights. In response to this scholarship and the protests against racial injustice, officials removed a Texas Ranger statue from the lobby of Dallas Love Field in June 2020. Mexican American scholars and activists praised this long-overdue removal, which many had advocated for several years. The renewed focus on these abuses has also prompted calls to rename the Texas Rangers baseball team. The Rangers' targeting of Indigenous people and Mexican Americans began in the early nineteenth century and continued during the US-Mexico War. While Mexican American scholars and activists might rejoice in these successful challenges to the nation's public history, the removal of statues of Spanish colonists like Juan de Oñate and Junípero Serra should serve as reminders of their ancestors' role in conquering Native Americans.[16] Indeed, historical reckoning can turn out in various ways.

The extraordinarily momentous war and subsequent treaty have reverberated through all these decades. The collective memories of the war and treaty will thus continue to inspire civil rights reform efforts.

Notes

Introduction

1. I have chosen to use Tejano, Chicano, and Latino, instead of Tejanx, Chicanx, and Latinx throughout. While these Spanish-language terms are gendered male, I employ them the way they are usually used in Spanish to refer to the entire Tejano, Chicano, and Latino community, including men, women, and children.

2. This explanation of collective memories as the interactions among individual, group, and public memories is based on my reading of the following works: Glassberg, "Public History and the Study of Memory," 10–11; Glassberg, *Sense of History*, 9–11; Van Wagenen, *Remembering the Forgotten War*, 4–5; Brundage, "No Deed but Memory," 5; Campbell, "History and Collective Memory in Texas," 270–71; Assmann, "Transformations between History and Memory," 52.

3. Brundage, "No Deed but Memory," 5.

4. Johannsen, "America's Forgotten War," 96–107.

5. Novick, *Holocaust in American Life*, 4.

6. For a selected overview of Mexican perspectives of the war, see Castillo Nájera, *Invasión norteamericana*; Fuentes Díaz, *La Intervención norteamericana en México*; Moyano Pahissa, *El Comercio de Santa Fe y la guerra del "47"*; López y Rivas, *La Guerra del 47 y la resistencia popular a la ocupación*; Zoraida Vázquez and Meyer, *United States and Mexico*. US perspectives of the war can be seen in the following selected works: Bancroft, *Works of Hubert Howe Bancroft*; Howe, *How We Robbed Mexico in 1848*; Smith, *The War with Mexico*; Johannsen, *To the Halls of the Montezumas*; Francaviglia and Richmond, *Dueling Eagles*.

7. Sánchez, *Telling Identities*; Mendoza, *Historia*; Pérez, *Remembering the Hacienda*; Rodríguez, *Literatures of the U.S.-Mexico War*; Saldaña-Portillo, "'Wavering on the Horizon of Social Being.'"

8. Kammen, *Mystic Chords of Memory*, 512, 701; Loewen, "Telling History on the Landscape," 2.

9. Since the 1990s, US scholars have been referring to the conflict as the "US-Mexican War" or the "US-Mexico War" while Mexico's scholars have long used the term "the War of '47."

10. Nguyen, "Just Memory," 144.

11. Confino, "Collective Memory and Cultural History," 1392.

12. Blight, *Beyond the Battlefield*, 191–92; Cantrell and Turner, "Study of History, Memory, and Collective Memory," 3.

13. Kammen, *Mystic Chords of Memory*; Nora, "Between Memory and History," 7–25; Wood, "Memory's Remains," 123–49; Anderson, *Imagined Communities*.

14. Martinez, *Injustice Never Leaves You*, 27, 104.

15. Green, *Taking History to Heart*; Bodnar, *Remaking America*; Gillis, *Commemorations*.

16. Campbell succinctly explains the existence of various collective memories among distinct ethnic and racial groups. Campbell, "History and Collective Memory in Texas," 274.

17. Glassberg, "Public History and the Study of Memory," 11–14; Glassberg, "Patriotism from the Ground Up," 2–3.

18. Brundage, "No Deed but Memory," 7.

19. Tijerina makes this point succinctly and also describes recent Tejano efforts at memorialization in Tijerina, "Constructing Tejano Memory," 176.

20. Brundage, "No Deed but Memory," 7.

21. Brundage, "No Deed but Memory," 5.

22. Blight, "Southerners Don't Lie," 351–52.

23. Valerio-Jiménez, *River of Hope*, 172–75.

24. I discuss these multiple uses of the border in *River of Hope*, chaps. 4–6.

25. Deverell refers to the pervasive anti-Mexican violence across the US Southwest as the "unending Mexican War." Deverell, *Whitewashed Adobe*, 24–25, 27.

26. Nguyen, *Nothing Ever Dies*, 25. Nguyen offers an insightful explanation of the limitations of the term "Vietnam War" in *Nothing Ever Dies*, 5–6.

27. M. G. Gonzales, *Mexicanos*, 88–89; Van Wagenen, *Remembering the Forgotten War*, 6, 41–58, 81–100.

28. Novick, *Holocaust in American Life*, 170.

29. The historical marker reads: "While marching to the conquest and occupation of California during the Mexican War, a detachment of 1st US Dragoons, under the command of Brig. Gen. Stephen W. Kearny, was met on this site by native California lancers, under the command of Gen. Andres Pico. In this battle, fought on December 6, 1846, severe losses were incurred by the American forces. The native Californians withdrew after Kearny had rallied his men on the field. Gallant action on the part of both forces characterized the battles of San Pasqual, one of the significant actions during the Mexican War of 1846–1848." Monument Lab database, https://monumentlab.com/audit#data.

30. Leuchtenburg, *American Places*. Another example is a practical guide to state parks in Texas, where the US-Mexico War began. Parent, *Official Guide to Texas State Parks and Historic Sites*.

31. Lichtenstein and Lichtenstein, *Marked, Unmarked, Remembered*; Bruggeman, *Born in the U.S.A.*

32. "The Spot Where 'American Blood Was Shed on American Soil,'" Cameron County, marker #5478, atlas #545061005478, 1936, Texas Historical Society, https://atlas.thc.texas.gov/.

33. The 1936 historical marker lists "Captain Philip Thornton," but most publications identify the captain as Seth Barton Thornton. Marker #5478, atlas #5061005478, Texas Historical Society, https://atlas.thc.texas.gov; Singletary, *The Mexican War*, 13; Tucker, *Encyclopedia of the Mexican-American War*, 653–54, 132.

34. Some of the US officers who expressed misgivings about entering Mexico's territory include Lieutenant Colonel Ethan Allen Hitchcock and Ulysses S. Grant. Greenberg, *Wicked War*, 101; Grant, *Memoirs and Selected Letters*, 50. The Thornton Skirmish site was one of five landmarks out of eleven hundred honored by the Texas Historical Commission with a granite monolith. Van Wagenen, *Remembering the Forgotten War*, 155.

35. Christensen and Christensen, *The U.S.-Mexican War*, 231.

Chapter One

1. Gómez, "I Am My Brother in the Same Struggle for Justice." The temperature in Oakland ranged from 51 to 55 degrees Fahrenheit on December 8, 1969. "Oakland, CA Weather History," Weather Underground, December 8, 1969, www.wunderground.com/history/daily/KOAK/date/1968-12-8.

2. Confino, "Collective Memory and Cultural History," 1392–93.

3. White, *"It's Your Misfortune,"* 59, 61, 74–75.

4. Native Americans' control over Texas and other parts of northeastern Mexico is explained in various recent books, including DeLay, *War of a Thousand Deserts*, 35–60; Hämäläinen, *The Comanche Empire*, 1–12, 18–106. According to Juliana Barr, "Eighteenth-century Texas . . . offers a story of Indian *dominance*." Barr, *Peace Came in the Form of a Woman*, 7; see also 2–6, 20–25.

5. Weber, *Mexican Frontier*, 10–11, 44–45, 83–86; DeLay, *War of a Thousand Deserts*, 16–24.

6. Reséndez, *Changing National Identities*, 93–106.

7. Chávez, *U.S. War with Mexico*, 3–4.

8. Valerio-Jiménez, *River of Hope*, 109–10; Hämäläinen, *The Comanche Empire*, 157–60; DeLay, *War of a Thousand Deserts*, 285–86; Weber, *Mexican Frontier*, 83–105; Henderson, *Glorious Defeat*, 10, 30–32, 58, 64.

9. Faragher, *Out of Many*, 218–19, 335.

10. Horsman, *Race and Manifest Destiny*, 219–21; Merk and Bannister, *Manifest Destiny*, 24–33; Hietala, *Manifest Design*, 111–12, 255–56; White, *"It's Your Misfortune,"* 74; Chávez, *U.S. War with Mexico*, 2.

11. Weber, *Mexican Frontier*, 159–60.

12. Weber, *Mexican Frontier*, 159–61.

13. Reséndez, *Changing National Identities*, 37–40; Weber, *Mexican Frontier*, 159–61.

14. Weber, *Mexican Frontier*, 161–62.

15. Weber, *Mexican Frontier*, 162, 166–70, 177; Flores, *Remembering the Alamo*, 23; Tijerina, *Tejanos and Texas*, 12.

16. Weber, *Mexican Frontier*, 170–72, 176–78.

17. Valerio-Jiménez, *River of Hope*, 115–28; Ramos, *Beyond the Alamo*, 144–53. Scholars of Texas history usually refer to European Americans in Texas as Anglo-Texans.

18. Weber, *Mexican Frontier*, 251–54; Ramos, *Beyond the Alamo*, 158–61; Flores, *Remembering the Alamo*, 28–31.

19. Seguín, *Revolution Remembered*, 40–44; De la Teja, "Juan N. Seguin," 226; Montejano, *Anglos and Mexicans*, 24–49.

20. Weber, *Mexican Frontier*, 245, 251–54, 266–69; Greenberg, *Wicked War*, 10–11.

21. De León, *Tejano Community*, 13–15; Montejano, *Anglos and Mexicans*, 1987, 26–34; Horgan, *Great River*, 589–600; Calvert and De León, *The History of Texas*, 91–95; Webb, *Texas Rangers*, 71–77; De León and Stewart, *Tejanos and the Numbers Game*, 90–91; Singletary, *The Mexican War*, 18–19; Johannsen, *To the Halls of the Montezumas*, 185; McCutchan, *Mier Expedition Diary*, 16–72.

22. Greenberg, *Wicked War*, 10–15, 268–69; Chávez, *U.S. War with Mexico*, 12–13; Griswold del Castillo, *Treaty of Guadalupe Hidalgo*, 12–14.

23. De León and Stewart, *Tejanos and the Numbers Game*, 92–93; Eisenhower, *So Far from God*, 17–26; Greenberg, *Wicked War*, 95, 100–104.

24. Horsman, *Race and Manifest Destiny*, 236–37; Gutiérrez, *Walls and Mirrors*, 15; Wolpert, *Gandhi's Passion*, 68, 72; Eisenhower, *So Far from God*, 284–85; Faragher, *Out of Many*, 404–5; Greenberg, *Wicked War*, 116, 193, 196–98, 248–49, 253–54.

25. Hietala, *Manifest Design*, 10–54; Merk and Bannister, *Manifest Destiny*, 29–31; White, *"It's Your Misfortune,"* 74; Horsman, *Race and Manifest Destiny*, 241; Limerick, *Legacy of Conquest*, 232–33.

26. DeLay, "Independent Indians and the U.S.-Mexican War," 58–62; DeLay, *War of a Thousand Deserts*, xv, 225; Van Wagenen, *Remembering the Forgotten War*, 225–26, 230–31; Greenberg, *Wicked War*, 203–4, 206, 208, 211–12, 223, 254.

27. Greenberg, *Wicked War*, 212–13, 247–48, 268; Johannsen, *To the Halls of the Montezumas*, 6; Henderson, *Glorious Defeat*, 177; Gómez, *Manifest Destinies*, 42; Bauer, *Mexican War*, 398; Gutiérrez, *Walls and Mirrors*, 13–14.

28. Van Wagenen, *Remembering the Forgotten War*, 247n1; Griswold del Castillo, "Treaty of Guadalupe Hidalgo," 437–38; Greenberg, *Wicked War*, 259. The land transferred totals about 525,000 square miles if Texas is not included in the Mexican Cession. With Texas included, the land totals some 725,000 square miles.

29. Valerio-Jiménez, *River of Hope*, 142–44; Martínez, *Border Boom Town*, 10.

30. Griswold del Castillo, *Treaty of Guadalupe Hidalgo*, 59–60; Chávez, *U.S. War with Mexico*, 27, 33n5; Mora, *Border Dilemmas*, 85–86.

31. Gutiérrez, *Walls and Mirrors*, 14–28; Montejano, *Anglos and Mexicans*, 311–15.

32. Greenberg, *Wicked War*, 268–69.

33. The most famous US officers who later fought in the Civil War were Ulysses S. Grant and Robert E. Lee. Gómez, *Manifest Destinies*, 20; Greenberg, *Wicked War*, 269; Christensen and Christensen, *The U.S.-Mexican War*, 222–23.

34. For the United States, General Zachary Taylor and Lieutenant Ulysses S. Grant became presidents, while for Mexico, generals José Joaquín de Herrera and Mariano Arista served as presidents. Christensen and Christensen, *The U.S.-Mexican War*, 222–24.

35. While both Mexican American men and women were considered US citizens, Mexican American women had limited citizenship rights (e.g., no voting rights). Kerber, *No Constitutional Right to be Ladies*, 13; Gross, *What Blood Won't Tell*, 8.

36. In 1898, Puerto Ricans became the nation's second group of Latinos to be incorporated into the nation by conquest with the end of the Spanish-American War. However, Puerto Ricans did not obtain US citizenship until 1917 with the passage of the Jones Act.

37. Martínez, "On the Size of the Chicano Population," 50–56.

38. Griswold, *Treaty of Guadalupe Hidalgo*, 62, 66, 189–90; Gómez, *Manifest Destinies*, 43, 83, 139; Lozano, *American Language*, 25.

39. Griswold del Castillo, *Treaty of Guadalupe Hidalgo*, 63; Lozano, *American Language*, 43.

40. Griswold del Castillo, *Treaty of Guadalupe Hidalgo*, 63–66.

41. Zoraida Vázquez, *México y el mundo*, 138; Délano, *Mexico and Its Diaspora in the United States*, 63. I discuss this repatriation issue in chapter 3.

42. Gross, "'Caucasian Cloak,'" 340; Gross, *What Blood Won't Tell*, 253–54.

43. In 1897, Ricardo Rodriguez, a Mexican citizen, applied to become a naturalized US citizen in San Antonio, Texas. According to the judge, Rodriguez would not be consid-

ered white, but he granted citizenship based on the Treaty of Guadalupe Hidalgo. For more on this case, see Haney López, *White by Law*, 43–44, 164; De León, *In Re Ricardo Rodríguez*.

44. *In re Ricardo Rodriguez* (1897) demonstrated the ambiguous racial status of Mexicans seeking naturalization. Gómez, *Manifest Destinies*, 138–42; Haney López, *White by Law*, 28–30, 43–44; Gross, "'Caucasian Cloak,'" 340; Gross, *What Blood Won't Tell*, 6–7, 257–60.

45. Griswold del Castillo, *Treaty of Guadalupe Hidalgo*, 50–52. Legal scholar Christopher David Ruiz Cameron offers an analysis of the treaty that employs Latino critical theory in "One Hundred Fifty Years of Solitude."

46. Griswold del Castillo, *Treaty of Guadalupe Hidalgo*, 48; Chávez, *U.S. War with Mexico*, 25–26.

47. Griswold del Castillo, *Treaty of Guadalupe Hidalgo*, 46–48, 179–80, 190 (emphasis mine).

48. Gómez, *Manifest Destinies*, 43–44 (italics in original).

49. Gómez, *Manifest Destinies*, 44; Greenberg, *Wicked War*, 268; Griswold del Castillo, *Treaty of Guadalupe Hidalgo*, 39–40, 55.

50. Gómez, *Manifest Destinies*, 44, 132; Griswold del Castillo, *Treaty of Guadalupe Hidalgo*, 8–9.

51. Gómez, *Manifest Destinies*, 7, 45; Nieto-Phillips, *Language of Blood*, 48, 53.

52. Griswold del Castillo, *Treaty of Guadalupe Hidalgo*, 70. Gómez argued that power of the US Congress to nullify any law passed by the territorial legislature probably led these legislators (majority ethnic Mexicans) to temper the laws they passed. Gómez, *Manifest Destinies*, 44–45.

53. Gómez, *Manifest Destinies*, 7, 16, 21.

54. P. B. Gonzales, "Struggle for Survival," 298; Griswold del Castillo, *Treaty of Guadalupe Hidalgo*, 44.

55. Griswold del Castillo, *Treaty of Guadalupe Hidalgo*, 34.

56. Griswold del Castillo, *Treaty of Guadalupe Hidalgo*, 36, 38, 44–45, 48.

57. Valerio-Jiménez, *River of Hope*, 227; Thompson, *Juan Cortina and the Texas-Mexico Frontier*, 17.

58. Griswold del Castillo, *Treaty of Guadalupe Hidalgo*, 150–53, 173; Gómez, *Manifest Destinies*, 117–47; Chávez, *U.S. War with Mexico*, 31–33.

59. Griswold del Castillo, *Treaty of Guadalupe Hidalgo*, 72–74.

60. Griswold del Castillo, *Treaty of Guadalupe Hidalgo*, 72–86.

61. Griswold del Castillo, *Treaty of Guadalupe Hidalgo*, 73–74; M. G. Gonzales, *Mexicanos*, 100; Chávez, *U.S. War with Mexico*, 28.

62. Chávez, *U.S. War with Mexico*, 28.

63. By contrast, European American arrivistes in Los Angeles outnumbered ethnic Mexicans by the 1860s. Unsurprisingly, ethnic Mexicans' dispossession occurred at a similar pace as their transition to a numerical minority, a mere 20 percent by 1880. Griswold del Castillo, *Los Angeles Barrio*, 35; Chávez-García, *Negotiating Conquest*, 163; M. G. Gonzales, *Mexicanos*, 100–101.

64. Griswold del Castillo, *Treaty of Guadalupe Hidalgo*, 72–77.

65. Griswold del Castillo, *Treaty of Guadalupe Hidalgo*, 77.

66. Ramos, *Beyond the Alamo*, 145, 158–59, 161–62.

67. Ramos, *Beyond the Alamo*, 156; Griswold del Castillo, *Treaty of Guadalupe Hidalgo*, 81–82; De León, *Tejano Community*, 14.

68. Montejano, *Anglos and Mexicans*, 51–53; Griswold del Castillo, *Treaty of Guadalupe Hidalgo*, 84.

69. Montejano, *Anglos and Mexicans*, 16–19; Valerio-Jiménez, *River of Hope*, 115–28. Montejano refers to the republic's "paper claim, of course, for the republic had no control or influence beyond the Nueces," 18.

70. Montejano, *Anglos and Mexicans*, 15–16.

71. Montejano, *Anglos and Mexicans*, 19.

72. Romero, "McKinney v. Saviego."

73. Griswold del Castillo, *Treaty of Guadalupe Hidalgo*, 190.

74. Romero, "McKinney v. Saviego"; Griswold del Castillo, *Treaty of Guadalupe Hidalgo*, 81, 92; *McKinney v. Saviego*, 59 U.S. (18 How.) 235 (1855).

75. Griswold del Castillo, *Treaty of Guadalupe Hidalgo*, 98.

76. P. B. Gonzales, "Struggle for Survival," 299–300; Griswold del Castillo, *Treaty of Guadalupe Hidalgo*, 53–55; Chávez, *U.S. War with Mexico*, 27.

77. Griswold del Castillo, *Treaty of Guadalupe Hidalgo*, 54–55, 82.

78. Griswold del Castillo, *Treaty of Guadalupe Hidalgo*, 82–86.

79. Griswold del Castillo, *Treaty of Guadalupe Hidalgo*, 83.

80. Griswold del Castillo, *Treaty of Guadalupe Hidalgo*, 77.

81. Public Acts of the 33rd Congress of the United States, sess. 1, ch. 103, 10 Stat. 308, July 22, 1854; Gonzales, "Struggle for Survival," 300–301; Griswold del Castillo, *Treaty of Guadalupe Hidalgo*, 77–78.

82. Gómez, *Manifest Destinies*, 123; P. B. Gonzales, "Struggle for Survival," 301; Griswold del Castillo, *Treaty of Guadalupe Hidalgo*, 78.

83. Nieto-Phillips, *Language of Blood*, 60–61; Griswold del Castillo, *Treaty of Guadalupe Hidalgo*, 78; P. B. Gonzales, "Struggle for Survival," 301–2.

84. P. B. Gonzales, "Struggle for Survival," 301–2.

85. Griswold del Castillo, *Treaty of Guadalupe Hidalgo*, 79.

86. Gómez, *Manifest Destinies*, 123.

87. Gómez, *Manifest Destinies*, 123.

88. Gómez, *Manifest Destinies*, 123.

89. Griswold del Castillo, *Treaty of Guadalupe Hidalgo*, 79.

90. Griswold del Castillo, *Treaty of Guadalupe Hidalgo*, 79–80.

91. Gómez, *Manifest Destinies*, 124.

92. Gómez, *Manifest Destinies*, 124.

93. Gómez, *Manifest Destinies*, 121–22.

94. Gómez, *Manifest Destinies*, 127.

95. Griswold del Castillo, *Treaty of Guadalupe Hidalgo*, 80–81.

96. Paredes and Bauman, *Folklore and Culture on the Texas-Mexican Border*, 29; Valerio-Jiménez, *River of Hope*, 12.

97. Nieto Phillips, *Language of Blood*, 53; John C. Calhoun, January 4, 1848, *Congressional Globe*, 96–100.

98. Nieto-Phillips, *Language of Blood*, 48; Gómez, *Manifest Destinies*, 71–79, 83–87.

99. Nieto-Phillips, *Language of Blood*, 81–82.

100. Nieto-Phillips, *Language of Blood*, 48.

101. Foley, "Becoming Hispanic," 63–66.

102. While there were more instances of conflict among African Americans and Mexican Americans, a few temporary alliances developed around support for farmworkers, protests against police brutality, ecumenical activism, and struggles against school segregation. Behnken, *Fighting Their Own Battles*, 124–26, 152–53, 174–75, 185–90, 220–21; Foley, *Quest for Equality*, 94–139; Krochmal, *Blue Texas*, 134–231.

103. Gómez, *Manifest Destinies*, 44–45.

104. Deverell, *Whitewashed Adobe*, 24–25, 27.

105. Pitt, *Decline of the Californios*, 132–33.

106. Pitt, *Decline of the Californios*, 134; Camarillo, *Chicanos in a Changing Society*, 22–23.

107. Deverell, *Whitewashed Adobe*, 36; Pitt, *Decline of the Californios*, 273.

108. Griswold del Castillo, *Los Angeles Barrio*, 158–59.

109. Deverell, *Whitewashed Adobe*, 36; Pitt, *Decline of the Californios*, 274.

110. In 2005, Antonio Villaraigosa won the mayor's seat. Garcia and Sanchez, *Hispanics and the U.S. Political System*, 155, 206.

111. Camarillo, *Chicanos in a Changing Society*, 22–23, 41–42.

112. Camarillo, *Chicanos in a Changing Society*, 31, 47.

113. Camarillo, *Chicanos in a Changing Society*, 74–75.

114. Pitt, *Decline of the Californios*, 273; Acuña, *Occupied America*, 117–18.

115. Ramos, *Beyond the Alamo*, 167.

116. Ramos, *Beyond the Alamo*, 161–62.

117. De León, *Tejano Community*, 25; Ramos, *Beyond the Alamo*, 170–72.

118. Ramos, *Beyond the Alamo*, 81–83.

119. Ramos, *Beyond the Alamo*, 83–84, 86, 96.

120. Ramos, *Beyond the Alamo*, 158–61.

121. Ramos, *Beyond the Alamo*, 174–76.

122. Seguín, *Revolution Remembered*, 35–39.

123. Seguín, *Revolution Remembered*, 40–43.

124. Ramos, *Beyond the Alamo*, 186; Seguín, *Revolution Remembered*, 43–44.

125. Cisneros served four terms as mayor. Garcia and Sanchez, *Hispanics and the U.S. Political System*, 175.

126. Ramos, *Beyond the Alamo*, 192; De León, *Tejano Community*, 28–34.

127. Ramos, *Beyond the Alamo*, 211, 227.

128. Ramos, *Beyond the Alamo*, 228.

129. De León, *They Called Them Greasers*, 53, 82–83; Ramos, *Beyond the Alamo*, 210–22.

130. De León, *Tejano Community*, 28–29, 33–34; Ramos, *Beyond the Alamo*, 230.

131. Montejano, *Anglos and Mexicans*, 34–37, 43–47; Valerio-Jiménez, *River of Hope*, 148–50.

132. Camarillo, *Chicanos in a Changing Society*, 19, 108; Griswold del Castillo, *Los Angeles Barrio*, 115.

133. Camarillo, *Chicanos in a Changing Society*, 113–41.

134. Griswold del Castillo, *Los Angeles Barrio*, 105–5.

135. Mexican Americans were also underrepresented on federal juries, where they made up only 8 percent of jurors. Griswold del Castillo, *Los Angeles Barrio*, 117–19; Camarillo, *Chicanos in a Changing Society*, 108–10.

136. Valerio-Jiménez, *River of Hope*, 151–58.

137. Valerio-Jiménez, *River of Hope*, 158–72.

138. The federal government broke up the territory of New Mexico to form Colorado (1861), Nevada (1861), and Arizona (1863). Nevertheless, New Mexico continued to boast the largest population of Mexican Americans throughout the nineteenth century. Gómez, *Manifest Destinies*, 6–7, 90, 164n21.

139. Mitchell, *Coyote Nation*, 16–17.

140. Gómez, *Manifest Destinies*, 89.

141. Gómez, *Manifest Destinies*, 89–90.

142. Gómez, *Manifest Destinies*, 87–89.

143. Gómez, *Manifest Destinies*, 87–89, 114.

144. Legal officials did disproportionately prosecute Hispanos for adultery (using federal rather than territorial statutes on adultery) in the late nineteenth century. Mitchell, *Coyote Nation*, 16.

145. Nieto-Phillips, *Language of Blood*, 92.

146. Mora, *Border Dilemmas*, 178–79.

147. Mora, *Border Dilemmas*, 178–79; Nieto-Phillips, *Language of Blood*, 51–59; Gómez, *Manifest Destinies*, 147.

148. Mora, *Border Dilemmas*, 174–75; Gómez, *Manifest Destinies*, 117, 119, 130.

149. Gómez, *Manifest Destinies*, 157.

150. Gómez, *Manifest Destinies*, 83–84, 149–50, 157.

151. Gómez, *Manifest Destinies*, 142.

152. Lozano, *American Language*, 5.

Chapter Two

1. *El Clamor Público*, April 5, 1856; translation from Kanellos, "El Clamor Público," 13.

2. Pitt, *Decline of the Californios*, 116–17; *El Clamor Público*, June 14, 1856; translation from Kanellos, "El Clamor Público," 13.

3. Nieto-Phillips, *Language of Blood*, 48; Mora, *Border Dilemmas*, 57; Griswold del Castillo, *Treaty of Guadalupe Hidalgo*, 71, 190.

4. John C. Calhoun, January 4, 1848, *Congressional Globe*, 96–100; Nieto-Phillips, *Language of Blood*, 52–53.

5. John A. Dix, January 26, 1848, *Congressional Globe*, 250–57.

6. Nieto-Phillips, *Language of Blood*, 47–49; Mora, *Border Dilemmas*, 56–57.

7. Mora, *Border Dilemmas*, 55.

8. Nieto-Phillips, *Language of Blood*, 55–56.

9. Griswold del Castillo, *Treaty of Guadalupe Hidalgo*, 70.

10. Nieto-Phillips, *Language of Blood*, 57, 77–78.

11. Nieto-Phillips, *Language of Blood*, 51–59; Mora, *Border Dilemmas*, 270–73.

12. Mora, *Border Dilemmas*, 63, 235.

13. Mora, *Border Dilemmas*, 224–25.

14. Nieto-Phillips, *Language of Blood*, 80–82.

15. While these statehood supporters did not actually forget their memories, they chose not to emphasize them. Similarly, they remembered only specific facts about the past that suited their social and political purposes. I use the terms "remembering" and "forgetting" without enclosing them in quotation marks to reflect this strategic use of memories.

16. Ramón Ortiz al Governador de Chihuahua, June 9, 1849, reprinted in Moyano Pahissa, *Protección consular*, 20–23.

17. Luis de la Rosa to Secretario de Estado de los Estados Unidos, September 18, 1849, in Moyano Pahissa, *Protección consular*, 33–34; Zoraida Vázquez, *México y el Mundo*, 138.

18. Zoraida Vázquez, *México y el Mundo*, 138; Délano, *Mexico and Its Diaspora*, 63.

19. Luis de la Rosa to Secretario de Estado de los Estados Unidos, October 19, 1849. in Moyano Pahissa, *Protección consular*, 31–32.

20. Zoraida Vázquez, *México y el Mundo*, 139.

21. Jorge Haphann to Ministro de Relaciones, April 15, 1850, in Moyano Pahissa, *Protección consular*, 35; Joaquín I. del Castillo to Ministro de Relaciones, September 30, 1853, in Moyano Pahissa, *Protección consular*, 36–37. The Mexican government also lodged complaints with the US government over violations of Article 11, which required both nations to contain Native American incursions across the international boundary, or to punish Native Americans for such incursions. Additionally, Mexico complained that the United States was not abiding by the laws of neutrality because it refused to stop incursions into Mexico by filibusters based in the United States. Zoraida Vázquez, *México y el Mundo*, 143–57.

22. Gómez-Quiñones, "Piedras contra la luna," 496.

23. Gómez-Quiñones, "Piedras contra la luna," 497–98.

24. Madley, *American Genocide*, 3.

25. S. L. Johnson, *Roaring Camp*, 31, 37, 125–26, 215, 247–49; Pitt, *Decline of the Californios*, 48–103.

26. Carrigan and Webb, *Forgotten Dead*, 63–64. Hurtado argues that Hubert Howe Bancroft "justified lynch-mob violence as 'the right of the governed at all times to instant and arbitrary control of the government.'" Hurtado, *Intimate Frontiers*, 134.

27. Carrigan and Webb, *Forgotten Dead*, 64–65.

28. Carrigan and Webb, *Forgotten Dead*, 67, 81.

29. Pitt, *Decline of the Californios*, 73.

30. Pitt identifies the doctor as Stephen J. Field, a future Supreme Court justice, in Pitt, *Decline of the Californios*, 73–74. However, California state senator David P. Barstow identifies the physician as Dr. Aiken in Caughey, *Their Majesties the Mob*, 49. Carrigan and Webb identify the physician as Cyrus Aiken based on their reading of various primary and secondary sources. Carrigan and Webb, *Forgotten Dead*, 70.

31. Rojas, "Re-Membering Josefa," 127; *Daily Alta California*, July 9, 1851.

32. Haas, *Conquests and Historical Identities in California*, 43; Valerio-Jiménez, *River of Hope*, 160–61; Mitchell, *Coyote Nation*, 6, 85, 153.

33. Rojas, "Re-Membering Josefa," 127–28.

34. Cutler, "Reading Nineteenth-Century Latino/a Fiction," 129.

35. Carrigan and Webb, *Forgotten Dead*, 34, 51, 58–59.

36. Carrigan and Webb, *Forgotten Dead*, 34–40.

284 Notes to Chapter Two

37. Carrigan and Webb, *Forgotten Dead*, 54.

38. Schedule of Mexican Claims against the United States, docket no. 904, S. Doc. No. 31, 44th Cong., 2nd Sess., at 94–95 (1868); Rojas, "Re-Membering Josefa," 143–44. The claim sets the date of the lynching as July 4, 1852, but this is probably a mistake, as various newspapers and personal accounts identify 1851 as the year of the lynching. José claimed $300,000 for his losses, which comprised not only his wife's death but also his banishment. It is unclear how he, or Mexican government officials, calculated this amount, but it presumably included the "value" of his wife's life and his loss of income in the ensuing years. *La Voz del Nuevo Mundo*, June 11, 1881, contains an account of the lynching and of José's claim.

39. Guidotti-Hernández, *Unspeakable Violence*, 52.

40. The Senate documents do not give a reason why the commissioners rejected José's claim, but an 1881 article titled "Recuerdos de California" in *La Voz del Nuevo Mundo* states that the claim was rejected "á instancias del comisionado mejicano" (at the request of the Mexican commissioner) because José could not prove his legal marriage to Josefa. *La Voz del Nuevo Mundo*, June 11, 1881.

41. Rojas, "Re-Membering Josefa," 135; *Daily Alta California*, July 14, 1851; *Marysville Herald*, July 8, 1851.

42. *Daily Alta California*, July 14, 1851.

43. Guidotti-Hernández, *Unspeakable Violence*, 44, 56, 304n42.

44. There are several possible explanations for José's failure to prove his legal marriage: neither he nor Mexican officials could obtain a copy of the marriage certificate while he lived in Mexico, or he had been in a common-law marriage with Josefa.

45. Guidotti-Hernández warns scholars of the dangers of reproducing sensationalized narratives of Josefa by overemphasizing resistance or victimhood. Guidotti-Hernández, *Unspeakable Violence*, 39–40, 68–69.

46. *Daily Alta California*, July 9, 1851.

47. *Steamer Pacific Star*, July 15, 1851, quoted in Rojas, "Re-Membering Josefa," 140 and McLure, "'I Suppose You Think Strange the Murder of Women and Children,'" 160. The *Daily Alta California* of July 9, 1851, reports a slightly different version.

48. *Steamer Pacific Star*, July 15, 1851, quoted in Rojas, "Re-Membering Josefa," 140.

49. Carrigan and Webb, *Forgotten Dead*, 69–74; McLure, "I Suppose You Think Strange the Murder of Women and Children," 9–10, 16–22.

50. A. I. Castañeda, "Sexual Violence in the Politics and Policies of Conquest."

51. Guidotti-Hernández, *Unspeakable Violence*, 78–80.

52. Gray, "Francisco P. Ramírez," 20–3; Carrigan and Webb, *Forgotten Dead*, 59–60.

53. Gray, "Francisco P. Ramírez," 24–5; Carrigan and Webb, *Forgotten Dead*, 59–60.

54. Gray, "Francisco P. Ramírez," 25–6; Carrigan and Webb, *Forgotten Dead*, 60.

55. *El Clamor Público*, July 26, 1856; Carrigan and Webb, *Forgotten Dead*, 104, 115.

56. *El Clamor Público*, April 25, 1857. Ramírez borrowed the term "*linchocracia*" from an unidentified Sacramento newspaper, whose editorial he republished. Paz Brownrigg, "Linchocracia," 72n18.

57. *El Clamor Público*, August 2, 1856; Paz Brownrigg, "Linchocracia," 43 (italics in original).

58. Carrigan and Webb, *Forgotten Dead*, 60.

59. *El Clamor Público*, June 5, 1858; *El Clamor Público*, January 29, 1859, quoted in Carrigan and Webb, *Forgotten Dead*, 60.

60. *El Clamor Público*, August 15, 1857, quoted in Gutiérrez, Benavides, and Deverell, introduction, 8.

61. Kanellos, "*El Clamor Público*," 14.

62. Kanellos, "*El Clamor Público*," 12.

63. Kanellos, "*El Clamor Público*," 10.

64. *El Clamor Público*, May 10, 1856. Gutiérrez, Benavides, and Deverell, introduction, 8.

65. Gray, "Francisco P. Ramirez," 29; Carrigan and Webb, *Forgotten Dead*, 116.

66. Kanellos, "*El Clamor Público*," 14.

67. Carrigan and Webb, *Forgotten Dead*, 56–60.

68. Kanellos, "*El Clamor Público*," 12, 14–15.

69. Paz Brownrigg, "Linchocracia," 51; Gutiérrez, Benavides, and Deverell, introduction, 5.

70. Gray, "Francisco P. Ramirez," 23–24.

71. *El Clamor Público*, February 7, 1857.

72. The editorial appeared originally in *La Crónica*, the first Spanish-language newspaper to be published in San Francisco. Kanellos, "*El Clamor Público*," 69n3; *El Clamor Público* republished *La Crónica*'s editorial under the title "Hospitalidad Californiana" on September 18, 1855; Gutiérrez, Benavides, and Deverell, introduction, 8.

73. Carrigan and Webb, *Forgotten Dead*, 115–16.

74. Ramos, *Beyond the Alamo*, 81–89.

75. Ramos, *Beyond the Alamo*, 200.

76. Seguín, *Revolution Remembered*, 48–50.

77. Seguín, *Revolution Remembered*, 50–51, 53–56.

78. Seguín, *Revolution Remembered*, 73; Ramos, *Beyond the Alamo*, 174.

79. Seguín, *Revolution Remembered*, 90.

80. Seguín, *Revolution Remembered*, 89, 101; *Beyond the Alamo*, 176–77.

81. Seguín, *Revolution Remembered*, 90.

82. Ramos, *Beyond the Alamo*, 176–77.

83. Seguín, *Revolution Remembered*, 89.

84. Seguín, *Revolution Remembered*, 101.

85. Seguín, *Revolution Remembered*, 44, 100–101; Ramos, *Beyond the Alamo*, 185–86.

86. Ramos, *Beyond the Alamo*, 184.

87. Seguín's use of the phrase "foreigner in my native land" in 1858 echoed the words of Pablo de la Guerra who characterized the Californios as "foreigners in their own land" in a speech to the California Senate in 1856. Seguín, *Revolution Remembered*, 73, 97; Weber, *Foreigners in Their Native Land*, vi.

88. Seguín, *Revolution Remembered*, vii, xi, 71.

89. Seguín, *Revolution Remembered*, 52.

90. Little is known about how his memoirs were received by the Tejano community.

91. Seguín, *Revolution Remembered*, 53–56.

92. Padilla, *My History, Not Yours*, 70.

93. Padilla, *My History, Not Yours*, 17.

94. Seguín, *Revolution Remembered*, 96.

286 Notes to Chapter Two

95. Padilla, *My History, Not Yours*, 71. Padilla makes a similar point about personal and collective trauma.

96. *Daily Alta California*, May 24, 1869; M. G. Gonzales, *Mexicanos*, 91; Pitt, *Decline of the Californios*, 43.

97. At least four of the petitioners had non-Spanish surnames, but one of them, Frank Lightston, was probably related to another petitioner, Juana Soto de Lightston. For a transcription of the petition with a list of all fifty petitioners, see Cleland, *Cattle on a Thousand Hills*, 238–43.

98. Petition of Antonio María Pico et al., to the Senate and House of Representatives of the United States, ms. HM 514, Huntington Library, San Marino, California, reprinted in Weber, *Foreigners in Their Native Land*, 195–99.

99. Petition of Antonio María Pico et al., reprinted in Weber, *Foreigners in Their Native Land*, 195–99.

100. Petition of Antonio María Pico et al., reprinted in Weber, *Foreigners in Their Native Land*, 196–99.

101. The petition begins by identifying the signatories as "some of us citizens of the United States, previously citizens of the Republic of Mexico." Cleland, *Cattle on a Thousand Hills*, 238.

102. Petition of Antonio María Pico et al., reprinted in Weber, *Foreigners in Their Native Land*, 199.

103. *Indianola Bulletin* (no date), reprinted in *Gonzales Inquirer*, September 17, 1853.

104. Secretaría de Relaciones al Ministro de México en Washington, December 28, 1853, reprinted in Moyano Pahissa, *Protección consular*, 38–39.

105. J. A. Hernández, *Mexican American Colonization*, 68–80.

106. Montejano, *Anglos and Mexicans in the Making of Texas*, 28.

107. Thompson, *Cortina*, 10.

108. Thompson, *Cortina*, 11–12, 15–16; Valerio-Jiménez, *River of Hope*, 137.

109. Goldfinch and Canales, *Juan N. Cortina*, 6; Valerio-Jiménez, *River of Hope*, 229.

110. Thompson, *Cortina*, 17–18.

111. Valerio-Jiménez, *River of Hope*, 158–72.

112. *Difficulties on Southwestern Frontier*, H.R. Doc. No. 52, 36th Cong., 1st Sess., at 70 (1860) (hereafter cited as DSF).

113. DSF, 70.

114. DSF, 71; Valerio-Jiménez, *River of Hope*, 226.

115. DSF, 71.

116. DSF, 70–72; Valerio-Jiménez, *River of Hope*, 224–28.

117. DSF, 80–81.

118. DSF, 81.

119. DSF, 81; Valerio-Jiménez, *River of Hope*, 165–72.

120. DSF, 81.

121. DSF, 70, 71, 80; *American Flag*, November 26, 1859.

122. James Fentress and Chris Wickham, *Social Memory* (Oxford: Blackwell, 1992), 25, quoted in Brundage, "No Deed but Memory," 4.

123. Brundage, "No Deed but Memory," 5.

124. While the proclamations do not use "conquest," they do refer to "conquerors" when explaining that the "[Mexican] race has never humbled itself before the conqueror." I ac-

knowledge that some Indigenous groups managed to survive, and in some cases thrive, under Spanish colonial rule. My argument here is that Spanish Mexican colonists did conquer, enslave, and decimate some Native American groups.

Chapter Three

1. *La Gaceta*, March 19, 1881. The battle of Resaca de Guerrero, commonly known in the United States as the battle of Resaca de la Palma, was the second major engagement between US and Mexican troops and took place on May 9, 1846. Yáñez, "Battle of Resaca de la Palma," 354–57.

2. More information on the Californio lancers is found in Christensen and Christensen, *U.S.-Mexican War*, 117–20; Frazier, *United States and Mexico at War*, 72–73, 159–60, 218–20.

3. Some Mexican nationals resettled in New Mexico and Texas during Mexico's battle against the French in the 1860s. For the case of Juarez loyalists seeking refuge and eventually settling in New Mexico, see Mora, *Border Dilemmas*, 94.

4. On colonization expeditions of Californios into Mexico in the 1850s and 1870s, see, respectively, Pitt, *Decline of the Californios*, 210–13, and Camarillo, *Chicanos in a Changing Society*, 65.

5. *La Gaceta*, March 19, 26, and April 2, 9, 16, 1881; Quiñonez, "De pronósticos, calendarios y almanaques," 344–45.

6. *La Gaceta*, March 19, 1881. According to Quiñonez, the retrospective series appeared between 1849 and 1851. Quiñonez, "De pronósticos, calendarios y almanaques," 344–45; Kanellos, "Brief History of Hispanic Periodicals," 91, 194, 313.

7. Quiñonez, "De pronósticos, calendarios y almanaques," 331, 349.

8. *La Gaceta*, April 16, 1881.

9. Weber, *Foreigners in Their Native Land*, 154.

10. *La Gaceta*, September 11, 1880.

11. Camarillo, *Chicanos in a Changing Society*, 74–76. According to Cary McWilliams, this impoverishment led European Americans to abandon the term "Californios" and begin referring to them as "Mexicans." McWilliams, *Southern California Country*, 63.

12. Camarillo, *Chicanos in a Changing Society*, 58–65, 69–72.

13. Camarillo, *Chicanos in a Changing Society*, 65. In several issues, *La Gaceta* covered the efforts of Manuel Castro and Samuel Brannan to establish a colony of settlers (Mexican and Anglo-American) in northern Sonora on behalf of Mexico's government. Editor Arzaga described Castro as someone who had "always been loyal to the mother country [Mexico] even though he was a native of this state [California]." See *La Gaceta*, March 12, April 23, May 7, May 14, 1881. Bringhurst, "Samuel Brannan and his Forgotten Final Years," 149.

14. Griswold del Castillo, *Treaty of Guadalupe Hidalgo*, 190 (emphasis mine). "The treaty made no mention of language rights, but over time former Mexican citizens used the treaty to advocate for their right to access their own language." Lozano, *American Language*, 5, 108.

15. Nieto-Phillips, *Language of Blood*, 76–77.

16. Approximately sixteen bilingual newspapers and thirteen Spanish-language newspapers were published in the 1880s. Meléndez, *So All Is Not Lost*, 26, 34, 42; Nieto-Phillips, *Language of Blood*, 105–6.

17. Nieto-Phillips, *Language of Blood*, 79.

18. Joseph introduced *House Bill 12646* in 1889. *El Tiempo*, March 21, 1889; Lozano, *American Language*, 102, 108.

19. Nieto-Phillips, *Language of Blood*, 74–77.

20. According to the 1880 census, the percentages of foreign-born population were as follows: New Mexico (7.0%), Washington (23.4%), Montana (41.6%), and Dakotas (62.1%). *Admission of New Mexico into Union*, S. Rep. No. 520, 54th Cong., 1st Sess., at 43–44 (1892).

21. *Admission of New Mexico into Union*, S. Rep. No. 520, 54th Cong., 1st Sess., at 44–45 (1892).

22. Fernández, *Biography of Casimiro Barela*, 69–71.

23. Fernández, *Biography of Casimiro Barela*, 71–72; Nieto-Phillips, *Language of Blood*, 77–78; *Santa Fe New Mexican Review*, March 30, 1885.

24. Fernández, *Biography of Casimiro Barela*, 72–73, 80–82; Nieto-Phillips, *Language of Blood*, 77–78.

25. Lozano, *American Language*, 95–96; J. R. Chávez, *Lost Land*, 61–62.

26. Fernández, *Biography of Casimiro Barela*, 46–47.

27. Fernández, *Biography of Casimiro Barela*, 49–54; Lozano, *American Language*, 95–98.

28. Like the different labels for the US-Mexico War, the various terms used for the Cuban War of Independence reveal the distinct subject positions, goals, and interpretations of the actors involved.

29. Fernández, *Biography of Casimiro Barela*, 113–19.

30. Lozano, *American Language*, 5.

31. Fernández, *Biography of Casimiro Barela*, xxxv, 50–52; Lozano, *American Language*, 95–98.

32. Fernández, *Biography of Casimiro Barela*, 49–54; Lozano, *American Language*, 95–98.

33. *Admission of New Mexico into Union*, S. Rep. No. 520, 54th Cong., 1st Sess., at 43 (1892).

34. *Admission of New Mexico into Union*, 43.

35. Stewart's bill was S. 4450, 51st Cong., 1st Sess. (1890), 10764; *La Estrella Mejicana*, October 11, 1890. The newspaper also carried a *décima* poem urging voters to reelect Joseph as New Mexico's congressional representative.

36. In addition to an article citing the accusation against Joseph, the newspaper carried a *décima* poem making the same accusation. *El Nuevo Mexicano*, October 18, 1890; Meyer, *Speaking for Themselves*, 24.

37. Fernández, *Biography of Casimiro Barela*, 84–86.

38. Gómez, *Manifest Destinies*, 123–24.

39. *Santa Fe Daily New Mexican*, September 5, 1891.

40. *Independent Democrat*, March 8, 1893.

41. Gonzales, *Mexicanos*, 104; Weber, *Foreigners in Their Native Land*, 156–57.

42. Weber, *Foreigners in Their Native Land*, 157.

43. *El Tiempo*, February 26, 1885, October 22, 1888. E. N. Ronquillo might have also worked as a journalist in New Mexico, as scholar A. Gabriel Meléndez identifies Elfego N. Ronquillo as a practicing journalist. Meléndez, *So All Is Not Lost*, 87.

44. *El Tiempo*, April 30, 1885.

45. *Boletin Popular*, May 27, 1886. These numbers in *Boletin Popular* were incorrect. The Treaty of Guadalupe Hidalgo transferred 525,000 square miles, while the Gadsden Treaty transferred 29,670 square miles from Mexico to the United States.

46. *Boletin Popular*, March 19, 1887. The grant was apparently made to Dr. Beales, who married a Mexican woman. The legality of the grant was questioned by various litigants. See Stanley, *Grant That Maxwell Bought*, 102–9.

47. *El Nuevo Mundo*, May 8, 1897.

48. Tinker Salas, *In the Shadows of Eagles*, 92–94.

49. Tinker Salas, *In the Shadows of Eagles*, 82–88.

50. Tinker Salas, *In the Shadows of Eagles*, 102.

51. Tinker Salas, *In the Shadows of Eagles*, 103–4.

52. Manuel Escalante, Mexican Consul in Tucson, Arizona, to Mexican Secretary of the Foreign Ministry, August 6, 1878, Archivo Histórico de la Secretaría de Relaciones Exteriores, 11-2-106, in Moyano Pahissa, *Protección consular*, 28–30.

53. Manuel Escalante to Mexican Secretary of the Foreign Ministry, August 6, 1878, 28–30.

54. Manuel Escalante to Mexican Secretary of the Foreign Ministry, August 6, 1878, 28–30.

55. Délano, *Mexico and Its Diaspora*, 63; Lajous, *México y el mundo*, 61.

56. Délano, *Mexico and Its Diaspora*, 63.

57. Lajous, *México y el mundo*, 61.

58. Délano, *Mexico and Its Diaspora*, 63; Lajous, *México y el mundo*, 61–62.

59. Gilbert González, *Mexican Consuls and Labor Organizing*, 1–5.

60. Historians have disagreed on whether Mexican consulates have played a positive or a negative role in support of Mexican Americans and Mexican immigrants in the United States. For summaries of this debate, see Gómez-Quiñones, "Piedras contra la luna," 495–97; Gilbert González, *Mexican Consuls and Labor Organizing*, 1–5.

61. Valerio-Jiménez, *River of Hope*, 106, 135–36, 158–63.

62. *El Progreso*, January 14, 1876. According to the Handbook of Texas, John Salmon "Rip" Ford had served in the Texas army during the republic period, served during the US-Mexico War, and later became a Texas Ranger. He became an editor of *Austin Texas Democrat* and Brownsville's *Sentinel*. Ford was also elected as Brownsville's mayor in 1874 and was a state senator from 1876 to 1879. Perhaps more importantly for this analysis, Ford was sent to the border region to try to quell Cortina's rebellion in 1859. Seymour V. Connor, "Ford, John Salmon [Rip]," *Handbook of Texas Online*, Texas State Historical Association, updated July 30, 2020, www.tshaonline.org/handbook/online/articles/ffo11.

63. *El Progreso*, January 14, 1876.

64. *El Progreso*, January 14, 1876. The editorial refers to the Rangers led by McKensie, which might have been a reference to Ranald Slidell MacKenzie, an army officer who was stationed along the border in the early 1870s when he led a series of raids into Mexico in pursuit of Native Americans believed to be engaged in cattle theft. Ernest Wallace, "MacKenzie, Ranald Slidell," *Handbook of Texas Online*, Texas State Historical Association, updated November 30, 2019, www.tshaonline.org/handbook/online/articles/fma07. A short list of the atrocities committed by Texas Rangers during the war can be found in Greenberg, *Wicked War*, 195, 223; Johannsen, *To the Halls of the Montezumas*, 37–38, 134–36; Foos, *Short, Offhand, Killing Affair*, 114, 119–21, 131–33.

65. Connor, "Ford, John Salmon [Rip]."

66. Sánchez, Pita, and Reyes, "Nineteenth Century Californio Testimonials," vii–viii; Sánchez, *Telling Identities*, ix–x.

67. Sánchez, *Telling Identities*, 3.

68. Sánchez, *Telling Identities*, 24.

69. Beebe and Senkewicz, *Testimonios*, 31, 145.

70. Sánchez, Pita, and Reyes, "Nineteenth Century Californio Testimonials," 46; Beebe and Senkewicz, *Testimonios*, 143–49.

71. Osuna de Marrón, "Recuerdos de Doña Felipa Osuna de Marrón," 50–51.

72. Osuna de Marrón, "Recuerdos de Doña Felipa Osuna de Marrón," 46, 51–52.

73. Osuna de Marrón, "Recuerdos de Doña Felipa Osuna de Marrón," 51–52; Christensen and Christensen, *U.S.-Mexican War*, 118–19.

74. Osuna de Marrón, "Recuerdos de Doña Felipa Osuna de Marrón," 46, 51–52.

75. Osuna de Marrón, "Recuerdos de Doña Felipa Osuna de Marrón," 52–53.

76. Sánchez, Pita, and Reyes, "Nineteenth Century Californio Testimonials," 124; Sánchez, *Telling Identities*, 108.

77. Pitt, *Decline of the Californios*, 134; Sánchez, Pita, and Reyes, "Nineteenth Century Californio Testimonials," 124; Sánchez, *Telling Identities*, 259–63.

78. Coronel, "De Cosas de California," 133, 136.

79. Coronel, "De Cosas de California," 129–32, 135.

80. Pitt, *Decline of the Californios*, 27–32; Davis, "Bear Flag Revolt," 40–41.

81. Coronel, "De Cosas de California," 129–30.

82. Coronel, "De Cosas de California," 131–32, 134.

83. Coronel, "De Cosas de California," 133.

84. Coronel, "De Cosas de California," 134.

85. Coronel, "De Cosas de California," 126.

86. Coronel, "De Cosas de California," 125–27.

87. Coronel, "De Cosas de California," 132–33.

88. After her second marriage, she became known as Juana Machado de Ridington. Sánchez, Pita, and Reyes, "Nineteenth Century Californio Testimonials," 16; Beebe and Senkewicz, *Testimonios*, 119–20.

89. Beebe and Senkewicz, *Testimonios*, 119–20; Sánchez, Pita, and Reyes, "Nineteenth Century Californio Testimonials," 16. Note that Juana Machado used a Spanish-sounding version of her surname.

90. Machado de Ridington (Wrightington), "Los Tiempos Pasados de la Alta California," 27–28.

91. Sánchez, Pita, and Reyes, "Nineteenth Century Californio Testimonials," 16.

92. Machado de Ridington (Wrightington), "Los Tiempos Pasados de la Alta California," 18.

93. Machado de Ridington (Wrightington), "Los Tiempos Pasados de la Alta California," 20–22; Beebe and Senkewicz, *Testimonios*, 128–33.

94. Machado de Ridington (Wrightington), "Los Tiempos Pasados de la Alta California," 28.

95. Sánchez, *Telling Identities*, 152.

96. Sánchez, Pita, and Reyes, "Nineteenth Century Californio Testimonials," 16–17.

97. Brandes and Savage, "Times Gone By in Alta California," 196–97.

98. Pérez, *Remembering the Hacienda*, 56.

99. Padilla, *My History, Not Yours*, 77–78; Pérez, *Remembering the Hacienda*, 56; Rosenus, "Mariano Guadalupe Vallejo," 455–56; Sánchez, Pita, and Reyes, "Nineteenth Century Californio Testimonials," 138.

100. Sánchez, Pita, and Reyes, "Nineteenth Century Californio Testimonials," 138; Sánchez, *Telling Identities*, 272.

101. Rosenus, "Mariano Guadalupe Vallejo," 455–56; Vallejo, "De recuerdos históricos y personales," 139.

102. Vallejo, "De recuerdos históricos y personales," 139, 142.

103. The number of confirmed land claims by Californios do not support Vallejo's claim, so his view is probably shaped by his own experience and the experience of close associates.

104. Vallejo, "De recuerdos históricos y personales," 139–40, 143.

105. Vallejo, "De recuerdos históricos y personales," 140–41.

106. Vallejo, "De recuerdos históricos y personales," 142. Vallejo blamed the increasing number of people in mental asylums on the introduction of hard liquor from France and Germany by European Americans.

107. Hernandez, *City of Inmates*, 14–15, 30–34.

108. Vallejo, "De recuerdos históricos y personales," 142–43.

109. Sanchez and Pita, "María Amparo Ruiz de Burton and the Power of Her Pen," 73.

110. MARB to Platón Vallejo, April 23, 1859, Jamul, California, in Ruiz de Burton, *Conflicts of Interest*, 157 (emphasis mine).

111. Sánchez and Pita, introduction to *Conflicts of Interest*, 97–100.

112. Sánchez and Pita, introduction to *Conflicts of Interest*, 386–88.

113. Ewence, "Memories of Suburbia," 141, 173.

114. Ruiz de Burton published *The Squatter and the Don* under the pseudonym "C. Loyal," standing for "Ciudadano Leal" or "Citizen Loyal," a common way of ending official government letters in nineteenth-century Mexico. Sánchez and Pita, "María Amparo Ruiz de Burton and the Power of Her Pen," 76–77.

115. Pérez, *Remembering the Hacienda*, 11.

116. Tuttle, "Symptoms of Conquest," 64.

117. Sánchez and Pita, "María Amparo Ruiz de Burton and the Power of Her Pen," 76–77; Montes, "We Were Born to Do Something," 297.

118. Aranda, "Returning California to the People," 23.

119. Pérez, "Remembering the Hacienda," 31; Sánchez and Pita, "María Amparo Ruiz de Burton and the Power of Her Pen," 77.

120. Ruiz de Burton, *Squatter and the Don*, 65–66.

121. Ruiz de Burton, *Squatter and the Don*, 162.

122. Sánchez and Pita, "María Amparo Ruiz de Burton and the Power of Her Pen," 79; Sánchez and Pita, introduction to *The Squatter and the Don*, 26–29; Warford, "'Eloquent and Impassioned Plea,'" 18; Aranda, "Returning California to the People," 13–15; Pérez, "Remembering the Hacienda," 28.

123. Ruiz de Burton, *Squatter and the Don*, 65–66; Pérez, "Remembering the Hacienda," 38.

124. Tuttle, "Symptoms of Conquest," 62–63; Alemán, "'Thank God, Lolita Is Away,'" 100, 104–5, J. M. González, "Whiteness of the Blush," 158–59.

125. Pérez, "Remembering the Hacienda," 28, 37.

126. Sánchez and Pita, "María Amparo Ruiz de Burton and the Power of Her Pen," 79–80.

127. Warford, "'Eloquent and Impassioned Plea,'" 8–11; Starr, *Americans and the California Dream*, 26.

128. Sánchez and Pita, "María Amparo Ruiz de Burton and the Power of Her Pen," 78; Ruiz, "Captive Identities," 114–15. Referring to *The Squatter and the Don*, Ernesto Chávez argues, "Although a fictionalized account, one could argue, of course, that these were Ruiz de Burton's sentiments for she was a displaced elite Mexican woman." E. Chávez, "U.S. War with Mexico in History and Memory," 7.

129. Sánchez and Pita, "María Amparo Ruiz de Burton and the Power of Her Pen," 81.

130. Sánchez and Pita, introduction to *The Squatter and the Don*, 10.

131. Sánchez and Pita, "María Amparo Ruiz de Burton and the Power of Her Pen," 79; Warford, "'Eloquent and Impassioned Plea,'" 8–10.

132. Ruiz de Burton, *Squatter and the Don*, 165; Sánchez and Pita, introduction to *The Squatter and the Don*, 25.

133. Ruiz de Burton, *Squatter and the Don*, 65.

134. Warford, "'Eloquent and Impassioned Plea,'" 5–7, 12, 19–20; Ruiz de Burton, *Conflicts of Interest*, 564–69.

135. Warford, "'Eloquent and Impassioned Plea,'" 9–10; Ruiz de Burton, *Conflicts of Interest*, 564–69.

Chapter Four

1. Clemente Idar, "Tantos los niños mexicanos como los mexico-americanos, son excluidos de las escuelas oficiales," *La Crónica*, December 24, 1910.

2. Gabriela González, *Redeeming La Raza*, 20.

3. Valerio-Jiménez, *River of Hope*, 182–84.

4. Gutiérrez, *Walls and Mirrors*, 40.

5. Valdés, *Al Norte*, 8–9.

6. Contrary to contemporary anti-immigrant views, Mexican immigrants rarely competed with non–Mexican Americans for jobs and housing, since they entered the labor market in agriculture, railroad, and construction—industries in which Mexican Americans were the main labor force. Gutiérrez, *Walls and Mirrors*, 60, 69–70, 158.

7. Gutiérrez, *Walls and Mirrors*, 59–65; Camarillo, *Chicanos in a Changing Society*, 188.

8. Sánchez, *Becoming Mexican American*, 151–54, 171–87.

9. Pycior, *Democratic Renewal*; Pycior, "La Raza Organizes," 26; De León, *Tejano Community*, 194–96; Zamora, *World of the Mexican Worker*, 72.

10. According to Pycior, while most *mutualista* members were laborers, skilled craftsmen and shopkeepers were among the founders of various mutual aid societies. Pycior, "La Raza Organizes," 34–36.

11. Pycior, "La Raza Organizes," 44.

12. Pycior, "La Raza Organizes," 27, 50, 55–56; Pycior, *Democratic Renewal*, 6–7; Zamora, *World of the Mexican Worker*, 72.

13. Pycior, "La Raza Organizes," 28, 56, 85–91, 105–6; Zamora, *World of the Mexican Worker*, 72; Pycior, *Democratic Renewal*, 42, 51.

14. Pycior, "La Raza Organizes," 102–4.

15. Pycior, "La Raza Organizes," 147–48, 150–54. For an example, see "Ley General de Instruccion Obligatoria," *Imparcial de Texas*, September 5, 1918, 6.

16. Pycior, *Democratic Renewal*, 52–53.

17. Pycior, "La Raza Organizes," 97–99.

18. Pycior, *Democratic Renewal*, 50.

19. The founding statement of Houston's Sociedad Mutualista Benito Juárez explained its deliberate naming choice: "'Benito Juárez' was the name proposed and accepted by unanimous applause. Everyone admitted that the Mexican heart has a passion for improvement and that the example of a true Indian, who by his civic virtues and self-worth rose to the first place among his compatriots and became a national Mexican symbol, was the name for their society." "Spirit and Solidarity of Brotherhood," 107; Pycior, "La Raza Organizes," 28, 38, 50, 61, 218.

20. Pycior, "La Raza Organizes," 28; Zamora, *World of the Mexican Worker*, 60, 74–76; Pycior, *Democratic Renewal*, 45–46.

21. Pycior, *Democratic Renewal*, 48–49.

22. González, *Redeeming La Raza*, 19–20.

23. González, *Redeeming La Raza*, 20–21, 29.

24. González, *Redeeming La Raza*, 6–7.

25. González, *Redeeming La Raza*, 26–27; Zamora, *World of the Mexican Worker*, 97.

26. Clemente Idar, "En pro de la raza mexicana del estado de Texas," *La Crónica*, November 26, 1910; González, *Redeeming La Raza*, 20.

27. Barragán-Goetz, *Reading, Writing, and Revolution*, 51.

28. Barragán-Goetz, *Reading, Writing, and Revolution*, 56.

29. Idar, "En pro de la raza mexicana."

30. Clemente Idar, "La exclusion de los miños mexicanos en la mayor parte de las escuelas oficiales de Texas, es positiva," *La Crónica*, December 17, 1910.

31. Idar, "La exclusion de los miños mexicanos."

32. Idar, "La exclusion de los miños mexicanos"; Barragán-Goetz, *Reading, Writing, and Revolution*, 61.

33. Idar, "Tantos los niños mexicanos."

34. Idar, "En pro de la raza mexicana."

35. "El Imparciál de Texas," *La Crónica*, December 10, 1910; Freund, *Modern American Metropolis*, 101.

36. F. M. Bralley, "Texas' Educational Outlook," *Houston Post*, December 29, 1910, 7 (emphasis mine). A partial Spanish-language account of Bralley's speech is found in "Extracto de un discurso del superintendente de instrucción pública de Texas," *La Crónica*, January 12, 1911.

37. Cited in Barragán-Goetz, *Reading, Writing, and Revolution*, 59.

38. "La Prensa de Mexico y de Texas se Interesa por el Bienestar de los Mexicanos en este Pais," *La Crónica*, January 12, 1911; Barragán-Goetz, *Reading, Writing, and Revolution*, 59.

39. "Teachers Meet in School Auditorium," *Abilene Daily Reporter*, December 29, 1910, 1.

40. De León, *Tejano West Texas*, 102.

41. De León, *Tejano West Texas*, 103; "Proceder injusto y ofensivo," *El Regidor*, June 30, 1910; Villanueva, *Lynching of Mexicans in the Texas Borderlands*, 37.

42. "Proceder injusto y ofensivo," *El Regidor*, June 30, 1910; De León, *Tejano West Texas*, 103.

43. Villanueva, *Lynching of Mexicans in the Texas Borderlands*, 37–38.

44. "Los mexicanos de San Angelo demandan a los sindicos," *La Crónica*, June 25, 1910; "La exclusion en el Condado de Guadalupe," *La Crónica*, December 31, 1910 (emphasis in original); Freund, *Modern American Metropolis*, 103; Villanueva, *Lynching of Mexicans in the Texas Borderlands*, 37.

45. Idar, "Tantos los niños mexicanos."

46. Villanueva, *Lynching of Mexicans in the Texas Borderlands*, 37.

47. "Los mexicanos de San Angelo demandan a los sindicos," *La Crónica*, June 25, 1910; "La exclusion en el Condado de Guadalupe"; Freund, *Modern American Metropolis*, 103; De León, *Tejano West Texas*, 103.

48. De León, *Tejano West Texas*, 104.

49. *San Angelo Standard*, June 20, 1910, quoted in De León, *Tejano West Texas*, 104. According to Villanueva, the Mexican parents' decision to withhold their school-age children's names from the census successfully reduced the amount of state funding for San Angelo, and this reduction was the reason the school board quickly offered to make improvements to the "Mexican school" and hire male teachers. A week after Mexican parents met with the school board, the city ordered the census to be retaken in the Mexican section of San Angelo, which yielded more school-age Mexican children. Villanueva, *Lynching of Mexicans in the Texas Borderlands*, 37.

50. "Los mexicanos de San Angelo demandan a los sindicos," *La Crónica*, June 25, 1910. At some point, the school board offered to enroll ethnic Mexican children in two "Mexican schools," but ethnic Mexican parents rejected this proposal. De León, *Tejano West Texas*, 105–6.

51. "El asunto de escuelas en San Angelo," *El Regidor*, August 4, 1910.

52. "San Angelo Wrong, Thinks Consul," *El Paso Herald*, September 23, 1910; De León, *Tejano West Texas*, 107.

53. "San Angelo Wrong, Thinks Consul"; De León, *Tejano West Texas*, 107; "Serious," *San Antonio Light*, October 1, 1910, cited in Villanueva, *Lynching of Mexicans in the Texas Borderlands*, 39.

54. *San Angelo Standard*, September 21, 1910, quoted in De León, *Tejano West Texas*, 106.

55. "Mexicans Refuse to Enter Own Schools," *Abilene Daily Reporter*, September 22, 1910; "Mexicans Scorn Isolation," *Victoria Advocate*, September 23, 1910.

56. De León, *Tejano West Texas*, 108. Villanueva argued that attending the Catholic school was "an improvement in the eyes of the Mexican families, because at least their children attended school on the same grounds as white children." Villanueva, *Lynching of Mexicans in the Texas Borderlands*, 39.

57. De León, *Tejano West Texas*, 109.

58. De León, *Tejano West Texas*, 108–9.

59. "La exclusion en el Condado de Guadalupe."

60. According to Haney López, the federal judge personally believed Rodríguez was not white but granted him citizenship based on the Treaty of Guadalupe Hidalgo. Haney López, *White by Law*, 43–44, 164; Villanueva, *Lynching of Mexicans in the Texas Borderlands*,

34. An early examination of the Rodríguez case is found in De León, *In Re Ricardo Rodríguez*.

61. Haney López, *White by Law*, 197n37.

62. "La repercusion de un linchamiento," *Regeneración*, November 11, 1910, 1; "Mexicano quemado vivo en Rock Springs, Texas," *El Tiempo*, November 19, 1910, 1, 3; "Los sucesos de México," *El Diario de Tampa*, November 11, 1910, 2–3.

63. "Mexico Prevents Further Rioting," *New York Times*, November 11, 1910; "Barbarismos," *La Crónica*, November 12, 1910; Martínez, *Injustice Never Leaves You*, 31.

64. "Barbarismos," *La Crónica*, November 12, 1910.

65. "Mexico Prevents Further Rioting," *New York Times*, November 11, 1910; "Barbarismos," *La Crónica*, November 12, 1910 (emphasis mine). Included in the *La Crónica* article was a summary of the news account of the killing published in an unnamed English-language newspaper.

66. Martínez, *Injustice Never Leaves You*, 40–41.

67. *El Imparcial*, November 9, 1910; "Protesta contra Estados Unidos," *Diario del Hogar*, November 10, 1910; Rosales, ¡*Pobre Raza!*, 11.

68. "Barbarismos," *La Crónica*, November 12, 1910; Rosales, ¡*Pobre Raza!*, 11; "El Mexicano Quemado," *El Imparcial*, November 9, 1910; "Un Mejicano fué lynchado en Tejas," *El País*, November 5, 1910; "Minister Creel Expresses his regret to U.S.," *The Mexican Herald*, November 12, 1910; "The Difference with Mexico," *Daily Star and Herald*, November 13, 1910; "Protesta contra Estados Unidos," *Diario del Hogar*, November 10, 1910.

69. Villanueva, *Lynching of Mexicans in the Texas Borderlands*, 56.

70. "Protesta contra Estados Unidos," *Diario del Hogar*, November 10, 1910; "Minister Creel Expresses his regret to U.S.," *The Mexican Herald*, November 12, 1910; "The Difference with Mexico," *Daily Star and Herald*, November 13, 1910; Martínez, *Injustice Never Leaves You*, 36–37.

71. "El lynchamiento de Antonio Rodriguez," *Diario del Hogar*, November 10, 1910.

72. "Un Mejicano fué lynchado en Tejas," *El País*, November 5, 1910. *El País* identified itself as a Catholic daily on its masthead.

73. "Barbarismos," *La Crónica*, November 12, 1910.

74. González, *Redeeming La Raza*, 16–17.

75. I do not discount the race, class, and gender divisions that existed in Mexico but want to highlight the different power relations and racial hierarchy in the United States.

76. Rosales, ¡*Pobre Raza!*, 110–11.

77. Villanueva, *Lynching of Mexicans in the Texas Borderlands*, 57; "Mexico Prevents Further Rioting," *New York Times*, November 11, 1910; "More Mexican Rumors," *New York Times*, November 21, 1910.

78. "Hard Fighting in Puebla," *New York Times*, May 8, 1911.

79. Villanueva, *Lynching of Mexicans in the Texas Borderlands*, 62.

80. De León, *They Called Them Greasers*, 49–62.

81. Campbell, "History and Collective Memory in Texas," 274–77.

82. Martínez, *Injustice Never Leaves You*, 36–37.

83. Villanueva, *Lynching of Mexicans in the Texas Borderlands*, 60.

84. Villanueva, *Lynching of Mexicans in the Texas Borderlands*, 59.

85. Villanueva, *Lynching of Mexicans in the Texas Borderlands*, 59. The letter is dated December 1913.

86. Arnoldo De León documented numerous examples of European American racism that led to accusations of disloyalty, criminality, and immorality against Mexicans. See De León, *They Called Them Greasers*. In interviews of residents of Nueces County conducted by Paul S. Taylor, he found that the state's public schools fostered European Americans' dislike and distrust of Tejanos, especially with discussions of the US-Mexico War. One informant stated, "My father and mother told us to hate the Mexicans because of the war with Mexico. They are treacherous and are always over the border for devilment." See Taylor, *An American-Mexican Frontier*, 273.

87. "El lynchamiento de Antonio Rodriguez," *Diario del Hogar*, November 10, 1910, 1; Villanueva, *Lynching of Mexicans in the Texas Borderlands*, 59; "Mexico Prevents Further Rioting," *New York Times*, November 11, 1910, 1.

88. Villanueva, *Lynching of Mexicans in the Texas Borderlands*, 56–57.

89. "Yankilandia," *Diario del Hogar*, November 9, 1910.

90. Martínez, *Injustice Never Leaves You*, 36–37.

91. Idar, "Tantos los niños mexicanos."

92. "Barbarismos," *La Crónica*, November 12, 1910.

93. Among US-based newspapers reporting on the lynching were "Lynching Angers Mexico," *New York Times*, June 26, 1911, 4; "Issue Warrants Lynching Case," *Austin Statesman*, June 24, 1911; "Notes on the Capitol," *Austin Statesman*, February 25, 1912; "Lynching Case to Come Up Monday," *San Antonio Express*, November 5, 1911; "Witness Tells of Lynching," *San Antonio Express*, November 11, 1911; "Arrests Follows Lynching," *Dallas Morning News*, June 25, 1911. Mexican newspapers' coverage of lynching of Mexicans and African Americans included "No hubo lynchamiento de mexicano en Texas," *El Diario*, June 3, 1911; "Supuesto lynchamiento," *Diario del Hogar*, June 3, 1911; "La secretaria de relaciones ordena una investigación por el lynchamiento," *El Diario*, June 22, 1911; "Antonio Gomez, lynchado en Texas era hijo de mexicanos," *El Diario*, June 23, 1911; "Linchamiento de un negro," *Nueva Era*, August 13, 1911; "Lynchamiento," *Nueva Era*, November 10, 1911; "Linchamiento de un pastor negro," *Nueva Era*, December 17, 1911.

94. "Cobarde, infame e inhumano lynchamiento de un jovencito mexicano en Thorndale, Milam Co., Texas," *La Crónica*, June 29, 1911, 1, 4; González, *Redeeming La Raza*, 199n2; "Lynching Angers Mexico," *New York Times*, June 26, 1911, 4.

95. "Cobarde, infame e inhumano lynchamiento"; translated quotation found in "Unhuman Lynching of a Young Mexican in Thor[n]dale, the Entire World Is Paying Attention to this Savage Crime . . . ," in Freund, *Modern American Metropolis*, 103–5.

96. Rosales, ¡*Pobre Raza!*, 37.

97. "Cobarde, infame e inhumano lynchamiento," 4.

98. Rosales, ¡*Pobre Raza!*, 37; Martínez, *Injustice Never Leaves You*, 41.

99. "Lynching Angers Mexico," *New York Times*, June 26, 1911, 4.

100. "Valentia cobardia de los lynchadores de Thorndale," *La Crónica*, July 13, 1911, 1.

101. Freund, *Modern American Metropolis*, 104.

102. "Valentia cobardia." According to Gabriela González, Nicasio Idar was one of the founders of the Order of the Knights of Honor, which was a fraternal organization that

promoted middle class respectability and cultural reform. González, *Redeeming La Raza*, 27.

103. "La barbarie en los Estados Unidos," *Regeneración*, August 5, 1911. In addition to publishing periodic updates on the Cárdenas Martínez case, Ricardo Flores Magón urged readers to contribute financially to the child's legal defense. "Para el neno mexicano," *Regeneración*, August 19, 1911; "A salvar un inocente," *Regeneración*, September 9, 1911; "El niño martir," *Regeneración*, September 16, 1911; "En defensa de los mexicanos," *Regeneración*, May 11, 1912; Flores Magón accused the Mexican government headed by Francisco Madero of inaction because Cárdenas Martínez was poor. Had the child been wealthy, argued Flores Magón, the Mexican government would have freed him. "El niño martir," *Regeneración*, June 15, 1912.

104. "Traduccion: Integra la narración que hizo el Lic. George Estes . . . ," *La Crónica*, October 26, 1911; "Barbarity in the United States," *Abilene Daily Reporter*, September 2, 1911; "Mexican Boy Will Appeal to Highest Court," *San Antonio Light*, April 9, 1912; "Mexican Must Pay Penalty for Crime," *Galveston Daily News*, May 9, 1914; "Honor Meet to Martinez," *Abilene Daily Reporter*, May 17, 1914; "Will Ask for Habeas Corpus," *Abilene Daily Reporter*, September 5, 1911; "Martinez Gets 30-Day Reprieve," *Pecos Enterprise*, December 19, 1973; Thomas Woods, "León Cárdenas Martínez, Jr., Trial," *Handbook of Texas Online*, Texas State Historical Association, updated April 27, 2021, www.tshaonline.org/handbook/online/articles/jrl02; González, *Redeeming La Raza*, 39; Martínez, *Injustice Never Leaves You*, 48.

105. "The Pardoning Power," *Houston Post*, September 17, 1911, 28.

106. "The Pardoning Power," 28; "Facultad de Perdonar," *La Crónica*, September 21, 1911; Martínez, *Injustice Never Leaves You*, 48; Limón, "El Primer Congreso Mexicanista," 89.

107. "El león despierta," *La Crónica*, July 13, 1911, 4; Zamora, *World of the Mexican Worker*, 97–98.

108. Lisandro Peña, "Introduccion," *Primer Congreso Mexicanista*; N. Idar, "Circular," *Primer Congreso Mexicanista*; Rosales, *Chicano!*, 62; Woods, "León Cárdenas Martínez, Jr., Trial."

109. Limón, "El Primer Congreso Mexicanista," 88.

110. Nicasio Idar was a mason and a member of Sociedad Mutualista Benito Juárez of Laredo and the fraternal lodge La Orden Caballeros de Honor. González, *Redeeming La Raza*, 27–29; Limón, "El Primer Congreso Mexicanista," 87, 91.

111. González, *Redeeming La Raza*, 29; Limón, "El Primer Congreso Mexicanista," 86–91.

112. "Discurso pronunciado por su autor J.M. Mora," *Primer Congreso Mexicanista*, 16.

113. Limón noted that the organizers selected the September date to take advantage of lower train fares and the large number of visitors in Laredo drawn to its *fiestas patrias*. Limón, "El Primer Congreso Mexicanista," 92; González, *Redeeming La Raza*, 30–31; Zamora, *World of the Mexican Worker*, 97.

114. González, *Redeeming La Raza*, 32; "Discurso pronunciado por su autor el Sr. Severo E. Peña," *El Primer Congreso Mexicanista*, 33.

115. "Discurso pronunciado por la Sra. Hortencia Moncayo," *El Primer Congreso Mexicanista*, 26.

116. Limón, "El Primer Congreso Mexicanista," 97–98; González, *Redeeming La Raza*, 37, 41–43.

117. "Cobarde, infame e inhumano lynchamiento"; Freund, *Modern American Metropolis*, 105.

118. "Cobarde, infame e inhumano lynchamiento."

119. "Cobarde, infame e inhumano lynchamiento."

120. Idar, "Tantos los niños mexicanos."

121. Idar, "Tantos los niños mexicanos." Idar might have been referring to the legal implication that Mexican immigrants could become naturalized US citizens, since the treaty had given Mexican Americans US citizenship.

122. Idar, "En pro de la raza mexicana."

123. Idar, "En pro de la raza mexicana."

124. "La exclusion en el Condado de Guadalupe"; Villanueva, *Lynching of Mexicans*, 34; Haney-López, *White by Law*, 43–44.

125. González, *Redeeming La Raza*, 20.

126. Idar, "Tantos los niños mexicanos."

127. Gross, "'Caucasian Cloak,'" 340; Foley, *Mexicans in the Making of America*, 55–56.

128. Idar, "Tantos los niños mexicanos"; *La Crónica*, February 9, 1911.

129. "Los niños mexicanos en Texas," *La Crónica*, November 26, 1910; Idar, "Tantos los niños mexicanos."

130. Idar, "Tantos los niños mexicanos."

131. "Barbarismos," *La Crónica*, November 12, 1910, 1; "La exclusion de los niños mexicanos," 1, 8; Idar, "Tantos los niños mexicanos." For more information on the exclusion of Japanese, Chinese, and Korean students by the San Francisco Board of Education in 1906, see Eng and McFarland, "Japanese Question."

132. Idar, "Tanto los niños Mexicanos."

133. Idar, "Tanto los niños Mexicanos."

134. Haney López, *White by Law*, 43–44, 88–89; Gómez, *Manifest Destinies*, 83–84.

135. "Nuestra labor es elogiada por la prensa mexicana," *La Crónica*, February 9, 1911, 4.

136. Nieto-Phillips, *Language of Blood*, 55, 58.

137. Kiser, *Borderlands of Slavery*, 123–27.

138. Nieto-Phillips, *Language of Blood*, 47, 54–55.

139. For an incisive analysis of the continued practice of peonage and Indian slavery in New Mexico after US annexation, see Kiser, *Borderlands of Slavery*.

140. Nieto-Phillips, *Language of Blood*, 56, 58.

141. Nieto-Phillips, *Language of Blood*, 52–53, 57–58.

142. Reprint of article in *Santa Fe New Mexican* appeared in *El Combate*, April 2, 1904; Nieto-Phillips, *Language of Blood*, 53.

143. *El Eco del Valle*, December 8, 1910, January 19, 1911.

144. *El Labrador*, March 6, 1903, February 4, 1910, August 25, 1911.

145. *El Labrador*, March 6, 1903. Senator Stephen Benton Elkins had previously served as a congressional delegate for the territory of New Mexico. As New Mexico's territorial representative, Elkins had advocated for statehood, given speeches in Congress, and cited the promises of self-government in the Treaty of Guadalupe Hidalgo as justification for statehood. Nieto-Phillips, *Language of Blood*, 67–69.

146. Nieto-Phillips, *Language of Blood*, 69.

147. Nieto-Phillips, *Language of Blood*, 74, 76, 82; Mora, *Border Dilemmas*, 231–32, 235.
148. Mora, *Border Dilemmas*, 241–42.
149. Mora, *Border Dilemmas*, 240.
150. Mora, *Border Dilemmas*, 237–40.
151. Mora, *Border Dilemmas*, 239–40; Montoya, "Dual World of Governor Miguel Otero," 19.
152. Mora, *Border Dilemmas*, 240.
153. Mora, *Border Dilemmas*, 241.
154. Mora, *Border Dilemmas*, 245.
155. Mora, *Border Dilemmas*, 246.
156. Mora, *Border Dilemmas*, 227, 232–34.
157. Meléndez, *So All Is Not Lost*, 5.
158. R. A. García, *Rise of the Mexican American Middle Class*, 222, 225, 235.
159. Van Wagenen, *Remembering the Forgotten War*, 135; Vázquez de Knauth, *Mexicanos y Norteamericanos*, 9–20, 146–49, 191–93; Alcaraz and Zoraida Vázquez, *Apuntes para la historia*.
160. "Las modificaciones al tratado de paz," *La Prensa*, May 16, 1920; "Las garantias que Mexico pidio al gobierno americano en el Tratado de Guadalupe Hidalgo, en 1848," *La Prensa*, June 16, 1921.
161. Luna Lawhn, "María Luisa Garza," 85; Kanellos, *Hispanic Literature*, 28.
162. García defines "permanency" as the "understanding, conscious and unconscious, that for Mexican Americans there was no retreat to Mexico." M. T. García, *Mexican Americans*, 15, 20, 85.
163. R. A. García, *Rise of the Mexican American Middle Class*, 236, 245.
164. Medeiros, "La Opinión," 73–75; R. A. García, *Rise of the Mexican American Middle Class*, 226–27.
165. Medeiros, "La Opinión," 68–74.
166. Hinojosa, *El México de afuera*, 9–10.
167. Griswold del Castillo, *Treaty of Guadalupe Hidalgo*, 158–59; Kramer, "A Border Crosses."
168. The controversy over El Chamizal was resolved with several ceremonies and a formal agreement beginning in 1964 and extending through 1968. Kramer, "A Border Crosses"; Griswold del Castillo, *Treaty of Guadalupe Hidalgo*, 161–63.
169. Cline, *United States and Mexico*, 13–14; Liss, "Chamizal Conflict," 70–77; Griswold del Castillo, *Treaty of Guadalupe Hidalgo*, 159–61; Vargas, "Abrazo at the Border," 393–94; Hill, "El Chamizal," 513–16; Kramer, "A Border Crosses."
170. "Cardenas Studies Note," *New York Times*, August 30, 1938, 6.
171. Payan, "Border Wars," 17–19.
172. Griswold del Castillo, *Treaty of Guadalupe Hidalgo*, 159; Kramer, "A Border Crosses."
173. According to Liss, the conflict over the Chamizal was more important to Mexicans than Americans as it influenced Mexican historical accounts of US-Mexico relations. Liss, "The Chamizal Conflict," 44, 93–94; Vargas notes that the disagreement over the Chamizal even surfaced in the platforms of presidential candidates. Vargas, "Abrazo at the Border," 390, 394; Kramer, "A Border Crosses"; Payan, "Border Wars," 16–17, 19; "Un punto de honra nacional," *La Prensa*, June 8, 1919, 3.

174. "El famoso asunto de 'El Chamizal,'" *El Labrador*, December 20, 1907, 1; "Las fronteras entre Mexico y los Estados Unidos," *La Prensa*, March 7, 1920, 3; "Ofrecen a Carranza tres millones por El Chamizal," *El Heraldo de Mexico*, September 17, 1919, 1.

175. "Land Disputed by US, Mexico," *Austin Statesman*, October 17, 1945, 2; "Land Seizure Arbitration Is Refused U.S. by Cardenas," *Washington Post*, August 4, 1938, 1; "Mexican Land," *New York Times*, July 24, 1938, 2E; "Border Riddles to Be Studied," *Los Angeles Times*, June 15, 1934, 10. One of the few articles that briefly mentioned the treaty that ended the US-Mexico War was "The Chamizal Zone Dispute," *Washington Post*, April 14, 1925, 6.

176. Griswold del Castillo, *Treaty of Guadalupe Hidalgo*, 161–63; Kramer, "A Border Crosses."

177. *La Prensa*, June 6, 1921; "Las modificaciones al tratado de paz," *La Prensa*, May 16, 1920, 3, 19; Griswold del Castillo, *Treaty of Guadalupe Hidalgo*, 96, 126; "Las garantias que Mexico pidio al gobierno americano en el Tratado de Guadalupe Hidalgo, en 1848," *La Prensa*, June 16, 1921, 1; "El reconocimiento se extendera dentro de cuarenta dias," *La Prensa*, August 28, 1921, 1, 13.

178. "Las garantias que Mexico pidio al gobierno Americano en el Tratado de Guadalupe Hidalgo, en 1848," *La Prensa*, June 16, 1921.

179. The interpretation of the Treaty of Guadalupe Hidalgo on which Aguirre based his arguments appeared in US newspapers again in 1946 with a series of stories regarding the nine islands. Bowman, "Question of Sovereignty," 291–92. According to a news story in the *Los Angeles Times*, the Mexican Foreign Office was preparing to submit the claim to the islands "before a century of United States occupation might seem to have settled title." "Mexico Will Claim Santa Catalina and Other Islands for Tax Levying," *Los Angeles Times*, July 23, 1946.

180. *La Prensa*, June 15, 1921. Aguirre based his interpretation on the following arguments: the US did not have rights to the nine islands because it had not discovered them, had not purchased them, and had not conquered them. According to the International Code of the United States, Aguirre maintained, the United States did not have legal jurisdiction over the islands because they were more than one maritime league off the coast of California.

181. Griswold del Castillo, *Treaty of Guadalupe Hidalgo*, 141–42.

182. "Los Estados Unidos no entregaran las islas que reclama Mexico como suyas," *La Prensa*, June 24, 1921.

183. "Se espera en Washington que haga pronto el gobierno Mexicano la reclamación por las nuevas islas," *La Prensa*, June 27, 1921.

184. "El concepto que de la Baja California tienen mexicanos y extranjeros," *La Prensa*, May 10, 1920.

185. "Presenta el Ministro de la Rosa el Tratado de Guadalupe Hidalgo," *La Prensa*, May 9, 1921. Griswold del Castillo, *Treaty of Guadalupe Hidalgo*, 53. Coincidentally, an editorial, "En defensa de humildes," appeared on the same page of *La Prensa* containing details on the plea by Mexican immigrants (in the United States) to the Mexican government to obtain aid so that they could repatriate to Mexico. The editorial mentioned that these workers could obtain only temporary employment in the United States but often lost such employment due to the economic crisis experienced there.

186. Walter, "Benjamin M. Read," 394; Nieto-Phillips, *Language of Blood*, 189.

187. Nieto-Phillips, *Language of Blood*, 43–45, 189; Walter, "Benjamin M. Read," 394; Twitchell, *Spanish Archives of New Mexico*, 185–86.

188. Mora, *Border Dilemmas*, 247; Walter, "Benjamin M. Read," 394. Meléndez, *So All Is Not Lost*, 125–26; Meyer, *Speaking for Themselves*, 191.

189. Nieto-Phillips, *Language of Blood*, 192–95.

190. Walter, "Benjamin M. Read," 394–95; Nieto-Phillips, *Language of Blood*, 189; Meyer, *Speaking for Themselves*, 192–94; Meléndez, *So All Is Not Lost*, 127, 129.

191. Van Wagonen, *Remembering the Forgotten War*, 11–13, 124.

192. Mora, *Border Dilemmas*, 250; Read, *Guerra México-Americana*, 181–87.

193. Read, *Guerra México-Americana*, 3–4. Read criticized Mexican historians for being "slow to censure" the U.S. government for the shedding of innocent blood. Meléndez, *So All Is Not Lost*, 128.

194. Read, *Guerra México-Americana*, 4; Nieto-Phillips, *Language of Blood*, 190.

195. Read, *Guerra México-Americana*, 4. Read did not explain why he stressed European Americans' racial hatred of the Spanish but not the French or British, who had also held jurisdiction over parts of Florida and Louisiana.

196. Read, *Guerra México-Americana*, 6; Read, *Illustrated History of New Mexico*, 5.

197. Nieto-Phillips, *Language of Blood*, 189; Meléndez, *So All Is Not Lost*, 126, 128.

198. Meyer, *Speaking for Themselves*, 250n32.

199. Read, *Guerra México-Americana*, 6; Meléndez, *So All Is Not Lost*, 127.

200. Meyer, *Speaking for Themselves*, 191; De León, *Racial Frontiers*, 106.

201. Read, *Illustrated History of New Mexico*, 395.

202. Mora, *Border Dilemmas*, 248–49.

203. Nieto-Phillips, *Language of Blood*, 81. The Spanish-language newspapers did not capitalize "Hispano-americanos," as is common in the Spanish language.

204. Nieto-Phillips, *Language of Blood*, 194; Mora, *Border Dilemmas*, 249.

205. Mora, *Border Dilemmas*, 249; Nieto-Phillips, *Language of Blood*, 81–82.

206. Nieto-Phillips, *Language of Blood*, 81–82.

207. Nieto-Phillips, *Language of Blood*, 81–82; Mora, *Border Dilemmas*, 249.

208. Meyer, *Speaking for Themselves*, 197.

209. Read was convinced that he was writing revisionist history that would result in "many of the so-called great men, so highly and wrongly praised, . . . be[ing] relegated to a shameful place in history and many of those overlooked . . . turn[ing] out to be the ones truly worthy of honor in the history pages of the land of their birth." Meyer, *Speaking for Themselves*, 195–96; Melendez, *So All Is Not Lost*, 129; Nieto-Phillips, *Language of Blood*, 190.

210. Read considered himself a native son of New Mexico even though he was one generation removed from Sonora, México, where his mother was likely born. Mora, *Border Dilemmas*, 249; Read, *Illustrated History of New Mexico*, 395.

211. Meyer, *Speaking for Themselves*, 195, 250n32.

212. Schwartz and Cook, "Archives, Records, and Power," 2.

213. Benjamin Read, letter to the editor, *La Revista de Taos*, September 24, 1909, quoted in Meyer, *Speaking for Themselves*, 196.

214. Nieto-Phillips, *Language of Blood*, 187–88.

215. Meyer, *Speaking for Themselves*, 199.

216. Meléndez, *So All Is Not Lost*, 129–30.

217. Nieto-Phillips, *Language of Blood*, 190–92.

218. Nieto-Phillips, *Language of Blood*, 196.

Chapter Five

1. Orozco, *No Mexicans, Women, or Dogs Allowed*, 120–73.
2. M. T. García, *Mexican Americans*, 31–32.
3. M. T. García, *Mexican Americans*, 32.
4. Gutiérrez, *Walls and Mirrors*, 82, 85.
5. Gutiérrez, *Walls and Mirrors*, 85; Alonso Perales, "La unificación de los méxico-americanos, parte I," *La Prensa*, September 4, 1929.
6. Gutiérrez, *Walls and Mirrors*, 82.
7. Gutiérrez, *Walls and Mirrors*, 84.
8. Gutiérrez, *Walls and Mirrors*, 85.
9. C. E. Castañeda, "Why I Chose History," 478; Almaráz, "Carlos Eduardo Castañeda, Mexican American Historian," 334; Félix D. Almaráz Jr., "Castaneda, Carlos Eduardo," *Handbook of Texas Online*, Texas State Historical Association, updated July 28, 2020, www.tshaonline.org/handbook/online/articles/fca85.
10. José T. Canales to Carlos E. Castañeda, July 17, 1935, Carlos E. Castañeda Papers, box 9.6, University of Texas at Austin; J. M. González, *Border Renaissance*, 113.
11. I use the term "Mexican Americans" to refer to US citizens of Mexican ancestry, "Mexican immigrants" to refer to Mexican citizens living in the United States, and "ethnic Mexicans" to refer to people of Mexican ancestry irrespective of citizenship.
12. M. T. García, *Mexican Americans*, 29–33, 35, 46; Márquez, *LULAC*, 19–22, 37–38; Orozco, *No Mexicans, Women, or Dogs Allowed*, 134–36; Gutiérrez, *Walls and Mirrors*, 74–78.
13. J. M. González, *Border Renaissance*, 110–11; R. Tijerina, "Constructing Tejano Memory," 193–96.
14. McLemore, "Early Historians and the Shaping of Texas Memory," 34–35.
15. On Canales as LULAC founder, see Orozco, *No Mexicans, Women, or Dogs Allowed*, 27, 163–66. While he remained a Mexican citizen, Castañeda was an "honorary member" of LULAC, and he became a regular member after becoming a naturalized US citizen. Almaráz, *Knight without Armor*, 80; Kaplowitz, *LULAC*, 44. Zamora O'Shea had joined LULAC by 1937. J. M. González, *Border Renaissance*, 5, 94; Tijerina, historical introduction, xviii.
16. Beginning in the early 1930s, Neil Foley argued, middle-class Mexican Americans, including LULAC members, "sought to overcome the stigma of being Mexican by asserting their Americanness. In the process, they equated Americanness with whiteness." Foley, "Partly Colored or Other White," 125.
17. Brown, "Counter-Memory and Race," 55–56; King, Crowley, and Brown, "Forgotten Legacy of Carter G. Woodson," 213–14.
18. Among the cohort of intellectuals and lay historians who published revisionist histories between the 1930s and the 1950s were Jovita González, Alonso Perales, Rubén Rendón Lozano, and J. Luz Sáenz. For a brief description of these intellectuals and their scholarship, see De León, "Texas Mexicans," 20–49.
19. In addition, some European immigrants left during World War I to serve in the military of their home countries. Mapes, "'Special Class of Labor,'" 66–67.
20. M. T. García, *Mexican Americans*, 27.

21. For examples of the effects of US conquest on Tejanos, see Montejano, *Anglos and Mexicans in the Making of Texas*; Alonzo, *Tejano Legacy*; A. Tijerina, *Tejano Empire*; Valerio-Jiménez, *River of Hope*.

22. Gutiérrez, *Walls and Mirrors*, 37–38, 46–65.

23. Balderrama and Rodriguez, *Decade of Betrayal*, 149–51, 336; Hoffman, *Unwanted Mexican Americans*, 126–27; Gutiérrez, *Walls and Mirrors*, 72; Guerin-Gonzales, *Mexican Workers and American Dreams*, 94, 111.

24. M. T. García, *Mexican Americans*, 26.

25. Blanton, "Citizenship Sacrifice," 300.

26. M. T. Garcia, *Mexican Americans*, 18–19.

27. Anthony Quiroz argues that returning World War I veterans combined with an increase in middle-class Mexican Americans fueled the beginning of the Mexican American movement to "claim citizenship" in the 1920s. Quiroz, *Claiming Citizenship*, xvii, 16.

28. According to Orozco, the League of Latin American Citizens (LLAC) was "sometimes also called the Latin American Citizens League (LACL)." Orozco, *No Mexicans, Women, or Dogs Allowed*, 125–26, 151, 156.

29. Orozco, *No Mexicans, Women, or Dogs Allowed*, 128–31, 138–43; R. García, "Alonso S. Perales," 99.

30. Blanton, "Citizenship Sacrifice," 299–300.

31. "Aims and Purposes of the League of United Latin American Citizens," *LULAC News*, April 30, 1932, 19; Gritter, *Mexican Inclusion*, 83; M. T. García, *Mexican Americans*, 29–33, 46; R. García, "Alonso S. Perales," 94, 99.

32. R. García, "Alonso S. Perales," 96.

33. Krochmal, *Blue Texas*, 126–27.

34. Almaráz, *Knight without Armor*, 3–4; Almaráz, "Carlos Eduardo Castañeda, Mexican American Historian," 320.

35. Almaráz, *Knight without Armor*, 5–13; Almaráz, "Carlos Eduardo Castañeda, Mexican American Historian," 321–22.

36. Almaráz, "Castaneda, Carlos Eduardo," 323–24; Almaráz, *Knight without Armor*, 18–42, 67; Lynch, "South Texas Renaissance Man," 43.

37. Almaráz, *Knight without Armor*, 68, 80–81, 153; Castañeda was invited to LULAC's founding convention but did not attend, writing, "I to this date am, in reality, a Mexican citizen and can't belong to the League," Orozco, *No Mexicans, Women, or Dogs Allowed*, 164.

38. Almaráz, *Knight without Armor*, 216–65; M. T. García, *Mexican Americans*, 241–44.

39. Gutiérrez, *Walls and Mirrors*, 74–78. M. T. García, *Mexican Americans*, 35.

40. Márquez, *LULAC*, 19–22, 37–38; Orozco, *No Mexicans, Women, or Dogs Allowed*, 134–36.

41. The editorial was unsigned but likely written by Valencia, the newsletter's editor. *LULAC News*, April 30, 1932.

42. Alonso Perales, quoted in Neil Foley, "Partly Colored or Other White," 131.

43. Goméz, *Manifest Destinies*, 83.

44. Foley, "Partly Colored or Other White," 129–30; R. García, "Alonso S. Perales," 99.

45. The United States formally granted Native Americans citizenship in 1924 with the Indian Citizenship Act, while the Jones Act (1917) granted Puerto Ricans US citizenship.

The United States did not remove barriers to naturalization for Chinese, South Asian, and Filipino immigrants until the 1940s. Spickard, *Almost All Aliens*, 308, 310, 327, 471.

46. Márquez, *LULAC*, 31; R. García, "Alonso S. Perales," 99.

47. Foley, "Partly Colored or Other White," 135.

48. Foley, *Quest for Equality*, 133–34; Foley, "Partly Colored or White," 125.

49. Márquez, LULAC, 30–34; Foley, "Partly Colored or White, 125; M. T. García, *Mexican Americans*, 48–49.

50. Foley, "Becoming Hispanic," 54–57, 63; Foley, "Partly Colored or Other White," 125; Johnson, "Cosmic Race in Texas," 414.

51. Blanton, "George I. Sánchez, Ideology, and Whiteness," 569–70, 572–74; Krochmal, *Blue Texas*, 126–31; Blanton, *George I. Sánchez*, 183, 202. Neil Foley acknowledges the variability of racial views and strategies among LULAC members. According to his research, several LULAC members condemned discrimination against African Americans. Foley, *Quest for Equality*, 134–35; Johnson, "Cosmic Race," 416n28.

52. Márquez, *LULAC*, 31.

53. Johnson, "Cosmic Race," 414–15; Carrigan and Webb, "*Muerto por unos desconocidos*," 58–59; Foley, "Becoming Hispanic," 54; M. T. García, *Mexican Americans*, 48; Lukens, *Quiet Victory for Latino Rights*, 97.

54. Márquez, *LULAC*, 33.

55. Márquez, "In Defense of My People," 34.

56. Krochmal, *Blue Texas*, 128–30.

57. José T. Canales, "The Romans of Today," *LULAC News*, February 1932, 5; M. T. García, *Mexican Americans*, 43.

58. M. T. García, *Mexican Americans*, 44.

59. Johnson, "Cosmic Race," 416–17. LULAC members often took pride in their Aztec, Mayan, or Toltec ancestry but denied any ancestry to non-sedentary Native groups. Thus, they embraced an Indigenous ancestry of groups with advanced civilizations. Lukens, *Quiet Victory for Latino Rights*, 97.

60. Márquez, "In Defense of My People," 35.

61. Johnson, "Cosmic Race," 404, 409–11; Lukens, *Quiet Victory for Latino Rights*, 83–84.

62. Johnson, "Cosmic Race," 417.

63. Lukens, *Quiet Victory for Latino Rights*, 98; Blanton, "George I. Sánchez, Ideology, and Whiteness," 604.

64. Márquez, "In Defense of My People," 34. Perales, like other LULAC members, understood that claiming whiteness (though not racial purity) also meant claiming to be "not Black" in the context of the US racial hierarchy in which they found themselves. Johnson, "Cosmic Race," 415.

65. Krochmal, *Blue Texas*, 126–30; Johnson, "Cosmic Race," 416–18.

66. De Zavala, *History and Legends of the Alamo*, vii; Raymond Estep, "Zavala, Lorenzo De," *Handbook of Texas Online*, Texas State Historical Association, updated March 21, 2019, www.tshaonline.org/handbook/online/articles/fza05. Adina De Zavala capitalized the "de" in her surname, while her father and grandfather did not. Flores, "Adina De Zavala and the Politics of Restoration," liiin3.

67. Robert L. Ables, "Zavala, Adina Emilia De," *Handbook of Texas Online*, Texas State Historical Association, updated January 15, 2021, www.tshaonline.org/handbook/online/articles/fzafg.

68. Flores, "Adina De Zavala and the Politics of Restoration," xl–lii; Cottraux, "Missed Identity," 2–4.

69. Flores, *Remembering the Alamo*, 89.

70. Cottraux, "Missed Identity," 64, 66–67; Ables, "Zavala, Adina Emilia De."

71. Adina De Zavala to Carlos E. Castañeda, April 30, 1933, and May 23, 1933, and Carlos E. Castañeda to Adina De Zavala, May 30, 1933, Carlos E. Castañeda Papers, box 15.4.

72. Adina De Zavala to Carlos E. Castañeda, March 20, 1934, and Carlos E. Castañeda to Adina De Zavala, March 24, 1934, Carlos E. Castañeda Papers, box 15.4.

73. Carlos E. Castañeda to Adina De Zavala, July 22, 1940, and Adina De Zavala to Carlos E. Castañeda, July 30, 1940, Carlos E. Castañeda Papers, box 15.4.

74. Adina De Zavala to Carlos E. Castañeda, July 30, 1940, and October 14, 1940, Carlos E. Castañeda Papers, box 15.4.

75. Flores, *Remembering the Alamo*, 71–75.

76. Ribb, "José Tomás Canales," 14–18; Johnson, *Revolution in Texas*, 43; Lynch, "South Texas Renaissance Man," 5–7; Orozco, *No Mexicans, Women, or Dogs Allowed*, 95; Evan Anders, "Canales, Jose Tomas," *Handbook of Texas Online*, Texas State Historical Association, updated January 11, 2023, www.tshaonline.org/handbook/online/articles/fcaag.

77. Ribb, "José Tomás Canales," 55, 118–19; Anders, "Canales, Jose Tomas."

78. J. M. González, *Border Renaissance*, 97. Benjamin Johnson argues that Tejano progressives petitioned the state and federal government to protect ethnic Mexicans during the racial violence of 1916–17, but neither President Woodrow Wilson nor Governor James Ferguson replied. Johnson, *Revolution in Texas*, 149–50.

79. Ribb, "José Tomás Canales," 1, 202–300, 302–48, 369–70; Johnson, *Revolution in Texas*, 171–75.

80. Alonzo, *Tejano Legacy*, 158; Montejano, *Anglos and Mexicans in the Making of Texas*, 43–47; Goldfinch and Canales, *Juan N. Cortina*, 17–41; Thompson, *Cortina*, 28–32, 37–38; Valerio-Jiménez, *River of Hope*, 179, 224.

81. Ribb, "José Tomás Canales," 204n685.

82. Ribb, "José Tomás Canales," 204n685; James A. Sandos, "Recovering the 1919 Canales Investigation" 221.

83. Ribb, "José Tomás Canales," 204n685.

84. Poole, "Strange Career of Jim Crow Archives," 24, 26.

85. José T. Canales to Carlos E. Castañeda, November 4, 1930, Carlos E. Castañeda Papers, box 9.6.

86. Schwartz and Cook, "Archives, Records, and Power," 2.

87. Carlos E. Castañeda to José T. Canales, November 12, 1930, Carlos E. Castañeda Papers, box 9.6.

88. On the important role of archivists in granting access to archives and how such access shaped historiography of the US South, see Poole, "Strange Career of Jim Crow Archives," 23–63.

89. José T. Canales to Carlos E. Castañeda, December 12, 1934, Carlos E. Castañeda Papers, Box 26.11.

90. According to Paul Lack and Raúl Ramos, the number of Tejanos who fought in the Texian Army during Texas's war of secession is difficult to calculate with precision due to incomplete records, but it was a significant number. Lack, *Texas Revolutionary Experience*, 132, 184; Ramos, *Beyond the Alamo*, 161–62. Various LULAC members explicitly criticized the state's history textbooks for anti-Tejano bias. For more information on LULAC's goals for the state's centennial celebrations, see J. M. González, *Border Renaissance*, 110–19.

91. J. M. González, *Border Renaissance*, 110–19.

92. Brown, "Counter-Memory and Race," 57.

93. J. M. González, *Border Renaissance*, 153.

94. Rubén Rendón Lozano would eventually complete the pamphlet. J. M. González, *Border Renaissance*, 116–19.

95. LULAC's limited finances prevented the organization from paying for Tejano Boy Scouts to lead tours of the missions. It is unclear if LULAC officially suggested to house a portrait of Seguín to the Texas Centennial Committee. J. M. González, *Border Renaissance*, 111–12.

96. DSF, 71, 79–82 DSF, Thompson, *Juan Cortina and the Texas-Mexico Frontier*, 23; Thompson, *Cortina*, 11–12, 39; Heintzelman, *Fifty Miles and a Fight*, 17–34; Valerio-Jiménez, *River of Hope*, 222–35; Jerry Thompson, "Cortina, Juan Nepomuceno," *Handbook of Texas Online*, Texas State Historical Association, updated on November 2, 2020, www.tshaonline.org/handbook/online/articles/fco73.

97. *American Flag*, November 26, 1859; DSF, 81; Goldfinch and Canales, *Juan N. Cortina*, 42–43.

98. Goldfinch and Canales, *Juan N. Cortina*, 1–71; Thompson, *Cortina*, 2–3; Anders, "Canales, Jose Tomas."

99. These negative characterizations are found in the following books: Dobie and Young, *Vaquero of the Brush Country*, xii, 49; Webb, *Texas Rangers*, 176; Woodman, *Cortina*, 8.

100. Canales, "Juan N. Cortina Presents His Motion," 1–19.

101. Thompson, *Cortina*, 1–2.

102. José T. Canales to Carlos E. Castañeda, December 3, 1949, and Carlos E. Castañeda to José T. Canales, December 19, 1949, Carlos E. Castañeda Papers, box 9.7.

103. Carlos E. Castañeda to José T. Canales, February 3, 1950, Carlos E. Castañeda Papers, box 9.7.

104. José T. Canales to Carlos E. Castañeda, February 7, 1950, Carlos E. Castañeda Papers, box 9.7.

105. Ribb, "José Tomás Canales," 402–9.

106. Ribb, "José Tomás Canales," 402–13.

107. José T. Canales to Carlos E. Castañeda, February 7, 1950, Carlos E. Castañeda Papers, box 9.7.

108. José T. Canales to Carlos E. Castañeda, March 8, 1950, Carlos E. Castañeda Papers, box 9.7.

109. José T. Canales to Carlos E. Castañeda, February 7, 1950, Carlos E. Castañeda Papers, box 9.7. Dobie's reference to the book, coauthored with John D. Young, related the

experiences of John Young in the nineteenth century. Dobie and Young, *Vaquero of the Brush Country*, xi–xvi.

110. José T. Canales to Carlos E. Castañeda, March 8, 1950, Carlos E. Castañeda Papers, box 9.7.

111. Reidt, "Unreconstructed History," 80–81.

112. J. M. González, *Border Renaissance*, 81.

113. Ribb, "José Tomás Canales," 18.

114. Taylor, *An American-Mexican Frontier*, 272–74.

115. José T. Canales to Carlos E. Castañeda, March 8, 1950, Carlos E. Castañeda Papers, box 9.7.

116. Anders, "Canales, Jose Tomas."

117. Lynch, "South Texas Renaissance Man," 37–39.

118. A. Tijerina, historical introduction, x–xi. Valerio-Jiménez, *River of Hope*, 17–91.

119. J. M. González, *Border Renaissance*, 71.

120. Her friendship with Canales had been crucial in gaining admission to Southwest Texas State. Garza-Falcón, "Renewal through Language," xxvii–xxx; J. M. González, *Border Renaissance*, 71–72; Cynthis E. Orozco, "O'Shea, Maria Elena Zamora," *Handbook of Texas Online*, Texas State Historical Association, updated May 21, 2020, www.tshaonline.org/handbook/online/articles/fos21.

121. A. Tijerina, historical introduction, xviii–xix. According to John Morán González, "By 1937, Zamora O'Shea had joined the League of United Latin American Citizens (LULAC), praising the organization for its efforts to improve access to public education for Mexican American children and for its antiracist work to restore Mexican American civil rights." González, *Border Renaissance*, 94.

122. Carlos Castañeda to Elena Zamora O'Shea, June 8, 1929, and June 8, 1929, Carlos E. Castañeda Papers, box 32.7.

123. Elena Zamora O'Shea to Carlos Castañeda, September 9, 1929, Carlos E. Castañeda Papers, box 32.7.

124. Elena Zamora O'Shea to Carlos Castañeda, September 9, 1929, and October 2, 1929, and Carlos Castañeda to Elena Zamora O'Shea, September 17, 1929, and October 24, 1929, Carlos E. Castañeda Papers, box 32.7.

125. Elena Zamora O'Shea to Carlos Castañeda, June 12, 1929, April 28, 1930, and February 3, 1931, and Carlos Castañeda to Elena Zamora O'Shea, May 13, 1931, Carlos E. Castañeda Papers, box 32.7.

126. Elena Zamora O'Shea to Carlos Castañeda, undated, and Carlos Castañeda to Elena Zamora O'Shea, August 21, 1929, Carlos E. Castañeda Papers, box 32.7; J. M. González, *Border Renaissance*, 84.

127. Elena Zamora O'Shea to Carlos Castañeda, June 29, 1929, October 2, 1929, April 28, 1930, July 22, 1930, February 3, 1931, and undated, and Carlos Castañeda to Elena Zamora O'Shea, July 20, 1929, October 24, 1929, May 11, 1930, and May 13, 1931, Carlos E. Castañeda Papers, box 32.7.

128. Elena Zamora O'Shea to Carlos Castañeda, June 12, 1929, Carlos E. Castañeda Papers, box 32.7.

129. Zamora O'Shea, "Ranches of Southwest Texas," lxxi.

130. Elena Zamora O'Shea to Carlos Castañeda, October 20, 1929, and Carlos Castañeda to Elena Zamora O'Shea, October 24, 1929, Carlos E. Castañeda Papers, box 32.7.

131. Elena Zamora O'Shea to Carlos Castañeda, October 28, 1929, Carlos E. Castañeda Papers, box 32.7.

132. Elena Zamora O'Shea to Carlos Castañeda, November 16, 1929, Carlos E. Castañeda Papers, box 32.7; J. M. González, *Border Renaissance*, 85–87; Pasternack, "History Should Be Told as Fact," 15–17.

133. Elena Zamora O'Shea to Carlos Castañeda, November 16, 1929, Carlos E. Castañeda Papers, box 32.7. It is unclear if the book to which Zamora O'Shea referred, "The Birth of Texas," was published.

134. Elena Zamora O'Shea to Carlos Castañeda, April 28, 1930, Carlos E. Castañeda Papers, box 32.7; J. M. González, *Border Renaissance*, 84. Zamora O'Shea might have been referring to the film *Heroes of the Alamo*, which opened in 1937. Flores, *Remembering the Alamo*, 110.

135. Flores, *Remembering the Alamo*, 98–103.

136. One example of this struggle is the efforts to create a Mexican American studies curriculum and textbook for use in the state's public schools. Tom Dart, "Classrooms: The Latest Battleground in Texas's Culture Wars," *Guardian*, September 19, 2018.

137. Laura E. Gómez argues that US society continues to portray Latinxs as "perpetual foreigners." Gómez, *Inventing Latinos*, 13.

138. Perales and Ben Garza were "careful to insist that LULAC would support the immigration bill if its sponsors could prove 'that Mexicans—that is Mexicans from Mexico—are a menace to the American working man because ... they ... lower wages,' rather than basing the legislation strictly on racial criteria." Gutiérrez, *Walls and Mirrors*, 85–86.

139. Gutiérrez, *Walls and Mirrors*, 86.

140. Orozco, "Alonso S. Perales," 24.

141. LULAC founder Manuel Carvajal Gonzales's surname is spelled as "Gonzales" and as "González" in various documents, such as the *LULAC News*. I have chosen to use "Gonzales" because he used it more often in his published articles, and most scholars use this surname for him.

142. M. C. Gonzalez, "¿Cual es Nuestro Deber?" *LULAC News*, October 1, 1931. For a similar view by contemporary historians, see Balderrama and Rodriguez, *Decade of Betrayal*, 99.

143. Gonzalez, "¿Cual es Nuestro Deber?"

144. Andres Hernandez Jr., "In Relation to Our Civil Liberties," *LULAC News*, August 1, 1932.

145. Gutiérrez, *Walls and Mirrors*, 86.

146. Nguyen, *Nothing Ever Dies*, 49.

147. Hernandez, "In Relation to Our Civil Liberties."

148. Hernandez, "In Relation to Our Civil Liberties."

149. F. Valencia, "Are Texas-Mexicans 'Americans'?," *LULAC News*, April 30, 1932.

150. Foley, "Partly Colored or Other White," 125.

151. Mora, *Border Dilemmas*, 231–36.

152. Native Americans' control over Texas and other parts of northeastern Mexico is explained in various books, including DeLay, *War of a Thousand Deserts*, 35–60; Hämäläinen, *Comanche Empire*, 1–12, 18–106. According to Juliana Barr, "Eighteenth-century Texas ... offers a story of Indian *dominance*." Barr, *Peace Came in the Form of a Woman*, 2–7, 20–25.

According to Benjamin Johnson, Valencia "drew heavily... from Vasconcelos and other prominent Latin American critics of US culture." Valencia acknowledged the significant roles of Native Americans and Africans in the racial fusion that created the Mexican "race," but he also believed in the benefits of modernization and Spanish civilization. Johnson, "Cosmic Race in Texas," 412–13, 416.

153. F. Valencia, "Are Texas-Mexicans 'Americans'?," *LULAC News*, April 30, 1932 (emphasis in original).

154. Because the Treaty of Guadalupe Hidalgo made Mexicans legally white, Mexican immigrants were eligible to become naturalized citizens while other people of color were not. According to legal scholar Ariela Gross, "Mexican Americans were held by federal and state courts to be white because they were citizens—'white by treaty.'" Gross, "'Caucasian Cloak,'" 340.

155. F. Valencia, "Are Texas-Mexicans 'Americans'?"

156. Juan N. Seguín famously wrote in his memoirs that he felt like a "foreigner in my native land" after experiencing the large demographic changes caused by the influx of Anglo-Americans to San Antonio while he served as mayor. Seguín was the last ethnic Mexican mayor of San Antonio before Henry Cisneros was elected in the 1980s. After attempting to defend ethnic Mexicans from attacks, Seguín fled the city after receiving deaths threat from Anglo-American vigilantes. Seguín, *Revolution Remembered*, 97; Roberto R. Calderón, "Tejano Politics," *Handbook of Texas Online*, Texas State Historical Association, updated February 15, 2020, www.tshaonline.org/handbook/online/articles/wmtkn.

157. F. Valencia, "Are Texas-Mexicans 'Americans'?"

158. McLemore, "Early Historians and the Shaping of Texas Memory," 24–25.

159. F. Valencia, "Are Texas-Mexicans 'Americans'?"; "Flanders' field" was a reference to the World War I battlefields in the Belgian and French regions of Flanders. The term became popular after the publication of a poem by Canadian officer Major John McCrae, "In Flanders Fields."

160. F. Valencia, "Are Texas-Mexicans 'Americans'?"

161. F. Valencia, editorial, *LULAC News*, December 1931, 1, cited in M. T. García, *Mexican Americans*, 34.

162. R. A. García, *Rise of the Mexican American Middle Class*, 294; M. T. García, *Mexican Americans*, 27.

163. Kaplowitz, *LULAC*, 31.

164. M. C. Gonzales quoted in Dickens, "Political Role of Mexican-Americans," 136.

165. R. A. García, *Rise of the Mexican American Middle Class*, 113–14.

166. M. T. García, *Mexican Americans*, 54–55.

167. Despite his support for Texas and for another breakaway republic, Carbajal sided with Mexico during the US-Mexico War and also fought in the Mexican army to repel the French in the early 1860s. Carbajal became the governor of the Mexican state of Tamaulipas in the 1860s. Orozco, *No Mexicans, Women, or Dogs Allowed*, 104; "Carbajal, Jose Maria Jesus," *Handbook of Texas Online*, Texas State Historical Association, updated May 4, 2022, www.tshaonline.org/handbook/online/articles/fca45.

168. R. A. García, *Rise of the Mexican American Middle Class*, 292–93.

169. Orozco, *No Mexicans, Women or Dogs Allowed*, 160; R. A. García, *Rise of the Mexican American Middle Class*, 266, 292, 294–95; M. T. García, *Mexican Americans*, 27.

170. R. A. García, *Rise of the Mexican American Middle Class*, 294–95.

171. "President General of L.U.L.A.C. Appeals to Members for Funds," *El Defensor*, June 19, 1931. According to the court ruling, the Del Rio ISD did not segregate schoolchildren on the basis of their Mexican ancestry but rather for pedagogical reasons. The court accepted the superintendent's arguments that Mexican American students attended separate schools through third grade because they often lacked sufficient English-language skills, enrolled in school late, and had irregular attendance due to their parents' migratory labor. LULAC and other organizations raised funds to appeal the case to the US Supreme Court, but the Supreme Court refused to hear the case. San Miguel, *"Let All of Them Take Heed,"* 78–80; Blanton, *Strange Career of Bilingual Education*, 95–96; Independent School Dist. v. Salvatierra, 33 S.W.2d 790 (Tex. Civ. App. 1930); Cynthia E. Orozco, "Del Rio ISD v. Salvatierra," *Handbook of Texas Online*, Texas State Historical Association, updated October 21, 2020, www.tshaonline.org/handbook/online/articles/jrd02.

172. R. A. García, *Rise of the Mexican American Middle Class*, 292.

173. "Prof. Loftin Is Teaching a Class of Teachers Who Will Undertake to Teach Pupils of Mexican Descent in Texas," *El Defensor*, June 19, 1931.

174. "Two Hundred Teachers Hear Address," *El Defensor*, July 10, 1931.

175. R. A. García, *Rise of the Mexican American Middle Class*, 294. Although not explicit, Gonzales was probably recalling Juan N. Seguín's famous phrase about appearing "as a foreigner in my own land" in this part of his speech.

176. "Two Hundred Teachers Hear Address."

177. "Two Hundred Teachers Hear Address."

178. "Two Hundred Teachers Hear Address."

179. "Two Hundred Teachers Hear Address."

180. "Two Hundred Teachers Hear Address."

181. "Two Hundred Teachers Hear Address"; M. C. Gonzales's speech was reprinted and translated into Spanish in the *LULAC News*, October 1, 1931, and September 1, 1931.

182. Kreneck, "Mr. LULAC," 231; Bernice Strong, "Ruiz, Jose Francisco," *Handbook of Texas Online*, Texas State Historical Association, updated August 4, 2020, www.tshaonline.org/handbook/online/articles/fru11.

183. Ramos, *Beyond the Alamo*, 139–40, 169–70; Strong, "Ruiz, Jose Francisco."

184. Kreneck, "Mr. LULAC," 234–35.

185. Kreneck, "Mr. LULAC," 235–36.

186. *Delgado v. Bastrop Indep. Sch. Dist.*, Civil Action No. 388 (W.D.Tex. 1948) (unreported); *Hernández v. Texas*, 347 U.S. 475 (1954); Márquez, *LULAC*, 54–55; M. T. García, *Mexican Americans*, 49–51, 57–58; Kreneck, "Mr. LULAC," 241–44.

187. John J. Herrera to the editor of the Mail Bag, *Houston Press*, June 9, 1941, John J. Herrera Papers, box 1, folder 8.

188. John J. Herrera to the editor of the Mail Bag, *Houston Press*, June 9, 1941.

189. Kreneck, "Mr. LULAC," 231.

190. Kreneck, "Mr. LULAC," 236–37.

191. John J. Herrera to Lassie Jackson, July 20, 1950, Portal to Texas History, University of North Texas, texashistory.unt.edu/ark:/67531/metapth250029. Ford Bend County is located in the southwest part of the Houston metropolitan area.

192. Nguyen, *Nothing Ever Dies*, 43.

193. John J. Herrera to Lassie Jackson, July 20, 1950.

194. For an example of Tejanos as a "suspect class" in San Antonio, see Ramos, *Beyond the Alamo*, 167–204.

195. There is a startling similarity in the arguments used by Herrera in 1950 and the resolutions passed by Tejanos of the Béxar County Democrats in 1855 who rejected the Know-Nothing Party's attacks on Tejanos. Consider the following resolution: "That we hold as a singular sentiment and desire to bear witness to the Honor, the Glory and the Prosperity of the country of our birth and the land of our affections; simultaneously contrast our obedience to the land [and] our interest in the welfare of Texas, against those that portend to take away our unalienable rights, and who, for the most part, are foreigners to our land, with at the most four years of residence in our State." Ramos, *Beyond the Alamo*, 212.

196. In his op-ed essay, Syers described the efforts of Corpus Christi resident W. M. Neyland, a realtor and Goliad native who, while traveling in Mexico, had discovered that Zaragoza was also born in Goliad (then La Bahia). In addition to working with American and Mexican groups to commemorate the centennial of Cinco de Mayo in Puebla, Neyland proposed a "commemorative shrine" in Goliad, Texas, to the "Man of Cinco de Mayo." Ed Syers, "The Man of Cinco de Mayo," *Houston Post*, February 24, 1964. Part of Syers's *Houston Post* op-ed essay also appeared in Ed Syers, "Memories of Goliad: Many Heroes Passed Her Way," *Corpus Christi Caller-Times*, February 21, 1964.

197. Syers, "Memories of Goliad."

198. John J. Herrera to the editor of Sound Off, *Houston Post*, February or March 1964, Portal to Texas History, University of North Texas, texashistory.unt.edu/ark:/67531/metapth24 8359.

199. Paredes, *Texas-Mexican Cancionero*, 24–25, 49–51; Paredes, "Folklore e historia," 216–20; *Daily Ranchero*, May 5, 1870, and May 7, 1870.

200. Mora, *Border Dilemmas*, 63, 235.

201. M. T. García, *Mexican Americans*, 200–201; Gómez-Quiñones, *Chicano Politics*, 50–51; Vargas, *Labor Rights Are Civil Rights*, 276–77; Behnken, *Fighting Their Own Battles*, 33.

202. M. T. García, *Mexican Americans*, 204; Pulido, "Checkered Choices, Political Assertions," 466.

203. "Breve historia del pueblo mexicano en E.U.," *Progreso*, June 1952 (author's translation).

204. Buelna, "Asociación Nacional México-Americana," 67; "Breve historia del pueblo mexicano."

205. M. T. García, *Mexican Americans*, 204.

206. "Breve historia del pueblo mexicano."

207. "Breve historia del pueblo mexicano."

208. "Breve historia del pueblo mexicano."

209. "El control del libre pensamiento en Los Angeles, California," *Progreso*, October 1950; "Convocatoria a la Segunda Convencion de la Asociacion Nacional Mexico-Americana," *Progreso*, June 1952; M. T. Garcia, *Mexican Americans*, 218.

210. "Segregan a los mexicanos aqui," *Progreso*, October 1950; Pulido, "Checkered Choices, Political Assertions," 472.

211. "Segregan a los mexicanos aqui"; M. T. García, *Mexican Americans*, 205–6.

212. "Segregan a los mexicanos aqui."

213. *Progreso*, June 1952 and October 1950.
214. "Tendremos razon?," *Progreso*, April 1952.
215. "El control del libre pensamiento."
216. "La Primer Convencion Nacional de ANMA"; "El control del libre pensamiento."
217. "Breve historia del pueblo mexicano."
218. "ANMA inicia su campaña," *Progreso*, October 1950; M. T. García, *Mexican Americans*, 217; Pulido, "Checkered Choices, Political Assertions," 468.
219. "Un dia con la señora secretaria general de ANMA," *Progreso*, October 1950.
220. M. T. García, *Mexican Americans*, 220.
221. M. T. García, *Mexican Americans*, 220–21.
222. M. T. García, *Mexican Americans*, 209.
223. M. T. García, *Mexican Americans*, 209.
224. "Saludo del presidente nacional," *Progreso*, April 1952.
225. M. T. García, *Mexican Americans*, 210.
226. "Paz o la guerra, *Progreso*, April 1952.
227. "El control del libre pensamiento."
228. M. T. García, *Mexican Americans*, 211.
229. M. T. García, *Mexican Americans*, 212.
230. "Convocatoria a la Segunda Convencion"; "El control del libre pensamiento"; M. T. García, *Mexican Americans*, 213.
231. M. T. García, *Mexican Americans*, 212.
232. M. T. García, *Mexican Americans*, 213.
233. Blanton, *George I. Sánchez*, 15, 19–20; García, *Mexican Americans*, 252.
234. Blanton, *George I. Sánchez*, 26, 46–63; M. T. García, foreword, xi.
235. G. I. Sánchez, *Forgotten People*, 12.
236. M. T. Garcia, *Mexican Americans*, 255.
237. M. T. García, foreword, xvii–xviii; Blanton, *George I. Sánchez*, 62; G. I. Sánchez, *Forgotten People*, 39.
238. G. I. Sánchez, *Forgotten People*, 12.
239. G. I. Sánchez, *Forgotten People*, 12.
240. G. I. Sánchez, *Forgotten People*, 3–5, 10–11; Blanton, *George I. Sánchez*, 62.
241. G. I. Sánchez, *Forgotten People*, 13, 19–25; M. T. García, *Mexican Americans*, 255–56, 270.
242. M. T. García, *Mexican Americans*, 271; Blanton, *George I. Sánchez*, 62–63; G. I. Sánchez, *Forgotten People*, 37–40.
243. M. T. García, *Mexican Americans*, 256–63; Blanton, *George I. Sánchez*, 16–17.
244. M. T. García, *Mexican Americans*, 270–71; M. T. García, foreword, xii–xiii; Blanton, *George I. Sánchez*, 167–68, 173, 177.
245. Coser, *Maurice Halbwachs on Collective Memory*, 52–53.
246. Kammen, *Mystic Chords of Memory*, 13.

Chapter Six

1. Sánchez, *Expedition through Aztlán*, 99.
2. Oropeza, *King of Adobe*, 14, 21; Rosales, *Chicano!*, 156–57; Busto, *King Tiger*, 35–36; Blawis, *Tijerina and the Land Grants*, 31.

3. Busto, *King Tiger*, 36, 38; Rosales, *Chicano!*, 157. Tijerina's schooling was sporadic, as he repeatedly left school when his family moved to join the migrant stream. Oropeza, *King of Adobe*, 18–19.

4. Busto, *King Tiger*, 39; Oropeza, *King of Adobe*, 18–19, 22–23; Rosales, *Chicano!*, 157.

5. The number of families (from a low of 7 to a high of 19) accompanying Tijerina to the Valle de Paz is in dispute by Tijerina (in his memoirs) and by scholars writing about him. For a discussion of these discrepancies, see Busto, *King Tiger*, 226n3. Tijerina, *They Called Me "King Tiger,"* 1–2; Oropeza, *King of Adobe*, 51; Rosales, *Chicano!*, 157; Busto, *King Tiger*, 9, 226n3; Blawis, *Tijerina and the Land Grants*, 33.

6. Busto, *King Tiger*, 39–40, 107–17.

7. Oropeza, *King of Adobe*, 52.

8. Oropeza, *King of Adobe*, 48; Busto, *King Tiger*, 118.

9. Busto, *King Tiger*, 118–19, 134–35; Oropeza, *King of Adobe*, 49–51.

10. Rosales, *Chicano!*, 157; Busto, *King Tiger*, 121–22, 130–32. Tijerina began learning about Nuevomexicanos' long history of land dispossession from the Penitente Brotherhood, whom he met during a 1956 trip to New Mexico after his religious commune in Arizona was flooded. Oropeza, *King of Adobe*, 45–53, 58–65.

11. Oropeza, *King of Adobe*, 73; Gardner, *¡Grito!*, 77.

12. Gardner, *¡Grito!*, 70–71; Rosales, *Chicano!*, 157.

13. Gardner, *¡Grito!*, 71; Oropeza, *King of Adobe*, 72–73.

14. Oropeza, *King of Adobe*, 125; Rosales, *Chicano!*, 157.

15. Busto, *King Tiger*, 46–47; Oropeza, *King of Adobe*, 94–95; Gardner, *¡Grito!*, 81.

16. Oropeza, *King of Adobe*, 68; Gardner, *¡Grito!*, 80–82; Rosales, *Chicano!*, 159.

17. Busto, *King Tiger*, 53; Oropeza, *King of Adobe*, 89.

18. Busto, *King Tiger*, 53.

19. Oropeza, *King of Adobe*, 114–15, 311n10.

20. Rosales, *Chicano!*, 158.

21. Oropeza, *King of Adobe*, 1–3.

22. Rosales, *Chicano!*, 168; Reies López Tijerina, interview.

23. Oropeza, *King of Adobe*, 233, 266.

24. Oropeza, *King of Adobe*, 266, 271–75.

25. Busto, *King Tiger*, 147, 149, 213n29; Calvin Kentfield, "Incident in Rio Arriba," *New York Times*, July 16, 1967; *Dallas Morning News*, September 3, 1967; "State Department Denies Land Claim," *New York Times*, June 8, 1968; Pete Herrera, "Land Grant Crusade Forged in Fire," *Dallas Morning News*, July 28, 1968; "What the Newspapers Wouldn't Publish," *El Grito del Norte*, September 15, 1968.

26. Armando Valdez, "Insurrection in New Mexico—the Land of Enchantment," *El Grito del Norte*, September 1, 1967.

27. Ed Meagher, "Seizure of N.M. Land Called Publicity Ploy: Tijerina Says Action Was Necessary to Get Officials to Reconsider Claims," *Los Angeles Times*, November 10, 1967; Ed Meagher, "Tijerina Forays Seen as Civil Rights Struggle: New Mexico Officials Fear Conviction of Leader, Followers Won't Deter Violence," *Los Angeles Times*, November 20, 1967.

28. Griswold del Castillo, *Treaty of Guadalupe Hidalgo*, 105.

29. "'The Anglo Has Lived His Time': Minorities' Time Coming, Tijerina Warns," *Los Angeles Times*, May 8, 1969.

30. Meagher, "Tijerina Forays."
31. Meagher, "Seizure of N.M. Land."
32. Meagher, "Tijerina Forays." During the same trial, Tijerina bluntly argued, "If through this land fight we protect our civil rights, that's our goal." Meagher, "Seizure of N.M. Land."
33. Meagher, "Cargo Relates New Mexican Rebels' Woes," *Los Angeles Times*, November 9, 1967; Meagher, "Tijerina Forays."
34. "Protesters Burn Draft Cards, Send Pieces Aloft on Balloons," *Los Angeles Times*, October 16, 1967.
35. Gardner, ¡*Grito!*, 141; Oropeza, *King of Adobe*, 222.
36. Oropeza, introduction, xxxiii.
37. Oropeza, introduction, xxxiii–xxxiv; Oropeza, *King of Adobe*, 275.
38. Enriqueta Longeaux y Vasquez, *El Grito del Norte*, November 27, 1968.
39. Enriqueta Longeaux y Vasquez, "Despierten! Hermanos," *El Grito del Norte*, August 24, 1968; Vasquez, *Enriqueta Vasquez and the Chicano Movement*, 6–7.
40. Vasquez, *Enriqueta Vasquez and the Chicano Movement*, 6–7, 68.
41. Vasquez, *Enriqueta Vasquez and the Chicano Movement*, 33–34.
42. Vasquez, *Enriqueta Vasquez and the Chicano Movement*, 34–35.
43. Vasquez, *Enriqueta Vasquez and the Chicano Movement*, 34–35, 39–41.
44. Martínez and Longeaux y Vasquez, *Viva la Raza!*
45. Vasquez, *Enriqueta Vasquez and the Chicano Movement*, 11.
46. Vasquez, *Enriqueta Vasquez and the Chicano Movement*, 48–49.
47. *Congressional Record*, June 23, 1969, republished in *El Grito del Norte*, "What Do You Mean U.S. Imperialism?," August 29, 1970. The editors of *El Grito del Norte* noted, "It takes pages of small print even to list the times and places of the wars waged by U.S. imperialism. This list names only a few. Only the wars between 1798 and 1945. Only the invasions made without Congressional approval.... This list stops before Vietnam and Korea. It doesn't name all the Indian wars. It doesn't name the wars that Congress approved. Think how long the list would be if you added them, too."
48. Vasquez, *Enriqueta Vasquez and the Chicano Movement*, 198.
49. Vasquez, *Enriqueta Vasquez and the Chicano Movement*, 93.
50. Vasquez, *Enriqueta Vasquez and the Chicano Movement*, 195–96.
51. Oropeza, ¡*Raza sí!* ¡*Guerra no!*, 151; Vasquez, *Enriqueta Vasquez and the Chicano Movement*, 198.
52. Vasquez, *Enriqueta Vasquez and the Chicano Movement*, 49–50.
53. Vasquez, *Enriqueta Vasquez and the Chicano Movement*, 33.
54. Vasquez, *Enriqueta Vasquez and the Chicano Movement*, 87. Alternatively, Vasquez might have been referencing Pablo de la Guerra's 1856 words. Weber, *Foreigners in Their Native Land*, vi.
55. Oropeza, "*Viviendo y luchando*," xxxii.
56. Chávez, "¡*Mi Raza Primero!*," 43–44. Chapter 5 of ¡*Mi Raza Primero!* provides a good overview of the Berets.
57. David Sánchez, interview, sess. 1, November 26, 2012.
58. Chávez, "¡*Mi Raza Primero!*," 45–48, 50, 56–60.
59. Oropeza, ¡*Raza sí!* ¡*Guerra no!*, 145–47, 160–67; Chávez, "¡*Mi Raza Primero!*," 65, 68–70; Rosales, *Chicano!*, 200–207.

60. Chávez, "¡Mi Raza Primero!," 72–77.

61. David Sánchez, interview, sess. 4, December 20, 2012; Sánchez, *Expedition through Aztlán*, 15–17.

62. Oropeza, ¡*Raza sí! ¡Guerra no!*, 69–72.

63. David Sánchez, interview, sess. 1, November 26, 2012.

64. Manuel Gómez, interview, September 7, 2017.

65. Chávez, "¡Mi Raza Primero!," 56.

66. Oropeza, ¡*Raza sí! ¡Guerra no!*, 186.

67. Jack Jones, "Chicanos March to 'Reconquer,'" *Los Angeles Times*, May 13, 1971; Jack Jones, "Chicanos 3-Month March to Capitol Reaches Salton Sea," *Los Angeles Times*, May 13, 1971; "Chicano March Ends in Near Skirmish," *Los Angeles Times*, August 8, 1971; Chávez, "¡Mi Raza Primero!," 56.

68. Jones, "Chicanos March to 'Reconquer.'"

69. Jones, "Chicanos 3-Month March."

70. Sánchez, *Expedition through Aztlán*, 18–51 (on problems with alcohol and drugs during the march, see pages, 34, 41, 45, 49); David Sánchez, interview, sess. 3, December 14, 2012.

71. "Chicano March Ends in Near-Skirmish," "Protesters Call Reagan a 'European Wetback,'" *Los Angeles Times*, August 14, 1971; Sánchez, *Expedition through Aztlán*, 51–54; David Sánchez, interview, sess. 4, December 20, 2012.

72. David Sánchez, interview, sess. 4, December 20, 2012; sess. 5, January 7, 2013.

73. Sánchez, interview, sess. 4, December 20, 2012; sess. 5, January 7, 2013.

74. Sánchez, interview, sess. 4, December 20, 2012; sess. 5, January 7, 2013.

75. Chávez, "¡Mi Raza Primero!," 56.

76. Gómez and Chilcott identify the golf course as El Río Golf Course, while Rosales identifies the golf course as Del Rio Golf Course. Gómez and Chilcott also identify the neighborhood as Barrio El Río and the adjacent neighborhoods (just south and southeast) as Barrio Manzo and Barrio Hollywood, respectively. See Gómez and Chilcott, *Outline of Mexican American Education*, 60–62; Rosales, *Chicano!*, 211.

77. Sánchez, *Expedition through Aztlán*, 73–76. Sánchez misspells the name of the park as "Joaquín Murietta."

78. Sánchez, *Expedition through Aztlán*, 74–75.

79. Sánchez, *Expedition through Aztlán*, 75.

80. Navarro, *La Raza Unida Party*, 208. This park was created through the grassroots efforts of the Chicano Leadership Coalition and the El Rio Coalition to create a neighborhood park from the city-owned El Rio Golf Course, located in a barrio on the west side of Tucson. The intransigence of city officials and their disrespect for community activists helped fuel the creation of La Raza Unida Party in Tucson, according to activist Salomon Baldenegro.

81. No unit in Villa's Division del Norte was named Los Tigres.

82. Sánchez, *Expedition through Aztlán*, 83–86.

83. Sánchez, *Expedition through Aztlán*, 86.

84. According to literary scholar Maythee Rojas, the woman referred to as "Juanita" was in reality Josefa (Juvera) Loaiza. Rojas, "Re-Membering Josefa," 144.

85. The Gadsden Treaty was signed in Mexico City. For more information on La Placita as a site of Mexican American community celebrations and the Mexican American women-led struggle against its redevelopment, see Otero, "La Placita Committee," 44–70.

86. Sánchez, *Expedition through Aztlán*, 90. Sánchez identifies Alvarez as a colonel and as a former U.S. ambassador to Spain. According to an oral history interview, Alvarez was attached to the American embassy in Madrid, Spain, during World War I. Cruz Richards Alvarez, interview, 1870.

87. Sánchez, *Expedition through Aztlán*, 90–91.

88. Sánchez, *Expedition through Aztlán*, 91–93.

89. *Valley Morning Star*, December 22, 1971.

90. Sánchez, *Expedition through Aztlán*, 150.

91. David Sánchez, interview, sess. 4, December 20, 2012.

92. "Brown Beret Leader Drubs 'Alien' Policy," *El Paso Herald-Post*, July 1, 1972; "Berets' Claim INS Passing Buck," *El Paso Herald-Post*, July 6, 1972; Sánchez, *Expedition through Aztlán*, 150–53.

93. Sánchez, *Expedition through Aztlán*, 153.

94. Sánchez, *Expedition through Aztlán*, 155.

95. Confino, "Collective Memory and Cultural History," 1398–1400.

96. Sánchez, *Expedition through Aztlán*, 156–57.

97. Sánchez, *Expedition through Aztlán*, 158–59. Their monument might also have been a response to several historical markers about the US-Mexico War that the group had seen on their visit to South Texas. After dedicating their monument to Cortina, the group visited the town of Santa Maria, where they read a historical marker with the following inscription: "This is the location where in April of 1848 [sic], the Mexican Cavalry killed 62 dragoons, perpetuating the Mexican-American War." Sánchez, *Expedition through Aztlán*, 160. The historical marker focuses on the so-called Thornton Skirmish, which precipitated the war. It reads, "The spot where 'American blood was shed on American soil' April 25, 1846; here Captain Seth B. Thornton and 62 dragoons were attacked by Mexican troops." Contrary to the information on the marker, this spot was not on US soil but rather on El Rancho de Carricitos, owned by a Mexican rancher and under Mexican jurisdiction. Valerio-Jiménez, *River of Hope*, 134–35.

98. Brundage, "No Deed but Memory," 8.

99. For more on the process of "disremembering," see Nguyen, *Nothing Ever Dies*, 63.

100. Brundage, "No Deed but Memory," 8.

101. Glassberg, *Sense of History*, 116.

102. Sánchez, *Expedition through Aztlán*, 173–74.

103. Griswold del Castillo traces the ownership of Catalina Island from California's Mexican governor Pio Pico's grant to Tomás Robbins in 1846 to William Wrigley Jr.'s purchase in 1919. Griswold del Castillo, *Treaty of Guadalupe Hidalgo*, 140–42. A detailed discussion of the transfer of ownership from Robbins to Wrigley is also found in chapter 6 of Doran, *Ranch That Was Robbins'*, 65–77.

104. Dial Torgerson, "Santa Catalina a Bit Uptight over 'Invasion,'" *Los Angeles Times*, August 31, 1972.

105. Chávez, "¡Mi Raza Primero!," 56. For more on Native Americans' occupation of Alcatraz Island, see Smith and Warrior, *Like a Hurricane*, 1–111.

106. Torgerson, "Rumors Are Rife in Avalon over Brown Beret Invasion," *Los Angeles Times*, August 31, 1972; Dial Torgerson, "Santa Catalina a Bit Uptight."

107. Torgerson, "Avalon 'Invaders' Now Just Tourist Attraction," *Los Angeles Times*, September 1, 1972; Torgerson, "Santa Catalina a Bit Uptight"; Brittny Mejia, "Nearly Half a

Century Ago, Chicano Activists Occupied Catalina Island. Locals Feared a Mexican 'Invasion,'" *Los Angeles Times*, August 16, 2020.

108. Chávez, "¡Mi Raza Primero!," 56–57.

109. Sánchez, *Expedition through Aztlán*, 180–82, 185–86; "Brown Berets Sit Tight on Catalina Hill," *Los Angeles Times*, September 2, 1972.

110. *La Guardia*, December 21, 1969, February 21, 1971; *Ideal*, September 5, 1972; *Latin Times*, September 19, 1969.

111. Sánchez, *Expedition through Aztlán*, 193–94.

112. Sánchez, *Expedition through Aztlán*, 180–82, 185–86.

113. Sánchez, *Expedition through Aztlán*, 193–94.

114. Torgerson, "Santa Catalina a Bit Uptight."

115. "Police Conspiracy to Intimidate La Raza," *La Causa*, May 23, 1969; "El Monte Shootout" and "78-Year-Old Chicano in Shoot-Out with Police," *La Causa*, August 29, 1970; "Brown Beret 13 Point Political Program," *La Causa*, December 1970; Sánchez, *Expedition through Aztlán*, 194, 196.

116. Sánchez, *Expedition through Aztlán*, 180–82.

117. Brundage, "No Deed but Memory," 8.

118. Confino, "Collective Memory and Cultural History," 1394.

119. Oropeza, ¡*Raza sí!* ¡*Guerra no!*, 61–66.

120. Oropeza, ¡*Raza sí!* ¡*Guerra no!*, 53–54.

121. Novick, *Holocaust in American Life*, 170.

122. Novick, *Holocaust in American Life*, 49.

123. Chávez, "¡Mi Raza Primero!," 63. Guzman calculated the percentage of Chicanos living in Arizona, California, Colorado, New Mexico, and Texas. Deborah Paredez, "Soldiers in la Guerra," *New York Times*, January 5, 2018.

124. Oropeza, ¡*Raza sí!* ¡*Guerra no!*, 67.

125. Paredez, "Soldiers in la Guerra."

126. Blanton, *George I. Sánchez*, 234; Oropeza, ¡*Raza sí!* ¡*Guerra no!*, 67.

127. Historian Lorena Oropeza suggested that Chicano activists at the October 1967 El Paso La Raza Unida conference might have been inspired by Martin Luther King Jr.'s April 1967 antiwar speech to make the links between budget cuts to domestic programs and increased military spending to wage war in Vietnam. Oropeza, ¡*Raza sí!* ¡*Guerra no!*, 57–58. Parts of the proclamation are found in Vigil, *Crusade for Justice*, 43–44.

128. Chávez, "¡Mi Raza Primero!," 64.

129. Oropeza, ¡*Raza sí!* ¡*Guerra no!*, 75.

130. Oropeza, ¡*Raza sí!* ¡*Guerra no!*, 68.

131. Ybarra, *Vietnam Veteranos*, 236; Chávez, "¡Mi Raza Primero!," 63; Oropeza, ¡*Raza sí!* ¡*Guerra no!*, 114.

132. Chávez, "¡Mi Raza Primero!," 61.

133. Oropeza, "¡*Raza sí!* ¡*Guerra no!*, 102; Mariscal, *Aztlán and Viet Nam*, 28.

134. Vigil is widely identified as the first Chicano to refuse induction. However, he argues that "no one then knew who was the *first* resister." Vigil, *Crusade for Justice*, 79.

135. Mariscal, *Aztlán and Viet Nam*, 28; Oropeza, ¡*Raza sí!* ¡*Guerra no!*, 58–59.

136. Mariscal, *Aztlán and Viet Nam*, 28.

137. Mariscal, *Aztlán and Viet Nam*, 217–18.

138. Vigil, *Crusade for Justice*, 73.

139. Vigil, *Crusade for Justice*, 74–78.

140. Vigil, *Crusade for Justice*, 27, 46, 50–51, 73, 79. Corky Gonzales' "Yo Soy Joaquín" poem was very influential in the Chicano movement, but it did not directly reference the US-Mexico War or the treaty.

141. Oropeza, ¡*Raza sí! ¡Guerra no!*, 65–66.

142. Vasquez, *El Grito del Norte*, November 27, 1968.

143. Mariscal, *Aztlán and Viet Nam*, 208; Oropeza, ¡*Raza sí! ¡Guerra no!*, 157. Irene Tovar described learning about Felix Longoria, the soldier killed during World War II but denied burial in a South Texas cemetery due to his Mexican ancestry. Through the intervention of the American GI Forum, Longoria's body was eventually buried in Arlington National Cemetery.

144. Rincón, *Bodies at War*, 55; Mariscal, *Aztlán and Viet Nam*, 189; Oropeza, ¡*Raza sí! ¡Guerra no!*, 104–5.

145. Oropeza, ¡*Raza sí! ¡Guerra no!*, 104–7.

146. Ybarra and Genera, *La batalla esta aquí*, 1–6.

147. Ybarra and Genera, *La batalla esta aquí*, 6; Rincón, *Bodies at War*, 56; Oropeza, ¡*Raza sí! ¡Guerra no!*, 106.

148. María Varela, "The U.S.A. Is an Outside Agitator: Vietnam, Chicago, New Mexico, Everywhere," *El Grito del Norte*, January 17, 1970.

149. Rincón, *Bodies at War*, 56; Oropeza, ¡*Raza sí! ¡Guerra no!*, 93–95.

150. Ybarra, *Vietnam Veteranos*, 4; Ybarra and Genera, *La batalla esta aquí*, 6–8.

151. Rincón, *Bodies at War*, 57; Oropeza, ¡*Raza sí! ¡Guerra no!*, 108, 112; Ybarra and Genera, *La batalla esta aquí*, 7–8.

152. Rincón, *Bodies at War*, 57; Ybarra and Genera, *La batalla esta aquí*, 1–4.

153. Ybarra and Genera, *La batalla esta aquí*, 10–25, 34–47.

154. Nancy Cleeland, "Building Better Bridges for All Students," *Los Angeles Times*, July 19, 1998; Oropeza, ¡*Raza sí! ¡Guerra no!*, 90.

155. Gómez, interview.

156. Gómez, interview; Oropeza, ¡*Raza sí! ¡Guerra no!*, 2.

157. Oropeza, ¡*Raza sí! ¡Guerra no!*, 90.

158. Gómez, interview. According to Gómez, he was the first and perhaps the only Chicano granted a conscientious objector classification by his board in Orange County.

159. Gómez, interview.

160. Gómez, interview.

161. *La Raza*, December 1969, 7. In a 2017 interview, Gómez vividly remembered learning about the US-Mexico War and realizing that this unjust war was the beginning of the US empire. Gómez, interview.

162. Gómez, interview.

163. Gómez, interview.

164. *La Raza*, December 1969, 7.

165. *La Raza*, December 1969, 7.

166. Gómez, interview.

167. Gómez, interview.

168. Oropeza, ¡*Raza sí! ¡Guerra no!*, 91.

169. *La Raza*, December 1969, 7.

170. Gómez, interview.

171. Gómez, interview.

172. Gómez, interview.

173. Gómez, interview.

174. Gómez, interview.

175. Oropeza, ¡*Raza sí!* ¡*Guerra no!*, 90; "Theodore Roszak" Gale Literature: *Contemporary Authors*.

176. Oropeza, ¡*Raza sí! Guerra no!*, 90.

177. Vigil briefly describes "the San Francisco Vietnam Moratorium" and the "Chicano Moratorium" at CSU Hayward, where Corky Gonzales and Rosalío Muñoz spoke, in Vigil, *Crusade for Justice*, 114–15. While El Plan Espiritual de Aztlán was extremely influential, this cultural nationalist manifesto only briefly references the war ("the brutal 'gringo' invasion of our territories").

178. Oropeza, ¡*Raza sí!* ¡*Guerra no!*, 74.

179. *Los Angeles Times*, November 19, 1969.

180. Chávez, "¡*Mi Raza Primero!*," 64; Oropeza, ¡*Raza sí!* ¡*Guerra no!*, 124; Rosales, *Chicano!*, 198–99; *El Grito del Norte*, October 29, 1969, found in Ernesto Vigil FOIA FBI Documents Collection, Herman Baca Papers, MSS 0649, Special Collections & Archives, UC San Diego.

181. *La Raza*, January 1970, 7–8, La Raza Collection, Chicano Studies Research Library, UCLA; *El Grito del Pueblo*, March 28, 1970; *Gidra*, October 1, 1970 (ddr-densho-297-18), 11.

182. Capps, *The Vietnam Reader*, 189–90; Oropeza, ¡*Raza sí!* ¡*Guerra no!*, 89–92; Morales, *Latinx*, 121; Martínez and Longeaux y Vasquez, *Viva la Raza!*, 287–89; Díaz, *Flying under the Radar*, 71–72, 176, 331; Mariscal, *Aztlán and Viet Nam*, 28–29.

183. Aguilar-San Juan, *Little Saigons*, 128; Nguyen, *Nothing Ever Dies*, 40.

Conclusion

1. Costanza-Chock, *Out of the Shadows*, 23–26.

2. According to Stan Steiner, the phrase was adapted from an earlier version, "We didn't come to America, America came to us," used by Chicano and Native American activists in the 1960s. These activists, in turn, probably revised the famous Malcolm X saying, "We didn't land on Plymouth Rock, my brothers and sisters—Plymouth Rock landed on us." Cisneros, *Border Crossed Us*, 11–12.

3. Cisneros, *Border Crossed Us*, 170n49.

4. Tim Weiner, "Mexico City Journal—of Gringos and Old Grudges: This Land Is Their Land," *New York Times*, January 9, 2004. The historian is identified as Miguel Soto.

5. Enrique Krauze, "Will Mexico Get Half of Its Territory Back?," *New York Times*, April 6, 2017.

6. Jaime Luis Brito, "Cárdenas y abogado presentan predemanda para recuperar territorio mexicano perdido ante EU," *Proceso*, March 9, 2017, www.proceso.com.mx/477516/cardenas-abogado-presentan-predemanda-recuperar-territorio-mexicano-perdido-ante-eu.

7. Krauze, "Will Mexico Get Half of Its Territory Back?"; Other recent examples of a historian invoking the U.S.-Mexico War and treaty are: "Every American needs to take a

history of Mexico class," Gabriela Soto Laveaga, *New York Times*, July 22, 2021; "History Professor Calls for U.S. Inclusion of Mexico Studies," National Public Radio, *All Things Considered*, August 1, 2021.

8. Van Wagenen, *Remembering the Forgotten War*, 188–89.

9. Weiner, "Of Gringos and Old Grudges"; Van Wagenen, *Remembering the Forgotten War*, 188–89.

10. Zavaleta-Reid and Flores, "Rapid Ethnographic Assessment of Brownsville-Matamoros," 313–30.

11. Van Wagenen, *Remembering the Forgotten War*, 3–4, 216–17.

12. Van Wagenen, *Remembering the Forgotten War*, 233–36.

13. I made these observations during a visit to the park on June 4, 2019, with a group of secondary-school teachers participating in a teachers' workshop, Historias Americanas, sponsored by the University of Texas–Rio Grande Valley.

14. Van Wagenen, *Remembering the Forgotten War*, 236.

15. Cox, *No Common Ground*.

16. Arielle Avila, "'A Watershed Moment': How Scholarship and Activism Finally Toppled a Texas Ranger Statue in Dallas, *Texas Monthly*, June 25, 2020; Maria Anglin, "A Long Overdue Departure from Love Field," *San Antonio Express-News*, June 12, 2020; John Morán González, "Removing Rangers Statue Acknowledges Their Brutal Past," *Austin American-Statesman*, June 9, 2020; Doug J. Swanson, "The Horrible Truth of Love Field's Texas—an Excerpt from *Cult of Glory*," *D Magazine*, June 2020; Russell Contreras, "Spanish Colonial Monuments Fuel Race Strife in the US Southwest," *Houston Chronicle*, June 27, 2020.

Bibliography

Archival Collections

Ernesto Chávez Collection, Chicano Studies Research Library, University of California, Los Angeles.

Ernesto Vigil FOIA FBI Documents Collection, Herman Baca Papers, MSS 0649, Special Collections & Archives, UC San Diego.

Carlos E. Castañeda Papers, Clemente Idar Papers, Clotilde García Papers, Cristóbal Aldrete Papers, League of United Latin American Citizens (LULAC) Archives, Mario Cantu Papers, Benson Latin American Collection, University of Texas at Austin.

John J. Herrera Papers, MSS 0160, Houston Metropolitan Research Center, Houston Public Library, Houston, TX.

La Raza Collection, Chicano Studies Research Library, University of California, Los Angeles.

Newspapers and Magazines

Abilene Daily Reporter (Abilene, TX)
American Flag (Brownsville, TX, and Matamoros, Tamaulipas)
Austin American-Statesman (Austin, TX)
Austin Statesman (Austin, TX)
Boletin Popular (Santa Fe, NM)
Congressional Globe (Washington, DC)
Daily Alta California (San Francisco, CA)
Daily Ranchero (Brownsville & Corpus Christi, TX, and Matamoros, Tamaulipas)
Daily Star and Herald (Panama City, Panama)
Dallas Morning News (Dallas, TX)
Diario del Hogar (Mexico City)
D Magazine (Dallas, TX)
El Clamor Público (Los Angeles, CA)
El Defensor (Edinburg, TX)
El Diario (Mexico City)
El Diario de Tampa (Tampa, FL)
El Eco del Valle (Las Cruces, NM)
El Grito del Norte (Española, NM)
El Heraldo de Mexico (Los Angeles, CA)
El Imparcial (Mexico City)
El Labrador (Las Cruces, NM)
El Nuevo Mexicano (Santa Fe, NM)
El Nuevo Mundo (Albuquerque, NM)
El País (Mexico City)
El Paso Herald (El Paso, TX)
El Paso Herald-Post (El Paso, TX)
El Progreso (Matamoros, Tamaulipas)
El Regidor (San Antonio, TX)
El Tiempo (Las Cruces, New Mexico)
Gidra (Los Angeles, CA)
Gonzales Inquirer (Gonzales, TX)
Guardian (New York City, NY)
Houston Chronicle (Houston, TX)
Houston Post (Houston, TX)
Ideal (Coachella, CA)
Independent Democrat (Las Cruces, NM)
La Cachiporrita del Condado de San Miguel (Las Vegas, NM)
La Causa (Los Angeles, CA)
La Crónica (Laredo, TX)

La Estrella Mexicana (Albuquerque, NM)
La Gaceta (Santa Barbara, CA)
La Guardia (Milwaukee, WI)
La Prensa (San Antonio, TX)
La Raza (Los Angeles, CA)
Latin Times (Chicago, IL)
La Voz del Nuevo Mundo (San Francisco, CA)
La Voz del Pueblo (Santa Fe, NM)
Los Angeles Times (Los Angeles, CA)
LULAC News (San Antonio, TX)
Marysville Herald (Marysville, CA)
Mexican Herald (Mexico City)
New York Times (New York City, NY)
Nueva Era (Mexico City)
Pecos Enterprise (Pecos, TX)
Regeneración (Los Angeles, CA)
San Angelo Standard (San Angelo, TX)
San Antonio Express (San Antonio, TX)
San Antonio Express-News (San Antonio, TX)
San Antonio Light (San Antonio, TX)
Santa Fe Daily New Mexican (Santa Fe, NM)
Steamer Pacific Star (San Francisco, CA)
Texas Monthly (Austin, TX)
Valley Morning Star (Harlingen, TX)
Victoria Advocate (Victoria, TX)
Washington Post (Washington, DC)

Oral History Interviews

Alvarez, Cruz Richards. Interview by Marie Carter. New Mexico. 1870. www.loc.gov/item/wpalh001139/.

Gómez, Manuel. Interview by author, digital recording of telephone interview, September 7, 2017.

Sánchez, David. Interview by Virginia Espino. UCLA Oral History Research. Session 1, November 26, 2012.

———. Interview by Virginia Espino. UCLA Oral History Research. Session 3, December 14, 2012.

———. Interview by Virginia Espino. UCLA Oral History Research. Session 4, December 20, 2012.

———. Interview by Virginia Espino. UCLA Oral History Research. Session 5, January 7, 2013.

Tijerina, Reies López. Interview by Luis Torres. December 29, 1989. In F. Arturo Rosales Collection, box 3, folder 59, Arizona State University, Special Collections Library.

Websites

Eng, Aimee, and Daniel McFarland. "The Japanese Question: San Francisco Education in 1906." Case 2006–03, Stanford GSE Case Library. 2006. https://caselib.stanford.edu/case/2006-03.

McCrae, John. "In Flanders Fields." The Great War, 1014–1918. May 1915. www.greatwar.co.uk/poems/john-mccrae-in-flanders-fields.htm.

Roszak, Theodore. In *Gale Literature: Contemporary Authors*. Farmington Hills, MI: Gale, 2011. Gale Literature Resource Center (accessed September 22, 2017). https://link.gale.com/apps/doc/H1000085161/LitRC?u=txshracd2604&sid=summon&xid=4ba0a5ac.

Court Cases

Delgado v. Bastrop Indep. Sch. Dist., Civil Action No. 388 (W.D.Tex. 1948) (unreported).
Hernández v. Texas, 347 U.S. 475 (1954).
McKinney v. Saviego, 59 U.S. (18 How.) 235 (1855).

Government Documents

Congress. *Public Acts of the 33rd Congress of the United States*, Sess. 1, ch. 103, 10 Stat. 308, July 22, 1854.
Congress, House of Representatives. *Difficulties on Southwestern Frontier*, H.R. Doc. No. 52, 36th Cong., 1st Sess., (1860).
Congress, Senate. *Admission of New Mexico into Union*, S. Rep. No. 520, 54th Cong., 1st Sess., (1892).
Congress, Senate. *Schedule of Mexican Claims against the United States*, docket no. 904, S. Doc. No. 31, 44th Cong., 2nd Sess., (1868).

Unpublished Works

Chávez, Ernesto. "The U.S. War with Mexico in History and Memory." Paper presented at the Center for the Study of Race, Politics, and Culture, University of Chicago, October 29, 2015, 7.

Published Works

DISSERTATIONS AND THESES

Cottraux, Suzanne Seifert. "Missed Identity: Collective Memory, Adina De Zavala, and the Tejana Heroine Who Wasn't." Master's thesis, University of Texas at Arlington, 2013.
Dickens, Edwin Larry. "The Political Role of Mexican-Americans in San Antonio, Texas." PhD diss., Texas Tech University, 1969.
Goldfinch, Charles W. "Juan N. Cortina, 1824–1892: A Re-Appraisal." Master's thesis, University of Chicago, 1950. Reprinted in Charles William Goldfinch and J. T. Canales. *Juan N. Cortina: Two Interpretations*. New York: Arno Press, 1974.
Liss, Sheldon. "The Chamizal Conflict, 1864–1964." PhD diss., American University, 1965.
Lynch, Michael John, III. "South Texas Renaissance Man: The Humanitarian, Political, and Philosophical Activities of Judge J.T. Canales." Master's thesis: Texas A&M University–Kingsville, 1996.
McLure, Helen. "'I Suppose You Think Strange the Murder of Women and Children': The American Culture of Collective Violence, 1652–1930." PhD diss., Southern Methodist University, 2019.
Pasternack, Natasha Miller. "'History Should Be Told as Fact': Elena Zamora O'Shea's Reconstruction of the Texas Past." Master's thesis, University of Texas at Austin, 2010.
Pycior, Julie Leininger. "La Raza Organizes: Mexican American Life in San Antonio, 1915–1930, as Reflected in Mutualista Activities." PhD diss., University of Notre Dame, 1979.
Ribb, Richard. "José Tomás Canales and the Texas Rangers: Myth, Identity, and Power, 1910–1920." PhD diss., University of Texas at Austin, 2001.

JOURNAL ARTICLES AND BOOK CHAPTERS

Alemán, Jesse. "'Thank God, Lolita Is Away from Those Horrid Savages': The Politics of Whiteness in *Who Would Have Thought It?*" In Montes and Goldman, *María Amparo Ruiz de Burton*, 95–111.

Almaráz, Felix D., Jr. "Carlos Eduardo Castañeda, Mexican-American Historian: The Formative Years, 1896–1927." *Pacific Historical Review* 42, no. 3 (August 1973): 319–34.

Aranda, José F., Jr. "Returning California to the People: Vigilantism in *The Squatter and the Don*." In Montes and Goldman, *María Amparo Ruiz de Burton*, 11–26.

Assmann, Aleida. "Transformations between History and Memory," *Social Research* 75, no. 1 (Spring 2008): 49–72.

Blanton, Carlos K. "The Citizenship Sacrifice: Mexican Americans, the Saunders-Leonard Report, and the Politics of Immigration, 1951–1952." *Western Historical Quarterly* 40, no. 3 (Autumn 2009): 299–320.

———. "George I. Sánchez, Ideology, and Whiteness in the Making of the Mexican American Civil Rights Movement, 1930–1960." *Journal of Southern History* 72, no. 3 (August 2006): 569–604.

Blight, David W. "Southerners Don't Lie: They Just Remember Big." In *Where These Memories Grow: History, Memory, and Southern Identity*, edited by W. Fitzhugh Brundage, 347–53. Chapel Hill: University of North Carolina Press, 2000.

Bowman, J. N. "The Question of Sovereignty over California's Off-Shore Islands." *Pacific Historical Review* 31, no. 3 (August 1962): 291–301.

Brandes, Raymond S., and Thomas Savage. "Times Gone By in Alta California: Recollections of Senora Dona Juana Machado Alipaz de Ridington (Wrightington) Bancroft Library, 1878." *The Historical Society of Southern California Quarterly* 41, no. 3 (1959): 195–240.

Bringhurst, Newell G. "Samuel Brannan and His Forgotten Final Years." *Southern California Quarterly* 79, no. 2 (1997): 139–60.

Brown, Anthony L. "Counter-Memory and Race: An Examination of African American Scholars' Challenges to Early Twentieth Century K–12 Historical Discourses." *Journal of Negro Education* 79, no. 1 (2010): 54–65.

Brownrigg, Coya Paz. "Linchocracia: Performing 'America' in *El Clamor Público*." *California History* 84, no. 2 (Winter 2006–7): 40–51.

Brundage, W. Fitzhugh. "No Deed but Memory." In *Where These Memories Grow: History, Memory, and Southern Identity*, edited by W. Fitzhugh Brundage, 1–28. Chapel Hill: University of North Carolina Press, 2000.

Buelna, Enrique M. "Asociación Nacional México-Americana (ANMA) (1949–1954)." In *Latinas in the United States: A Historical Encyclopedia*, edited by Vicki L. Ruiz and Virginia Sánchez Korrol, 67–68. New York: Oxford University Press, 2006.

Campbell, Randolph B. "History and Collective Memory in Texas: The Entangled Stories of the Lone Star State." In *Lone Star Pasts: Memory and History in Texas*, edited by Gregg Cantrell and Elizabeth Hayes Turner, 270–82. College Station: Texas A&M University, 2007.

Canales, José T. "Juan N. Cortina Presents His Motion for a New Trial." In *Juan N. Cortina: Two Interpretations*, edited by Charles William Goldfinch and J. T. Canales, 1–19. New York: Arno Press, 1974.

Cantrell, Gregg, and Elizabeth Hayes Turner. "A Study of History, Memory, and Collective Memory in Texas." In *Lone Star Pasts: Memory and History in Texas*, edited by Gregg Cantrell and Elizabeth Hayes Turner, 1–14. College Station: Texas A&M University, 2007.

Carrigan, William D., and Clive Webb. "*Muerto por unos desconocidos* (Killed by Persons Unknown): Mob Violence against Blacks and Mexicans." In *Beyond Black and White: Race, Ethnicity, and Gender in the U.S. South and Southwest*, edited by Stephanie Cole and Alison M. Parker, 35–74. College Station: Texas A&M University Press, 2004.

Castañeda, Antonia I. "Sexual Violence in the Politics and Policies of Conquest: Amerindian Women and the Spanish Conquest of Alta California." In *Building with Our Hands: New Directions in Chicana Studies*, edited by Adela de la Torre and Beatriz M. Pesqueras, 39–55. Berkeley: University of California Press, 1993.

Castañeda, Carlos E. "Why I Chose History." *Americas* 8, no. 4 (April 1952): 475–92.

Confino, Alon. "Collective Memory and Cultural History: Problems of Method." *American Historical Review* 102, no. 5 (December 1997): 1386–1403.

Coronel, Antonio Franco. "De Cosas de California." In "Nineteenth Century Californio Testimonials," edited by Rosaura Sánchez, Beatrice Pita, and Bárbara Reyes. Special issue, *Crítica: A Journal of Critical Essays*, Spring 1994, 124–37.

Cutler, John Alba. "Toward a Reading of Nineteenth-Century Latino/a Short Fiction." In *The Latino Nineteenth Century: Archival Encounters in American Literary History*, edited by Rodrigo Lazo and Jesse Alemán, 124–45. New York: New York University Press, 2016.

Davis, Carlyn E. "Bear Flag Revolt." In *The United States and Mexico at War: Nineteenth Century Expansion and Conflict*, edited by Donald S. Frazier. New York: Macmillan Reference Books, 1998.

De la Teja, Jesús F., "Juan N. Seguin: Federalist, Rebel, Exile." In *Tejano Leadership in Mexican and Revolutionary Texas*, edited by Jesús F. De la Teja, 212–30. College Station: Texas A&M University, 2010.

DeLay, Brian. "Independent Indians and the U.S.-Mexican War." *American Historical Review* 112, no. 1 (February 2007): 35–68.

De León, Arnoldo. "Texas Mexicans: Twentieth-Century Interpretations." In *Texas through Time: Evolving Interpretations*, edited by Walter L. Buenger and Robert A. Calvert, 20–49. College Station: Texas A&M University Press, 1991.

Ewence, Hannah. "Memories of Suburbia: Autobiographical Fiction and Minority Narratives." In *Memory and History: Understanding Memory as Source and Subject*, edited by Joan Tumblety, 160–76. New York: Routledge, 2013.

Flores, Richard. "Adina De Zavala and the Politics of Restoration." Introduction to *History and Legends of the Alamo and Other Missions in and around San Antonio*, by Adina De Zavala, edited by Richard R. Flores. Houston: Arte Público Press, 1996.

Foley, Neil. "Becoming Hispanic: Mexican Americans and the Faustian Pact with Whiteness." In *Reflexiones 1997: New Directions in Mexican American Studies*, edited by Neil Foley, 53–70. Austin: Center for Mexican American Studies and University of Texas Press, 1998.

———. "Partly Colored or Other White: Mexican Americans and Their Problem with the Color Line." In *Beyond Black and White: Race, Ethnicity, and Gender in the U.S. South and Southwest*, edited by Stephanie Cole and Alison M. Parker, 123–44. College Station: Texas A&M University Press, 2004.

García, Mario T. Foreword to *Forgotten People: A Study of New Mexicans*, by George I. Sánchez, xi–xxx. Albuquerque: University of New Mexico Press, 1996.

García, Richard. "Alonso S. Perales: The Voice and Visions of a Citizen Intellectual." In *Leaders of the Mexican American Generation*, edited by Anthony Quiroz, 85–118. Boulder: University Press of Colorado, 2015.

Garza-Falcón, Leticia M. "Renewal through Language in Elena Zamora O'Shea's Novel *El Mesquite*." In *El Mesquite: A Story of the Early Spanish Settlements between the Nueces and the Rio Grande*, by Elena Zamora O'Shea, xxiii–lxiv. College Station: Texas A&M University Press, 2000.

Glassberg, David. "Patriotism from the Ground Up." *Reviews in American History* 21 (1993): 1–7.

———. "Public History and the Study of Memory." *Public Historian* 18, no. 2 (Spring 1996): 7–23.

Gómez, Manuel. "I Am My Brother in the Same Struggle for Justice." December 8, 1969. www.geocities.ws/college_chicano_warrior/poems/same.htm.

Gómez-Quiñones, Juan. "Piedras contra la luna: México en Aztlán y Aztlán en México: Chicano-Mexican Relations and the Consulates, 1900–1920." In *Contemporary Mexico: Papers of the IV International Congress of Mexican History*, edited by James W. Wilkie, Michael C. Meyer, and Edna Monzon de Wilkie. Berkeley: University of California Press, 1976.

Gonzales, Phillip B. "Struggle for Survival: The Hispanic Land Grants of New Mexico, 1848–2001." *Agricultural History* 77, no. 2 (Spring 2003): 293–324.

González, John M. "The Whiteness of the Blush: The Cultural Politics of Racial Formation in *The Squatter and the Don*." In Montes and Goldman, *María Amparo Ruiz de Burton*, 153–68.

Gray, Paul Bryan. "Francisco P. Ramírez: A Short Biography." *California History* 84, no. 2 (Winter 2006–7): 20–38.

Griswold del Castillo, Richard. "Treaty of Guadalupe Hidalgo." In *The United States and Mexico at War: Nineteenth Century Expansion and Conflict*, edited by Donald S. Frazier, 437–38. New York: Macmillan Reference Books, 1998.

Gross, Ariela J. "'The Caucasian Cloak': Mexican Americans and the Politics of Whiteness in the Twentieth-Century Southwest." *Georgetown Law Journal* 95, no. 2 (January 2007): 337–92.

Gutiérrez, Félix, José Luis Benavides, and William Deverell. Introduction to *California History* 84, no. 2 (Winter 2006–7): 4–9.

Hill, James E. "El Chamizal: A Century-Old Boundary Dispute." *Geographical Review* 55, no. 4 (October 1965): 510–22.

Johannsen, Robert W. "America's Forgotten War." *Wilson Quarterly* 20, no. 2 (Spring 1996): 96–107.

Johnson, Benjamin H. "The Cosmic Race in Texas: Racial Fusion, White Supremacy, and Civil Rights Politics." *Journal of American History* 98, no. 2 (September 2011): 404–19.

Kanellos, Nicolás. "A Brief History of Hispanic Periodicals in the United States." In *Hispanic Periodicals in the United States, Origins to 1960: A Brief History and Comprehensive Bibliography*, edited by Nicolás Kanellos and Helvetia Martell. Houston: Arte Público Press, 1999.

———. "*El clamor público*: Resisting the American Empire." *California History* 84, no. 2 (Winter 2006–7): 10–18.

King, LaGarrett J., Ryan M. Crowley, and Anthony L. Brown. "The Forgotten Legacy of Carter G. Woodson: Contributions to Multicultural Social Studies and African American History." *Social Studies* 101 (2010): 211–15.

Kramer, Paul. "A Border Crosses." *New Yorker*, September 20, 2014, www.newyorker.com/news/news-desk/moving-mexican-border.

Kreneck, Thomas H. "Mr. LULAC: The Fabulous Life of John J. Herrera." In *Leaders of the Mexican American Generation Biographical Essays*, edited by Anthony Quiroz. Boulder: University of Colorado Press, 2015.

Limón, José E. "El Primer Congreso Mexicanista de 1911: A Precursor to Contemporary Chicanismo." *Aztlán* 5 (Spring–Fall 1974): 85–117.

Loewen, James. "Telling History on the Landscape." *Poverty and Race Research Action Council* 8, no. 2 (1999), 1–2, 5–6.

Luna Lawhn, Juanita. "María Luisa Garza: Novelist of *El México de Afuera*." In *Double crossings/Entre Cruzamientos*, edited by Mario Martín Flores and Carlos von Son. New Jersey: Ediciones Nuevo Espacio, Academia, 2001.

Machado de Ridington (Wrightington), Juana. "Los tiempos pasados de la Alta California: Recuerdos de la Sra. Doña Juana Machado de Ridington." In "Nineteenth Century Californio Testimonials," edited by Rosaura Sánchez, Beatrice Pita, and Bárbara Reyes. Special issue, *Crítica: A Journal of Critical Essays*, Spring 1994, 17–30.

Mapes, Kathleen. "'A Special Class of Labor': Mexican (Im)Migrants, Immigration Debate, and Industrial Agriculture in the Rural Midwest." *Labor: Studies in Working-Class History of the Americas* 1, no. 2 (2004): 65–88.

Márquez, Benjamin. "In Defense of My People: Alonso S. Perales and the Moral Construction of Citizenship." In *In Defense of My People: Alonso S. Perales and the Development of Mexican-American Public Intellectuals*, edited by Michael A. Olivas. Houston: Arte Público Press, 2012.

Martínez, Oscar J. "On the Size of the Chicano Population: New Estimates, 1850–1900." *Aztlán* 6, no. 1 (Spring 1975): 43–67.

McLemore, Laura Lyons. "Early Historians and the Shaping of Texas Memory." In *Lone Star Pasts: Memory and History in Texas*, edited by Gregg Cantrell and Elizabeth Hayes Turner, 15–38. College Station: Texas A&M University, 2007.

Medeiros, Francine. "La Opinión, A Mexican Exile Newspaper: A Content Analysis of Its First Years, 1926–1929." *Aztlán* 11 (Spring 1980): 65–87.

Montes, Amelia M. de la Luz. "'We Were Born to Do Something More Than Simply Live': María Amparo Ruiz de Burton and the Nineteenth Century." *Symbolism: An International Journal of Critical Aesthetics* 4 (2005): 293–309.

Montoya, María E. "The Dual World of Governor Miguel Otero: Myth and Reality in Turn-of-the-Century New Mexico." *New Mexico Historical Review* 67, no. 1 (January 1992): 13–31.

Nguyen, Viet Thanh. "Just Memory: War and the Ethics of Remembrance." *American Literary History* 25, no. 1 (January 2013): 144–63.

Nora, Pierre. "Between Memory and History: Les Lieux de Mémoire." *Representations* 26 (Spring 1989): 7–24.

Oropeza, Lorena. Introduction to *Enriqueta Vasquez and the Chicano Movement: Writings from "El Grito del Norte,"* by Enriqueta Vasquez. Edited by Dionne Espinoza and Lorena Oropeza. Houston: Arte Público Press, 2006.

———. "*Viviendo y luchando*: The Life and Times of Enriqueta Vasquez." In *Enriqueta Vasquez and the Chicano Movement: Writings from "El Grito del Norte,"* by Enriqueta Vasquez, xix–liii. Edited by Lorena Oropeza and Dionne Espinoza. Houston: Arte Público Press, 2006.

Orozco, Cynthia E. "Alonso S. Perales and His Struggle for the Civil Rights of *La Raza* through the League of United Latin American Citizens (LULAC) in Texas in the 1930s: *Incansable Soldado del Civismo Por-Raza*." In *In Defense of My People: Alonso S. Perales and the Development of Mexican-American Public Intellectuals*, edited by Michael A. Olivas, 3–28. Houston: Arte Público Press, 2012.

Osuna de Marrón, Felipa. "Recuerdos de Doña Felipa Osuna de Marrón natural de San Diego donde vive actualmente con varios papeles originales pertenecientes al archivo particular de la misma señora, que los obsequió a la Bancroft Library 1878." In "Nineteenth Century Californio Testimonials," edited by Rosaura Sánchez, Beatrice Pita, and Bárbara Reyes. Special issue, *Crítica: A Journal of Critical Essays*, Spring 1994, 46–53.

Otero, Lydia. "La Placita Committee: Claiming Place and History." In *Memories and Migrations: Mapping Boricua and Chicana Histories*, edited by Vicki Ruiz and John R. Chávez, 44–68. Urbana: University of Illinois Press, 2008.

Paredes, Américo. "Folklore e historia: Dos cantares de la frontera del norte." In *25 Estudios de Folklore*, edited by Fernando Anaya Monroy and Luz Gorráez Arcaute, 209–22. Vol. 4. Mexico City: Instituto de Investigaciones Estéticas, Universidad Nacional Autónoma de México, 1971.

Payan, Tony. "Border Wars: The (Mostly) Forgotten Story of How a Parched Patch of Land Tormented U.S.-Mexico Relations for 100 Years." *Americas Quarterly* 1 (2016): 14–19.

Pérez, Vincent. "Remembering the Hacienda: Land and Community in Californio Narratives." In Montes and Goldman, *María Amparo Ruiz de Burton*, 27–55.

Poole, Alex H. "The Strange Career of Jim Crow Archives: Race, Space, and History in the Mid-Twentieth Century American South." *American Archivist* 77, no. 1 (Spring/Summer 2014): 24–63.

Pulido, Laura. "Checkered Choices, Political Assertions: The Unarticulated Racial Identity of La Asociación Nacional México-Americana." In *Critical Ethnic Studies: A Reader*, edited by Nada Elia, David M. Hernández, Jodi Kim, Shana L. Redmond, Dylan Rodriguez, and Sarita Echavez See, 463–76. Durham, NC: Duke University Press, 2016.

Quiñonez, Isabel. "De pronósticos, calendarios y almanaques." In *La república de las letras: Asomos a la cultura escrita del México decimonónico*. Vol. 2, *Publicaciones periódicas y otros impresos*, edited by Belem Clark de Lara and Elisa Speckman Guerra, 331–52. Mexico City: Universidad Nacional Autónoma de México, 2005.

Reidt, Kelly. "Unreconstructed History: Anna Pennybacker's *A New History of Texas* and the Politics of Texas Textbooks in the Early Twentieth Century." *American Educational History Journal* 31, no. 1 (2004): 79–86.

Rojas, Maythee. "Re-Membering Josefa: Reading the Mexican Female Body in California Gold Rush Chronicles." *Women's Studies Quarterly* 35, no. 1/2 (Spring/Summer 2007): 126–48.

Romero, Victor C. "*McKinney v. Saviego.*" In *The Oxford Encyclopedia of Latinos and Latinas in the United States*. Vol. 3. Oxford: Oxford University Press, 2005, 90–91. www.oxfordreference.com/view/10.1093/acref/9780195156003.001.0001/acref-9780195156003-e-587.

Rosenus, Alan. "Mariano Guadalupe Vallejo." In *The United States and Mexico at War: Nineteenth-Century Expansionism and Conflict*, edited by Donald S. Frazier. New York: Macmillan Reference Books, 1998.

Ruiz, Julie. "Captive Identities: The Gendered Conquest of Mexico in *Who Would Have Thought It?*" In Montes and Goldman, *María Amparo Ruiz de Burton*, 112–32.

Ruiz Cameron, Christopher David. "One Hundred Fifty Years of Solitude: Reflections on the End of the History Academy's Dominance of Scholarship on the Treaty of Guadalupe Hidalgo." *Bilingual Review/La Revista Bilingüe* 25, no. 1 (January–April 2000): 1–22.

Saldaña-Portillo, María Josefina. "'Wavering on the Horizon of Social Being': The Treaty of Guadalupe-Hidalgo and the Legacy of Its Racial Character in Americo Paredes's George Washington Gomez." *Radical History Review* 89 (Spring 2004): 135–64.

Sánchez, Rosaura, and Beatrice Pita. Introduction to *Conflicts of Interest: The Letters of María Amparo Ruiz de Burton*, by María Amparo Ruiz de Burton. Edited with a commentary by Rosaura Sánchez and Beatrice Pita, ix–xxii. Houston: Arte Público Press, 2001.

———. Introduction to *The Squatter and the Don*, by María Amparo Ruiz de Burton. Edited and introduced by Rosaura Sánchez and Beatrice Pita. 2nd ed., 7–49. Houston: Arte Público Press, 1997.

———. "María Amparo Ruiz de Burton and the Power of Her Pen." In *Latina Legacies: Identity, Biography, and Community*, edited by Vicki L. Ruiz and Virginia Sánchez Korrol, 72–83. New York: Oxford University Press, 2005.

Sandos, James A. "Recovering the 1919 Canales Investigation of the Texas Ranger Force: Archival Investigation and Its Consequences, 1975-2010." In *Reverberations of Racial Violence: Critical Reflections on the History of the Border*, edited by Sonia Hernández and John Morán González, 219–228. Austin: University of Texas Press, 2021.

Schwartz, Joan M., and Terry Cook. "Archives, Records, and Power: The Making of Modern Memory." *Archival Science* 2, no. 1–2 (2002): 1–19.

"The Spirit and Solidarity of Brotherhood." In *Testimonio: A Documentary History of the Mexican American Struggle for Civil Rights*, edited by Francisco Arturo Rosales, 107. Houston: Arte Público Press, 2000.

Tijerina, Andrés. "Constructing Tejano Memory." In *Lone Star Pasts: Memory and History in Texas*, edited by Gregg Cantrell and Elizabeth Hayes Turner, 176–202. College Station: Texas A&M University, 2007.

———. Historical introduction to *El Mesquite: A Story of the Early Spanish Settlements between the Nueces and the Rio Grande*, by Elena Zamora O'Shea, ix–xxii. College Station: Texas A&M University Press, 2000.

Tuttle, Jennifer. "The Symptoms of Conquest: Race, Class, and the Nervous Body in *The Squatter and the Don*." In Montes and Goldman, *María Amparo Ruiz de Burton*, 56–72.

Vallejo, Mariano Guadalupe. "De recuerdos históricos y personales tocante a la Alta California, 1769–1849." In "Nineteenth Century Californio Testimonials," edited by Rosaura Sánchez, Beatrice Pita, and Bárbara Reyes. Special issue, *Crítica: A Journal of Critical Essays* (Spring 1994), 139–43.

Vargas, Robert L. "Abrazo at the Border: El Chamizal Returns to Mexico." *Southwest Review* 51, no. 4 (Autumn 1966): 390–98.

Walter, Paul A. F. "Benjamin M. Read." *New Mexico Historical Review* 2, no. 4 (October 1927): 394–97.

Warford, Elisa. "'An Eloquent and Impassioned Plea': The Rhetoric of Ruiz de Burton's *The Squatter and the Don*." *Western American Literature* 44, no. 1 (Spring 2009): 5–21.

Wood, Nancy. "Memory's Remains: Lieux de Mémoire." *History and Memory* 6 (Spring–Summer 1994): 123–49.

Yáñez, Aaron P. Mahr. "Battle of Resaca de la Palma." In *The United States and Mexico at War: Nineteenth Century Expansion and Conflict*, edited by Donald S. Frazier, 354–57. New York: Macmillan Reference Books, 1998.

Zamora O'Shea, Elena. "The Ranches of Southwest Texas as They Were in the '80–'90's." In *El Mesquite: A Story of the Early Spanish Settlements between the Nueces and the Rio Grande*, by Elena Zamora O'Shea, lxxi. College Station: Texas A&M University Press, 2000

Zavaleta-Reid, Antonio Noé, and Rodolfo R. Flores. "Rapid Ethnographic Assessment of Brownsville-Matamoros Concerning the Development of a Palo Alto National Historic Battlefield Site." In *Still More Studies in Rio Grande Valley History*, edited by Milo Kearney, Anthony Knopp, and Antonio Zavaleta. Brownsville: Texas Center for Border and Transnational Studies, 2014.

BOOKS

Acuña, Rodolfo. *Occupied America: A History of Chicanos*. 3rd ed. New York: Harper & Row, 1988.

Aguilar-San Juan, Karin. *Little Saigons: Staying Vietnamese in America*. Minneapolis: University of Minnesota Press, 2009.

Alcaraz, Ramón, and Josefina Zoraida Vázquez. *Apuntes para la historia de la guerra entre México y los Estados Unidos*. México, D.F.: Consejo Nacional para la Cultura y las Artes, 1991.

Almaráz, Félix D., Jr. *Knight without Armor: Carlos Eduardo Castañeda, 1896–1958*. College Station: Texas A&M University Press, 1999.

Alonzo, Armando C. *Tejano Legacy: Rancheros and Settlers in South Texas, 1734–1900*. Albuquerque: University of New Mexico Press, 1998.

Anderson, Benedict. *Imagined Communities: Reflections on the Origins and Spread of Nationalism*. Rev. ed. New York: Verso, 1991.

Balderrama, Francisco, and Raymond Rodriguez. *Decade of Betrayal: Mexican Repatriation in the 1930s*. Rev. ed. Albuquerque: University of New Mexico Press, 2006.

Bancroft, Hubert Howe. *The Works of Hubert Howe Bancroft*. 39 vols. San Francisco: A. J. Bancroft, 1885.

Barr, Juliana. *Peace Came in the Form of a Woman: Indians and Spaniards in the Texas Borderlands*. Chapel Hill: University of North Carolina Press, 2007.

Barragán-Goetz, Philis. *Reading, Writing, and Revolution: Escuelitas and the Emergence of a Mexican American Identity in Texas*. Austin: University of Texas Press, 2020.

Bauer, Jack. *The Mexican War, 1846–1848*. New York: Macmillan, 1974.

Beebe, Rose Marie, and Robert M. Senkewicz, eds. *Testimonios: Early California through the Eyes of Women, 1815–1848*. Norman: University of Oklahoma Press, 2016.

Behnken, Brian D. *Fighting Their Own Battles: Mexican Americans, African Americans, and the Struggle for Civil Rights in Texas.* Chapel Hill: University of North Carolina Press, 2011.

Blanton, Carlos Kevin. *George I. Sánchez: The Long Fight for Mexican American Integration.* New Haven. CT: Yale University Press, 2014.

———. *The Strange Career of Bilingual Education in Texas, 1836–1981.* College Station: Texas A&M University Press, 2004.

Blawis, Patricia Bell. *Tijerina and the Land Grants: Mexican Americans in Struggle for Their Heritage.* New York: International, 1971.

Blight, David W. *Beyond the Battlefield: Race, Memory, and the American Civil War.* Amherst: University of Massachusetts Press, 2002.

Bodnar, John. *Remaking America: Public Memory, Commemoration, and Patriotism in the Twentieth Century.* Princeton, NJ: Princeton University Press, 1992.

Bruggeman, Seth C. *Born in the U.S.A.: Birth, Commemoration, and American Public Memory.* Amherst: University of Massachusetts Press, 2012.

Brundage, W. Fitzhugh, ed. *Where These Memories Grow: History, Memory, and Southern Identity.* Chapel Hill: University of North Carolina Press, 2000.

Busto, Rudy V. *King Tiger: The Religious Vision of Reies López Tijerina.* Albuquerque: University of New Mexico Press, 2005.

Calvert, Robert A., and Arnoldo De León. *The History of Texas.* Arlington Heights: Harlan Davidson, 1990.

Camarillo, Albert. *Chicanos in a Changing Society: From Mexican Pueblos to American Barrios in Santa Barbara and Southern California.* Cambridge, MA: Harvard University Press, 1979.

Cantrell, Gregg, and Elizabeth Hayes Turner, eds. *Lone Star Pasts: Memory and History in Texas.* College Station: Texas A&M University, 2007.

Capps, Walter, ed. *The Vietnam Reader.* New York: Routledge, 1991.

Carrigan, William D., and Clive Webb. *Forgotten Dead: Mob Violence against Mexicans in the United States, 1848–1928.* New York: Oxford University Press, 2013.

Castillo Nájera, Francisco. *Invasión norteamericana: Efectivos y estado de los ejércitos beligerantes, consideraciones sobre la campana.* Mexico City: Congreso Mexicano de Historia, 1947.

Caughey, John W. *Their Majesties the Mob: The Vigilante Impulse in America.* Chicago: University of Chicago Press, 1960.

Chávez, Ernesto. *"¡Mi Raza Primero!" (My People First!): Nationalism, Identity, and Insurgency in the Chicano Movement in Los Angeles, 1966–1978.* Berkeley: University of California Press, 2002.

———. *The U.S. War with Mexico: A Brief History with Documents.* Boston: Bedford/St. Martin's, 2008.

Chávez, John R. *The Lost Land: The Chicano Image of the Southwest.* Albuquerque: University of New Mexico Press, 1984.

Chávez-García, Miroslava. *Negotiating Conquest: Gender and Power in California, 1770s to 1880s.* Tucson: University of Arizona Press, 2004.

Christensen, Carol, and Thomas Christensen. *The U.S.-Mexican War.* San Francisco: Bay Books, 1998.

Cisneros, Josué David. *The Border Crossed Us: Rhetorics of Borders, Citizenship, and Latina/o Identity.* Tuscaloosa: University of Alabama Press, 2014.

Cleland, Robert Glass. *The Cattle on a Thousand Hills: Southern California, 1850–1880*. San Marino, CA: Huntington Library, 1969.
Cline, Howard F. *The United States and Mexico*. Cambridge, MA: Harvard University Press, 1967.
Coser, Lewis A., ed. and trans. *Maurice Halbwachs on Collective Memory*. Chicago: University of Chicago Press, 1992.
Costanza-Chock, Sasha. *Out of the Shadows, into the Streets! Transmedia Organizing and the Immigrant Rights Movement*. Cambridge, MA: MIT Press, 2014.
Cox, Karen L. *No Common Ground: Confederate Monuments and the Ongoing Fight for Racial Justice*. Chapel Hill: University of North Carolina Press, 2021.
DeLay, Brian. *War of a Thousand Deserts: Indian Raids and the U.S.-Mexican War*. New Haven, CT: Yale University Press, 2009.
De León, Arnoldo. *In Re Ricardo Rodríguez: An Attempt at Chicano Disenfranchisement in San Antonio, 1896–1897*. San Antonio: Caravel Press, 1979.
———. *Racial Frontiers: Africans, Chinese, and Mexicans in Western America, 1848–1890*. Albuquerque: University of New Mexico Press, 2002.
———. *The Tejano Community, 1836–1900*. Albuquerque: University of New Mexico Press, 1982.
———. *Tejano West Texas*. College Station: Texas A&M University Press, 2015.
———. *They Called Them Greasers: Anglo Attitudes toward Mexicans in Texas, 1821–1900*. Austin: University of Texas Press, 1983.
De León, Arnoldo, and Kenneth L. Stewart. *Tejanos and the Numbers Game: A Socio-Historical Interpretation from the Federal Censuses, 1850–1900*. Albuquerque: University of New Mexico Press, 1989.
Délano, Alexandra. *Mexico and Its Diaspora in the United States: Policies of Emigration since 1848*. New York: Cambridge University Press, 2011.
Deverell, William. *Whitewashed Adobe: The Rise of Los Angeles and the Remaking of Its Mexican Past*. Berkeley: University of California Press, 2004.
De Zavala, Adina. *History and Legends of the Alamo and Other Missions in and around San Antonio*. Edited by Richard R. Flores. Houston: Arte Público Press, 1996.
Díaz, Ella María. *Flying under the Radar with the Royal Chicano Air Force: Mapping a Chicano/a Art History*. Austin: University of Texas Press, 2017.
Dobie, J. Frank, and John D. Young. *A Vaquero of the Brush Country: The Life and Times of John D. Young*. Austin: University of Texas Press, 1998.
Doran, Adelaide LeMert. *The Ranch That Was Robbins': Santa Catalina Island*. Glendale, CA: Arthur H. Clark, 1963.
Eisenhower, John S. D. *So Far from God: U.S. War with Mexico 1846–1848*. New York: Random House, 1989.
Faragher, John Mack. *Out of Many: A History of the American People*. 6th ed. Upper Saddle River, NJ: Pearson/Prentice Hall, 2009.
Fernández, José Emilio. *The Biography of Casimiro Barela*. Translated by A. Gabriel Meléndez. Albuquerque: University of New Mexico Press, 2003.
Flores, Richard R. *Remembering the Alamo: Memory, Modernity, and the Master Symbol*. Austin: University of Texas Press, 2002.
Foley, Neil. *Mexicans in the Making of America*. Cambridge, MA: Harvard University Press, 2014.

---. *Quest for Equality: The Failed Promise of Black-Brown Solidarity.* Cambridge, MA: Harvard University Press, 2010.
Foos, Paul. *A Short, Offhand, Killing Affair: Soldiers and Social Conflict during the Mexican-American War.* Chapel Hill: University of North Carolina Press, 2002.
Francaviglia, Richard V., and Douglas W. Richmond, eds. *Dueling Eagles: Reinterpreting the U.S.-Mexican War, 1846–1848.* Fort Worth: Texas Christian University Press, 2000.
Frazier, Donald S., ed. *The United States and Mexico at War: Nineteenth-Century Expansionism and Conflict.* New York: Macmillan Reference Books, 1998.
Freund, David M. P., ed. *The Modern American Metropolis: A Documentary Reader.* West Sussex, UK: Wiley-Blackwell, 2015.
Fuentes Díaz, Vicente. *La Intervención norteamericana en México [1847].* Mexico City: Imprenta Nuevo Mundo, 1947.
Garcia, F. Chris, and Gabriel Sanchez. *Hispanics and the U.S. Political System: Moving into the Mainstream.* New York: Routledge, 2016.
García, Mario T. *Mexican Americans: Leadership, Ideology, and Identity, 1930–1960.* New Haven, CT: Yale University Press, 1989.
García, Richard A. *Rise of the Mexican American Middle Class: San Antonio, 1929–1941.* College Station: Texas A&M University Press, 1991.
Gardner, Richard. *¡Grito! Reies Tijerina and the New Mexico Land Grant War of 1967.* Indianapolis: Bobbs-Merrill, 1970.
Gillis, John, ed. *Commemorations: The Politics of National Identity.* Princeton, NJ: Princeton University Press, 1994.
Glassberg, David. *Sense of History: The Place of the Past in American Life.* Amherst: University of Massachusetts Press, 2001.
Goldfinch, Charles William, and J. T. Canales. *Juan N. Cortina: Two Interpretations.* New York: Arno Press, 1974.
Gómez, Angel Ignacio, and John Henry Chilcott. *Outline of Mexican American Education.* Tucson: Impresora Sahuaro, 1973.
Gómez, Laura E. *Inventing Latinos: A New Story of American Racism.* New York: New Press, 2020.
---. *Manifest Destinies: The Making of the Mexican American Race.* New York: New York University Press, 2007.
Gómez-Quiñones, Juan. *Chicano Politics: Reality and Promise, 1940–1990.* Albuquerque: University of New Mexico Press, 1990.
González, Gabriela. *Redeeming la Raza: Transborder Modernity, Race, Respectability, and Rights.* New York: Oxford University Press, 2018.
González, Gilbert. *Mexican Consuls and Labor Organizing: Imperial Politics in the American Southwest.* Austin: University of Texas Press, 1999.
González, John Morán. *Border Renaissance: The Texas Centennial and the Emergence of Mexican American Literature.* Austin: University of Texas Press, 2009.
Gonzales, Manuel G. *Mexicanos: A History of Mexicans in the United States.* 2nd ed. Bloomington: Indiana University Press, 2019.
Grant, Ulysses S. *Memoirs and Selected Letters: Personal Memoirs of U.S. Grant, Selected Letters 1839–1865.* New York: Library of America, 1990.
Green, James. *Taking History to Heart: The Power of the Past in Building Social Movements.* Amherst: University of Massachusetts Press, 2000.

Greenberg, Amy S. *A Wicked War: Polk, Clay, Lincoln, and the 1846 U.S. Invasion of Mexico.* New York: Knopf, 2012.

Griswold del Castillo, Richard. *The Los Angeles Barrio, 1850–1890: A Social History.* Berkeley: University of California Press, 1979.

———. *The Treaty of Guadalupe Hidalgo: A Legacy of Conflict.* Norman: University of Oklahoma Press, 1990.

Gritter, Matthew. *Mexican Inclusion: The Origins of Anti-discrimination Policy in Texas and the Southwest.* College Station: Texas A&M University Press, 2012.

Gross, Ariela J. *What Blood Won't Tell: A History of Race on Trial in America.* Cambridge, MA: Harvard University Press, 2008.

Guerin-Gonzales, Camille. *Mexican Workers and American Dreams: Immigration, Repatriation, and California Farm Labor, 1900–1939.* New Brunswick, NJ: Rutgers University Press, 1996.

Guidotti-Hernández, Nicole Marie. *Unspeakable Violence: Remapping U.S. and Mexican National Imaginaries.* Durham, NC: Duke University Press, 2011.

Gutiérrez, David G. *Walls and Mirrors: Mexican Americans, Mexican Immigrants, and the Politics of Ethnicity.* Berkeley: University of California Press, 1995.

Haas, Lisbeth. *Conquests and Historical Identities in California, 1769–1936.* Berkeley: University of California Press, 1995.

Hämäläinen, Pekka. *The Comanche Empire.* New Haven, CT: Yale University Press, 2008.

Haney López, Ian. *White by Law: The Legal Construction of Race.* New York: New York University, 2006.

Heintzelman, Samuel Peter. *Fifty Miles and a Fight: Major Samuel Heintzelman's Journal of Texas and the Cortina War.* Edited by Jerry D. Thompson. Austin: Texas State Historical Association, 1998.

Henderson, Timothy J. *A Glorious Defeat: Mexico and Its War with the United States.* New York: Hill & Wang, 2007.

Hernández, José Angel. *Mexican American Colonization during the Nineteenth Century: A History of the U.S.-Mexico Borderlands.* New York: Cambridge University Press, 2012.

Hernández, Kelly Lytle. *City of Inmates: Conquest, Rebellion, and the Rise of Human Caging in Los Angeles, 1771–1965.* Chapel Hill: University of North Carolina Press, 2017.

Hietala, Thomas R. *Manifest Design: Anxious Aggrandizement in Late Jacksonian America.* Ithaca, NY: Cornell University Press, 1985.

Hinojosa, Federico Allen. *El México de afuera.* San Antonio: Artes Graficas, 1940.

Hoffman, Abraham. *Unwanted Mexican Americans in the Great Depression.* Tucson: University of Arizona Press, 1974.

Horgan, Paul. *Great River: The Rio Grande in North American History.* 2 vols. New York: Holt, Rinehart, and Wilson, 1954.

Horsman, Reginald. *Race and Manifest Destiny: The Origins of American Racial Anglo-Saxonism.* Cambridge, MA: Harvard University Press, 1981.

Howe, Robert H. *How We Robbed Mexico in 1848.* New York: Latin American News Association, 1916.

Hurtado, Albert L. *Intimate Frontiers: Sex, Gender, and Culture in Old California.* Albuquerque: University of New Mexico Press, 1999.

Johannsen, Robert W. *To the Halls of the Montezumas: The Mexican War in the American Imagination.* New York: Oxford University Press, 1985.

Johnson, Benjamin Heber. *Revolution in Texas: How a Forgotten Rebellion and Its Bloody Suppression Turned Mexicans into Americans.* New Haven, CT: Yale University Press, 2003.

Johnson, Susan Lee. *Roaring Camp: The Social World of the California Gold Rush.* New York: W. W. Norton, 2001.

Kammen, Michael. *Mystic Chords of Memory: The Transformation of Tradition in American Culture.* New York: Knopf, 1991.

Kanellos, Nicolás. *Hispanic Literature of the United States: A Comprehensive Reference.* Westport, CT: Greenwood Press, 2003.

Kaplowitz, Craig A. *LULAC, Mexican Americans, and National Policy.* College Station: Texas A&M University Press, 2005.

Kerber, Linda K. *No Constitutional Right to Be Ladies: Women and the Obligations of Citizenship.* New York: Hill and Wang, 1998.

Kiser, William S. *Borderlands of Slavery: The Struggle over Captivity and Peonage in the American Southwest.* Philadelphia: University of Pennsylvania Press, 2017.

Krochmal, Max. *Blue Texas: The Making of a Multiracial Democratic Coalition in the Civil Rights Era.* Chapel Hill: University of North Carolina Press, 2016.

Lack, Paul D. *The Texas Revolutionary Experience: A Political and Social History, 1835–1836.* College Station: Texas A&M University Press, 1996.

Lajous, Roberta. *México y el mundo: Historia de sus relaciones exteriores.* Vol. 4. Mexico City: Senado de la Republica, 1990.

Leuchtenburg, William E., ed. *American Places: Encounters with History.* New York: Oxford University Press, 2000.

Lichtenstein, Andrew, and Alex Lichtenstein. *Marked, Unmarked, Remembered; A Geography of American Memory.* Morgantown: West Virginia University Press, 2017.

Limerick, Patricia Nelson. *The Legacy of Conquest: The Unbroken Past of the American West.* New York: Norton, 1987.

Longeaux y Vásquez, Enriqueta., Dionne. Espinoza, and Lorena Oropeza. *Enriqueta Vasquez and the Chicano Movement: Writings from El Grito Del Norte.* Houston, Texas: Arte Público Press, 2006.

López y Rivas, Gilberto. *La Guerra del 47 y la resistencia popular a la ocupación.* Mexico City: Editorial Nuestro Tiempo, 1976.

Lozano, Rosina. *An American Language: The History of Spanish in the United States.* Berkeley: University of California Press, 2018.

Lukens, Patrick D. *A Quiet Victory for Latino Rights: FDR and the Controversy over "Whiteness."* Tucson: University of Arizona Press, 2012.

Madley, Benjamin. *An American Genocide: The United States and the California Indian Catastrophe, 1846–1873.* New Haven, CT: Yale University Press, 2016.

Mariscal, George. *Aztlán and Viet Nam: Chicano and Chicana Experiences of the War.* Berkeley: University of California Press, 1999.

Márquez, Benjamin. *LULAC: The Evolution of a Mexican American Political Organization.* Austin: University of Texas Press, 1993.

Martínez, Elizabeth Sutherland, and Enriqueta Longeaux y Vasquez. *Viva la Raza! The Struggle of the Mexican-American People.* Garden City, NY: Doubleday, 1974.

Martinez, Monica Muñoz. *The Injustice Never Leaves You: Anti-Mexican Violence in Texas.* Cambridge, MA: Harvard University Press, 2018.

Martínez, Oscar J. *Border Boom Town: Ciudad Juárez since 1848.* Austin: University of Texas Press, 1978.
McCutchan, Joseph D. *Mier Expedition Diary: A Texan Prisoner's Account.* Edited by Joseph Milton Nance. Austin: University of Texas Press, 1978.
McWilliams, Carey. *Southern California Country, an Island on the Land.* New York: Duell, Sloan & Pearce, 1946.
Meléndez, A. Gabriel. *So All Is Not Lost: The Poetics of Print in Nuevomexicano Communities, 1834–1958.* Albuquerque: University of New Mexico Press, 1997.
Mendoza, Louis Gerard. *Historia: The Literary Making of Chicana and Chicano History.* College Station: Texas A&M University Press, 2001.
Merk, Frederick, and Lois Bannister. *Manifest Destiny and Mission in American History: A Reinterpretation.* New York: Knopf, 1963.
Meyer, Doris. *Speaking for Themselves: Neomexicano Cultural Identity and the Spanish-Language Press, 1880–1920.* Albuquerque: University of New Mexico Press, 1996.
Mitchell, Pablo. *Coyote Nation: Sexuality, Race, and Conquest in Modernizing New Mexico, 1880–1920.* Chicago: University of Chicago Press, 2005.
Montejano, David. *Anglos and Mexicans in the Making of Texas, 1836–1986.* Austin: University of Texas Press.
Montes, Amelia María de la Luz, and Anna Elizabeth Goldman, eds. *María Amparo Ruiz de Burton: Critical and Pedagogical Perspectives.* Lincoln: University of Nebraska Press, 2004.
Mora, Anthony. *Border Dilemmas: Racial and National Uncertainties in New Mexico, 1848–1912.* Durham, NC: Duke University Press, 2011.
Morales, Ed. *Latinx: The New Force in American Politics and Culture.* London: Verso, 2018.
Moyano Pahissa, Ángela. *El comercio de Santa Fe y la guerra del "47."* Mexico City: Sep Setentas, 1976.
———. *Protección consular a mexicanos en los Estados Unidos, 1849–1900.* Mexico City: Secretaría de Relaciones Exteriores, 1989.
Navarro, Armando. *La Raza Unida Party: A Chicano Challenge to the U.S. Two-Party Dictatorship.* Philadelphia: Temple University Press, 2000.
Nguyen, Viet Thanh. *Nothing Ever Dies: Vietnam and the Memory of War.* Cambridge, MA: Harvard University Press, 2016.
Nieto-Phillips, John M. *The Language of Blood: The Making of Spanish-American Identity in New Mexico, 1880s–1930s.* Albuquerque: University of New Mexico Press, 2004.
Novick, Peter. *The Holocaust in American Life.* Boston: Houghton Mifflin, 2000.
Oropeza, Lorena. *The King of Adobe: Reies López Tijerina, Lost Prophet of the Chicano Movement.* Chapel Hill: University of North Carolina Press, 2019.
———. *¡Raza sí! ¡Guerra no! Chicano Protest and Patriotism during the Viet Nam War Era.* Berkeley: University of California Press, 2005.
Orozco, Cynthia. *No Mexicans, Women, or Dogs Allowed: The Rise of the Mexican American Civil Rights Movement.* Austin: University of Texas Press, 2009.
Padilla, Genaro M. *My History, Not Yours: The Formation of Mexican American Autobiography.* Madison: University of Wisconsin Press, 1993.
Paredes, Américo. *A Texas-Mexican Cancionero: Folksongs of the Lower Border.* Urbana: University of Illinois Press, 1976.

Paredes, Américo, and Richard Bauman. *Folklore and Culture on the Texas-Mexican Border.* Austin: CMAS Books, Center for Mexican American Studies, University of Texas at Austin, 1993.

Parent, Laurence. *Official Guide to Texas State Parks and Historic Sites.* New ed. Austin: University of Texas Press, 2018.

Pérez, Vincent. *Remembering the Hacienda: History and Memory in the Mexican American Southwest.* College Station: Texas A&M University Press, 2006.

Pitt, Leonard. *The Decline of the Californios: A Social History of the Spanish-Speaking Californians, 1846–1890.* 1966. Updated with a new foreword, Berkeley: University of California Press, 1998.

Primer Congreso mexicanista verificado en Laredo, Texas, EE. UU. de A. los días 14 al 22 de septiembre de 1911. Discursos y conferencias. Por la raza y para la raza. Laredo, TX: Tipografía de N. Idar., 1912.

Pycior, Julie Leininger. *Democratic Renewal and the Mutual Aid Legacy of US Mexicans.* College Station: Texas A&M University Press, 2014.

Quiroz, Anthony. *Claiming Citizenship: Mexican Americans in Victoria, Texas.* College Station: Texas A&M University Press, 2005.

Ramos, Raúl A. *Beyond the Alamo: Forging Mexican Ethnicity in San Antonio, 1821–1861.* Chapel Hill: University of North Carolina Press, 2008.

Read, Benjamin M. *Guerra México-Americana.* Santa Fe, NM: Compania impresora del Nuevo Mexico, 1910.

Reséndez, Andrés. *Changing National Identities at the Frontier: Texas and New Mexico, 1800–1850.* New York: Cambridge University Press, 2005.

Rincón, Belinda Linn. *Bodies at War: Genealogies of Militarism in Chicana Literature and Culture.* Tucson: University of Arizona Press, 2017.

Rodríguez, Jaime Javier. *The Literatures of the U.S.-Mexico War.* Austin: University of Texas Press, 2010.

Rosales, Francisco Arturo. *¡Pobre Raza! Violence, Justice, and Mobilization among México Lindo Immigrants, 1900–1936.* Austin: University of Texas Press, 1999.

———, ed. *Testimonio: A Documentary History of the Mexican American Struggle for Civil Rights.* Houston: Arte Público Press, 2000.

Ruiz de Burton, María Amparo. *Conflicts of Interest: The Letters of María Amparo Ruiz de Burton.* Edited with a commentary by Rosaura Sánchez and Beatrice Pita. Houston: Arte Público Press, 2001.

———. *The Squatter and the Don.* Edited and introduced by Rosaura Sánchez and Beatrice Pita. 2nd ed. Houston: Arte Público Press, 1997.

Sánchez, David. *Expedition through Aztlán.* La Puente, CA: Perspective, 1978.

Sánchez, George I. *Forgotten People: A Study of New Mexicans.* Albuquerque: University of New Mexico Press, 1996.

Sánchez, Rosaura. *Telling Identities: The Californio Testimonios.* Minneapolis: University of Minnesota Press, 1995.

Sánchez, Rosaura, Beatrice Pita, and Bárbara Reyes, eds. "Nineteenth Century Californio Testimonials." Special issue, *Crítica: A Journal of Critical Essays,* Spring 1994.

San Miguel, Guadalupe, Jr. *"Let All of Them Take Heed": Mexican Americans and the Campaign for Educational Equality in Texas, 1910–1981.* Austin: University of Texas Press, 1987.

Seguín, Juan N. *A Revolution Remembered: The Memoirs and Selected Correspondence of Juan N. Seguín*. Edited by Jesús F. De la Teja. Austin: State House Press, 1991.

Singletary, Otis A. *The Mexican War*. Chicago: University of Chicago Press, 1960.

Smith, Justin H. *The War with Mexico*. 2 vols. New York: Macmillan, 1919.

Smith, Paul Chaat, and Robert Allen Warrior. *Like a Hurricane: The Indian Movement from Alcatraz to Wounded Knee*. New York: New Press, 1996.

Spickard, Paul. *Almost All Aliens: Immigration, Race, and Colonialism in American History and Identity*. New York: Routledge, 2007.

Stanley, F. *The Grant That Maxwell Bought*. Santa Fe: Sunstone Press, 2008.

Starr, Kevin. *Americans and the California Dream, 1850–1915*. New York: Oxford University Press, 1986.

Taylor, Paul S. *An American-Mexican Frontier*. Chapel Hill: University of North Carolina Press, 1934.

Thompson, Jerry D. *Cortina: Defending the Mexican Name in Texas*. College Station: Texas A&M University Press, 2007.

———. *Juan Cortina and the Texas-Mexico Frontier, 1859–1877*. El Paso: Texas Western Press, University of Texas at El Paso, 1994.

Tijerina, Andrés. *Tejano Empire: Life on the South Texas Ranchos*. College Station: Texas A&M University Press, 1998.

———. *Tejanos and Texas under the Mexican Flag, 1821–1836*. College Station: Texas A&M University Press, 1994.

Tijerina, Reies. *They Called Me "King Tiger": My Struggle for the Land and Our Rights*. Translated and edited by José Angel Gutiérrez. Houston: Arte Público Press, 2000.

Tinker Salas, Miguel. *In the Shadows of Eagles: Sonora and the Transformation of the Border During the Porfiriato*. Berkeley: University of California Press, 1997.

Tucker, Spencer C., ed. *Encyclopedia of the Mexican-American War: A Political, Social, and Military History*. Santa Barbara, CA: ABC-CLIO, 2013.

Twitchell, Ralph Emerson. *The Spanish Archives of New Mexico Comp. and Chronologically Arranged with Historical, Genealogical, Geographical, and Other Annotations, by Authority of the State of New Mexico*. Cedar Rapids, IA: Torch Press, 1914.

Valdés, Dennis Nodin. *Al Norte: Agricultural Workers in the Great Lakes Region, 1917–1970*. Austin: University of Texas Press, 1991.

Valerio-Jiménez, Omar S. *River of Hope: Forging Identity and Nation in the Rio Grande Borderlands*. Durham, NC: Duke University Press, 2013.

Van Wagenen, Michael Scott. *Remembering the Forgotten War: The Enduring Legacies of the U.S.-Mexico War*. Amherst: University of Massachusetts Press, 2012.

Vargas, Zaragoza. *Labor Rights Are Civil Rights: Mexican American Workers in Twentieth-Century America*. Princeton, NJ: Princeton University Press, 2005.

Vázquez de Knauth, Josefina. *Mexicanos y Norteamericanos Ante la Guerra del 47*. Mexico City: Secretaría de Educación Pública, 1972.

Vigil, Ernesto B. *The Crusade for Justice: Chicano Militancy and the Government's War on Dissent*. Madison: University of Wisconsin Press, 1999.

Villanueva, Nicholas, Jr. *The Lynching of Mexicans in the Texas Borderlands*. Albuquerque: University of New Mexico Press, 2017.

Webb, Walter Prescott. *The Texas Rangers: A Century of Frontier Defense*. Boston: Houghton Mifflin, 1935.

Weber, David J., ed. *Foreigners in Their Native Land: Historical Roots of the Mexican Americans*. Albuquerque: University of New Mexico Press, 2003.

———. *The Mexican Frontier, 1821–1846: The American Southwest under Mexico*. Albuquerque: University of New Mexico Press, 1982.

White, Richard. *"It's Your Misfortune and None of My Own": A New History of the American West*. Norman: University of Oklahoma Press, 1991.

Wolpert, Stanley. *Gandhi's Passion: The Life and Legacy of Mahatma Gandhi*. New York: Oxford University Press, 2001.

Woodman, Lyman L. *Cortina: Rogue of the Rio Grande*. San Antonio, TX: Naylor, 1950.

Ybarra, Lea. *Vietnam Veteranos: Chicanos Recall the War*. Austin: University of Texas Press, 2004.

Ybarra, Lea, and Nina Genera. *La batalla esta aquí: Chicanos and the War*. El Cerrito, California: Chicano Draft Help, 1972.

Zamora, Emilio. *The World of the Mexican Worker in Texas*. College Station: Texas A&M University Press, 1993.

Zamora O'Shea, Elena. *El Mesquite: A Story of the Early Spanish Settlements between the Nueces and the Rio Grande*. College Station: Texas A&M University Press, 2000.

Zoraida Vázquez, Josefina. *México y el mundo: Historia de sus relaciones exteriores*. Vol. 1. Mexico City: El Colegio de México, Centro de Estudios Internacionales, 2010.

Zoraida Vázquez, Josefina, and Lorenzo Meyer. *The United States and Mexico*. Chicago: University of Chicago Press, 1985.

Index

Page numbers in italics refer to illustrations.

Acuña, Rodolfo, 247
Aguilar, José Cristóbal, 48
Aguirre, Amado, 169, 300n179–300n180
Alamar, Mariano (fictional character), 126–28. *See also* Ruiz de Burton, María Amparo; *The Squatter and the Don* (Ruiz de Burton)
the Alamo, 25, 49, 190, 192, 195, 205, 210–11. *See also* De Zavala, Adina Emilia; Texas
Alatorre, Richard, 236
Alianza Hispano Americana, 135. *See also* mutual aid societies
Alvarez, Cruz (colonel), 245–46, 316n86
American GI Forum, 211, 255–56, 267. *See also* League of United Latin American Citizens (LULAC)
American Indian Movement (AIM), 251, 253
Ampudia, Pedro de, 28
annexation: citizenship and, 55, 61–62, 81, 94, 195; Mexico and, 29–30, 123, 130, 223; New Mexico and, 282 n138; Texas and, 26–27, 30, 33, 41, 87, 94, 206
anti-Mexican sentiment, 25–26, 30, 64, 180, 202–3
Arizona: citizenship and, 4, 34, 37, 48, 59, 160–61, 243; consuls in, 92, 109; Native American attacks in, 108; property rights in, 92, 108–9
Arzaga, José, 93–95
Asociación Nacional México-Americana (ANMA), 4–5, 184, 217–22, 224–25. *See also* civil rights
Assmann, Aleida, 2
Austin, Moses, 23, 49–50
Austin, Stephen F., 49, 209
Axelrod, Beverly, 233
Aztlán, 235–36, 248, 250

Bancroft, Hubert Howe, 114
Barela, Casimiro, 98–103
Battle of Buena Vista, 29–30, 75
Battle of Cinco de Mayo, 215
Battle of San Jacinto, 25, 50, 76, 211
Battle of San Pasqual, 14, 115, 119
Bear Flag Revolt, 117, 121
Béxar Auxiliary Squadron, 75
Béxar Defenders, 75
The Birth of Texas, 201
Bits of Texas History in the Melting Pot of America (Canales), 198
Blanton, Carlos, 184, 188–89
Blight, David W., 10
Boletin Popular, 105
Border War, 192–93
boycott: economic, 268; school and, 142–44, 178. *See also* education rights
Bracero Program, 221–22. *See also* immigrants
Bralley, F. M., 140–41
"Breve Historia del Pueblo Mexicano," 217–18. *See also* González, Isabel
Brown Berets, 226, 236–45, 242, 247, 250–54, 252, 265, 267, 270. *See also* Chicanos; La Caravana de la Reconquista (Caravan of the Reconquest); Sánchez, David
Brundage, W. Fitzhugh, 2, 10
Burton, Henry, 125

Calendario de Ontiveros, 93–94
Calhoun, John C. (senator), 46, 60
California: gold in, 5, 31–32, 43, 63–66, 81, 116–17; land loss in, 5, 39–40, 69–71, 80–82; politics in, 48–49; Spanish in, 200. *See also* Californios
California Land Act of 1851, 38, 58, 70, 81, 126

Californios: activism of, 58–59; citizenship and, 58, 67–68, 71; land and, 58, 69–71, 94–95, 121–23, 126; politics and, 48–49, 71, 287n11; testimonios, 114, 120–23; violence against, 64–65, 122. *See also* California; Chicanos; Latinos; Mexican Americans; social subordination

Camarillo, Albert, 133

Campo Tecolote (Owl Camp), 251

Canales, José T., 180, *181*, 182, 184–85, 188, 192–201. *See also* Castañeda, Carlos E.; De Zavala, Adina Emilia; League of United Latin American Citizens (LULAC); Tejanos; Zamora O'Shea, Elena

Canales, Teresa, 249

Cannon, Fredrick, 65–66

Cano, Ignacia, 170–71

Caravana de la Reconquista, 226, 242, 270. *See also* Brown Berets

Carbajal, José María Jesús, 208–9, 309n167

Cardenas, Cuauhtémoc, 269

Cargo, David (governor), 232

Carrigan, William, 65, 72–73

Carson, Kit, 233

Carta Editorial, 258

Castañeda, Carlos E., 180, 182, 185, *186*, 190–94, 196, 198–201, 224, 302n15. *See also* Canales, José T.; De Zavala, Adina Emilia; Zamora O'Shea, Elena

Castillo, Richard Griswold del, 35, 40, 43, 251

Catalina Island. *See* Santa Catalina Island

Catholicism, 23, 29–30, 160

Catron, Thomas B., 43

Cavazos, Sabas, 84

Cavelier, René-Robert, 200

centralists, 24, 30

Channel Islands, 169, 250

Chavez, Cesar, 237, 265

Chávez, Ernesto, 251–52

Chicano Draft help, 259

Chicano Liberation symposium, 265

Chicano Moratorium Committee, 238, 241, 246, 259

Chicanos: activism of, 5, 16–19, 226–33, 237–54, 261–67, 317n127; antiwar movement of, 255–66; discrimination of, 16; history of, 222–23, 254, 275n1; military service of, 235; violence against, 238. *See also* Brown Berets; Californios; Hispanos; Latinos; Mexican Americans; Nuevomexicanos; social subordination; Tejanos; Tijerina, Reies López; Vietnam War

Chicano Youth Conference, 236, 265

Christianity. *See* Catholicism

citizenship: annexation and, 61–62, 81, 94, 195; Arizona and, 4, 34, 37, 48, 59, 160–61, 243; Californios and, 58, 67–68, 71; Hispanos and, 102, 107; Latinos and, 33, 70–71; Mexican Americans and, 155, 186–88, 219–20, 235–36; Mexico and, 61–62; Native Americans and, 21, 162, 303n45; Nuevomexicanos and, 37, 46–47, 107, 162–63, 223–24; Treaty of Guadalupe Hidalgo and, 3–5, 7–8, 33–36, 56, 70–71, 80–82, 95–97, 99–101, 159–60, 187, 204–6, 218–19, 239. *See also* annexation; Arizona; Californios; Hispanos; Latinos; Mexican Americans; Mexico; naturalization; Nuevomexicanos; social subordination; Treaty of Guadalupe Hidalgo

"Civil Disobedience" (Thoreau), 29, 272

civil rights: African Americans and, 47, 72–73, 188, 230, 232, 255, 272, 281n102; collective memories and, 3–7, 11, 213, 273; fiction and, 129; journalism and, 68–73, 132, 136–41, 143–51, 154–58, 162–63, 268; language rights, 100; marches for, 237–41, 247–50; Mexican Americans and, 154–58; organizations of, 179–90; organized movements for, 152–54, 227–33, 236–54, 256–57. *See also* American GI Forum; Asociación Nacional México-Americana (ANMA); Brown Berets; League of United Latin American Citizens (LULAC); newspapers; social subordination

Civil War, 33
Clay, Henry, 27
Cold War, 214, 220
collective memories: family and community, 176–77, 192, 198, 213, 215–16, 248–49; politics and, 4–5, 7–9, 16, 88–89, 128–31, 180, 185–86, 230, 245–46, 253–55, 266–67, 270; of US-Mexico War, 1–13, 56–57, 148, 161, 226, 246, 252–53, 263–64, 268. *See also* identity; newspapers; US-Mexico War
colonization plan, 22–24
communism, 214
Community Service Organization (CSO), 236
Compromise of 1850, 33
Congressional Record, 234–35
Cook, Terry, 176–77, 194
Coronel, Antonio Franco, 116–18
Cortina, Juan, 38, 83–86, 85, 90, 112–13, 130, 180, 195–200, 244–45. *See also* Tejanos
Court of Private Land Claims, 44–45, 104
criminalization: cultural practices and, 52–53; ethnic Mexicans and, 151–52; jury exclusion and, 211, 282n135; Mexican Americans and, 5, 51–53, 253; New Mexico and, 54–55; role of press, 53; Tejanos and, 87–88
Crusade for Justice, 257
Cuban War of Independence, 100–101, 288n28
cultural pluralism, 184
cultural practices, 52–53, 95, 163–64, 178, 220
Czech Hour, 213

Daughters of the Republic of Texas (DRT), 190, 192
A Day without an Immigrant, 268
Defensores de Béjar (Béxar Defenders), 75
Defensores de la Patria, 84
de la Barra, Francisco, 137
de la Rosa, Luis, 62, 170
Delgado v. Bastrop Independent School District, 211
Del Rio ISD v. Salvatierra, 208, 310n171

Democratic Party of Bexar County, 75
Democratic Review, 22
De Zavala, Adina Emilia, 182, 185, 190–92, 191. *See also* Canales, José T.; Castañeda, Carlos E.; Zamora O'Shea, Elena; Zavala, Lorenzo de
de Zavala, Lorenzo, 190–91, 206, 210, 215–16. *See also* De Zavala, Adina Emilia
Diario del Hogar, 148, 149
Díaz, Porfirio, 111, 133, 145–46
Diébold, Miguel, 137, 139
Dobie, J. Frank, 195–97
Dominguez, Dominga, 38
Douglass, Frederick, 29
draft. *See* US government
Dred Scott decision, 33
Driscoll, Clara, 192
Du Bois, W. E. B., 10

education rights: history omissions and, 234, 308n136; lack of access to, 155; school funding and, 156–57, 294n49; segregation and, 5, 132, 137–44, 156, 178, 207–11, 294n56; textbooks and, 181–82, 195, 197, 200–202, 209–10, 234–35. *See also* segregation
Edwards, Hayden, 197
Eimer, Margaret, 6
El Bejareño, 51
El Chamizal, 166–68, 169, 178, 299n168, 299n173
El Clamor Público, 58, 59, 68–73
El Eco de la Sierra, 158
El Fronterizo, 73
El Grito del Norte, 233, 235, 266, 314n47
El Imparcial de Texas, 135
Elkins, Stephen (senator), 159–60, 298n145
El Luchador, 208
El Mesquite, 200
El Nuevo Mexicano, 103
El Nuevo Mundo, 107
El País, 145
El Paso Herald, 143

El Primer Congreso Mexicanista (First Mexicanist Congress), 152–54, 297n113
El Progreso, 112–13
El Tiempo, 96, 105, *106*
empresario, 24, 50, 73
Escalante, Manuel, 109–10
Escobar, Mary, 228
Escuadrón auxiliar de Béjar, 75
European Americans, 23–24
Evans, T. L., 211
Ewence, Hannah, 125
Expedition through Aztlán, 248. *See also* Sánchez, David

federalists, 24, 30
Flores, Francisca, 258
Flores, José María, 91
Flores, Richard, 190, 192, 201
Foley, Neil, 187–88
Ford, John S. (colonel), 112–13, 289n62
Foreign Miners' Tax, 64, 66, 218
Forgotten People, 222–23. *See also* Sánchez, George I.
Fourteenth Amendment (1868), 35
fraternal organizations, 151

Gadsden Treaty, 31, 105, 245–46
Galveston Historical Society (GHS), 191–92
Gárcia, Alberto, 188
García, Gus, 211
García, Macario, 214
García, Mario, 185
García, Richard, 207
Garner, John Nance, 147
Garrison, William Lloyd, 29
Garza Falcón, Blas María de la, 84
Garza, José Saldívar de la, 83
Genaro García Collection, 180, 185, 194. *See also* Castañeda, Carlos E.
Genera, Nina, 259–61. See also *La batalla esta aquí* (Ybarra & Genera)
Goldfinch, Charles, 196–97
Goliad, 25, 200
Gómez, Antonio, 150–51. *See also* lynching
Gómez, Laura, 36, 43, 45, 54–55, 187, 279n52

Gómez, Manuel, 6, 16–18, 17, 261–66, 318n158, 318n161. *See also* Chicanos; US government
Gonzales, M. C., 202–3, 207–10
Gonzales, Rodolfo "Corky," 256, 258, 265
González, Deena, 15
González, Gabriela, 137, 153
González, Isabel, 217–18
González, John Morán, 193, 197
González, Jovita, 6
González, Macedonio, 115, 120
Goseascochea, José Manuel, 84
Grant, Ulysses S. (president), 272, 278n33–34
Great Depression, 182–83, 202, 229
Green Berets, 263
Griffith, D. W., 201
Gross, Ariela, 35, 156–57
Guerra México-Americana, 171–74, 177. *See also* Read, Benjamin Maurice
guerrilla tactics, 30
Gutiérrez, David, 133
Guzman, Ralph, 255

Halbwachs, Maurice, 2, 224
Henderson, Effie Greer, 144–45
Hermandad Penitente, 136. *See also* mutual aid societies
Hernández, Andrés, 203–4
Hernández v. the State of Texas, 211
Herrera, John J., 188, 210–17, 311n195
Hidalgo, Miguel, 136. *See also* mutual aid societies
Hinojosa, Federico Allen, 165
Hispanos: citizenship rights and, 102, 107; identity of, 46–47, 55, 61, 70, 175–77; land grants and, 43–45; politics and, 53–55, 101–2. *See also* Chicanos; Latinos; Mexican Americans; New Mexico; Nuevomexicanos; social subordination
History and Legends of the Alamo (De Zavala), 192. *See also* De Zavala, Adina Emilia
Houston Post, 152
Houston, Sam, 26, 75

Idar, Clemente. *See* Idar Family
Idar, Eduardo. *See* Idar Family
Idar Family, 132, 136–41, 138, 144, 146, 150–58. *See also La Crónica*
Idar, Jovita. *See* Idar Family
Idar, Nicasio, 298n121. *See also* Idar Family
identity: boundary and, 45–47; collective memories and, 2, 7, 10–11, 46, 233–34; education system and, 263–64; land loss and, 4, 253; political disenfranchisement and, 4; race and, 60–61. *See also* collective memories; newspapers
Illustrated History of New Mexico, 174, 177–78. *See also* Read, Benjamin Maurice
immigrants: agriculture and, 183; cultural impacts of, 132–33; deportation of, 183, 202–3, 221–22, 247; economy and, 133, 182–85, 292n6; quotas and, 183; reform and, 269–70; rights and, 111, 239, 248, 268; social standing of, 146, 179–80; violence against, 144–45. *See also* Mexican exiles; Mexican nationals; Mexican Revolution; Operation Wetback; xenophobia
immigration agent. *See* empresario
Immigration Bureau, 183
imperialism, 166, 233, 259, 261, 265, 269
Independent Democrat, 104
Indianola Bulletin, 82
intermarriages, 108, 127–28
International Boundary Commission, 166

Jackson, Andrew (president), 26
Jeffersonian ideals, 29
Johnson, Benjamin, 188–89
Jones, Anson (president), 75
Joseph, Antonio, 96–97, 102–3, 288n36
Juárez, Benito, 136, 251. *See also* mutual aid societies

Kammen, Michael, 8
Kanellos, Nicholás, 71
Kansas-Nebraska Act of 1854, 33

Kearny, Stephen Watts, 29, 99, 226, 246–47
King, Martin Luther, Jr., 231
Kingsbury, Robert, 82
Know-Nothing Party, 51, 75
Krauze, Enrique, 269–70
Krochmal, Max, 188

La Alianza Federal de las Mercedes (the Federal Land Grant Alliance), 229–33, 238. *See also* land grants
La batalla esta aquí (Ybarra & Genera), 259–60, 260
labor rights, 111, 222. *See also* civil rights; immigrants
labor unions, 133, 183, 256
La Caravana de la Reconquista (Caravan of the Reconquest), 241, 242. *See also* Brown Berets
La Causa, 242, 249, 253
La Crónica, 132, 136–41, 138, 142, 145–46, 150, 152–58. *See also* Idar Family
La Estrella Mejicana, 103
La Gaceta, 91, 93–94, 287n13
La Gran Liga Mexicanista de Beneficencia y Protección (Great Mexican League for Beneficence and Protection), 153. *See also* civil rights
La Liga Protectora (Phoenix), 135–36. *See also* mutual aid societies
La Liga Protectora Mexicana of San Antonio, 135. *See also* mutual aid societies
land dispossession, 5, 38–40, 105, 279n63. *See also* land grants
land grants: *La Alianza* and, 67–68, 230, 232, 238; legality of, 41–43, 45, 80, 104, 122; opposition of, 103; Treaty of Guadalupe of Hidalgo and, 35, 37, 103–5, 129, 256. *See also* land dispossession; Treaty of Guadalupe Hidalgo
La Piranya, 237
La Prensa, 165, 170
La Raza (magazine), 6, 17, 266
Larrazolo, Ambrosio, 162
Las Gorras Blancas (the White Caps), 56

Latinos: citizenship and, 33, 70–71; heritage of, 275n1; Puerto Ricans and, 278n36, 303n45; violence against, 68–69. *See also* Californios; Chicanos; Hispanos; Mexican Americans; Nuevomexicanos; Tejanos
La Voz del Nuevo Mundo, 67, 73
League of United Latin American Citizens (LULAC), 5, 47, 179–82, 184–90, 194–95, 202–4, 206–11, 224–25, 302n16. *See also* American GI Forum; Canales, José T.; civil rights; Mexican nationals; nationalism; whiteness
Liga Femenil Mexicanista (League of Mexican Women), 153. *See also* civil rights
Lincoln, Abraham, 29, 33, 272
Loaiza, José, 66–68, 284n38, 284n40, 284n44
Loaiza, Josefa Juvera, 65–68. *See also* lynching
Los Tigres del Norte, 268
Louisiana, 23, 173, 301n195
Lozano, Rosina, 102
Lukens, Patrick, 189
Luz Sáenz, José de la, 189
lynching, 53, 64–69, 144–45, 147, 150–51, 154. *See also* Gómez, Antonio; Loaiza, Josefa Juvera; Rodríguez, Antonio; vigilantes

Machado de Ridington (Wrightington), Juana, 118–20, 290n88
Machete (Rodriguez), 269
Magón, Ricardo Flores, 151, 297n103
manifest destiny, 22, 30, 234, 271
The Man of Cinco de Mayo (Syers), 215
Marcha de la Reconquista, 238–41, 239
march to El Paso, 247–50
Mariscal, George, 257
Márquez, Benjamin, 186, 188–89
Marrón, Juan María, 114
Marshall, John, 36, 63–64
Martínez, Elizabeth "Betita," 233–34
Martínez, León Cárdenas, Jr., 151–52
Martinez, Monica Muñoz, 9

Martyrs of the Alamo (Griffith), 201
McWilliams, Carey, 265
media. *See* newspapers
Meléndez, A. Gabriel, 171
memorials, 98–99, 101. *See also* monuments
Mexican American Political Association (MAPA), 255
Mexican Americans: citizenship rights of, 155, 186–88, 219–20, 235–36; civil rights of, 154–57, 179–80, 226–27, 232, 255; housing discrimination and, 219; identity of, 188–89, 264, 302n11; military service of, 163, 255–58; violence against, 220. *See also* Californios; Chicanos; criminalization; Hispanos; Latinos; League of United Latin American Citizens (LULAC); Nuevomexicanos; Tejanos
Mexican American Student Confederation, 265
Mexican American Youth Leadership Conference, 236
Mexican Cession, 36–37
Mexican consuls, 61–63, 82–83, 90, 108–11, 129, 137, 142–44, 150–52, 155, 208, 289n60
Mexican exiles, 163–65. *See also* immigrants
Mexican nationals: immigration and, 146, 164, 202–3, 222; League of United Latin American Citizens (LULAC) and, 179–80, 204; rights of, 31, 48, 61, 88–89, 110–11, 132, 155–56, 158, 183; US-Mexico War and, 8, 14, 46, 92–93, 167, 169, 270–71. *See also* immigrants; League of United Latin American Citizens (LULAC); Mexico
Mexican Revolution, 111, 133, 147, 150, 164–65, 167, 169, 182–83, 244–45. *See also* immigrants
Mexican Texans. *See* Tejanos
Mexico: anti-American sentiment and, 145–46; borderlands and, 21–22; citizenship and, 61–62; government and, 21–22, 24–25, 30, 62–63, 110–11; Independence of, 19–21, 23; map of land boundaries, 20, 32; military of, 25, 30, 75, 199; slavery and, 22, 24, 110. *See also* land grants; Mexican nationals; US-Mexico War

Mier expedition, 27
minute men, 109. *See also* vigilantes
Missouri Compromise, 33
Montejano, David, 41, 51
Montoya, Alfredo, 221
monuments, 14, 226, 243–44, 249–50, 254, 270–73, 276 n29, 315n80, 316n97. *See also* memorials; Palo Alto Battlefield National Historical Park
Mora, Anthony, 61, 162
Mora, J. M., 153
Moreno, José Matías, 115
Muñoz, Rosalío, 237–38, 257–58, 265
Murrieta, Joaquín, 56, 122, 243–44, 250, 254, 265
mutual aid societies, 134–37, 178, 293n19
mutualistas. *See* mutual aid societies

National Association for the Advancement of Colored People, 195
nationalism, 29, 164, 241. *See also* League of United Latin American Citizens (LULAC)
National Museum of Interventions, 270
National Youth Conference (1970), 235
Native Americans: citizenship and, 21, 162, 303n45; gold rush and, 64; relations in Mexico and, 19–23, 30, 89; slave trade and, 20; treaty and, 31–33, 263; violence against, 115–20
nativism, 30, 64, 66, 182
naturalization, 18, 34–35, 156. *See also* Rodríguez, Ricardo
Naturalization Act of 1790, 18, 21, 34, 144
Navarro, Angel, 51
Navarro, José Antonio, 206, 210
Nazi propaganda, 212
A New History of Texas (Pennybacker), 197
New Mexico: criminalization and, 54–55; land grants in, 42–45; politics and, 53–55; slavery in, 159; statehood in, 4–5, 46, 55, 59–61, 95–100, 129, 159–60, 175–76, 178. *See also* Hispanos; Nuevomexicanos
New Mexico Historical Review, 176
New Spain: borderlands of, 19–20, 23; government of, 22–23. *See also* Spain

newspapers: civil rights and, 68, 72–73, 83, 90, 111–13, 132, 144, 178, 231, 259, 265, 268; identity and, 61, 163–65, 175; politics and, 58–59, 62, 96–97, 101–5, 111, 129, 139, 145–47, 158, 160; role of English-language, 53, 72, 89, 129, 146–47, 151; war memories and, 4–5, 57, 92–93, 107, 113, 129, 146, 161, 166–67, 169–70. *See also* civil rights; collective memories; identity; New Mexico; transnationalism
New York Times, 146, 151
Nguyen, Viet Thanh, 8, 14, 214, 250
Nieto-Phillips, John, 47, 61
North from Mexico (Carey McWilliams), 265
Novick, Peter, 7, 14, 255
Nueces Strip, 27–28, 31, 40–41, 84, 112, 200, 215–16
Nuevomexicanos: citizenship and, 37, 46–47, 107, 162–63, 223–24; identity of, 60–61, 161–62, 170–77; language and, 101–2; New Mexico statehood and, 95–96; property rights and, 42–43. *See also* Chicanos; Hispanos; Latinos; Mexican Americans; New Mexico; social subordination

Office of the Fair Employment Practice Committee, 185
Operation Wetback, 222. *See also* immigrants
Organic Act of 1850, 159
Ornelas, Enrique, 142–43
Oropeza, Lorena, 255, 264
Orozco, Cynthia, 186
Ortiz, Ramón, 62
O'Sullivan, John, 22
Osuna de Marrón, Felipa, 114–16
Otero, Miguel, 161–62
Our Catholic Heritage in Texas (Castañeda), 192. *See also* Castañeda, Carlos E.

Padilla, Genaro, 79
Padilla, Juan, 117
Palo Alto Battlefield National Historical Park, 270–71. *See also* monuments

Paredes, Mariano, 271
Partido Liberal Mexicano, 151
Paz Brownrigg, Coya, 72
Pelirojos (Redheads), 30. *See also* San Patricios (Saint Patrick's Battalion)
Pennybacker, Anna J. Hardwicke, 197–98, 200, 210
peonage, 160
Perales, Alonso, 179, 187, 189
Pico, Andrés, 117
Pico, Antonio María, 80–82
Pico, Pío, 80, 115, 125
Pita, Beatrice, 128
police brutality, 195, 220, 227, 238, 240–41, 247, 249, 258, 262
Polk, James (president), 15, 27–29, 37, 235, 248, 271
Poole, Alex, 194
Poor People's March (1968), 231
Primer Congreso Mexicanista (First Mexicanist Congress), 152–54. *See also* civil rights
Progreso, 217, 219–21, 223
Protocol of Querétaro, 42
Pycior, Julie Leininger, 136

race prejudice, 147–48
race war of 1850s, 52
radio, 213–14, 268
railroad monopolies, 127
Raleigh, Eve. *See* Eimer, Margaret
Ramírez, Francisco, 58, 59, 68–72
Ramos, Raúl, 75
Read, Benjamin Maurice, 170–77, 172, 178, 301n209–301n210. *See also Guerra México-Americana*; *Illustrated History of New Mexico*; Nuevomexicanos
Reagan, Ronald (governor), 240
Regeneración, 151–52
religious commune. *See* Tijerina, Reies López
repatriation, 34, 62–63, 92, 107, 283n21. *See also* Mexican consuls
Ribb, Robert, 193, 196

Rio Grande: battles of, 15, 25, 27, 75; borderland and, 1, 27–28, 31, 45–46, 51, 105, 166–68, 215; trade and, 41; use of, 53
Rodríguez, Antonio, 144–45, 147–48, 149, 150–51, 153, 278–79n43, 294n60
Rodríguez, Ricardo, 144, 156. *See also* naturalization
Rodriguez, Robert, 269. See also *Machete* (Rodriguez)
Roosevelt, Franklin Delano (president), 213
Roybal, Edward, 219, 256
Ruiz, Antonio, 69, 213
Ruiz de Burton, María Amparo, 6, 92, 123–29, 124, 130–31, 291n114. See also *The Squatter and the Don* (Ruiz de Burton)
Ruiz, Francisco, 210–11

Salazar, Rubén, 238, 246
San Antonio de Béxar. *See* the Alamo
Sánchez, Alfonso, 230
Sánchez, David, 226, 236–38, 243, 245–51, 253. *See also* Brown Berets; *Expedition through Aztlán*
Sánchez, George I., 222–24, 256. *See also Forgotten People*
Sánchez, Rosaura, 120, 128
Sandos, James, 194, 305n78
San Patricios (Saint Patrick's Battalion), 30. *See also* Pelirojos
Santa Anna, Antonio López de, 24–25, 29–30, 37, 197, 200
Santa Catalina Island, 236, 250–53, 252, 267, 316n103
Santa Fe Daily New Mexican, 104
Santa Fe expedition, 26–27, 74
Santa Fe Ring, 43
Schwartz, Joan, 176–77, 194
Scott, Winfield, 30
segregation, 6, 132, 137–39, 141–44, 152–54, 156, 162, 206–7, 219. See also *Delgado v. Bastrop Independent School District*; education rights
Seguín, Erasmo, 49–50
Seguín, Juan N., 26, 49–51, 73–79, 74, 195, 216, 260, 264, 285n87, 309n156. *See also* Tejanos

selective remembering: of conquest, 61, 89, 107, 118, 161–62, 204, 206–7, 224, 254–55, 283n15; of Texas Rebellion, 140–41; of US-Mexico War, 14, 90, 158, 204, 267
Sena, José D., 97–98
Shears, Robert, 195
slavery: expansion of, 19, 22, 26–29, 33, 159–60, 164, 173, 175; Mexico and, 22, 24, 140; opposition of, 60, 70, 99, 196; US Constitution and, 21
Slidell, John, 27
social subordination: activism against, 5; African Americans and, 188; archives and, 194; Californios and, 118; Chicanos and, 235, 240, 267; education and, 182, 234; Hispanos and, 55; legal system and, 13; Nuevomexicanos and, 160–61; Tejanos and, 130, 205; Treaty of Guadalupe Hidalgo and, 3, 14, 16, 36, 39, 139, 183, 205, 223, 226. *See also* Californios; Chicanos; civil rights; Hispanos; Nuevomexicanos; Tejanos
Sociedad Protección Mutua de Trabajadores Unidos, 135. *See also* mutual aid societies
Somervell expedition, 27
"Somos más Americanos" (We are more Americans), 268, 319n2
Sonorans. *See* Arizona; California
Spain: Bourbon leaders of, 20; heritage and, 46–47, 56, 61, 95–96, 161–62, 175, 187, 189, 209, 217; land and, 19–21, 23, 169, 173, 200–201, 234; land grants from, 38, 41–42, 45, 67, 80–81, 98, 100, 104, 109, 193; Native Americans and, 116, 118–22, 130, 214, 286–87n124; New Spain and, 22–23
Spanish-American War. *See* Cuban War of Independence
Spot Resolutions, 29, 272. *See also* Lincoln, Abraham
The Squatter and the Don (Ruiz de Burton), 6, 92, 125–26, 128, 292n128. *See also* Ruiz de Burton, María Amparo
statues. *See* monuments
Step-Children of a Nation, 217. *See also* González, Isabel

Stewart, William, 103
Stockholm Peace Appeal, 220
Sutter, John, 63–64
Syers, Ed, 215–16, 311n196. *See also* The Man of Cinco de Mayo (Syers)

Taft, William Howard (president), 142
Taylor, Paul S., 197–98
Taylor, Zachary (president), 15, 28, 28–30, 99, 160, 278n34
Tejanos: criminalization of, 87–88, 112; discrimination against, 208–10, 212; history of, 180–82, 194–95, 197–202, 205–6, 212, 214–15; identity of, 87–88, 275n1; land loss of, 40–42, 77, 87–88, 113; loyalty of, 76–79, 186, 194, 204, 206–7, 306n90; lynchings and, 53; politics and, 49–51; rebellions led by, 24–26, 40–41, 79, 83–90, 112, 130, 140–41, 165, 180, 195–96, 210; rights of, 76–77, 195, 212–13. *See also* Canales, José T.; Chicanos; Cortina, Juan; criminalization; Latinos; Mexican Americans; Seguín, Juan N.; social subordination; Texas
Texas: agricultural workers in, 110; Cortina rebellion of, 84–89, 112, 130, 195–96; expulsion of Ethnic Mexicans in, 82–83; history and, 190–202; independence of, 33, 79, 140–41, 165, 180, 182, 210; land loss in, 40–42; politics in, 49–51; separatist rebellion of, 25–26. *See also* the Alamo; Cortina, Juan; Seguín, Juan N.; Tejanos
Texas Patriots, 206
Texas Rangers, 66, 86, 113, 193–97, 248, 263, 272–73, 289n64
The Texas Rangers (Webb), 196. *See also* Webb, Walter Prescott
Thoreau, Henry David, 29, 272. *See also* "Civil Disobedience" (Thoreau)
Thornton Skirmish, 15, 271–72, 276 n33–34
Tierra Amarilla courthouse, 230, 232, 238
Tijerina, Reies López, 6, 227–33, 236, 238, 265–66, 313n3, 313n5, 313n10. *See also* land grants

Tovar sisters, 259
Trade and Intercourse Act (1790), 21
transcontinental railroad, 6, 31, 64, 108
transnationalism: collective memories and, 2–3, 57, 153, 215–16, 245, 251, 270; identity and, 61, 153, 164; newspapers and, 4–5, 57, 91–94, 111–13, 129, 144–45, 178. *See also* newspapers
Tratado de Mesilla. *See* Gadsden Treaty
Treaties of Velasco, 25
Treaty of Fort Laramie (1868), 251
Treaty of Guadalupe Hidalgo: boundary and, 31, 165–67, 169–70, 268, 278n28; citizenship guarantees of, 3–5, 7–8, 33–36, 56, 70–71, 80–82, 95–97, 99–101, 159–60, 187, 204–6, 218–19, 239; Cortina rebellion and, 83–90; expulsion of ethnic Mexicans and, 82–83; language rights and, 57, 101–3, 231–32, 287n14; nullification of, 269; property rights and, 33–38, 41–42, 70, 167–70, 229, 249, 251–53; unfulfilled promises of, 16–19, 38, 62–63, 86–89, 99–100, 122–23, 126–27, 155–56, 205, 222, 226, 230, 249, 257–58, 263, 266–67. *See also* land grants
Treaty of Louisiana, 168
Trujillo, Charley, 256
Tyler, John, 27

Ulibarri, Sabine, 230
Unión Fraternal Mutualista La Protectora, 135–36. *See also* mutual aid societies
United States: Constitution of, 36; democratic ideals and, 221; Immigration Bureau of, 247; legal system of, 148; map of land boundaries, 20, 32; military campaigns of, 29–30; westward expansion of, 19, 22, 27, 29, 89, 126, 130, 243–45, 249, 254
Uranga, Rodolfo, 164
US government: draft and, 235, 255–57, 261–66; treaty enforcement by, 40–42, 45, 62–63, 86–89, 110, 122–23, 126–27, 155–56, 223–24, 230, 239, 263–67. *See also* Treaty of Guadalupe Hidalgo
US-Korean War, 214, 221

US-Mexican Claims Commission, 67–68
US-Mexico War: alternate views of, 2–4, 7–8, 164, 167, 171–73, 226, 234, 248, 252–53, 275n9; causes of, 26–28, 91, 173; consequences of, 6–7, 14–15, 93–94, 99–101, 158, 161, 175, 253, 265–66, 272; opposition of, 28–29; public schools and, 1, 148; treaty and, 30–31; Vietnam War and, 257–58, 262–63, 266–67. *See also* collective memories

Valencia, F., 186–87, 204–7, 212, 308–9n152
Vallejo, Mariano Guadalupe, 39, 117, 121–23, 125–28, 291n103, 291n106
A Vaquero of the Brush Country (Dobie), 197
Varela, María, 260–61
Vasconcelos, José, 189
Vasquez, Enriqueta, 233–36, 259
Vásquez, Tiburcio, 56
Vázquez, Rafael (general), 78
Vietnam War: activists and, 16, 255, 259, 262, 267; collective memories and, 11, 14, 227; opposition against, 221, 232–33, 235, 256, 265. *See also* Chicanos; US-Mexico War and, 18, 235, 257–58, 261, 263, 266–67
vigilantes: consuls and, 109; journalists and, 144–45, 147; politics and, 64; punishing of, 69, 147–48, 150–51; race war and, 52; Tejanos and, 26, 50, 53; workers and, 66, 90, 129. *See also* lynching
Vigil, Ernesto, 257–58, 317n134
Villanueva, Nicholas, Jr., 147
Villa, Pancho, 244
Viva la Raza!, 234. *See also* Martínez, Elizabeth "Betita"; Vasquez, Enriqueta
Viva Tejas: The Story of the Mexican-Born Patriots of the Republic of Texas, 195. *See also* Canales, José T.
voting: obstacles to, 5, 31, 37, 55–56, 206; rights and, 19, 47–48, 54, 71, 92, 135, 184, 187–88, 219

Wallace, Henry, 217
Warford, Elisa, 127

war memorials. *See* monuments
Warren, Earl, 231
Webb, Clive, 65, 72–73
Webb, Walter Prescott, 194–97
Weber, David, 24, 104
Webster, Daniel, 272
"What Is Our Duty" (Gonzales), 202. *See also* immigrants
Whig Party, 27–29, 272
whiteness: Asociación Nacional México-Americana (ANMA), 217; education and, 142, 158; League of United Latin American Citizens (LULAC), 185–89; New Mexico statehood and, 160, 174–75, 178; rights and, 4, 47, 56, 127, 182, 204, 225, 309n154. *See also* League of United Latin American Citizens (LULAC)
white supremacy, 21–22, 65, 67–68, 189, 197, 272
Who Would Have Thought It? (Ruiz de Burton), 125. *See also* Ruiz de Burton, María Amparo
Wilmot, David, 29
Wilmot Provisio, 29
Woll, Adrián (general), 75
World War I, 183, 206–7, 303n27, 309n159
World War II, 221–22
Wrigthington, Thomas, 119

xenophobia, 47, 117, 181, 202, 269. *See also* immigrants

Ybarra, Lea, 259–61. See also *La batalla esta aquí* (Ybarra & Genera)
Yeaman, Caldwell, 101–2
Young Citizens for Community Action (YCCA), 236–37

Zamora O'Shea, Elena, 182, 185, 198–201, 199, 307n121. *See also* Canales, José T.; Castañeda, Carlos E.; De Zavala, Adina Emilia
Zaragoza, Ignacio, 136, 215–16. *See also* mutual aid societies
Zieschang, Charles, 150

www.ingramcontent.com/pod-product-compliance
Lightning Source LLC
Chambersburg PA
CBHW021848230426
43671CB00006B/308